THE STORY
OF
SOCIAL
PHILOSOPHY

AUGUSTE COMTE

(Chapter XXIII)

THE STORY

OF

SOCIAL

PHILOSOPHY

BY

CHARLES A. ELLWOOD

Professor of Sociology
Duke University

NEW YORK
PRENTICE-HALL, INC.
1938

To The
SOCIOLOGISTS
of the
FUTURE

Preface

THE STORY OF SOCIAL PHILOSOPHY, of all that man
has thought regarding human relations, their origin
and destiny, is even more thrilling than the story of
philosophy, because it is more vital to human welfare. What man has thought regarding his universe, his mind, and the meaning of his individual
existence is, of course, of the deepest interest; but it
hardly has the tragic significance for his welfare
that is possessed by his thought about his institutions, his culture, and the meaning of his history.

The story is too long, however, to be told in any
single work. Moreover, it is only just beginning to
be written. That is true regarding even the great
currents of social thought that have guided the development of our own civilization. Regarding the
social thought of peoples and civilizations other
than our own, we know as yet very little. We know,
indeed, that there must have been thought to guide
the development of their cultures and institutions;
for some sort of thought, some sort of a philosophy
of social values, has always guided man in the development of his institutions and human relations,
even though sufficient allowance is made for uncon-

scious adaptation. It still remains true, no matter how large a part has been played in human history by the unintended, that men everywhere have had social values, and have usually had some reflective thought to support and justify them. This was true of the American Indians, of the African Negroes, and of the South Sea Islanders. In India and China, we find a voluminous social philosophy analogous in some respects to that developed by western Europe, though utterly lacking in scientific method.

With all of the social philosophies of peoples and civilizations other than our own, we shall not be concerned. They are of interest to the historian of culture, but they are not vitally connected with the problems of our own civilization. We shall even leave aside the social philosophies of Russia and the Near Orient, though they have many vital interconnections with our own. We shall confine ourselves mainly to the social theories developed by the four leading peoples of western Europe, the Italians, the French, the English, and the German, though the fountain source of all of these social philosophies in Greek thought will necessarily claim our attention. It is these social philosophies of western Europe that control the social tradition of our civilization, and hence are interwoven with its many social problems.

We call this the story of social philosophy, rather than of sociology, because, according to the views of certain sociologists, scientific sociology did not begin until about a generation ago, although we shall see that from the time of Aristotle onward the social thought of our western nations was not unaffected by scientific methods. It was, however, so interwoven with the development of general philosophy and with philosophical implications of various sorts that it is better to speak of the social thought previous to the twentieth century, for the most part, as social philosophy; and this will happily save us the trouble of trying to draw a line between science and philosophy. Then, too, historically, "science is not to be dissociated from philosophy, any more than philosophy from science." Both have developed together; and practically we shall see that Professor Flint's dictum, that "science can only prosper when it strives to become philosophic, as philosophy can only prosper when it strives to become scientific," has been especially exemplified in the social sciences.

As I have just implied, this survey will come to an end shortly after the opening of the twentieth century. It is always unsafe to attempt to pass judgment upon one's living contemporaries. We are too near them to see them in a fair perspective, and this is especially true in the social sciences because many men with different points of view are working in this field, and it will probably be a long time before there is among them any general agreement. Indeed, the whole field of the social sciences is a field of controversy, and one object of this historical survey is to shed light upon the origin of existing controversies, and, if possible, make some little contribution to their solution.

Because this is the story of social philosophy, we

shall not be overcareful about the boundaries between the social sciences. This is, indeed, impossible in the early development of social thought,
because, as Herbert Spencer would say, social
thought proceeds from the homogeneous to the heterogeneous, from the indefinite to the definite. In
early times it was predominantly religious, at a
later stage it was predominantly political, and in
recent times it has been predominantly economic.
Nevertheless, the main problems of sociology as a
science will furnish the outline of our analysis.

For many reasons, the biographical method has
been chosen to tell the story of this development.
We shall select outstanding individuals in the history of social thought, outline their doctrines, and
briefly describe the conditions under which their
thinking took place. One reason for using the
biographical method is the obvious importance of
unique biographical incidents in determining thinking. This importance of strictly individual biographical elements has often been denied by social
and cultural determinists of the rigid sort; but we
hope to show that the evidence for the influence of
unique biographical incidents is overwhelming. To
recognize the influence of the uniquely biographical
will not prevent us from recognizing fully the influence of general cultural and social conditions also,
nor from tracing the growth of social and political
traditions in western civilization. Indeed, the purpose of this book is to trace and evaluate the great
currents of social thought in our civilization. To
paraphrase Flint's words, we propose, therefore,

not merely to pass in historical review some of the more famous of the many attempts that have been made in western civilization to discover the laws and principles that regulate human affairs, but also to pass judgment on the truth or falsity of what is essential and characteristic in them, indicating their chief merits and defects from the standpoint of impartial social science.

In the life of each of our thinkers, accordingly, we shall briefly outline the biographical incidents that may have influenced his social thought, noting the general social and cultural conditions that surrounded him, and the immediate predecessors who may have influenced him. Then we shall take up the scientific method, or lack of method, of each thinker; for we shall find that thinking is always limited, if not determined, by the method employed. Next, we shall outline the thinker's doctrine, if he has such, of social origins, then his doctrine of social development, then his doctrine of social organization and functioning, and, finally, his doctrines of social order and of social progress. But it will not always be possible to follow this order of presentation in a systematic way, because social thinking, with most thinkers, has been so fragmentary that it has rarely covered the whole field of problems outlined.

The thinkers selected have been chosen with a view to making the story of the development of sociological theories in western civilization down to the year 1900 as complete and systematic as possible. No doubt many important thinkers have been omitted; but they are not important for the understanding of the confusion of social philosophies that now prevails in our western world.

It is idle to try to indicate even the chief authorities to whom the author is indebted. Montesquieu put on the title page of his famous treatise the legend, "Offspring without a mother;" we, on the contrary, would claim that our story of social philosophy has had so many mothers that we cannot enumerate them! The only originality we would claim for the book is its interpretation.

CHARLES A. ELLWOOD

Contents

PART I

THE PRECURSORS OF SOCIOLOGY

THE STORY
OF
SOCIAL
PHILOSOPHY

PART I

THE PRECURSORS OF SOCIOLOGY

CHAPTER I

Introduction

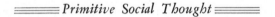 *Primitive Social Thought*

ALL PEOPLES OF WHOM we have records have had some thought about their institutions, customs, and human relations.[1] Most of this earlier social thought was a part of folk-lore and religion. A single example will suffice for our purpose. The Cheyenne Indians, an Algonquian tribe that had wandered westward to the Rocky Mountains, and that had reverted practically to savagery, had in their legends and folk-lore what seemed to them adequate explanations of the origin and form of practically all of their institutions, customs, and social behavior. This was true not only of their tribal organization, but of their family life, their property

---

1 See Bogardus, *A History of Social Thought,* Second Edition, Chapters I, II, III.

3

relations, and their forms of religion and government. Yet, the Cheyennes were among the lowest in cultural development of the North American Indians. Other tribes had much more elaborate social philosophies embedded in their legends and folklore. On account of the connection of primitive social philosophy with myths and legends, we may properly say that it was in the mythological stage. This stage has not yet been outgrown altogether by the peoples of the world. Only in very recent times have some of the peoples of the world begun to think of their institutions, customs, and relations in a scientific, matter-of-fact way.

When we pass from the New World to the earliest civilized peoples in the Old World, we find the same conditions. The origin of institutions is conceived of in a mythological way. However, the social development of these peoples of the Old World had gone further than the social development of most American Indian tribes. Consequently, in some cases, the mythological element in their social thinking was not so pronounced. For example, the famous code of laws of Hammurabi, who is supposed to have been king of Babylon from 2067–2025 B. C., contains many reflections upon institutions and customs and social relations, but most of them are in matter-of-fact terms. There is only one way to explain this, and that is that the code of Hammurabi had behind it at least one thousand years of civilization with written records. This implies that the Babylonians already had centuries of social and political experience before the code of Hammurabi was formulated. It was probably preceded by many other codes, most of them much more mythological in form. However, even the code of Hammurabi had a mythological setting. As a code, dealing with the most fundamental human relations, it was doubtless regarded by the early Babylonians as essentially a part of their religion.

The code of Manu in India, though formulated nearly two thousand years later, was much more mythological in its form. It was preceded by a cosmogony that contained practically all of the essential myths of early India, with many reflections upon the origin, development, and meaning of customs and institutions. Upon this mythological social philosophy as a basis, an elaborate code of laws was developed, covering every form of human relation from the family and property to ritualistic observances in religious ceremonies. The laws of Manu were thus simply a part of early Brahmanism. This illustrates again how early social thought was deeply embedded in religion.

The Chinese seem to have preceded the peoples of India in their social development by several centuries. The writings of Confucius and Mencius show very considerable social maturity, and suggest that many centuries of experience must have lain behind them. Nevertheless, these writings are still essentially religious in their outlook. Confucius takes for granted the worship of ancestors and the reverence of the political ruler. Practically everything in his teachings rests upon filial piety and reverence for the established social and political order. When it is said that the teachings of these two Chinese sages were ethical rather than religious, we can mean by such an expression only that the religious setting of these teachings is taken for granted.

Even the social thought of the Hebrews, though in some ways more advanced than any of the peoples that we have mentioned, is deeply embedded in Hebrew religion. Not only is the theory of the origin of institutions in the Old Testament mythological, but even in the New Testament there is no thought of separating the teachings that concern human relations from those that concern the relations of men and the Deity. We may admit that this was an element of strength rather than of weakness. Nevertheless, it is an admission that there was no attempt among the ancient Jews to base thought about human relations upon scientifically established facts and reasoning. We may conclude that religion, as has often been said, was the primitive matrix out of which has come our law, our philosophy, and our science. In this respect, early social life showed much greater unity than our own. It was reserved for one people in antiquity, however, to make the break between religion and philosophy and science. That people was the Greeks.

Social Thought of the Greeks

It is difficult to say why the people of Greece separated their philosophy and science from religion, thereby laying independent foundations for both of these phases of culture. The Greeks were not the original inhabitants of what we now call Greece, but came down into this peninsula from the north at various times between 1200 B. C. and 900 B. C. They seem to have been originally pastoral nomads like the Slavic tribes to the north of them. But in the peninsula of Greece they came into contact with an ancient civilization that had developed in Troy and Crete and to some extent on the mainland of Greece. This civilization has been named by archaeologists "the Aegean civilization." Although it was relatively advanced in many respects, it was overthrown by the Greeks, who called themselves "Hellenes." Perhaps it was this contact of the early Greeks with the old Aegean civilization that stimulated the development of their own culture. At any rate, they soon absorbed all that it had to give, and then they began to surpass it. The cross-fertilization of dissimilar cultures in this case, surely enough, did produce a new and higher culture.

Yet, the social thought of the Greeks at the earliest point in which we catch sight of them in history was still in the mythological stage, as, for example, in the poems of Homer and Hesiod. In the works of both of these early Greek poets, and particularly in Homer's *Odyssey,* we find an elaborate social philosophy. But it is all mythological, all still in terms of the will of the gods or of superhuman heroes. Moreover, this social philosophy of the early Greeks, in common with that of all early peoples, represented the perfect stage of human society to be in the past. The gods had created man and human institutions perfect, or nearly so, and man by his sinfulness had destroyed that original perfection. The similar view among the Hebrews is found in the legend of the Garden of Eden. Among the Greeks it gave rise to the legend of the Golden Age, which was placed at the beginning of human history and which was gradually succeeded by the Age of Silver and the Age of Iron. Thus the development of human society was represented as a degeneration from an original state of perfection. This particular myth, down to comparatively recent times, continued to influence the social thinking of even the civilized peoples of Europe. It is for this reason that some writers on the history of social thought hold that the entire ancient and medieval world did not have anything that corresponded to our conception of progress. We shall see that this statement is a mistake, if taken in an unqualified sense. But nothing could illustrate more clearly the power of ancient religious myths over the social thinking of even civilized peoples than this legend of a perfect state of human society at the beginning, with a fall from that perfect state through sin, and followed since then by progressive degeneration.

In their social thinking, then, the Greeks did not achieve any independence from their mythological religious beliefs until comparatively late. The independence of their social philosophy from their religion is therefore not to be ascribed to any particular genius of the Greek people. The Greeks were, if judged by their later achievements, no doubt a gifted, superior people, but their superiority did not express itself in any independent social thinking in the early stages of their history. It was not until Athens had risen to power and had come into conflict with Sparta, especially during the long Peloponnesian War (430–400 B. C.), that social thought independent of religious tradition began to manifest itself. Here, then, at the very threshold of the story of social thought in the western world, we come upon the crisis theory of thought. According to this theory, we think only when practical problems arise, when our old habits no longer work well, and we need to build new habits. Put in social terms, this theory would be that social thinking arises when the institutions and customs of the past no longer work well, perhaps break down, and have to be replaced by new adjustments, new values, which result in new customs and institutions. This theory seems to assume that only through compulsion do human individuals and human groups think about the situations in which they find themselves. However, the word "crisis" in this theory must not be taken to mean more than that some situation has arisen that creates a problem and demands intelligent thinking for its solution.

Now, a major crisis in Greek institutions and social life occurred when Sparta overthrew Athens in the Peloponnesian War. Athens had built up a great empire after the Persian wars, and it must have been indeed a shock to the Athenians to see the imperial power of Athens overthrown by Sparta and her allies. It was no wonder that men began to ask what was wrong. There is little wonder also that they found no adequate solution in their religion; for Greek religion, unlike the Hebrew, had failed to get a rational philosophical basis. It had degenerated into a nature worship, in which the gods manifested all the imperfections of conduct known in Greek society itself. There was nothing in popular religion that could be appealed to for the elevation either of private morals or of public affairs. Hence, the Greek mind was thrown back upon the examination of the facts of experience.

Now it must be admitted that Greek society had had a very varied experience upon which to reflect. Greece had been divided into a great number of petty city-states, each with a different political and social organization, varying from the military aristocracy of Sparta to the equalitarian democracy of later Athens. All of this experience afforded material for social thinking. Moreover, after the Persian wars, Athens had grown rich and powerful, and its citizens had come to think only of their own happiness and comfort. Individualism was rampant in Athens, and this had already, to a great extent, undermined ancient customs, institutions, and even beliefs. The situation, therefore, was ripe for the stimulation of thinking about social and political problems. Perhaps the crisis of the Peloponnesian War could not have resulted in such fruitful thinking if all this experience within Greek society had not furnished material for thought.

Apparently the stimulus to think was felt quite generally among the citizens of Athens. There had been among them, however, for a long time, a class of private teachers who called themselves Sophists, or "wise men." There was no public education in ancient cities, and in Athens this class of private teachers had grown up, recruited from many occupations and professions. The object of their teaching was to make their pupils successful in some line of endeavor. Political life, especially, offered at the time an attractive career to Athenian youth, and therefore, the Sophists taught what they claimed would bring success in political life and in the affairs of the community. The defeat of Athens by Sparta stimulated among them a variety of social and political theories. Dr. Will Durant goes so far as to say: "Every school of social thought had there its representatives and perhaps its origin." At any rate, there were those who claimed that, in the life of the state, "might makes right"; others who claimed that right and justice were mere conventions of the community, agreed upon by the domi-

nant majority; while still others, taking a more individualistic view, said that pleasure or happiness was
the only thing that could be considered a rational
aim for either the individual or the community.
Moreover, many of these Sophists were sceptics,
and made light of the old gods and the old traditions. They were regarded by the more conservative as disturbers of society, and hence, as a group,
acquired a bad reputation. Most of them taught
their views for hire; but among them was one who
refused to take any money for his teaching, and who
questioned whether the Sophists really had the
knowledge that they claimed to possess. This man
was Socrates.

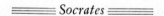

Socrates

Socrates, whom we must regard as the greatest
of the Sophists, even though he was their chief
critic, was born about 470 B. C. and died in 399 B. C.
He evidently came from a good family, as his father
was a sculptor, and he himself was trained in that
art. As a leading citizen of Athens, he had participated in many public activities. He had been both
a soldier and a judge. He knew the excesses of the
Athenian democracy and the foolishness of its politicians, as well as of his fellow teachers. Moreover,
he felt within himself a divine commission to convict
his fellow citizens of their foolishness and ignorance. He claimed that a "voice" within him gave

him this commission. This voice, which Socrates believed to be that of a demon or familiar spirit, has been variously explained by his biographers. Perhaps the most plausible explanation is that the intensity of Socrates' thought produced what is called an "internal audition," a not infrequent psychological phenomenon. We may remember also that this sense of a divine commission is not infrequent in the history of leadership in early societies. At any rate, Socrates felt it his duty to convict his fellow citizens of their ignorance. During the Peloponnesian War, he went from camp to camp, propounding questions and cross-examining those who claimed any validity for their social and political opinions. He saw that he himself did not know, and that the people did not know, and that the thing needful was a search for trustworthy knowledge. He soon gained, however, a reputation for wisdom; but it is said that when the Delphic oracle declared him the wisest of Athenians, he said: "One thing only I know, and that is that I know nothing." This, he said, was his sole claim to wisdom.

Socrates' fellow citizens of Athens did not take kindly to his attempt to convict them of ignorance. Perhaps there are even today very few communities that would be tolerant to such a teacher. They probably felt that he slandered and derided them, and they lodged against him the charge that he denied the gods and was corrupting the youth. There was probably some basis for the charge, because Socrates, like many preceding Greek thinkers, saw that the popular polytheism was without any rational basis. Socrates himself believed in one God, and also came to believe in the immortality of the soul; but, from the point of view of the populace, he was a dangerous sceptic in both morals and religion. He had surrounded himself, moreover, with some of the leading youths of Athens, who had become his ardent disciples. Nevertheless, it is said that it is probable that the Athenian democracy would have acquitted Socrates if he had said nothing in his own behalf, but had let himself be defended by his friends. Instead, he openly defied his prosecutors, ridiculed their charges, and told the populace that, instead of trying him for impiety, they should be erecting a monument of gratitude. The result was an overwhelming vote for his conviction and execution. He was allowed, however, one month in which to commune with his friends and prepare for death. During this time, if we may believe Plato, he delivered to his pupils some of his most remarkable discourses.

We cannot close this biographical sketch without pointing out the remarkable parallel that has often been noted between Socrates and Jesus. Both were occasional teachers. Neither left any writings of his own. We know Socrates only through his disciples, chiefly Plato and Xenophon. Both felt a divine commission. Both were unfortunate enough to enrage their communities against them, and both were put to death by their own communities.

Scientific method. It may seem strange that the world looks back to such an occasional teacher as Socrates as the founder, for the European world at least, of both the method of science and the method of philosophy. No modern philosopher would deny this; but Socrates' method of doubt and definition was equally the starting point of scientific method. He saw, as he said, that he did not know; and he was certain also that others did not know what they were talking about. He saw that the first step to knowledge must be clearness in ideas, in concepts. Now the exact definition of terms, or concepts, is one of the most difficult tasks in philosophy and science. But, as Socrates also knew, it must be undertaken at the very beginning, if we are to arrive at any truth that can have social currency. We must know the meaning of the terms we use before we can convey truth from one mind to another. Definition is, therefore, the first step in science, as well as perhaps the mark of its final completion.

It is perhaps unfortunate that Socrates did not devise a method of interrogating nature, as well as a method of interrogation as to the meaning of terms. But his demand for clarity in the use of terms was the indispensable first step in clarity of thought. Incidentally, too, in demanding clear and exact meanings of terms, Socrates demonstrated the need of logic as the foundation for all scientific and philosophical methods.

Social philosophy. It is not certain that we can speak of Socrates' having a social philosophy. As we have just said, he left no writings of his own, but Plato makes him the chief interlocutor in his dialogues. It is impossible to say, however, from Plato's dialogues, what is the teaching of Socrates and what is the teaching of Plato. It will be safer to ascribe most of the teachings in the dialogues to Plato. But one teaching does stand out as unmistakably Socrates' own, and that is that intelligence is the foundation of all excellence, in customs, institutions, and human relations, as well as in private conduct. This is Socrates' famous doctrine that good conduct is practically synonymous with intelligent conduct; that knowledge leads to virtue, and is practically synonymous with it. This doctrine Socrates derived easily from his knowledge of the art of the sculptor and of the practice of artisans generally. Socrates said that if we know how to do a thing rightly, we do it that way. The artisan who knows the right way to make a thing makes it that way. All excellence has its basis in knowledge. Hence, Socrates insisted upon the value of knowledge for the guidance of conduct. A just man, for example, must know what the laws are. But Socrates escapes the charge of superficiality, because he points out that besides the laws of men, there are also the laws of God; and justice is the virtue that springs from knowledge of law in this higher sense. Therefore, Socrates seems to imply that goodness or virtue is not mere compliance with the customs and wishes of the community. He also seems to teach that goodness is something discoverable by human intelligence, even though his own method went no further than the cross-examination of peoples' beliefs and ideas concerning goodness. It would seem, in conclusion, that we must recognize Socrates as the first great protagonist of the general idea that if we are to reconstruct human society successfully, it must be reconstructed upon the basis of scientific knowledge. So far from believing that human intelligence could do little or nothing to improve human society, Socrates apparently believed that intelligence could do everything. In fact, the main criticism of his social philosophy is that it is too intellectualistic. Perhaps, if we knew how to control impulses, emotions, and habits perfectly through intelligence, knowledge would be synonymous with virtue. But thus far we can lay claim to no such knowledge, and the animal impulses, baser emotions, and unsocialized habits of men frequently dominate their conduct when their knowledge and intelligence point in another direction. In fact, it has been the universal experience of intelligent men that they not infrequently know the right, yet the wrong pursue. Socrates might well reply, however, that they do not know the right in the fullest sense, and how it might be attained. If they did, they would not continue to pursue the wrong. Something like this faith lies at the basis of the development of the human sciences, and so the spirit of Socrates may be said still to inspire the scientific world.

CHAPTER II

Plato

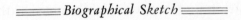

Biographical Sketch

PLATO WAS BORN about 427 B. C. and died 347 B. C. He came from an old aristocratic family of Athens. His sympathies were all aristocratic. It is said that on his deathbed he thanked God that he was born a Greek and not a barbarian, a free man and not a slave, a man and not a woman, and above all, that he was born in the time of Socrates. He was Socrates' most distinguished pupil. Like Socrates, he became the greatest teacher of his time. When Socrates was put to death, he entered upon a long period of travel, visiting Egypt, Asia Minor, Sicily, and southern Italy. He was, therefore, familiar with the Mediterranean world of his time, and the influence of his extensive travels is easily discerned in his writing. Moreover, in southern Italy, he

18

came into contact with the philosophical school of Pythagoras. In 387 B. C. he returned to Athens and founded his famous Academy, which, because it attracted so many of the intellectual youths of Greece, might almost be said to have been the first European university. He lived to be more than eighty years of age, and during the last forty years of his life he seems to have been constantly occupied with teaching and writing.[1]

Certain things must be remembered about Plato, apart from these external biographical details. He became early interested in politics, but withdrew from political life upon the death of Socrates, and even more than Socrates was disgusted with the results of Athenian democracy. It must be remembered, too, that Plato was perhaps predominantly of the artistic, or poetic, temperament. What he wrote was always suffused with warm human interest and emotion. This added greatly to the literary quality of his writings, but it probably injured his work as a scientific thinker. Nevertheless, Plato was interested in the science of his time.

In the multitude of Plato's Dialogues, only three need concern us as containing his leading social and political ideas. The first is *The Republic,* written when he was about the age of forty, and published soon after his return to Athens. It was the first great attempt to describe an ideal society in which justice would be realized. The second dialogue that

---

[1] An excellent sketch of Plato's life and teachings can be found in Durant's, *The Story of Philosophy,* Chapter I.

concerns us is *The Laws,* which was an outline of a practical social and political constitution, written in his extreme old age when he saw that the ideals of *The Republic* could not be carried out. The third dialogue is *The Statesman,* another discussion of a political constitution, which some think the work of one of Plato's pupils rather than his own.

═══ Plato's Scientific Method ═══

Plato's method does not mark any great advance on that of Socrates. It is a development of the dialectical method of Socrates in a purely speculative direction. We have seen how Socrates began the interrogation of the concepts of the mind. Gradually there grew up in Plato's mind the idea that these concepts were not obtained from experience, but were forms which lay back of all experience and from which we could obtain our truest knowledge. We could find out more about man, for example, by considering the general notion or idea of man than by studying particular men. The laws and the nature of man were therefore to be found in the concept man. This is the so-called Platonic "idealism," which, however, as a method, we would prefer to call "conceptualism"—the doctrine that truth is to be found in the examination and in the criticism of concepts. Now this method of Plato almost completely reverses the method of modern science. Modern science insists that we should study the particular and the individual, from which we may generalize universal truth. But according to Plato, universal truth is not to be sought in phenomena. Phenomena, as the very word implies in Greek, are mere appearances. They are local and temporary embodiments of the universal ideas that lie behind them. The real world is better revealed by the criticism of the concepts of the mind than by the study of phenomena.

Now, we cannot deny a certain validity to this method of the criticism of concepts. It often serves to make thinking more exact and to expose fallacies. It has been found particularly useful in philosophy. Indeed, it may be said that philosophy from Plato's time down almost to the twentieth century was dominated by this method. But it has been a method that has given much trouble in the social sciences. It is opposed to the realism of modern science, and, to a certain extent, to the inductive spirit.

However, we must not give the impression that Plato ignored objective social reality. On the contrary, there is much evidence that he was greatly influenced by his observations of Athenian society and of the lands which he visited on his travels; and it is universally acknowledged by all students of Plato that he was particularly influenced by his knowledge of the Spartan military aristocracy. Indeed, the prestige of Sparta as the victor in the Peloponnesian War colors Plato's social and political ideals.

"The Republic." In Plato's writings we find for the first time a coherent, well-organized social philosophy. We shall depart, however, from the general outline that we have laid down, because in Plato's case, it will be most convenient to treat of his social and political ideas under the heading of each of the three dialogues that we have mentioned. Of these three, *The Republic* is the one of outstanding importance. It is primarily a treatise in social ethics, a sketch of an ideal society, although Professor MacIver has called it "the first and greatest of all sociological treatises." [2] It is only indirectly sociological, however, as we understand the word, for it is purely an ideal construction to define justice.

We have already spoken of the immense influence of Sparta upon Plato's thought. But the influence of his conceptualistic method is not less evident. He tells us, first of all, that the ideal community must be an enlarged likeness of the individual human soul. It must be a sort of an enlargement of the concept man. Thus Plato has an implicit parallelism between the individual and society; we might almost say, therefore, an organic view of society, except that the community of men should be likened to the human mind rather than to the human body.

---

2 MacIver, *Community, A Sociological Study*, p. 51.

Just as there are in human nature three levels of
activity—(1) the appetites or the senses, (2) the
spirit or the will, and (3) intelligence, reason, and
judgment—so there are inevitably in the human
world and in every human community three classes
of individuals: (1) those who devote themselves to
the gratification of the senses, the enjoyment of
their bodily appetites; (2) those who devote themselves to action for the sake of honor and distinction; and (3) those who devote themselves to the
cultivation of the intellect and the pursuit of truth.
Now Plato proposes that these three types of human
beings, which do in fact exist in every human community, shall be recognized as distinct social classes
and each given its appropriate work. Just as the
appetites and the senses must sustain and nourish
the animal body, so those who are devoted to the
gratification of their appetites and senses should
sustain the community. Just as will and animal
spirit defends and protects the body, so those who
are devoted to action for the sake of honor and distinction should protect the community. Finally,
just as intelligence and rational judgment should
guide and govern human life, so the class devoted to
the cultivation of intelligence and reason should govern the community. Thus the ideal community will
have three classes among its citizens: first, the class
of producers or artisans, which we would call the
manual workers; second, a citizen-soldier class to
guard the community against invasion and internal
strife; and third, a class of magistrates or rulers

who are to supervise and govern the entire life of the community.

In the ideal society, these three social classes or orders will not only be recognized, but each will perform its proper functions. In the social division of labor, the class of artisans or manual workers should perform all agricultural and mechanical work, carry on necessary trade and commerce, and support by their labor the other two classes. This class will constitute the bulk of the population. Unlike the Helots of Sparta, they were not to be slaves; neither were they to be given the full rights and privileges of citizens, because their function was to produce, and hence they could not be expected to cultivate either will or intelligence. Moreover, as their motive was self-interest, they would be incapable of unselfish devotion to the life of the community. They were, however, to have the privileges appropriate to those who live lives of self-interest and devote themselves to the gratification of their appetites and senses. They were therefore to have private family life and a limited right of private property; and unlike the two classes above them, they were not expected to merge their life entirely in the life of the community.

The soldier-citizen class, whose chief function was to guard the community against internal strife and against invasion from without, was to be the real citizen class. Like the Spartan citizen class, its members were to be mobilized from the beginning and to live in barracks. They were to be carefully

trained in gymnastics, music, and military science.
Their interests were to be the interests of the community. They were therefore to live in complete
communism and have no private life, their sole reward being the glory and honor of serving the community. Their children were to be brought up in
communal homes, nurseries, and schools, without
being known by their own mothers, much less by
their fathers. For men and women were to be
mated upon a rigidly eugenic basis, wholly with
reference to the inherited character of their offspring. Romance was to have no place. Men were
permitted to become fathers between the ages of
thirty and fifty-five, and women were permitted to
become mothers between the ages of twenty and
forty. Immediately at birth, the children, until they
were seven years of age, were placed in the hands of
women who were especially trained in child care.
Children begotten or born outside of the age limits,
as well as illegitimate and defective children, were
to be put to death.

The class of magistrates or ''guardians'' were
to be recruited chiefly from this soldier-citizen class.
They were to be selected upon the basis of intellectual ability, but could not assume the duties of
magistrates until they had reached the age of fifty.
For twenty years previous to this age they were
to be trained in philosophy and in the practical
tasks of life. During this whole period, as well as
after they became magistrates, they were to undergo
a severe physical and intellectual discipline, to live

in tents, to have no property of their own, to touch neither gold nor silver, and to be sustained without luxury by the community. Women were equally eligible with men to enter this class. The functions of these magistrates were very different from those we ordinarily associate with political rulers. While they were to promulgate the laws, look after the mating of men and women, and the general good of the community, yet their supreme function was to be teachers of the young. They were to be not only philosophers and statesmen, but above all teachers, for Plato argued that laws could do little unless they were voluntarily observed by the community, and laws would be observed only in proportion as the people from childhood up were educated to observe them. In fact, Plato's whole social scheme rested fundamentally upon his educational system. It was his conception of the place of education in the ideal community which, through the ages, has indeed given to this dialogue of *The Republic* much of its vitality and interest.

Equality of educational opportunity for all children was the very foundation of Plato's social system. In his educational scheme, sex was to be ignored. Not only were girls to be given the same opportunities as boys in education, but women were to be given military training and serve in the army the same as men. Everyone, through education, was to have the same chance of finding his proper place in the life of the community. While Plato divided the community into the three social classes whose life we have just described, yet these were not to be castes, for he provided for the free passage of children from one class to the other. While the artisans were to have their private family life and the rearing of their own children, yet if any child was born into the laboring class which showed ability to enter the higher classes, then this child was to be given the same opportunities as the child of the soldier-citizen class. The education of all children was to be predominantly physical up to the age of ten years. Then they were to be trained in the fundamental sciences, in music, including literature, and in military science. At the age of twenty they were to be given a comprehensive physical and intellectual examination. Those who were found to be unfitted for the two higher classes were to be returned to the class of manual workers. The rest were to enter the soldier-citizen class, and after ten years more of training in the fundamental sciences, in philosophy, and in military science, they were to be given another comprehensive examination. From this final examination were selected those who were to be trained to be the future magistrates or "guardians." For five years they were to receive intensive training in dialectics. Those who showed sufficient philosophical ability were then to be given fifteen years of practical training in the affairs of the community, in minor offices, and as assistants to the "guardians" in performing their duties. This last fifteen years might be said to be a training in practical politics and statesmanship.

Thus Plato hoped to make the rulers of the community at once philosophers and statesmen. This combination of the philosopher and the statesman in the ruler, is, as has often been pointed out, the key to Plato's social and political philosophy. Only thus could the evils that characterize the Greek city-states be overcome and the ideal community be produced. "Until philosophers are kings," Plato said, "or the kings and princes of this world have the spirit and power of philosophers . . . cities will never cease from ill, nor the human race."

It is evident that Plato considered the ideal community to be an intellectual aristocracy, and that all of the arrangements of the community should be such as to place the power of social control in the hands of the most highly educated and intelligent class. Any departure from this pattern Plato regarded as a degradation of the social ideal. He admitted that Sparta had had something which resembled this social and political organization. But Spartan society was organized upon the basis of military efficiency and achievement. It honored the warrior and not the philosopher, and therefore Plato regarded it as relatively degenerate. Even more degenerate were those communities in which wealth was honored and given power, or where power was given to all citizens regardless of their qualifications. Plato's ideal was therefore not at all democratic. It was wholly aristocratic; except that Plato aimed at an aristocracy of intellect rather than of blood. As to his communism, we must note that it was confined to the two upper classes and did not extend to the whole of the population. It was therefore entirely an outcome of the Platonic ideal that these two higher classes should have no private interests, but should merge their entire life in that of the community.

The Republic, as we said at the beginning, was written to define justice. Only in such a state, Plato said, could justice be realized. A just man could exist only in a just society. Hence we see that Plato's conception of justice was a social conception. He conceived justice as a relation among individuals depending upon the social organization. Indeed, the whole method of *The Republic* presupposes that ethics has a social basis and is essentially a social science. The approach to our conceptions of right and wrong, Plato argued, must be through a critical consideration of our social ideals. While it will be well to reserve our criticisms till we have finished with a consideration of Plato's other dialogues, it is appropriate that we should end this discussion of *The Republic* with these memorable words of Professor Franklin H. Giddings:

> The imperishable contribution which this work makes to our reasoned knowledge of human society is found not in its communistic plan of life, but rather in its analysis and its correlation of moral and social forces; above all, in its actual solution of the problem of social reaction upon individual character. Assuming that man as a personal cause can in fact mold the commonwealth to his will, assuming also that the final

end of endeavor is the attainment of a good life
—which should consist substantially of those
kinds and degrees of pleasurable activity that
reason can approve of—*The Republic* demonstrates that the "good life" so conceived, after all
depends upon a certain objective condition which
reason and the human will may create, and which
is called "justice." Moreover, reason and will
cannot create justice directly. They can establish it only through the fine adjustments of a
social order. Thus, in the thought of Plato, the
"good life" is a function of "justice" and to
maintain justice is the function of social organization.[3]

"*The Laws.*" In his extreme old age, Plato
wrote another dialogue, not to set forth a social
ideal, but to provide a practical constitution for
Greek city-states. He called it himself a sketch of
"a second best commonwealth." This was the dialogue known as *The Laws,* published soon after his
death. While it contains a good many of the same
ideas that are found in *The Republic,* yet it contains other social theories that are worthy of notice.

The first of these theories is an outline of the
stages of social development. Plato represents human society as passing through five stages: (1) the
stage of isolated families living by grazing or hunting (this Plato identifies with the Golden Age);
(2) patriarchal societies in which families are consolidated into clans and tribes, but still live by grazing flocks and herds; (3) agricultural cities in which

---

3 Lichtenberger, *Development of Social Theory,* p. 28, quoted from
Giddings' *Studies in the Theory of Human Society,* p. 102.

villages depending upon agriculture are consolidated into city-states; (4) commercial cities like Corinth, located on the seacoast, and because commercial, corrupt in morals; (5) mixed cities like Sparta and Athens, partly agricultural and partly commercial.

This crude classification is notable because it is the first recognition that we have of marked stages in social development. This dialogue, however, contains another classification of societies which is even more suggestive, closely following the classes recognized in *The Republic*. Southern nations, like Phoenicia and Egypt, Plato said, are sensuous, devoted to the gratification of their senses and appetites, and therefore essentially like the artisan class pictured in *The Republic*. The northern nations, like the Thracians and the Scythians, are distinguished for their courage, and so, like the soldier-citizen class, live for military honor and distinction. But the Greeks represent the intellect. This suggestion is not merely a manifestation of Greek snobbishness, but also implies that peoples can be classified according to their stage of development. It also suggests the influence of geographical conditions on human society.

But the dialogue of *The Laws* is noted chiefly for the concessions that it makes to the political and social customs already existing among the Greeks. While Plato holds that the citizen class should be strictly limited in numbers, as it was in all the Greek city-states, he regretfully gives up his ideal of communism for that class. He concedes the necessity of a private family life of the monogamic form and of private property. He holds, however, that private property should be strictly limited in amount, as it was in some of the Greek states. The council of the state should decide the minimum amount of property that should be guaranteed to every family of the citizen class. No family was to be permitted to fall below this minimum, and in that way, poverty and its dangers were to be avoided. The second class of citizens might have twice as much as the first class; the third class three times the minimum; and the fourth class up to four times the minimum amount of property. All above four times the minimum was subject to a one hundred per cent tax, and so was confiscated to the state. Thus Plato concedes the necessity of different degrees of wealth among the families of the citizen class. To lessen the opportunities for amassing wealth and to make the scheme more practical, he would prohibit the citizen class from engaging in trade and commerce and forbid the existence of monopolies within the state.

The general political and social organization followed that of Grecian states, with boards of magistrates chosen by lot and rotating in office. As Plato was opposed to democracy, however, he still provided that the making of laws should be in the hands of a small select council particularly fitted for the task.

Only a word is necessary concerning Plato's third

PLATO

political dialogue, *The Statesman*. The whole purpose of this dialogue is to show the necessity, in ordinary human society, of a political constitution, whether actual rule is exercised by one, by a few, or by many. In this dialogue, which is probably again a product of his old age, Plato favors monarchy, which he defines as the rule of one under a constitution. He favors it because it best secures the unity of the state. However, the rule of one without a constitution becomes a tyranny, the worst of all forms of government. The rule of a few with a constitution is aristocracy; but the rule of a few without a constitution becomes a selfish and corrupt oligarchy. While democracy with a constitution is not as desirable as either aristocracy or monarchy, yet democracy without a constitution is less intolerable than tyranny or oligarchy. Thus Plato seems indirectly to reach the conclusion that government should be a rule of law and not of persons. It is noteworthy also that in this dialogue Plato anticipates Aristotle's famous classification of governments.

Criticism

Probably no writing of classical antiquity, besides the New Testament, has had such influence in recent times as Plato's *Republic*. Its influence upon the Russian Soviet Government is beyond question, as well as upon every recent experiment in com-

munism. Plato must be considered the first great apostle of communism, even though, as we have seen, he limited his communism to the upper classes. One American political scientist has recently declared that "Plato was even more Bolshevist than the Bolshevists of our time." He points out that "the ideal state of Plato and that of the Russian communists have many elements in common: both hate commerce and money economy; both regard private property as the sole source of all evil; both would eliminate wealth and poverty; both favor a collective education of the children, exempted from paternal care; both regard art and literature only as a means of state education; both would control all science and ideology in the interest of the state; both have a rigid central dogma, a kind of state religion to which all individual and social activity must be subordinated." He adds that both schemes are "capable of realization only under the protection and violence of armed force."[4]

Let us remember, too, that Plato was also the first great apostle of the absolute social equality of the two sexes, and of the necessity of a eugenic control of marriage. We have already quoted Professor Giddings' appreciation of Plato's contributions to sociological theory. Let us add that Plato was perhaps the very first to appreciate to the full the value of expert knowledge in human society. He saw not only the need for intelligent leadership, but the so-

---

[4] See Engelmann's *Political Philosophy from Plato to Jeremy Bentham*, with Introductions by O. Jaszi, pp. 4, 5.

cial advantage of a government by the wisest. Perhaps here we should add that modern Fascism is almost as dependent upon Plato as modern communism. Fascism makes its central principle government by the intelligent few. Like Fascism, too, Plato emphasizes the necessity of the unity of the state. Again let us note that, unlike Soviet communism, Plato does not believe in a classless society. He believes that every society necessarily has classes, and moreover, that the essential psychological classes are, so to speak, fixed by nature.

But in criticism we need hardly point out that Plato overemphasized the differences among individuals. While his classes are not castes, yet there are no such lines in the population of a community as he tried to make out. His classes are too hard and fast, just as was Augustine's division of human society into sinners and saved. All ordinary human beings have something in their nature corresponding to each of the three classes that Plato described, and the differences are wholly differences of degree, and not of qualities. Finally, we might raise the question as to whether the aristocratic ideal of human society can be ultimate any more than Plato's ideal of the state as essentially like a Greek city-state can be ultimate. After all, Plato's social ideals hardly rose into the universal, although to make them such was the task that he essayed in *The Republic.*

CHAPTER III

Aristotle

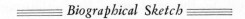

=== *Biographical Sketch* ===

IN A CERTAIN SENSE, Aristotle was the only truly scientific mind in antiquity. Measured by his achievements, he was by far the greatest thinker of the ancient world. He was born in 384 B. C. at Stagira, an Ionian colony in Macedonia, and he died in 322 B. C. at the age of sixty-two years. His father was court physician to Amyntas II, the grandfather of Alexander the Great. It is well to remember that even as a youth Aristotle was brought up in contact with the royal court. But the Macedonian court was permeated with all of the influences of Greek culture. Aristotle's father, however, was a physician, a dissector of animals, and a student of nature. This certainly gave Aristotle his interest in natural history and perhaps, in a certain sense, gave all of

36

his thinking a naturalistic bent. Upon the death of his father, Aristotle, then in his eighteenth year, went to Athens to study under Plato, whose Academy was already famous throughout Greece, and he continued his relations with Plato until the latter's death nearly twenty years later. Plato regarded Aristotle as his most brilliant pupil, although they often disagreed. Aristotle was too great to be molded by any teacher. Apparently, even as a student, he could pursue an independent course and think for himself. Nevertheless, the relations of Aristotle and Plato seem to have been almost ideal student and teacher relations, despite what has often been said to the contrary. Each thoroughly respected the other. At the death of Plato, Aristotle had every right to expect that he would succeed him as the head of the Academy, for Aristotle had already demonstrated his ability as a teacher. However, the headship went to a nephew of Plato of whom no one would ever have heard had it not been for this accident. There is no evidence that Aristotle held any grudge on this account. On the contrary, when Plato's name and reputation were slanderously assailed after his death, Aristotle was among the very first to defend his former teacher. Nevertheless, he felt it necessary to leave Athens rather than open up a school in competition with the Academy. He finally found refuge at the court of Hermias, the tyrant of a petty Greek city-state in Asia Minor. Here he remained nearly three years till Hermias was captured by the Persians. In the meantime, he had married a niece and adopted daughter of Hermias by the name of Pythias. There was nearly twenty years difference in their ages, and Aristotle always claimed that something like this difference made the ideal marriage, which is perhaps as striking an illustration as we can find of how even the greatest minds "rationalize" their personal behavior.

In 342 B. C., Aristotle was recalled to the court of Macedonia by Philip II to become the tutor to his son, Alexander, then in his thirteenth year. For about four years Alexander seems to have been under Aristotle's tutorship. He was a relatively apt pupil and seems to have got some of his ideas of statecraft from Aristotle. Aristotle, in accordance with his own educational ideas, did not teach Alexander as a private pupil, but in a school that apparently was made up largely of the sons of Macedonian nobles. He continued at the Macedonian court for eight years until Alexander ascended the throne. From this time on, however, Aristotle, in a sense, was under Alexander's patronage. According to one story, Alexander gave Aristotle eight hundred talents in gold, the equivalent of about four million dollars in our money, to purchase books, to establish a library and a museum, and to collect scientific information. If this is so, it is the first instance in history of the endowment of scientific research by a wealthy patron. In any case, it is certain that Aristotle was the first Greek to amass a library and to establish a museum, and also that

Alexander's government gave him great aid in making these collections. It is probably in this way that Aristotle was able to make his collection of a hundred and fifty-eight constitutions of the city-states of his time; and it was this collection that enabled him to make his wide, inductive study of both Greek and non-Greek communities.

Aristotle had remained very much attached to Athens. Accordingly, after Alexander's ascent of the throne, Aristotle, then fifty years of age, returned to Athens, taking his library and museum with him. His fame as a teacher had preceded him, and he had no difficulty in establishing in the Lyceum of Apollo a school that soon became the rival of Plato's Academy. Aristotle's school came to be known as the Peripatetic School, because, it is said, Aristotle lectured to his students while walking through the garden, a fact which would seem to preclude the belief that many of Aristotle's treatises are simply lecture notes taken by students; on the other hand, there is good ground for thinking that many of them are simply lecture memoranda which Aristotle used and expanded in oral teaching.

Aristotle remained twelve years in Athens; but after Alexander's death, there came a rebellion of Athens against Macedonia, and the anti-Macedonian party charged Aristotle with impiety, because they knew that he was friendly to Macedonia. Aristotle had not the courage of Socrates and fled to Calchis, near his old home, dying shortly thereafter.

Aristotle's mind was encyclopedic. He was the

virtual founder of many sciences and philosophical disciplines. We should especially remember him, however, as the founder of the social sciences. More than thirty treatises are still extant which are justly ascribed to Aristotle, but we shall be concerned mainly only with two, the *Politics,* which is in the nature of lecture memoranda of which we have just spoken, and *The Nicomachean Ethics,* a more finished treatise written for the instruction of his illegitimate son, Nicomachus. In these two books, Aristotle laid the foundations for all the social sciences.

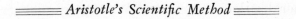

Aristotle's Scientific Method

Plato talks of ideals; Aristotle talks of nature and the world of reality. Hence, his method was almost the opposite of Plato's, even though he owed much to Plato. Aristotle's mind was objective and realistic in the best sense of those words. He tried to build up his theories on the basis of facts, even though at times he was a careless observer and knew his facts imperfectly. Such faults do not detract from the fact that Aristotle found his sources of truth in experience, and discredited ideas and concepts as the chief sources. That Aristotle was inductive in a high degree may be seen from the fact that he studied extensively all of the communities of his time and collected a hundred and fifty-eight different political constitutions. The single one of these which has come down to us, *The Constitution of Athens,* shows that he studied these constitutions, not only as they existed, but also in their historical development. Hence, we can say that Aristotle was probably the first to use the historical method in the study of social facts. It goes without saying that his method was also comparative. Moreover, his knowledge of human nature enabled him to use psychological analysis to throw light upon the conditions that he discusses.

Although Aristotle always sought his truth in experience, yet his mind was highly speculative, and he never dreamed of repudiating entirely the speculative method. But he wished his speculations to be generalizations from facts. While he was not always as careful as Plato in defining his terms and in criticizing concepts, yet we must remember that Aristotle was virtually the founder of logic, the science of correct thinking, which, according to his common-sense way of looking at things, was the main method of every science. Every science, according to Aristotle, was necessarily a reasoned body of knowledge and, in this sense, philosophical.

We owe to Aristotle's analytic mind the divisions among many of the sciences. In the field of the social sciences, however, he did not carry his analysis very far. He recognized a broad general field dealing with human affairs, which he called "political science," and this he subdivided into ethics and into political science in the narrow sense. Ethics was one half of the field of social science, and politics the other half. Ethics, according to Aristotle, looked at the problem of life from the standpoint of individual character and happiness, while political science in the narrow sense looked at the same problem from the standpoint of the welfare of the community or the state. Like Plato, Aristotle thought of the individual, not as isolated, but in his social and political setting. To solve the problem of individual character and happiness, the community or state must be rightly organized. Hence, Aristotle's ethics and politics were the two sides of what we would call his social philosophy. He did not separate the two subjects in any absolute way. Their separation was one of convenience and point of view. Hence, Aristotle considers social and political ideals in his *Politics* quite as freely as did Plato; but he considers them in relation to the facts studied. He lets his ideals grow out of the facts. Apparently Aristotle never dreamed of the absolute separation of the study of what is and of what ought to be, such as was proposed centuries later. In Aristotle's mind, the "right" was the same in human affairs as in mathematics. It was simply the "correct," and could be determined only through a careful study of facts and their relations.

Aristotle's Social Philosophy

The *Politics* of Aristotle discusses political problems upon a background of social philosophy. It is this social philosophy of Aristotle that we are particularly interested in examining.

Doctrine of social origins. Aristotle begins with the simple assumption that there are two primary and essential forms of human association—the association of male and female for the procreation of children, and the association of natural rulers and natural subjects for safety. Both these forms of association are natural, not deliberative; and both are found exemplified in the family, in the relations of husband and wife, of parents and children, of master and slave. All other human associations grow out of these two fundamental associations. The household, for example, is the association naturally formed for the supply of daily wants. The village in its most natural form is derived from the household; it is the association of several households for more than ephemeral purposes. The state in its complete form is the association of several villages. Like the household and the village, the state is a natural growth; for in it the simpler forms of human association attain their complete development. For the criterion of the state is full independence, self-sufficiency, and self-government.

Thus the state is a natural group, and man is naturally a political animal. Let us remember again that Aristotle is thinking of the city-state of his time, the Greek *Polis,* which more nearly resembles our community. We might almost translate Aristotle's famous aphorism, therefore, as "man is naturally a community animal," if we understand that in Aristotle's mind the community has a political organization. The stateless man, the individual not living in organized society, if his isolation is natural and not accidental, is either superhuman or else very low in the scale of development. The impulse to political association, Aristotle says, is innate; for even where there is no utilitarian advantage to be derived from it, men are none the less anxious to live together. At the same time, it must not be denied that the common advantage is also a motive of union. Organized social life is essential to the existence of man as man; one who has no need of such association is either a brute or a god. Aristotle is thinking of the claim of the Sophists that society had its origin in the perception of the utilities to be derived from it, or as we would say, in a "social contract." Moreover, Aristotle points out that the human individual has been developed in and through human society. In the order of nature, therefore, the state or community is prior to the individual, just as the whole must be prior to its parts.

Aristotle recognized the social life of animals. But he says that man is a social animal in a higher sense than a bee or any other gregarious creature. Aristotle is aware that vast differences separate man from the animals. Man, he says, is the only animal endowed with articulate speech. It follows that human society has a moral as well as a natural basis; for by means of speech man can indicate advantage and disadvantage, justice and injustice. Therefore, perceptions of justice and injustice are bound up with all human relations. Human society, we would now say, has a cultural as well as a natural basis.

Doctrine of social organization. A large part of Book I of the *Politics* is taken up with the consideration of what Aristotle calls the "science of the household," in which he founds not only what we would call the science of economics, but also household economics. He divides the science of the household into four parts: (1) the relations of master and slave; (2) the relations of husband and wife; (3) the relations of parents and children; and (4) the science or art of finance. Let us note briefly Aristotle's position upon each of these vital social questions.

Aristotle defends slavery. His theory is that there are persons for whom a life of slavery is advantageous and just; there are natural slaves, who by nature are not their own masters, but belong to someone else. Indeed, the principle of rule and subjection is universal throughout nature, and is equally inevitable and beneficent. Where several parts combine to form one common whole, the relation of ruler and subject invariably manifests itself. The relation of master and slave is, therefore, but one manifestation of this law of subordination which holds good throughout nature generally. Those who are rational beings only so far as to understand reason without possessing it are natural slaves. But natural slavery must not be confused with legal slavery. Legal slavery is partly right and partly wrong. In some cases actual slaves are not so naturally; yet on the other hand there are cases where this distinction does not exist and where the relation of master and slave is mutually advantageous and just. Wherever the relation is in accordance with Nature's ordinance, there is mutual helpfulness and friendship between master and slave. But just the contrary is the case where it is unnatural and depends upon law or force.

As regards the relations between husband and wife, Aristotle says that they are not the relations of a king and his subject. In this view, Aristotle was non-Greek, and probably reflected the influence of Plato. However, Aristotle held that man is naturally superior and that the wife should obey the husband, as the husband is naturally the head of the household. But the relations between husband and wife are those of moral equality. Therefore, they are like the relations of ruler and subject under a constitutional form of government. Moreover, the husband is to be guided in all that he does by the consideration of the interest of his wife and children. His rule over his wife and children is in both cases a rule over free persons; but while in the wife's case the rule is constitutional, in the children's case the rule is regal. In the former case, both ruler and subject are naturally equal, but no such equality exists between parents and children, and Aristotle says that here the relation is that of monarch and subject.

After this discussion of the relations of persons

in the household, Aristotle devotes considerable attention to the art of money-getting, or finance. Here his attitude is that characteristic of the whole ancient world. He does not favor the acquisition of money for money's sake. There should be a definite limit to one's possessions; the amount should be enough for independence and a good life, but not more. The mere acquisition of money is not the function of true finance; its end is in something beyond mere accumulation—in living well. Aristotle looks with disfavor upon trade and commercial pursuits; for he believes that the agricultural pursuits are the only source of true wealth. Manufactures he does not refer to, for manufactures in his time, unless ranked among the arts, were mostly included in the agricultural pursuits. Finance, so far as it follows nature, he says, depends universally upon the fruits of the earth and animals. Hence Aristotle's opposition to interest-taking. Of all forms of money-getting, he says, there is none which so well deserves abhorrence as interest-taking; for by it, it is money itself which produces the gain, instead of serving the purpose of a mere medium of exchange for which it was devised. No form of money-getting does so much violence to nature as this. Here Aristotle is one with practically the whole antique world. It must be remembered, of course, that in ancient times loans were made more to meet distress than to promote productive enterprises. To charge interest on such loans seemed to the ethical thinkers of ancient times the height of immorality. Conditions have vastly changed in the modern world, but we should not forget that, on the whole, modern socialists still contend against the taking of interest. We may say, of course, that Aristotle's economics was very primitive, but some of his economic ideas still persist.

The more fundamental of Aristotle's economic ideas come out, however, in Book II of the *Politics,* in which he reviews practically all of the social systems that had been proposed in his time, criticizing especially the ideas set forth in Plato's *Republic.* Aristotle is strongly in favor of private property, though he holds that it should be limited and regulated by the state. He admits, with Plato, the desirability of the unity of the state, but holds that communism is not necessary to attain such unity. He criticizes Plato's communism severely. In relation to property, it will occasion constant dispute. It will destroy the pleasure which arises from the sense of ownership and it will make impossible the virtue of liberality or generosity. What is needed is not suppression, but reform of private property. In effect, Aristotle says that communism is psychologically all wrong and that it destroys the very virtues that are necessary for its success. Communism presupposes generosity and altruism, but it furnishes no means to cultivate generosity and altruism. It is even worse when it comes to communism of wives and children. Such communism would prevent the development of family affections and lead to constant quarrels. Aristotle says fi-

ARISTOTLE

nally that the unity of the state which is desirable is a moral unity, and that this unity must be effected by moral and not mechanical means; that is, by the education of citizens rather than by the communistic organization of society. He also criticizes Plato for not making any provision for the limitation of the increase of population, and implies that under a communistic scheme, population will increase with little or no restraint. In many points, however, Aristotle agrees with Plato. While he would not apparently endorse Plato's division of society into three classes fixed by nature, yet he agrees with Plato that artisans and laborers are not fitted to become citizens. On account of their dependent economic condition they cannot be expected to have that independence of judgment which is necessary for good citizenship.

Doctrine of political organization. In his doctrine of political organization, Aristotle anticipates many modern ideas. He not only holds that the best government is to be secured by lodging the main political power in the middle class, but even anticipates the division of government into legislative, executive, and judicial branches, with some hint that these will mutually check one another. Aristotle recognizes only six fundamental forms of the state, according to the number of persons exercising sovereignty and according to whether the government itself is good or bad, pure or corrupt. Government by one, when good, is monarchy; when bad, tyranny; government by a few, when good, is aristocracy; when bad, oligarchy; rule by the many, either good or bad, Aristotle calls democracy. However, his idea of a good democracy is one which is controlled by a fundamental law or constitution: a constitutional republic. Oligarchy is usually the rule of the rich for selfish purposes, while tyranny is the rule of a monarch who has discarded all legal restraints and rules selfishly. Thus Aristotle accepts with very little change the classification of governments suggested in Plato's dialogue, *The Statesman.*

Aristotle holds that there is no one best form of government, but what is best will depend upon social conditions. Ideally, monarchy would be best, provided we could always find a wise and good man to be monarch; but this is not possible, and monarchy easily degenerates into tyranny. For the Greeks, Aristotle holds that the constitutional republic is the best form of the state. Athens at its best seems to have been Aristotle's ideal almost as much as Sparta was Plato's.

Doctrine of social development. Aristotle makes no attempt to survey history in its widest sense or to suggest general stages of social and political evolution. He had a keen eye, however, to recent historical events, particularly in the Greek city-states, and seems always to have studied the development of their constitutions as far as he could in an historical way. As one of the purposes of the *Politics* was to show how governments might be made stable and avoid disastrous changes, Aristotle was bound to consider the problem of political revolutions, of which there had been numerous illustrations in the history of the Greek states. Thus Aristotle became the first to give to the world a definite and carefully worked out theory of political revolutions. This theory seems to border upon a cataclysmical theory of social development, though there is no reason for supposing that Aristotle so intended it. Aristotle finds the source of all political revolution in inequality in the organization of the state; not necessarily absolute inequality, but what he calls "proportional inequality." Each class in the state must have the power to which it is entitled for the good of the whole. Besides this general cause of all political revolutions, Aristotle finds many minor causes for each special type of revolution. In fact, his whole theory of revolutions is worked out with such care and with such a fund of historical knowledge as its background that it still creates in us astonishment. Aristotle holds that monarchy is the oldest and most primitive form of government, springing directly from the power of the patriarch in the patriarchical family. Monarchy in this original form was unselfish and controlled by considerations of the welfare of all. But in time, monarchs become corrupt, rule for their own selfish purposes, and the government becomes a tyranny. Then the landed nobility arise, overthrow the tyranny, and establish an aristocracy, a government by the nobles for the good of the whole. But after a time the aristocracy becomes corrupted by riches, forgets its obligations to the whole body of citizens, and becomes an oligarchy, a government by a few ruling for their own selfish purposes. Then the mass of citizens arise, drive out the oligarchs, and organize a constitutional republic, a rule of law for the good of all classes. After a time, however, through the influence of demagogues, the rule of law is replaced by the rule of the mob, and a degenerate democracy takes the place of a constitutional republic. Then some strong man with a few supporters sees the necessity of restoring order, becomes what we would call a dictator or, as Aristotle would say, a monarch, and the cycle is begun again.

This theory of Aristotle has often been represented not only as a cycle theory of political revolutions, but also as fatalistic. It is certain, however, that Aristotle did not intend to formulate any theory of an inevitable cycle, because he discusses at length the preventives for each form of revolution. But he saw clearly enough how power frequently led to social inequality and social corruption. Indeed, his theory might be formulated in terms of the corruption of the ruling class. In Aristotle's mind, the causes of revolution, both remote and immediate, were psychological and therefore preventable.

Doctrine of social ethics. Aristotle holds that a state is an association not merely for mutual protection or to promote commercial prosperity, but rather for what he calls "well-living." His doctrine of the state contains a carefully elaborated doctrine of social welfare. According to Aristotle, the principles of morality are the same for states and for individuals. The good life is not one thing for the individual and another thing for the state, as Machiavelli proclaimed. It is essentially the same for both. Hence, the most desirable life for the state can be known through knowing the nature of the most desirable life for the individual. Now the elements of welfare or of a happy life for the individual, Aristotle says, are three: (1) external goods, or wealth; (2) goods of the body, or health; and (3) goods of the soul, or intelligence and character. The happy man must possess all three, but in different proportions. External goods, like instruments, have a limit, namely, their utility; and it follows that the excess of them is either hurtful or in no way beneficial to their possessors. Excess of wealth and excess of health may tempt to harmful behavior. Hence external goods and goods of the body have a limit; whereas the goods of the soul, intelligence and character, have no limit. The greater the amount of these we possess, the greater their utility. Happiness for the individual, therefore, depends ultimately upon the accumulation of these goods of the soul, but the happy individual must also have wealth and health in proper amount to be happy and to live virtuously. Now it is the same, Aristotle says, with the community and the state. The state must have reasonable prosperity and wealth and a physically sound population in order to develop the best and most virtuous life.

The best life, Aristotle says, whether for the individual or for the state, is one which possesses virtue furnished with external advantages to such a degree as to be capable of action according to virtue. The best social system, therefore, is a system under which anybody can do best and live happily. But happiness, Aristotle is careful to add, is to be defined as "well-doing," or as we would say, welfare. Hence, his ideal of the community is a balanced ideal of material prosperity, physical soundness, diffused intelligence, and character; but Aristotle would add that the intelligence and character of a community have no limit in their utility, but external goods have. We must remember that both Sparta and Athens limited wealth, and that this ideal of a balanced life for both the individual and the state represents Greek social thought at its best.

Doctrine of social progress. Aristotle is generally represented as having no doctrine of social progress, and he did not advocate anything by that name. Yet, implicitly he had one, notwithstanding what Professor Bury says to the contrary. For Aristotle had a doctrine of how to achieve the ideal society that we have just sketched. In other words, he had a doctrine of social improvement, and a doctrine of social improvement is essentially a doctrine of progress, though, of course, Aristotle's theory of progress must not be confused with the modern theories that have masqueraded under the same name. Aristotle is at one with Plato, that the only way to achieve the ideal human community is by education. He did not conceive that social ideals might be realized by the blind processes of nature, such as evolution by automatic selection. The virtuous character of a state, he says, is not an affair of fortune, but of knowledge and of moral purpose. Movement toward the social ideal must be through education and the diffusion of moral purposes. The virtuous character for the community can be realized only when all who enjoy political rights are virtuous. The point to be considered, therefore, is the means by which individuals become virtuous. Now there are three ways by which men become good and virtuous; namely, nature, habit, and reason. Like his master, Plato, Aristotle holds that nature should be looked after by a eugenic program in the community, to secure proper mating and a proper physical heredity for every child born. Like Plato, he would limit the period of reproduction to the prime of life and destroy all deformed and defective children, though he would not, as we have already seen, abolish the private family. But Aristotle seems to hold that the control of nature or heredity is possible only to a limited degree. It is habit and reason which are within our control, and these can be directed by education. Education consists of two parts: habituation, or what we would call training of the habits; and the education of the rational powers, or reasoning. Education of the habits is important and should precede that of the reason, just as the education of the body should precede that of the intellect. Habituation of the impulses and the passions to the standards of civilization is the first thing. In Aristotle's own words, the education of the irrational part of the soul, the appetites, should precede the education of the rational part, the intellect; for the principle to be observed in education, as in everything, is that the lower is for the sake of the higher. Thus in Aristotle's view, the senses and the appetites should be trained to minister to our higher intelligence, for it is chiefly through intelligence that men become good.

It follows from all of this that the education of the young, as Aristotle says, is a matter that has a paramount claim upon the attention of the legislator. The provision for such education, he says, should be in public rather than in private hands. He adds that it is not right to suppose that any citizen should be his own master in this regard, but rather that all belong to the state; for each individual is a member of the state and the supervision of any part is naturally relative to the whole. Furthermore, Aristotle claims that the general education of all citizens should be one and the same. For in all states, to a certain extent, all the citizens must alike participate in the alternation of rule and subjection. As the same person is to become first a subject and afterward a ruler, particularly in a constitutional republic, the legislator should endeavor through education to make all citizens good. But Aristotle acknowledges that the educational system must always be relative to the particular polity in which it exists. As to the general character of education, Aristotle says it should be liberal and noble, and that the utilitarian elements should be subordinated. Citizens should be taught what is indispensable and salutary, but still more what is moral. Here Aristotle anticipates the necessity of education for leisure, for he says education should fit men not only to engage in business rightly, but to spend their leisure nobly. For the right employment of leisure, he adds, necessitates a higher degree of virtue than either business or war. Finally, the end to be sought in all education is always the moral character of the citizen, for the higher this character, the higher the social order it produces. Education, Aristotle would apparently say, agreeing with Lester F. Ward, is the proximate means of social progress. After discovering so many anticipations of modern ideas concerning education in Aristotle's writings, it is a pity to add that, unlike Plato, he had practically no program for the education of women.

Criticism

Outstanding intellectual leaders in history have always been centers of controversy. The controversy regarding Aristotle has not yet died down. Only very recently Bertrand Russell has declared, ''Aristotle has been one of the great misfortunes of the human race.''[2] Peter Ramus, one of the edu-

[2] Russell, *The Scientific Outlook*, p. 42.

cational leaders of the period of the Renaissance and Reformation, similarly declared that "All that Aristotle said was false," [3] and, surprising as it may seem, he received his Master's degree from the University of Paris in defending this thesis. The opposition of Francis Bacon and his followers to Aristotle is well known. But surely the controversy over Aristotle has now sufficiently subsided for us to be able to form a dispassionate estimate of the man and his work. There can be only one rational judgment upon this matter, and that is that, if Aristotle is taken rightly and placed at the beginning of the scientific movement in the western world, not at the end, his work was remarkable. To be sure, like every great thinker that we know, he showed the limitations of his environment and was to a certain extent the child of his time and of his people. Many of his ideas were characteristically Greek. This was true of his attitude toward trade and commerce, his low valuation of manual workers, his ideas on slavery, and many of his ideas regarding forms of government. Yet there were other elements in Aristotle which are universal, not the product of his time and place, but of a mind that sensed the foundations of universal scientific and philosophic truth. Such universal elements in his work were his inductive spirit, his use of the comparative and historical method, his conception of the unity of the social sciences, his conception of the indi-

---

[3] Graves, *Peter Ramus*, p. 26.

vidual as largely the product of society, his view of the origin of human association, his perception that the virtues of the community are not different from the virtues of the individual, and many of his educational ideals. If it be asked how it is possible for the human mind to think in universal terms and reach conclusions universally valid, and whether it is possible to do this without contradicting the very principle which Aristotle himself laid down, namely, the relativity of the individual to his social environment, it may be replied that this is because there are common elements in all human social life. Aristotle found these common elements by his very method of study. But we should also remember that there are common elements in the working of the human mind everywhere, and that the mind of man is after all not strictly limited by its environment of time and place. Through imagination and reasoning the human mind comes to the perception of universal truths, and this discovery of universal truth is the very essence of science in the true sense of the word. Aristotle's mind was not only encyclopedic; it was scientific, in the sense that it penetrated to the perception of universal truth. It is just because Aristotle did this that we must count him as the founder of the social sciences.

Yet Aristotle must be put at the beginning, not at the end, of scientific social thinking. Just because he was the first truly scientific social thinker, his theories must not be taken as final. Their true worth can be perceived only when they are viewed in their historical perspective. Yet, if our social thinking would take Aristotle as a starting point, it might possibly serve to clarify the atmosphere of our present-day social sciences.

There is only one sense in which Bertrand Russell's remark might be held to have even a modicum of truth; and that is, that the historical prestige and reputation of Aristotle as an authority from whom there was no appeal has often been an impediment to the development of science. This was especially true in the Middle Ages. Aristotle's own time apparently paid little attention to his ideas. Some revival of the Aristotelian philosophy began after about two centuries, and it was prevalent in early Roman times. But with the fall of the western empire, Aristotle's writings almost totally disappeared from Europe. They were brought in again with the Crusades, and from 1260 onward, Aristotle became the great authority of the scholastic philosophers. He was regarded as semi-inspired and an authority from whom there was no appeal. In this way for nearly three centuries Aristotle's prestige became an impediment to the advancement of learning and science. This Francis Bacon perceived and he, along with other Reformation scholars, led the revolt against Aristotle. The revolt became general in all Protestant countries, and only recently has a more just estimate of Aristotle as a social and political thinker begun to become general.

CHAPTER IV

Late Greek and Early Roman Thinkers

IT IS PROBABLY near the truth to say, as Nietzsche affirmed, that Socrates, Plato, and Aristotle were not truly representative of Greek society and civilization. At any rate, their teachings had no appreciable effect in determining the development of Greek social and political life. The social thinking that was to guide the development of later Greek social attitudes was rather to be found in the philosophy of Epicurus.

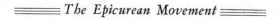

The Epicurean Movement

Epicurus was born 341 B. C., eighteen years before Aristotle died, and he lived until 270 B. C. Apparently he was a typical Greek gentleman of his age, with fine culture and a pleasing, genial, social character. Little has survived of his writings, but

61

he seems to have looked at things from the standpoint of his age. He was apparently indifferent to the course of political events, as Athens had now given up the struggle against Macedon. He counseled devotion to art and to the intellectual pleasures of literature and philosophy. He surrounded himself with a school of like-minded, admiring disciples. They represented an easygoing, simplicitarian view of life and of the universe. They were not vicious men, or even crude hedonists, but believed that the good of life was to be found in refined pleasures. This philosophy appealed to the masses, and, becoming popularized, became degraded, so that the word "Epicurean" came to mean a devotee of sensual pleasures. In its popular form, the movement finally numbered its adherents by the million in the Roman Empire, and perhaps must be regarded as the chief competitor of early Christianity.

Epicurean social philosophy. According to Epicurus, self-interest rules all men. What they seek is their own pleasure or good. Man is not naturally a social animal, as Aristotle taught, but enters into association with his fellow men to gain some pleasure or advantage for himself. Epicurus therefore implies a contract theory of the origin and nature of human society. Its basis is to be sought in the self-interest of the individuals who make it up. Its end is in ministering to their happiness. The idea that right or justice is something in the nature of things was therefore rejected by the Epicureans.

Justice is a social convention, and the conventions of society can make anything right. These views of Epicurus were elaborated and embodied in a long philosophical poem, "Concerning the Nature of Things," by the Latin poet, Lucretius. In this remarkable poem is set forth a simple materialistic view of the universe and of human life which often anticipates modern scientific views. It is particularly remarkable for the anticipation of the doctrine of evolution, both in its cosmic and biological aspects. Indeed, it contains even the rudiments of a doctrine of cultural evolution, but Bury is probably right in saying that it contains no doctrine of social progress, because it has no doctrine for the improvement of human society. Indeed, Epicureanism even at its best was essentially a doctrine of individualism, of personal pleasure and happiness. It never rose to the consideration of the general improvement of human society. Perhaps this explains why the movement was so popular in the decadent days of Rome.

The Stoic Movement

If the Epicurean movement reflected Greek life and character, the same can hardly be said of the Stoic movement. Some critics think that it was essentially Semitic in character. At any rate, it was founded by Zeno, the son of a Phoenician merchant, who was born in 340 B. C. and died in 260 B. C.

Zeno, however, studied in all the philosophical schools of Athens. He became dissatisfied with all of their teachings and set up a school of his own in the Stoa, from whence the movement received its name. However, it must be said that in many respects his teachings closely resemble those of Plato and Aristotle. Like the Epicureans, the Stoics found the supreme values of life in inner, subjective states, and counseled indifference to external things. The Stoics were pantheists, and this fact explains much in their social philosophy. Stoicism was never a popular movement, and especially not in Greece. It was, however, taken up by the Romans, among whom it found some illustrious disciples. Probably at the height of its popularity it never had more than a hundred thousand followers at most within the Roman Empire. But even so, it did much to prepare the way for Christianity, as some of its social teachings were identical with those of the Christian movement.

Stoic social philosophy. According to the Stoics, all nature is pervaded by a moral law, and virtue in the individual is the observance of this moral order in the universe. The good life is therefore not necessarily one of pleasure, but is a certain harmony between one's own nature and the moral order of the universe. The social order is, or should be, a projection and embodiment of the universal moral order. Any disturbance of this order of nature and of rational human society is injustice. Justice, therefore, is not a convention of society. Man is

made to live with his fellow man, but in order to do
so most happily and successfully, he must live according to the moral law which pervades all things
and which manifests itself particularly in his own
reason.

Inasmuch as the Stoics threw their whole emphasis upon the inner harmony of self with the universe, upon the internal mood instead of upon external conditions, they held that the good life was
possible for all men regardless of external conditions. A slave could realize the good life not less
than those blest with wealth and power. Indeed
Epictetus, the Roman slave, became the almost
perfect embodiment of the Stoic spirit. However,
Marcus Aurelius, the Roman emperor, was a not less
perfect embodiment, and his *Thoughts* have usually
been taken as the perfect expression of Stoicism
from his day down to the present, although we must
remember that Marcus Aurelius was exposed in
many ways to the influence of early Christianity.

The doctrine of the Stoics almost necessarily led
to the belief that all men are essentially the same,
inasmuch as all could realize the good life, no matter what their external condition might be, whether
bond or free, rich or poor, white or black, male or
female. Moreover, this doctrine of the moral and
social equality of men led easily to a doctrine of human brotherhood. While the Roman Stoics were
not lacking in national loyalty, yet their doctrine
of universal human brotherhood led them also to
a doctrine of the citizenship of the world. Theo-

retically they held to cosmopolitanism, though practically their world citizenship was citizenship in the Roman empire.

Finally, let us note that the Stoics anticipated the doctrine of natural law which was to play such a large part in the social and political thinking of the next eighteen hundred years. If both the universe and the social order were pervaded by a principle of reason that was the basis of all discriminations of good and evil, justice and injustice, then it followed that there was a law of nature to which all human institutions and behavior should conform. Thus the Stoics, while few in number, have had an influence upon social thought out of all proportion to their numbers.

The Social Philosophy of Rome

It is perhaps hardly correct to say that Rome did almost nothing in the way of social and political thinking, except to be a seed-ground for the various schools of Greek thought; for the influence of Rome upon modern civilization has been tremendous. Nevertheless, its influence was not mainly through its thinkers, but rather through its men of action and its practical policies. The Romans were a conquering people, and having conquered the world, they had to govern it. Nevertheless, except in the realm of law, they added almost nothing new to social and political theories. They never seemed

to get time to formulate their concepts. Hence, in
social philosophy, they were essentially imitators of
the Greeks. The leading writers of their classical
period deserve from us scarcely more than a passing
notice. The greatest of their social and political
thinkers of this early period was the lawyer Cicero.
Cicero was born 106 B. C. and died 42 B. C. He came
from the patrician class, and was carefully educated
not only in law, but in all the schools of Greek philosophy. He was scarcely capable of synthesizing
these schools, but he was eclectic in his method, and
borrowed freely from all schools, particularly from
the Stoic. Among his numerous writings, the two
which contain the most of his social and political
philosophy were *De Republica* and *De Legibus,* mod-
eled after Plato's dialogues of the same names. The
very titles rightly suggest that Cicero was essentially a popularizer of Greek philosophy for the
Romans. Indeed, he himself never professed to be
anything else.

At first, we may be inclined to dismiss Cicero as
simply an orator and politician; but to do so would
be to overlook the fact that he did play a very considerable part as a mediator of Greek ideas in Roman culture.

In general, Cicero followed Aristotle and the
Stoics, rather than Plato. With Aristotle he held
that man is naturally a social animal, spontaneously
seeking the society of his fellow men without being
motivated by perceptions of utility. The origin of
society is to be sought in the social instincts of man,

we would say. Hence, the state and most other human institutions are natural growths. Cicero rejects in just so many words the hypothesis of a primal convention or compact as the beginning of the state or society. Therefore, he is also opposed to the idea that justice and right are mere social conventions. "Man," he says, "is born for justice, and law and equity are not mere establishment of opinion, but an institution of nature." Justice, accordingly, is something independent of the character and consciousness of man.

This is obviously in harmony with the Stoic doctrine that the principle of reason runs through nature and should rule human society. Justice is, therefore, necessary in human relations if they are to prosper. This, Cicero holds, is a law of nature that is more or less imperfectly recognized in the laws and institutions of all peoples. The rights of individuals, of groups, and even of nations spring from the fact that there is such a law of nature to which individuals and institutions ideally should conform.

Moreover, Cicero defends the Stoic doctrine of the natural equality of all men. All men are capable of living the good and virtuous life. All men have the same reason to guide them, and the capacity of acquiring knowledge, though the knowledge itself may be endlessly diversified. The doctrine of natural equality, of course, sweeps away the differences among men due to social and economic status, and

lays a foundation for a doctrine of human brotherhood.

After such an exhibition of Stoic principles, one
would expect that Cicero would become an ardent
advocate of the Stoic doctrine of cosmopolitanism.
But he was too much of a Roman and perhaps too
much of a politician to take that stand.   Instead,
he claimed that the Roman constitution was the best
of which we have knowledge, which is what we would
expect an orator and a politician to say.   However,
we will have to remember that ethnocentrism is common to all peoples, and that Rome in particular was
one of the first nations to develop strongly nationalistic traits and a chauvinistic loyalty to her institutions.

CHAPTER V

Early and Medieval Church Thinkers

We shall not attempt to deal with the Christian movement in this story of social philosophy, even though it has had such profound influence upon the currents of social thought in western civilization. So much has been written upon this movement and the currents of thought that have accompanied it that it would be idle, if not presumptuous, to try to add anything. It is necessary, however, that a sharp distinction should be made between the teachings of Jesus and the historical Christian movement. The teachings of Jesus seem to have been a logical development of the teachings of the later Jewish prophets, while the historical Christian movement gathered elements from many sources until perhaps even the founder of the movement would have been unable to recognize it. Moreover, the teachings of Jesus were concerned mainly with developing the ethical content of religion, but the Christian movement, absorbing much from Greek philosophy, soon became very largely theological in character. It centered about doctrines that were no part of Jesus' teaching, such as the doctrines of the atonement, of sacraments, and of the Trinity. The world was not ready for the revolution in morals and in social attitudes that Jesus advocated, and theology was an easily accepted substitute for such a revolution. Thus, as time went on, the Christian movement tended to become more and more centered upon theological, rather than upon social and ethical, questions.

Nevertheless, it is true that the early fathers of the Christian church were the social thinkers of their time. It is often asked why no great thinkers are found in the later days of the Roman empire. The answer is that there was no dearth of great thinkers, but that they were absorbed in the religiosocial movement that we call "early Christianity." The best minds throughout the Greco-Roman world turned to the new religion as the medium for their ideas. Yet this religious movement did not favor the development of scientific social thought. Instead of going forward to attack the problems of their civilization in a scientific manner, the Church Fathers went back to the theological way of looking at things. Social and political thinking became again subservient to religion. To this extent the Christian movement must be considered a retrograde movement. Nevertheless, the Church Fathers, even though primarily theologians, were the chief

social thinkers and organizers of their time; and
as Flint says in effect, "Christianity almost spontaneously and inevitably produced a sort of social
philosophy; but a philosophy excessively one-sided,
owing to the life of society on earth being viewed
so exclusively in relation to religion, that the interests of industry, commerce, and wealth almost faded
out of sight." Chief among these social thinkers of
the early church was Augustine of Hippo, commonly
known as Saint Augustine.

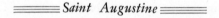 *Saint Augustine*

Biographical sketch. Augustine was borne 354
A. D. and died 430 A. D. Although his father settled at
Tagaste, Numidia (now a part of Algeria), he was
apparently of an old patrician Roman family, and
a man of wealth and considerable culture. The an-
cestry of Augustine's mother is not known, but she
was a Christian, while the father remained a pagan.
Augustine was brought up in the lap of luxury, and
apparently had able private tutors, who acquainted
him with the whole field of Greek philosophy. At
seventeen, he went to Carthage to study rhetoric,
and became involved with the debauched and dis-
solute youth of the city. He identified himself with
their pleasure seeking, and became hostile to Christianity. At first he was an Aristotelian, but at nine-
teen he became a Manichean, still later a Platonist,
and finally a sceptic. At the age of twenty-eight,

after the death of his father, he went to Rome, and later to Milan, to become a teacher of rhetoric. At Milan he came under the influence of Ambrose, and was finally converted to Christianity. He returned to North Africa in 388, and shortly thereafter became a priest. A little later he was made Bishop of Hippo, now Bona, in Algeria. He devoted the rest of his life to organizing the church in North Africa and writing in defense of Christianity.

Augustine was a man of very great force and ability. He wrote voluminously, but mainly along theological lines. However, in 410, the Goths under Alaric sacked the city of Rome. Pagan worship had been forbidden about twenty years earlier, but many of the Romans remained pagans, and said that the fall of Rome was due to the failure to worship the old gods who had hitherto protected the city, and also to the new religion, which made men effeminate and incapable of defending themselves. In reply to this talk, Augustine wrote his greatest work. He entitled it *De Civitate Dei,* and we ordinarily translate it *The City of God.* *Civitas* in Latin originally meant "city," but in Augustine's time it had come to mean "the state," or almost "human society." It would not be far wrong to translate the title of this work as "The Divine Society." This voluminous work was written from 413 to 426. It was not a scientific work in any sense. We should call it a polemic directed against paganism and in defense of Christianity. But it was much more than a theological polemic. It contained a whole social philosophy based upon Augustine's understanding of Christianity.

Scientific method. Though Augustine's method was wholly unscientific, it deserves consideration, because it still prevails in some of our social thinking. Augustine got his social philosophy from the Bible, from the Old Testament in particular, and from the doctrines of the church. He considered these authoritative, but he was acquainted, as we have seen, with the whole field of Greek philosophy and with Greek and Roman history. He undertook to show how the best philosophical thinking and the course of human history supported the Bible and the church of his time. It should be hardly necessary to say that Augustine's method is to be condemned from the standpoint both of religion and science; for if religion is true and socially valuable, it must stand the light of independent investigation; while science cannot build itself upon presupposed assumptions. Nevertheless, Augustine had the greatest influence upon the whole thinking of the church in the Middle Ages, and still is recognized as one of the great authorities by the Roman Catholic Church. Many Protestant denominations, also, have been considerably influenced by his theories.

Social philosophy. The City of God, as we may call Augustine's most important work, contains, as we have just said, a whole social philosophy devoted to the defense of Christian ideals and to the criticism of the practices of the pagan world. In it, Augustine asserts that the downfall of Rome was due to the weakening effect of pagan vices, but to prove this he found it necessary to survey the whole of history, so far as he knew it. He asserts that the human species was created by God less than six thousand years before his time. All theories which assign a greater antiquity than that to man are mendacious. All men are descended from a single primitive pair, Adam and Eve. They are all bound together by ties of kinship and are similar in their nature. In a certain sense, Augustine thinks the whole subsequent history of man was bound up in this primitive pair. But God placed them in a world of law and order. Everything in the physical world is ruled by the laws of nature, which represent the will of God. Therefore law must also rule in human affairs, in the growth and decay of nations, in their victories and defeats. The vicissitudes of the Roman empire are to be explained neither by chance nor by fate, but by moral causes. Over all human events are the laws of God's providence; but Augustine holds that this is not inconsistent with man's freedom, although the general plan of history is divinely foreordained.

Human society, naturally one, had its unity broken by the fall or sin of Adam, from whom have issued in consequence two kinds of men, two societies: the one ruled by self-will and self-love, degenerate, lawless, and predestined to perdition; the other ruled by the love of God and man, regenerate, law-abiding, and predestined to eternal bliss. Outwardly, visibly, these two societies or cities of men may be confused; but inwardly and spiritually, they are essentially and eternally distinct. This distinction of sinners and saved is greater than any other distinction, such as race, birth, or economic condition. But man, even in the sinful state, is endowed with the power to progress. Through his intelligence he can make inventions and develop the countless arts of life. The virtues of the heathen people, for a time, may merit and receive dominion and temporal rewards. Such especially was the case with Rome. The earlier Romans, by their industry, moderation, freedom from luxury and licentiousness, and skill in government, achieved great power. But the later Romans, by their vices and corruption, brought on because they lacked an understanding of true religion, reversed all this and brought about their own destruction.

At this point, Augustine brings in the parallel between the development of the individual and of the race, which is perhaps his chief contribution to social philosophy. The comparison of the individual and society, as we have already seen, was a common social thought among Greek thinkers; but none of them reached the point of making it a parallel in the development of the individual and of human society. It is a testimony to Augustine's intellectual penetration that he first set forth the theory that the development of the race is analogous to the development and education of an individual. The historical records that he uses to demonstrate this are those of the Old Testament. He makes a three-fold division of human history into youth, manhood, and old age. The epoch of youth is characterized by the absence of law, and comprehends infancy and adolescence. In this period, which extends from Adam to Noah, man is absorbed in the satisfaction of his physical wants; in the second, which extends from Noah to Abraham, the development and confusion of languages take place, and historical records begin to be written. The manhood of the race, or reign of law, extends from Abraham to Christ. It is marked by the growth of reason and the sense of sin. Augustine divides this epoch up into three periods without clearly indicating reasons for doing so: (1) Abraham to Moses; (2) Moses to the Captivity; and (3) the Captivity to Christ. The old age of humanity, or reign of grace, begins with the birth of Christ. Here Augustine sees that his elaborate parallel breaks down. Old age in the individual is a period of weakness, but in humanity it marks the period of perfection. With the coming of Christ comes the reign of grace that will last until the victory of Christianity is complete and the saints inherit the earth.

However, Augustine, with all early Christians, looked for the early end of the world. Christ will come again to judge the quick and the dead and finally to separate the good from the evil. The heavenly Jerusalem is to come down on the earth and the saved are to be gathered into it and the sinful are to be cast out. Thus the city of God which has grown up alongside the kingdoms of this world will outlast them all.   It will draw into itself all the saved out of all the nations, tribes, and peoples of the world, and a new peaceful and perfectly happy human society will be built upon the ruins of the cities and kingdoms of this world that has passed away.   Thus, as Bury says, Augustine had scarcely any theory as to the future progress of mankind.

Augustine's conception of social order was based wholly upon the realization of this ideal divine society.   It was to be an order of love, in which justice was to be done, not only to man, but to God.   The peace of the divine city was therefore to be a peace of brotherly love, reflecting the eternal peace of God. Apparently the state, as we understand the word, is superseded entirely by the heavenly kingdom.

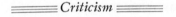

Criticism

Augustine's social philosophy has had very great influence upon the social thought of western civilization.   There are still many, not only within the Roman Catholic Church, but also in Protestant denominations, who think that no other social philosophy is possible.   They agree with Augustine that "nothing is to be accepted save on the authority of Scripture, since greater is that authority than all the powers of the human mind."   They hold, as Professor Lichtenberger has said, that "the Bible supplied man with a history of his origin and his institutions. Not only was there no need for scientific research or social philosophy, but its very pursuit was impious and its conclusions, in so far as they differed, blasphemous.'' The Protestant theology of Calvin, as well as the Roman Catholic theology of St. Thomas Aquinas, is based directly upon Augustine's work. The prestige of Augustine's authority has therefore often hindered the development of scientific social thinking.

As to the content of his social philosophy, only one judgment is possible regarding it, and that is that it is a poetic religious conception. If there is truth in it, it needs corroboration by scientific research. One cannot but remark, however, the relative harshness and inhumanitarianism of Augustine's conceptions. Like Plato, he divided human society into predetermined classes. The social dualism which he created between the sinners and the saved was even more impassable than the gulf between artisans and citizens in Plato's *Republic*. This dualism has persisted in our social thinking down even to the present, and has often interfered with the scientific solution of social problems.

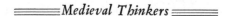

Medieval Thinkers

The Middle Ages are historically and sociologically of great interest, but they produced little or no original social thinking, for their task was to assimilate and harmonize the past Greek, Roman, and Jewish-Christian thought.   Culturally, the Middle Ages were a period of profound reversion toward barbarism, especially in southern Europe, where Greek and Roman learning for a time almost disappeared. As northern Europe had never had any high culture, we can scarcely speak of reversion there.   Indeed, the cultural development of northern and western Europe was only beginning. The various cultural elements received from Greek, Roman, and Jewish-Christian sources did not easily harmonize, and gave rise to many social problems, some of which have persisted to this day.   The great problem that occupied the thinkers of the Middle Ages, however, was the relation between the authority of the church and the authority of the state or empire. As the church grew into power, more and more it began to claim that it should be supreme in political and social affairs, just as the spiritual in man should be supreme over the physical.   This conflict between the authority of the church and the authority of the state reached its height in the twelfth and thirteenth centuries.   The partisans of the state held that the temporal power had always been in the hands of the Roman emperor and was therefore in the hands of his successors. The schoolmen, or scholastics, who represented the church, held, on the other hand, that supreme power, in all matters that pertained to human welfare, had been given to the church and its head, the pope. Medieval social thought cannot be understood without keeping this conflict between the church and the state steadily in mind.

Even the greatest academic work of the schoolmen centered around this problem. This was the task of interpreting Aristotle, and harmonizing his philosophy with the teachings of the Bible and the traditions of the church. In the early Middle Ages, only Latin fragments of Aristotle's work were known. His full works did not come into Europe until about the middle of the twelfth century. Then they came in through the Saracens in Spain and through the returning Crusaders. The returning Crusaders brought back with them the full Greek text of most of Aristotle's works, and the reconciliation of Aristotle with the teachings of the church now became the main task of the schoolmen. Greatest and most famous among these was Thomas Aquinas.

Thomas Aquinas. Aquinas was born about 1225 in the territory of Naples of a noble family. He was educated at the University of Naples, and it is said that his parents destined him for military life. At the age of seventeen, however, he entered the Dominican order. Later he studied philosophy at the University of Cologne and in 1245 entered the University of Paris, then the largest university in Europe, and studied there for three years. Soon after, he became a teacher at the University of Paris and attracted students from all over Europe. He seems to have been the most popular teacher of the

Middle Ages.   His students called him "the Angelic
Doctor," a compliment that has been very rare in
academic history. He wrote many works, including
a *Commentary on Aristotle,* though some of his social teachings are found in his *Summa Theologica.*
He died in 1274 at a relatively early age.   Along
with Augustine, he is still the orthodox social philosopher and theologian of the Roman Catholic
Church.

Scientific method. Aquinas distinguished two
sources of truth: revelation and reason.   By "revelation," he meant the Bible plus the traditions of
the church. His method was to show how these
two sources of knowledge harmonized, though he
gave primacy to revelation. The proper use of
reason and the proper interpretation of Aristotle's
teachings would lead, he argued, to the same conclusions as those that had been given by revelation.
In this way, Thomas Aquinas used all of the resources of logic and philosophy, as he understood
them, to support the Christian tradition, which in
his mind was the tradition of the church.   Thus he
became the great defender of the power of the
church and the power of the popes. His method
is still employed by some Roman Catholic social
thinkers. He has often been called a Roman Catholic edition of Aristotle.

Social philosophy. In the main, his social philosophy is that of Aristotle. His belief is that the state
arose from social necessity and from the fact that
man is by nature a social animal. But Aquinas

argues that the authority of the state has not only a natural, but also a divine source. This source he finds in the nature of law which ultimately comes from the nature of the universe itself, and so from the will of God. It is this insistence upon law that makes Aquinas the great philosopher of authority, perhaps for our time as well as for his own. Law, he says, is of four kinds: (1) *Eternal law,* which is the design or plan of the universe; (2) *Natural law,* which is the perception of this constitution of the universe as rational by man; (3) *Human law,* which is the attempt of human society more or less imperfectly to embody natural law in statutes and institutions; and (4) *Divine law,* which is the church's interpretation and mediation of eternal law and natural law in their application to human problems. More strictly, Aquinas conceived of divine law, as we have already said, as the law of revelation. But as the church must interpret this revelation, it is the court of last resort. Through it, all other forms of law should be mediated to man. Justice, therefore, has more than a social implication. It has a theological application as well. A just social order must acknowledge God, render to him his due, and respect the authority of his church, as well as harmonize human relations. The divine law of revelation interpreted by the church must supplement the inadequacies of human reason and build up among men the divine society that Augustine described.

In most other respects, Aquinas accepts Aristotle.

His views on slavery, for example, are similar to Aristotle's, though, with Augustine, he agrees that slavery is a result of sin. His economic ideas were also similar to Aristotle's, though he held that the poor should be cared for by the state. He argues for monarchy as the best form of government for the state, because it best secures social unity.

Dante. Dante, the great Italian poet, merits a word because he reflects the opposite views from Thomas Aquinas. He was born in 1265 and died in 1321. Unlike Aquinas, he was educated for the church, and then turned away from it to enter political life. He held several offices of importance in his native city of Florence. But when the opposition party came into power, he was exiled and spent the remainder of his life wandering from one Italian city to another, writing at the same time his great poem, *The Divine Comedy,* which represents at once both medieval theology and medieval social philosophy. However, when the Holy Roman Emperor, Henry VII, came into Italy in 1310, Dante, to strengthen the position of the Empire among Italians, published his celebrated treatise, *De Monarchia.* This work is notable for us, not because it defended the Empire and advocated monarchy as the best form of government, but because it insisted that there should be one world state as well as one world religion. The world state, according to Dante, should be made up of semi-independent principalities and kingdoms, all united, however, in one world empire. All states should be under one central government, Dante argued, because only thus could universal peace be secured. Moreover, Dante continued, this world state should not be subject to the church. While the power of the church comes from God, yet the power of the Empire, as it existed in the Roman Empire, was prior. According to Dante, there are two sides to man's nature: the religious, and the secular; hence, there are two sets of interests: the temporal, and the spiritual. These should co-operate, but each should attend to its own business. The Emperor should be supreme in the state, while the pope and the church should be supreme in spiritual matters. Quite evidently, Dante drew the inspiration for his ideal of a world state from the Roman Empire. He imagined that the Roman Empire had been one great state, and he persuaded himself that Christendom also might be such.

Perhaps Dante should be remembered chiefly, however, as "the first conscious pacifistic thinker of the world." He was an advocate of a world state because he believed that only through such political organization could permanent peace be achieved, and he seems to have been thoroughly convinced, in reaction to the disorders of his time, that the best means of promoting the welfare of mankind is peace; but peace, he thought, could not be secured without some world-wide political organization. In this thought, Dante must be ranked among the moderns.

CHAPTER VI

Early Modern Thinkers

 *Niccolo Machiavelli*

Biographical sketch. Niccolo Machiavelli, states-man and historian of Florence, was born in 1469 and died in 1527. Machiavelli is the gateway to modern social and political thinking, for he marks the end of the medieval point of view. As has often been pointed out, his thinking constitutes a break so complete that it is as if medieval social and political thinkers had never existed. Machiavelli lived in a most momentous epoch. The Renaissance movement, with its purpose of restoring not only ancient learning, but also Greek and Roman social and political ideals, had completely triumphed. Moreover, nationalism and patriotism were being reborn. Absolutism, too, had come to dominate political life. Because Machiavelli represented in an extreme degree all of these new tendencies, he was able not only to reflect the spirit of his time, but to become an enduring influence in all subsequent social and political thought.

The Italy of Machiavelli's time, in every department of life, had become almost completely paganized by the triumph of the Renaissance movement. Even the church was influenced, and became paganized and corrupt beyond our imagination. As one of the most reliable of Machiavelli's commentators says:

> At the beginning of the sixteenth century Italy was rotten to the core. In the close competition of great wickedness the Vicar of Christ easily carried off the palm, and the court of Alexander VI was probably the wickedest meeting place of men that has ever existed upon earth. No virtue, Christian or Pagan, was there to be found; little art that was not sensuous or sensual. It seemed as if Bacchus and Venus and Priapus had come to their own again, and yet Rome had not ceased to call herself Christian.[1]

It was an era of strong, unscrupulous men; none was more unscrupulous than Alexander VI, who ascended the Papal throne in 1492. He was a man who apparently stopped at nothing in his determination to extend the power of the church and even of his own family. His illegitimate son, Cesare Borgia, was probably one of the most unprincipled

---

[1] Cust, "Introduction to Machiavelli," in *Tudor Translations*, Vol. I, p. xvii; quoted by Lichtenberger, *Development of Social Theory*, p. 127.

political adventurers that Europe has ever known. Since Machiavelli's native city of Florence was threatened in this situation, he became an envoy of the city to the camp of Cesare Borgia, whom he came to admire greatly. He also was the ambassador of Florence to the Papal See, to France, and to the court of the Emperor Maximilian. Thus Machiavelli was in the midst of all the political turmoil of his time. He witnessed constantly the use of force and of intrigue. It is no wonder that in such a world he concluded that might was the only possible right, and that he saw no possible relation between politics and morals and religion.

We cannot understand Machiavelli except as a child of his time and as a patriotic citizen of the little city republic of Florence. It may be well also to remember that, considering the age in which he lived, he was a highly cultured man. In 1512 the family of the Medici came again into autocratic power in Florence, and Machiavelli lost his official position. He believed, however, that in Lorenzo de Medici he had found a strong man who might be able not only to free Florence from the menace of its enemies, but also expand its power, possibly over all Italy. Hence, Machiavelli wrote the book which we call *The Prince,* dedicating it to Lorenzo de Medici and counselling him in effect to adopt the same methods that Alexander VI and his son, Cesare Borgia, Duke Valentino, had used.

This is how Machiavelli happened to elaborate the doctrine that we now call "political immoralism."

It is simply the doctrine that in politics might is right, and that the only possible end of the state is power. There is hardly any doubt that Machiavelli himself was a worshipper of power, not only in the state, but also in individuals. We would say that he was an advocate of success at any price.

Machiavelli's political theories startled the world. Many people of his time and since have refused to believe that he meant what he said, and have claimed that he wrote in irony. But his private correspondence and his *Discourses on Livy* prove that he was absolutely sincere. As we have already said, he must not be judged out of his setting. It has often been said that Machiavelli wrote without any presupposition, and described things just as he found them; but this is hardly correct. His presupposition was patriotism—unscrupulous patriotism, to be sure, but nevertheless patriotism. We should also remember that Machiavelli had no knowledge of or interest in science as we understand it. He was a man of the world, a politician and a diplomat, who attained to a cold, detached view of things which approached a scientific view; but he seemed to lack the scientific imagination that might have enabled him to see the possibility of another sort of social and political world than the one which he experienced.

It is hardly necessary to add that we must not think of Machiavelli's political and social views as the depth of depravity and wickedness. In Machiavelli's mind, they represented merely the practices of the successful rulers and states around him, and not only around him, but also essentially the practices of Imperial Rome, which was, as we have said, his model in all things political. Moreover, to him, all these practices were an expression of patriotism, and if we grant Machiavelli's belief that the power and prosperity of the state are the only ends to be sought in politics, then we must concede that his doctrine, that the end justifies the means, was logical. It is easy, therefore, to construct a defense of Machiavelli as a super-patriot, and many such defenses have been written. As early as 1771 a book, *The Thoughts of a Statesman,* was published by an Italian jurist to show the injustice of the charges against Machiavelli. It must also be added that many rulers and statesmen who have repudiated Machiavelli's teachings in theory have followed them in practice. For example, Frederick II of Prussia, before he came to the throne, wrote a book whose title was *Anti-Machiavelli;* yet it would be difficult to point to a modern ruler more Machiavellian in his practices than Frederick II when he became King of Prussia. The competition of states and nations for power, and even of politicians and statesmen for prestige, therefore, have lent an air of plausibility to Machiavelli's views. This is doubtless the reason why the principles that he advocated still survive in the minds of many. Machiavelli must be considered, therefore, the great formulator of the doctrine of political immorality, a doctrine that has too frequently been followed in the modern

world in political practices, even though generally
repudiated in theory.

Scientific method. Machiavelli has been called
the founder of the science of politics, but that honor,
as we have seen, belongs to Aristotle. Like Aristotle, his familiarity with men and with affairs enabled him to develop a cold, impersonal view, somewhat like that of science. Machiavelli knew little
of Aristotle, however, and perhaps if he had known
more he would not have completely severed politics
and ethics. His problem was not that of the truth,
but rather that of the practical success of the state
and the ruler. To understand the conditions of this
success, he adopted a completely empirical method,
cutting loose from all authority and from all moral
scruples as well. However, he studied things dy-
namically, as moving. Thus, he invoked history,
and is often counted as one of the founders of the
historical method in politics. But his view of human history was narrow. Practically, he knew the
history only of his own time and of the Roman Empire. Again, he was acquainted only with the political side of history, and knew little or nothing of the
general history of civilization. Now the historical
method is of fundamental importance in the social
sciences, but no method lends itself more easily to
abuse. Machiavelli used the historical method, but
he used it simply to bolster up his own theories. He
found in world-conquering Rome his political ideal,
and from the history of Rome, as well as from his
experience with the politics of his time, he induced

his social and political theories. Such a use of the historical method is not only narrow, but superficial, and bound to lead to very superficial conclusions.

Quite as narrow as Machiavelli's theory of history was his theory of human nature. Very few modern writers have surpassed this Italian of the Renaissance in cynicism. He saw only the evil in human nature, and again we must say that his views were a reflection of his environment. "Whoever desires to found a state and give it laws," Machiavelli tells us in his *Discourses on Livy*, "must start with assuming that all men are bad and ever ready to display their vicious nature." This simple, egoistic theory of human nature, not less than his practical experiences, must account for much that Machiavelli says. Even if at times he acknowledges that there are some individuals who are not all bad, he makes no use of his exceptions in his political theorizing.

Machiavelli's Social Philosophy

Origin of society and the state. Machiavelli's theory of the origin and nature of society and the state is found chiefly in his *Discourses on Livy*, which perhaps must be considered his chief contribution to social philosophy. His theory is implied more often than explicit. He does not distinguish between society and the state. In Machiavelli's thinking, the state is society, and the state is the

only unit of his thought. He assumes, as we have
seen, that the whole conduct of man is dictated by
selfish interests. Self-interest is a sufficient explanation of all things social and political. Therefore,
it would seem that Machiavelli held to something
like the contract theory of the origin and nature of
the state. At any rate, he considered that everything in the social world originated and was sustained by the egoistic desires of individuals or of
some class.

Doctrine of social organization. A much neglected phase of Machiavelli's social philosophy is
his views on the place of religion in social order.
He is one of the first modern writers to take a
purely pragmatic and social view of religion. He
says in the *Discourses* that religion is "the most
useful and assured support of any civil society,"
Moreover, in contradiction to the views which he
expresses in *The Prince,* he holds that religion is a
"chief cause of prosperity." He tells us therefore
that "Everything that tends to favor religion (even
though it were believed to be false) should be received and availed of to strengthen it." He praises
especially the religion of early Rome as a source
of Roman strength of character. But he seems to
hold that Christianity has "emasculated mankind."
Nevertheless, a purer form of Christianity than that
which obtains in Italy would strengthen religion
and so strengthen Italian society. Though a Roman
Catholic, he goes so far as to say "the evil example
of the court of Rome has destroyed all piety and

religion in Italy," and "The nearer people are to the church of Rome, the less religious they are." It is in this doctrine of the part that religion plays in social order that Machiavelli approaches nearest to a sociological interpretation of history. He even goes so far as to anticipate the doctrine that the decay of religion is a sure symptom of a decay of the civilization. For, he says, "No greater indication of the ruin of a country can be found than to see religion contemned." With Bodin, therefore, he would seem to hold that superstition from a social and political point of view is preferable to atheism.

Doctrine of political organization. Is is Machiavelli's doctrine of political organization that has especially shocked the world. This is to be found chiefly in *The Prince,* a book which was written, as we have seen, for one of the Medici. The book had two problems: first, how to get political power for a state; and second, how princes or rulers could retain their power. It is not certain that Machiavelli favored absolutism. He was thoroughly an opportunist, and favored any strong government that could assure political success. He considered that the success of the prince or the ruler was the same thing as the success of the state. He argued that the end of the state is power, and that whatever conduces to that end is justified in politics. In other words, he thoroughly indorsed the maxim that in politics the end justifies the means. Politics and morals, therefore, have no necessary relation. The state is immoral, or rather, amoral. Therefore, the things that are done by the state and in political life cannot be judged by the ordinary standards. The state and the ruler must aim at success, no matter what the price may be; and Machiavelli says that history teaches that only those rulers succeed who do not shun deceit and breach of faith as well, while those who always deal honestly nearly always fare badly. Hypocrisy and deceit, he believes, are at the bottom of political success. Even cruelty and assassination may be employed if used discreetly. Goodness, virtue, and religion are to be considered, but only in so far as it is profitable to consider them. They should be cultivated in the state by rulers, because they give rulers power over the populace and preserve order. Vices, too, should be encouraged when they help to keep the populace contented. Such a policy is just as necessary in a democracy as in a monarchy, if the state is to achieve success. But Machiavelli seems to catch a slight glimpse of a moral law pervading human society when he adds that a free government cannot be maintained in a corrupt state.

The internal end of the state is not justice or morality, as Aristotle and Plato argued, but industrial and commercial prosperity. It is for this that the state is organized. Any other way of looking at the political life is utopian. The success of political parties and of diplomacy is solely for this end. It follows that if the internal end of the state is industrial and commercial prosperity for its citizens, the external end is expansion. Expansion is the very life of the state, according to Machiavelli.   This can come about by two methods: conquest, or diplomacy. Machiavelli much prefers diplomacy, and he says that the great basis of diplomacy is craft.   After a state has expanded, however, there is always the troublesome problem of keeping what it gets. Machiavelli advocates that subject populations should be given some liberty, but not too much. Rulers should not interfere too greatly with the customs of conquered people.   But if such peoples are overly troublesome, they should be wiped out or deported, and colonists should be planted in their place.

The main reliance of the prince or the ruler, whether over his own people or over a subject population, is fear. Fear, according to Machiavelli, can always be depended upon. Princes keep their thrones only by force of arms. The ruler should seek the love of his people, but love cannot be counted on as much as fear. People may be permitted to have things to keep them contented, but nevertheless, a ruler should always inspire them with a wholesome fear. He should never forget that he must maintain and increase the power of the state.

Machiavelli gives five specific methods for expanding the power of the state: (1) Increase of population. Numbers, according to Machiavelli, are a source of power, and everything should be done to encourage the increase of numbers, especially by increased births. (2) Expansion of

NICCOLO MACHIAVELLI

trade and commerce. Machiavelli might be called the father of commercial imperialism. (3) The formation of fortunate alliances. Machiavelli believed that alliances of the proper kind are a great source of increased power to the state. (4) The keeping of a standing army. But Machiavelli held that mercenary troops always weaken the power of the state, and that the whole citizen class should be drilled in times of peace, and be ready for military duty. To this end he advocated the method of universal conscription, which has been so widely followed by European nations. It is not too much to say that Machiavelli is the father of modern militarism. (5) Diplomacy. As we have already said, Machiavelli thought that the best method for expanding the power of the state is diplomacy, which, if properly used, is stronger than any army. Nevertheless, when a place in the sun cannot be secured by diplomacy, then the sword should be used for conquest. War is a natural and inevitable means of expansion, and expansion, in Machiavelli's mind, is the life of the state.

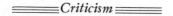

Criticism

Machiavelli was not only the formulator of the doctrines of political immorality and unscrupulous patriotism, but, as we have seen, he was also the father of modern militarism and one of the earliest protagonists, through his doctrine of the necessity

of political and commercial expansion, of both political and commercial imperialism. In all of this,
he was simply reflecting the tendencies of his time.
He was doubtless a realistic thinker, but his thought
was completely in bondage to the practice of his age.
Just as a physicist of the sixteenth century might
have been unable to imagine modern machines, so a
different sort of human world seems to have been
beyond Machiavelli's imagination. It is a great
mistake, therefore, to find anything universal in
Machiavelli. His principles are still active in our
political and economic life, for the simple reason
that the practices which generated them in Machiavelli's mind are still all too common in our own society, and we must recognize that we cannot refute
Machiavelli completely until we get rid of such
practices.

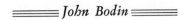

John Bodin

Biographical sketch.   A very different sort of political thinker was John Bodin. He was born about
1530 and died in 1596. He, too, lived in a stormy
period, the period of the Huguenot wars in France.
He studied law and took his degree at the University
of Toulouse, where later, for a time, he was a professor of jurisprudence. In 1561 he moved to Paris
and held a number of positions of professional and
public importance. He held himself aloof from the
religious controversies that were going on all about

him, and was one of the earliest advocates of religious toleration. He endeavored to be neutral, but
in this way incurred the displeasure of both Catholics and Huguenots, and was at times accused of
being an atheist. His interest was in establishing
a sure and stable government for France. His passion was the peace and unity of France. Like
Machiavelli, he was undoubtedly highly patriotic, but
unlike Machiavelli, he was not an unscrupulous patriot. Like Aristotle, he saw political life as a
means to peace and justice, and not as an end. For
his time, he was a man of great learning, both in
history and in knowledge of comparative jurisprudence. In 1566 he published a work in Latin entitled
A Method for the Easy Understanding of History,
which contained an attempt at the interpretation
of history and which has led to his being counted
among the founders of the philosophy of history.
In 1576 he published in French his chief work, ten
years later translated into Latin, entitled *Six Books
of the Republic.* This book gained more recognition in England than in France, where it was almost
unknown for a whole century. While it was largely
a repetition of Aristotle's teachings, it was so sane
and well balanced that by some it has been considered the greatest work in social and political thought
published between Aristotle and Montesquieu.

Scientific method. Bodin represents a return
essentially to the point of view and methods of
Aristotle, with qualifications. While he may be considered a sixteenth-century representative of Aris-

totle, yet he used the historical method much more than Aristotle, and much better than did Machiavelli, because his knowledge of history was greater. He knew something of the history of all European peoples, in medieval and modern, as well as in ancient times. Further, he was familiar with the accounts of travelers in America, Asia, and Africa, and was one of the first social thinkers to make use of this material. Thus, he might be considered as one of the modern founders of comparative method, for he insisted that the customs and laws of all peoples must be studied in order to understand either government or history. In a certain sense, he thus combined the comparative and the historical methods. Like Aristotle, Bodin insisted that there could be no complete severance of politics and ethics, but that the correct position here was the middle ground.

===== *Bodin's Social Philosophy* =====

Origin of society and the state. Bodin was the first social thinker to distinguish society from the state. He kept society and the state apart as two distinct things to be considered separately. He agrees with Aristotle, so far as society is concerned, that it (society) is natural. Like Aristotle, he regards the family as the original social group, and, of course, he accepts the Biblical theory that the whole human race is descended from one primitive pair. He says that it would be natural for the descendants of a family to continue to live in close proximity. In this way, "the beginning of all civil societies is derived from the family." Natural affection or a feeling of kinship is thus the basis of society. "Amity and friendship," Bodin tells us, "are the only foundation of all human society, and much more requisite for the keeping and maintaining thereof than justice itself;" for "Justice often makes of friends foes, whereas amity and friendship best establish true natural justice." Therefore, "The manner of the government of a house or family is the true model for the government of a commonwealth." Bodin goes even further, and anticipates a Christian philosophy of society when he proclaims that "The principal end of all laws, both human and divine, is to keep and maintain the love of men towards one another." But here we are concerned only with noting that, according to Bodin, society is natural, growing out of the family, and vastly antedates the origin of the state.

The state, on the other hand, Bodin conceives as something different. It did not arise through natural affection or the sentiment of kinship, but arose through force. Force and violence, Bodin tells us, are in the beginning of the state, and history shows us that the first monarchs were military leaders. It is primarily a union for self-defense. In other words, the origin of the state is to be found in war. War, Bodin says, leads to the concentration of power in the hands of one chief, and this chief gradually rises to the rank of a king. So the state arose through military necessities. From this Bodin derives his theory of sovereignty. Sovereignty, he says, is "supreme power unrestrained by the laws." "A sovereign gives laws unto his subjects without their consent." It is the power ultimately attained by the victorious war chief who becomes a monarch, although this power may also rest in the hands of a council or of a majority. All this Bodin considers an act of Providence, and therefore argues for the divine right of the sovereign. Government, then, according to Bodin, unlike society, did not have its birth in natural needs and tendencies, but in military necessities.

Doctrine of social organization. Bodin's general view of society is more interesting than that of any previous writer. He views society as made up of units, or groups, some small, some larger, ranging in size from the family to the state. The most important of these units is the family, but others are fraternities, corporations, and "colleges." The function of these various groups, families, communities, civil associations, and corporations should be recognized, although the state is the inclusive organization which includes them all and to which all should be subject. Just as Bodin favors the monarchical type of the state, so he thinks that the patriarchal family is best fitted to preserve the unity of the family. Like Aristotle, he is opposed to the communism advocated by Plato and Sir Thomas More, and defends private property. For some reason not clear, he seems to think that communism will tend to decrease the population. With Aristotle, he is opposed to interest-taking, because he says the low rates of interest will lead to higher rates. Like Aristotle, too, he would not allow the ruling classes to participate in trade and commerce. But he departs from Aristotle in that he holds that "slavery is not natural, profitable, or just." Negro slavery was at this time being introduced into Spain, Portugal, and France, and Bodin opposed it. The fact that slavery has been universal, he claims, does not show that it is natural. Human sacrifices in religious ceremonies have also been universal. They are not therefore on that account natural; neither is slavery. Nor is slavery a useful institution. If there are persons who are unfitted to be their own masters, as Aristotle argued, society should train these people and develop them. Here Bodin strikes a very modern note by saying that these lower classes should receive industrial education, in publically provided schools.

One of Bodin's greatest contributions to social and political theory was his doctrine of religious toleration. Since he holds that even superstition is preferable to atheism, religion of some sort is necessary in the state. But Bodin sees the great religious wars around him, and he advocates religious toleration as the only solution of the problem of conflicting religions. On account of this neutrality, as we have already seen, he was accused by the religious factions of his time of being an atheist.

But in general, in the interest of establishing social peace and justice, Bodin is greatly in favor of extending the regulatory and controlling functions of government. He even favored the strict censorship of morals by the state rather than by the church.

Doctrine of political development. Bodin accepted Aristotle's classification of governments into democracies, aristocracies, and monarchies. Monarchy he considered the primitive, natural, and divinely instituted form of government. It was best fitted to secure unity and order in the state, as in it sovereignty was simple and undivided. Hence, it was the most durable form of government. Other forms were more liable to become corrupt and to promote disorders within the state, and hence were less durable. Monarchy, by becoming corrupt, might give birth to these other forms. Like Aristotle then, Bodin considered that government had a tendency under certain conditions to run through these different forms. His theory of revolutions was not very different from Aristotle's. As there were only three fundamental types of government, so there could be only six varieties of revolution. Bodin was the first to give a clear definition of revolutions. He said that a revolution was to be distinguished from other political changes in that it always involved a change in the location of sovereignty, or a change from one type of government to another. Ordinary changes in law and in wealth should not be considered revolutions. The main causes of revolutions Bodin found, like Aristotle, in the cruelties and corruption of governments. Fear and force will not preserve a government, Machiavelli to the contrary notwithstanding, but only the love and respect of the people, built up by the virtue, wisdom, and justice of the sovereign. We are sorry to add that Bodin also held that the position of the stars operated in causing revolutions. He was a child of his age, and like Machiavelli and Bacon, believed firmly in astrology.

Doctrine of social development. Bodin holds that human history has been a course of development, not of retrogression. He refutes the idea that the Golden Age lay in the past. While he does not say that the primitive state of human society was one of savagery, he strongly implies that this is so, for he says that if the so-called Golden Age could be recalled and compared with our own, we should consider it iron. In spite of the oscillations of history, there has been progress, a slow but gradual progress, which has been governed by natural law. His conception of natural law, however, is not clear. He seems to consider that it is something that lies behind not only human laws, but human society. The laws of human society, he thinks, have grown out of natural law. Thus natural laws are abstract principles that govern nature and human society, and that are capable of being understood. Therefore, history as a whole is capable of being understood and of being studied as a science.

He thinks that there are two main classes of causes at work in human history: geographical causes, and divine causes. History rests upon geographical factors on the one side, and on revealed religion on the other side. Man is influenced in his development by both of these factors. Here again, we may note, Bodin takes the truth of revealed religion for granted, and argues at length that Christianity has had a great influence upon progress through promoting good will among men. But he also considers that geographical factors have had a strong influence on particular nations. He holds that the people of the north differ from the people of the south mainly on account of climate; that people who live on the plains differ from those who live in the mountains chiefly because of geographical conditions. Democracy has been successful in Switzerland, for example, mainly because mountain peoples love freedom. The southeastern peoples who founded the first great empires were dominantly religious; the Mediterranean peoples, especially the Romans, were practical; while the northern nations were warlike and inventive. All this Bodin attributes mainly to geographical factors. Bodin thus goes on to give a great number of crude generalizations regarding the effects of geographical factors. He was among the first to call forcible attention to the influence of these factors upon the course of human development.

===== *Criticism* =====

Bodin represents a curious combination of the medieval and the modern mind. While it is not certain that he believed in absolutism in government (for at times he contradicts himself), yet he believed in divine right, and exalted the state to a position of almost supreme authority. But he advocated freedom and tolerance in religion, opposed slavery, and held that love and good will are stronger social bonds than fear and force. He anticipated many modern ideas, such as the distinction between society and the state, the origin of the state in force, the primacy of the historical method in the social sciences, and the belief in progress through inventions and discoveries. But he is vague in the statement of these ideas and rarely develops them. For example, he believes in a general progress in the past, but fails to predict that inventions and discoveries will bring progress in the future. If he is "safe and dull," as Bury says, yet it was almost two centuries before even French social thought caught up with his thinking.

===== *Reformation Social Thinkers* =====

There were three contemporaries of Bodin who deserve more than passing notice, because of their great influence on modern social thinking, even though they themselves were not primarily social thinkers. These were the three great leaders of the Protestant Reformation—Martin Luther, Philip Melancthon, and John Calvin. While their social ideas were secondary to their religious teachings, yet all three have had a profound influence not only upon social and political thought, but also upon social, political, and economic life. The Reformation, in general, was an individualistic movement, essentially revolutionary in character. Its great principle was the individualistic one of the right of every man to decide for himself questions in religion and morality. This was called the principle of "the freedom of conscience"; but it had vast effects in the political and economic, as well as in the religious, realm. Next to the Renaissance, the Reformation was the great movement toward individual emancipation in early modern history. As a revolutionary movement, its leaders were not so much thinkers as men of action. Nevertheless, they had a profound influence upon thought.

Luther. Luther (1483–1546) was essentially a warrior, a man of brute-like force, of great courage, and of splendid moral aims. His book, *Table Talk,* contains the bulk of his ideas in the field of social philosophy. Like Dante, he held that the church and the state in general should be separate in field and function; but the church should help the state in moral matters, while the state should support the church and punish impiety and heresy.

The state, as well as the church, is a divine institution—the state to look after the temporal needs, the church to look after the spiritual needs. It is the duty of Christians to submit to the state. This is Luther's famous doctrine of "passive obedience." The state will always be necessary, Luther thinks, because men will always be wicked, and it is necessary that such an institution exist to punish human misdeeds. He says that we would not need government at all if all the people were good. But the masses and the world will never be Christian. Therefore, the need of government will continually exist. It is evident than Luther held to what we would now call the "police-power" conception of government, and that he approached the conception of philosophical anarchism that government is a necessary evil. It is evident also that Luther did not consider that religious ideals could be realized in this world, and that the purpose of religion was mainly to save souls in a future life. We should add also that in many of his conceptions Luther remained even to the end of his days essentially scholastic and Roman Catholic.

Melancthon. Melancthon (1497–1560), whose real name in German was Schwarzerd, was much more than Luther the philosopher of the Protestant Reformation. In one sense he was a product of the Renaissance. Yet, in another, he represented the influence of scholasticism within the Protestant movement. Like the scholastics, his effort was to harmonize the Bible and Aristotle. Hence, he was a sort of a Protestant Thomas Aquinas, and his method was no different from that of Aquinas. It was to take the Bible and Aristotle as authorities and reconcile them. Like Aquinas, he held that the order of human society has a double basis: the nature of man, and divine authority. In other words, the social order should rest upon the decalogue and the nature of man. Laws arise out of the nature of man, but they are also instituted by the will of God. Melancthon holds to the ancient idea that there is a law of nature which stands back of all human laws, and of which human laws should be an expression. The state has a different work from the church. Its work is external and temporal, while that of the church is internal and spiritual. While the church should be supported by the state, the state should not interfere in its religious work.

Calvin. Calvin (1509–1564) was a more remarkable man than either Luther or Melancthon. He was trained both for the law and for the church, but early accepted Protestant ideas and found it impossible to remain in France. He fled to the little city state of Geneva, which had already accepted the Protestant movement. There he helped to organize not only a Protestant church that should accord with his religious ideas, but also a civil government that he thought would be consistent with these ideas. Thus Geneva became the great center for the diffusion of Calvin's ideas. Most of these are to be found in his celebrated work, *The Institutes of the Chris-*

tian Religion, which, it is said, next to the Bible, was the greatest influence in early New England.

Essentially, Calvin's ideas were like those of Luther and Melancthon. But he was clearer as to the exact relation of church and state. Calvin held for a free church in a free state; but personally he can hardly be said to have practiced this principle. Not only did he organize Geneva in a theocratic way, but he insisted that the civil government ought to punish impiety and heresy; and therefore he caused his own friend, Michael Servetus, whom he accused of heresy, to be burned at the stake. Yet, in general, he held that the church was to have power only in its ranks, and that power was to be limited to excommunication. He leans strongly to aristocracy in government, and this was reflected not only in the government of Geneva, but also in the polity of the Calvinistic churches, especially the Presbyterian. Like Luther, he advocated, in general, passive obedience to the state; yet he insisted that Christians should resist and rebel when the commands of the civil ruler were contrary to the commands of God. As this was to be decided by the conscience of the individual citizen, it left with the mass of the citizens a large right of revolution.

But perhaps the chief social influence of the leaders of the Reformation was upon the economic and industrial life of modern nations. This, at least, was the opinion of Professor Max Weber, who found that their teachings created the psychological conditions that made possible the rise of modern capitalism.   Weber pointed out that the Reformation was accompanied by a vocational or industrial ethics that made work not something incidental, but the main purpose of life.   A man's work, therefore, became his calling through which he was to glorify God, and hence was the principal function of his life.   The very qualities that economic success demanded, namely, diligence, sobriety, frugality, and thrift, Protestantism made also the foundation for the Christian life.   These teachings were especially emphasized in Calvin's *Institutes of the Christian Religion*.   Hence, Professor R. H. Tawney [1] claimed that Calvin did for the bourgeoisie of the sixteenth century what Marx did for the proletariat of the nineteenth century—he gave an ethical and idealistic basis to the business life of the commercial classes.   Calvin saw that capital and credit were indispensable to society; that the financier is not a pariah, but a useful member of society; that lending money at interest, provided the rate is reasonable, is not sinful.   Calvin put the profits of trade and finance, in other words, upon the same level of respectability as the earnings of the laborer.   Not wealth, but its misuse for self-indulgence, according to Calvin, is evil.   Material interests should therefore be dedicated to the service of God.   Thus the pursuit of riches, which once had been regarded as the enemy of religion, was now welcomed as its ally.

---

[1] See Tawney, *Religion and the Rise of Capitalism,* Chapter II.

This teaching was admirably designed to liberate economic energies and to give a status to the rising class of the bourgeoisie. However, one must be careful not to attribute too much to Calvin's teaching and overlook the spirit of the time. In the Protestant countries where Calvin's teachings found lodging, individualism and commercialism were rising. It was the religious individualism of a great majority of early Protestants that gave free reign to the development of modern capitalistic industry and commerce. This individualism was destined to become more and more marked as the Protestant movement developed. However, the doctrines of the Protestant reformers helped to create a social atmosphere that was favorable to the development of capitalism as we now know it.

The Utopians. Perhaps we should at least mention here the great Utopians of the sixteenth and seventeenth centuries, whose work has received so much attention and has been so often written up that we need not dwell upon it. The work is significant in the history of social thinking not only because it projects social ideas, but because the writing of Utopias was often a means of concealing social ideas that otherwise it would have been unsafe to publish. This was particularly true of the *Utopia* of Sir Thomas More (1478–1535), a work that was fundamentally directed to the advocacy of communism as the best solution of the problem of human relations, because More, like Plato, considered that covetousness was the great source of evil in human society.   Somewhat similar ideas were set forth by Thomas Campanella (1568–1639) in his *City of the Sun*.   James Harrington (1611–1677) set forth an ideal democratic constitution for England in his *The Commonwealth of Oceana,* which had a great influence upon later political thinking; while Sir Francis Bacon, in his *New Atlantis,* sketched the first Utopia based upon the results of modern science, in which the government was to be conducted by scientific men, and social ideals were to be realized through the development and diffusion of scientific knowledge.   All of these Utopias, while primarily works of imagination, have had great influence upon the social and political thinking of the modern world. As has just been said, that influence is so well known that there is scarcely need to dwell upon it.   We cannot, however, admit the contention of Mr. H. G. Wells that the principal business of social philosophy is to construct such social Utopias.   In a certain sense, the social sciences have been developed to correct this unrestricted play of the imagination. The social sciences and social philosophy must be built upon critically established knowledge and the careful interpretation of verified facts, rather than upon imagination.

We may note in passing that, for social thinking, Sir Francis Bacon is much more significant as one of the founders of scientific method in the modern world than as a social Utopian.   Bacon, more than any other thinker at the beginning of the modern era, stressed the importance of empirical methods in all scientific work. He seemed to regard the building of the sciences as entirely a matter of fact-gathering and generalization from these facts. While the greatest achievements in modern science have not been the result of such a pure inductive process, yet we must recognize that the inductive spirit has come to dominate all scientific work and hence all modern social thought.

CHAPTER VII

Thomas Hobbes

WE NOW COME TO the first of the great English social philosophers. We have intentionally passed over Sir Thomas More, because his Utopian dream added very little to either Plato or Augustine. Hobbes was the first great English-speaking social philosopher in the strict sense that he attempted to state the abstract principles of social and political life. He is great also in another sense, and that is in his influence upon succeeding generations. He stamped his thought upon the whole English-speaking world, and we still have not emancipated ourselves entirely from his influence.

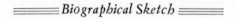 *Biographical Sketch*

Thomas Hobbes was born in 1588, during the descent of the Spanish Armada on the coast of Eng-

land. To this fact he always attributed his timidity.
He died in 1679, so that his life spanned practically
the whole seventeenth century. He was the son of
a vicar of the Church of England, and was educated
at Magdalen College, Oxford, one of the chief schools
of the Church. But neither the scholasticism of
Magdalen nor the growing Puritanism of the England of his time greatly affected him. Either he
was too original, or else some other elements in his
environment affected him more. In 1608, upon the
recommendation of the principal of his college, he
became a tutor in the family of the Earl of Devonshire. As this powerful noble family was one of
the chief supporters of the Royalist cause, he came
into close contact with the Royalist party. In 1610,
with his pupil, the young Earl of Devonshire, he
made a trip to France and Italy, in which he seems
to have come into some contact with the scientific
and philosophical movements in both countries. He
continued to remain in the service of the Earl of
Devonshire, and in this service met, among others,
Sir Francis Bacon, for whom he seems to have had
considerable admiration, and who probably had some
influence upon him; for we remember that Bacon
was in England the arch foe of Aristotle and of
scholasticism. Hobbes' mind and Bacon's, however,
were divergent. While Bacon seems to have interested Hobbes in the physical sciences, he did not
in the least succeed in conveying to Hobbes his enthusiasm for inductive, empirical methods. Probably much more influential in Hobbes' thinking was

the influence of Galileo, whom he met in 1636 on a
second trip to the Continent. Galileo had already
performed his notable experiments and outlined his
mechanical philosophy. Hobbes became an enthusiastic convert of Galileo's point of view in physics,
and it became his ambition to do for politics, or, as
we would say, for the social sciences, what Galileo
was doing for physics; for Hobbes was keen enough
to see that the mechanistic interpretation could be
applied to the world of human relations. Hobbes,
even at this early date, was saying that there was
only one reality in the world, and that was "motion." All motion, whether in the world of nature
or of human society, must be according to the same
principle. Thus Hobbes began to anticipate in his
thought the "social physics" of the nineteenth century.

On account of his Royalist sympathies and his
natural timidity, Hobbes feared the possibility of
revolution growing out of the Puritan movement.
Accordingly, he fled to Paris in 1640, as he said himself "the first of all to flee." There, somewhat
later, he became the tutor of the Prince of Wales,
who later became Charles II of England. In 1647,
he published his first political treatise, *De Cive.*
This was followed by other publications, and all
these were gathered together in 1651 in the *Leviathan.* A copy of this work was presented with
much pride to the Prince of Wales, but the Royalist
court, then in exile in Paris, received the work with
much suspicion, because it was on the mechanistic

principle, and evidently denied God's direct hand
in present human affairs. Therefore, the court
turned a cold shoulder toward Hobbes. He was
seized with another attack of his timidity and fled
back to London, where he was rather coldly received
by Cromwell's government. Upon the Restoration,
he went into hiding, but Charles II seemed to be
able to take a fairly generous attitude toward his
old tutor, and gave him a pension of a hundred
pounds a year. He found refuge with one of the
minor English nobility, and finally died, as we have
seen, in extreme old age. He never married. In
many respects his life and thinking closely parallel
that of Herbert Spencer in the nineteenth century.

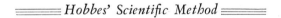

Hobbes' Scientific Method

Hobbes' scientific knowledge was limited principally to the physical sciences and to mathematics.
He considered geometry as the only true and perfect
science, and his idea was to make political science
on the same pattern. The *Leviathan* is therefore
filled with definitions and propositions that were
carefully reasoned out deductively. If one granted
Hobbes' premises, it was very difficult not to accept his conclusions. His general premise was the
materialistic one that there were only motions and
particles in motion in the universe. Here we may
remark that if we ever come to a mechanistic view
of human society, we shall have to reinstate Hobbes

as the founder of the social sciences. We must criticize Hobbes, however, because he did not have enough of an inductive method. Even in the physical sciences he was not much of an experimenter or concrete investigator; and in his social thinking he paid little or no attention to human history or to the actual social life around him. He thought that a few simple egoistic principles, such as self-interest, could adequately explain human behavior. His social thinking, however, was based upon a doctrine of human nature, and Hobbes is usually counted as one of the founders of psychology in modern times; but he considered that human nature was passive rather than active. All knowledge, he held, is the result of sense impressions. All ideas are the result of impressions on some organ of sense by the motion of some external object. As to internal feelings, they are also to be explained, according to Hobbes, on the basis of matter in motion. Human appetites and desires are but slight motions toward an object which stimulates the appetite or desire. Thus appetites and desires are stimulated by external objects. Aversion is exactly the opposite. It is a slight motion away from an object. Human appetites and desires arise through attraction and aversion. What attracts us we call good or pleasing; what repels us we call the bad or the displeasing. Originally, the only distinction between good and bad was this distinction between the pleasing and the displeasing. All of man's movements are controlled by self-interest, and are in the direction of maximizing the agreeable, or pleasing, and minimizing the disagreeable, or displeasing. They all aim at happiness; and happiness Hobbes defines as continual success in gratifying desires. Hence, there is on the part of all men a perpetual desire for power, since power is the effective means of gratifying all desires.

Although in philosophy Hobbes was materialistic and mechanistic, yet in theology he was not an atheist, but a deist. Deism is a form of theism that is consistent with the materialistic and mechanistic conception of the universe, since it makes God merely a first cause back of and behind material nature. Hobbes therefore did not need to let his religion affect his scientific thinking.

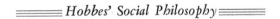

===== *Hobbes' Social Philosophy* =====

Origin of society. Hobbes deduced from his egoistic theory of human nature the conclusion that the natural state of man was one of war, of all and against all. It was a state in which the hand of every man was against every other man. In this state of nature, according to Hobbes, men lived solitary, poor, nasty, brutal, and sordid lives. Granting that every individual seeks the gratification of his own appetites and desires, and has no other end in life, this is an inevitable conclusion. Moreover, Hobbes holds to the natural equality of all men. They are naturally nearly equal in strength and in ability to gratify their appetites and desires. In the state of nature, this led to perpetual strife or war. Hobbes gives three sources for unceasing strife among men: (1) Competition to gratify appetites. (2) Fear in each one lest another surpass him in power, and so in ability to gratify appetite. (3) Craving in human nature for admiration through being superior to another, or the love of glory.

These continually lead to actual or potential war among men. Accordingly, every man rests on his arms, ready to do the other fellow when he has a chance. Here Hobbes deigns to use an illustration from the human society around him. He says if you want to know how human beings lived in a state of nature, you have but to look around and see how nations live with one another now. The nations are, with reference to one another, still in a state of nature, since there is no power above them; and they live in a state of actual or potential war. Every nation sleeps on its arms, in the belief that every other nation would attack it if it did not do so. Again, Hobbes says that if a man goes on a journey, he arms himself. He expects to be attacked by bandits and to defend himself. We may remark that in the England of Hobbes' time this was literally true.

Now in this natural state of man, Hobbes says, there is no distinction between right and wrong, no distinction between just and unjust, because there is no power to define such terms. How did these distinctions come to be? Hobbes says that there is in a state of nature what we might call natural right, which is simply the liberty of every man to do what seems best to him for his own preservation and for his own existence. There is also natural law, which is something different from natural right, since it implies the restraint of reason. Natural right is the absence of any impediment to the doing of that which seems best for self-preservation; but natural law is a rule found out by reason, and reason forbids any act or omission unfavorable to self-preservation. Natural law therefore imposes three fundamental precepts: (1) Men must seek peace and observe it. This means fhat they must escape from the state of actual or potential war. (2) Men must mutually abandon their natural right to all things. (3) All promises made must be kept, or else men will be back in the state of nature again. The individual, however, would have difficulty in doing this, and hence there must be a power or force above individuals to enforce promises or covenants. The law of nature that leads men to give up their natural rights and to covenant with their neighbors, therefore, leads to mutual agreement for the establishment of some external power to enforce covenants.

It is this mutual agreement to set up a power to enforce covenants or promises that creates the state. But it also creates society, according to Hobbes, because no society exists until it is organized. The origin of the state and the origin of society are one and the same. Thus the origin of both the state and society is in contract. It is, however, Hobbes says, an implicit, not a formal or historical contract. Previous to such organization, there is only the natural state of war. Right consists in the keeping of promises; wrong, in breaking them; and justice is the same as right. Hence, justice is impossible outside of the state. The sovereign is the third party chosen to enforce promises. Hence, Hobbes argues that the sovereign is outside and above the contract or the law of the state. He is not a party to the contract, but undertakes to enforce promises and thus keep peace within the body politic. Hence, Hobbes argues: (1) The sovereign power must be absolute, and all citizens must submit to the sovereign. (2) The sovereign power is indivisible, whether it is held by one person, by an assembly, or by the majority of the people.

Doctrine of social and political organization. According to Hobbes, every man, by accepting the social order in which he lives, tacitly accepts the social contract. If he rebels against this order and is put to death by the sovereign, whether the sovereign be king, parliament, or a popular majority, he has no right to complain, because he is virtually a suicide. As the sovereign power of the state is the power that makes the laws, it is above the law. It is also above justice and morality, because these are made by the social contract. Hence, the sovereign power has no duties toward the people. It is the absolutist theory of the state for which Hobbes argues. The state, he says, is a mortal god to whom, under the immortal God, we owe our safety and defense.

It should be noted that Hobbes is not necessarily arguing for monarchy, or for "the divine right of kings." He is arguing for the absolute power of the state, whether its sovereign is a monarch, an aristocracy, or the majority in the democracy. He favors monarchy only because he thinks it is the type of sovereignty which best maintains the unity of the state. In all cases, the sovereign power must be absolute, whether it be monarchy, aristocracy, or democracy, if peace and justice are to exist within the state. It will be noted also that Hobbes sets up an absolutism the very opposite of that claimed by the medieval church. Not only could the sovereign do no wrong, according to Hobbes, but the sovereign alone could interpret the will of God. Right and justice rest upon the contract that forms the state. Morality is simply synonymous with good citizenship; and the good citizen is the one who obeys the sovereign. Moreover, the sovereign power must decide what opinions and ideas may be circulated within the state. The subject has no right to express opinions at all against his government unless his government permits it. Agitators may cause revolutions, and should not be permitted. Hence Hobbes subordinates individual opinion, intellectual and religious life, as well as social behavior, to the state. As God's will must be interpreted by the state, the sovereign is the head of the church as well as of the state. Thus the state, according to Hobbes, is absolute in its power over the individual.

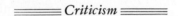

Criticism

If one grants Hobbes' premises, it is difficult, as we have said, to avoid his conclusions. He is arguing simply for an absolutist theory of the state, whether the state be a democracy, aristocracy, or monarchy. If the sovereign is a monarch, then Hobbes would support "the divine right of kings." If the sovereign is the people, then Hobbes would say that "the voice of the people is the voice of God." This way of thinking was not at all new in Hobbes' world, and it has not completely disappeared even in the most enlightened countries at the present time. Again, we must remember that this is a mechanistic theory of the state and society. A mechanistic theory of society leaves no room for liberty and makes little or no room for progress. We may criticize Hobbes as having a static view of social and political life. He was concerned simply with the way in which things should be organized. The reason for this was that he was essentially unhistorical in his view. He had no theory of social development worth mentioning, and certainly none of social progress. In social and political life, he concerned himself only with certain elements that he regarded as fixed. We may say that he was not only mechanical in his thinking, but in a certain sense, scholastic. Above all, Hobbes made no place for ethics, as we understand the word, in his social and political thinking. We have seen that with Hobbes, ethics was absorbed by politics. He therefore had a certain type of social ethics, and did much to discredit the idea that social ethics might find a basis in the social sciences.

CHAPTER VIII

Puritan Social Thinkers

A LARGE PART OF the social and political literature of England in the seventeenth and eighteenth centuries was taken up with the replies to Thomas Hobbes. The political movement did not go in Hobbes' direction, but rather toward a liberal, constitutional monarchy, with democracy in the distance. Puritanism was a movement of revolt in the state as well as in the church, and on the whole was an effort to find a basis for a more liberal and a more just social order. Among the Puritan thinkers who replied, directly or indirectly, to Hobbes was the poet John Milton (1608–1674). Milton had remarkably elevated and liberal ideas for his time, but his training was wholly literary, and he shows hardly any vestige of scientific interest. He protested against the blue laws of the Puritans and is remembered in social and political thought chiefly as one of the great advocates of the freedom of the press

in his treatise, *Areopagitica*. Even more remarkable, he wrote a very liberal treatise on divorce, in
which he advocated divorce by mutual consent. But
as the secretary of Cromwell, Milton felt it especially
incumbent upon him to defend the execution of King
Charles and to stand for popular sovereignty. This
he did in his tract on *The Tenure of Kings and
Magistrates*. He assumes the contract theory, even
as Hobbes did, but he says that kings and magistrates are but the agents of the people, and the
people have the right to remove them. The people's
election of the king is an act of God; but when the
people depose the king, that is also an act of God.
Kings and magistrates are chosen to administer law
and government, and when they do not do this to
the satisfaction of the people, the people have the
right to remove them. Thus Milton goes a long way
toward a democratic conception of the social and
political order.

But the real social philosopher of Puritan England was John Locke. Strangely enough, he wrote
more in reply to Robert Filmer than in reply to
Hobbes, because Filmer, a rather ludicrous social
and political thinker according to our standards, had
set forth a political philosophy that defended absolutism and that was acceptable to the royal family
and their supporters. Filmer's view was that the
right of the king was derived from the right of the
father in the patriarchal family. The patriarchal
father was absolute in his rule over his group. The
early kings were patriarchs. Therefore the kings

of Stuart England, he argued, had inherited all the legal rights of the patriarchs. Let us now see how Locke replied to both Filmer and Hobbes.

====== *John Locke* ======

Biographical sketch.   Locke was born in 1632 and died in 1704. His father had served as a captain in the parliamentary army. He was educated at Christ Church, Oxford, and took his degree there in 1656. Upon the Restoration, he became a member of the Church of England, although he remained a Puritan at heart. In 1664 he entered the British diplomatic service and spent some time in Germany and France. In 1679 he entered the service of Lord Chancellor Shaftesbury. The latter was involved in a plot against the king, and Locke fell into official disfavor. He fled to Holland in 1683 ostensibly for his health, but really because of political conditions. When James II was driven from his throne by the revolution of 1688, Locke was employed to defend the revolution and to refute the theories of Filmer and Hobbes. That is how he came to write his *Two Treatises of Government*. It will be noted that Locke was a liberal in both politics and religion. He was a strong defender of individual liberty, and incidentally of the doctrine of religious toleration. But while Hobbes was fundamentally a social and political thinker, Locke was fundamentally a metaphysical thinker. His main interest was in the philosophical problems involved in a theory of knowledge, as is shown by his famous *Essay concerning Human Understanding.* Thus Locke's social and political writings were subordinate, or a sideline, with him. As a social and political thinker, he did not have the depth or the penetration of Hobbes.

Scientific method. Locke may be considered as one of the founders of the psychological method in the social sciences. His fundamental philosophical doctrine was that all of our knowledge comes from experience and through the senses. There are no innate ideas of truth or of right or wrong. There is nothing in the human mind, he says, except what was first in the senses. At birth, the mind of the individual is a *tabula rasa,* so far as particular ideas and beliefs are concerned; but it has certain formal faculties and powers, such as perception, memory, desire, judgment, and reason. Locke was therefore inclined to be very regardful of experience, and was a close observer of facts. In general, his method was inductive, but it was also deductive in so far as he makes use of careful definitions of terms and a very definite theory of human nature.

Social philosophy. Let us note first of all Locke's theory of the origin of society and of the state. He does not confuse these two. Like Bodin, he keeps them separate. Locke does not believe in a presocial state. There was no presocial state, but there was a prepolitical. Man has always been a social creature. We do not need to conceive his natural condition as one of war. The law of nature is a law of reason, and as men are by nature equal, it leads, even in a state of nature, to the respect for natural rights and the keeping of peace. The state of nature was one of peace, good will, and mutual helpfulness. The primitive state of man was not therefore a state of war, and social life existed before there was any social contract. Nevertheless, in the state of nature, there are intolerable conditions that would necessitate the organization of the state or government. For in the state of nature, every man would have to redress his own wrongs, and that would lead to unnecessary conflicts. Furthermore, men would vary in the way in which they would redress their wrongs; some would mete out a greater amount of punishment than would others. So it became necessary to adopt a standard of proper punishment for violations of natural rights. These are three: life, liberty, and property. Government is organized to protect these natural rights. But, unlike Hobbes' theory, power is not turned over to a third party. The community, or society, organizes itself and thus becomes the state. The community turns over to the government as its trustee only the punishment for the violation of these natural rights of life, liberty, and property. Through their fundamental laws, agreed to by the majority, the people determine what are violations of these natural rights, and how such violations should be punished. Thus, political organization takes place through a contract and rests upon the consent of the governed, and government is strictly limited to police powers.

It will be noted that Locke, in opposition to Hobbes, regards rights as natural and inherent in the individual.   Thus Locke places the individual and his rights at the center of social and political organization.   Nevertheless, Locke's state of nature is social in character, and with him society is antecedent to the state.   The state exists only to prevent and redress the wrongs that are incident to the uncertainties of human nature.   Locke's ideal seems to have been a state of nongovernment; for he says "if men could live peaceably and quietly together, there would be no need at all of magistrates or politics, which are only made to preserve man in this world from the fraud and violence of one another." To this extent Locke agrees with Hobbes.   However, his conception of sovereignty is totally different.   It remains with the community.   The governments that are instituted by communities are only trustees for the community; and Locke says "it cannot be supposed that people should give any one or more of their fellowmen an authority over them for any other purpose than their own preservation or to extend the limits of their jurisdiction."

Locke seems to think that this was the way in which governments were actually formed.   The contract, however, is limited to political and governmental matters.   It is renewed whenever anyone accepts the state's protection.   So it is a contract theory of the state or government, but not a contract theory of society, that Locke advocated.   Popular will is the basis, for popular will makes and unmakes governments. Therefore, governments may be dissolved while society remains intact. Thus Locke puts forth the theory of popular sovereignty in an even more emphatic way than did Milton, and so shatters the pretensions of divine right.

Doctrine of political organization. "The essence and union of society," Locke tells us, "consists in having one will"; but in his state the one will is the will of the majority. Governments, he tells us, are to be classified by the number concerned in making laws. If the laws are made by the majority, the government is a democracy; if by few, an oligarchy; if by one, a monarchy. Legislation is the essential part of government, and this must depend in any case upon the support of the majority. While Locke maintains that there may be mixed governments in reference to the execution of laws, yet in legislation, governments represent either the will of the majority, or of a few, or of one. Locke advocates a government that represents a majority of the people, such as England had developed in its parliamentary system without any theory at all about it. Hence, according to Locke's own definition, he would incline so far as legislation is concerned to democracy, but he believed that the will of the majority of the people could be best secured through representation in a legislative body such as parliament. Hence we may say that Locke stands as the great advocate of parliamentary government.

Locke finds that there are three necessary compartments of government. The first makes the laws, the second enforces them, and the third protects the citizens. These necessary compartments of government Locke called the legislative, the executive, and the federative. He says that these compartments should be separate to work well, and that the legislative should represent the people and should be subject to its own laws. It is the source of all government. The executive should enforce the law and impose the penalties prescribed by the legislative for its violation. The federative is to protect citizens against foreign governments, and Locke admits that for the time it necessarily has to be in the hands of the executive. This classification of the compartments of government is of interest to us because it foreshadows the famous classification by Montesquieu into legislative, executive, and judicial. It will be noted, however, that Locke does not make the judicial a separate department of government, but includes it in the executive.

Doctrine of social progress. It can scarcely be said that Locke had any definite theory of social progress, but in accordance with his psychology, he consistently laid great stress upon education. According to Locke's psychology, education should be all-powerful, and he devoted a good deal of his time in the later years of his life to setting forth his theory of education, which was broadly conceived along Aristotelian lines as an education of the habits and passions before the education of the intellect, although intellectual training was to crown the whole system. Locke also threw much stress upon religion, concentrating on the essential things rather than the nonessentials.   If attention was paid to these essentials, he thought that Protestant sects could be harmonized, and that even the whole enlightened world would agree upon what he called "The Reasonableness of Christianity."

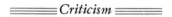

Criticism

The influence of Locke was out of all proportion to the brilliance of his work.   Especially did his ideas take root in America, where we find them voiced in both the Declaration of Independence and in the Federal Constitution.   But he had hardly less influence on the liberal thought of Great Britain; probably because he voiced the spirit or tendencies of his time, he became recognized for over a century as the leading political thinker of the English-speaking world.   He stood for individual rights and for democracy in the sense of popular sovereignty.   It is not too much to say that the doctrine of natural rights culminated in Locke, at least in the English-speaking world.   He is to be remembered especially for two important political doctrines which have had great influence upon the development of political movements.   (1) Governments originate by compact and rest upon the consent of the governed. There is therefore the right of revolution when government no longer represents the will of the majority.   (2) Governments should be limited to police powers. No absolute power can be given governments by the popular consent upon which they are based, but only power to protect life, liberty, and property.

Practically all students of the social sciences would now say that there is no good historical basis for the idea that governments originated by compact or originally rested upon the consent of the governed. Such a generalization has almost nothing to warrant it in human history. As to the limitation of governments to police powers, that doctrine has also been transcended both in practice and in theory in modern experience. Locke seems to have had very little idea that government might become an agency for the promotion of social welfare. His views on the functions of government were very circumscribed and even his views on political organization were limited almost to the England of his time. Nevertheless, we must regard Locke as one of the founders of modern political liberalism.

CHAPTER IX

Giambattista Vico and Social Evolution

ITALIAN SOCIAL THOUGHT during the eighteenth century was for the most part sterile and unproductive. An exception, however, was Giambattista Vico (1668–1744), who came a little after Locke and a little before the great English and French social thinkers of the middle and later part of the eighteenth century. Vico was born of a very poor family in Naples. He was educated by the Jesuits and prepared himself for the practice of law; but he became even more interested in the study of history and language. In 1697 he was elected professor of rhetoric in the University of Naples on a very small yearly salary that would not equal more than a few hundred dollars in terms of the purchasing power of our own money. He lived in poverty all of his life, and supplemented his slender salary by giving private lessons in grammar and doing hack literary work. Moreover, he was called upon to teach a wide range of subjects from rhetoric and literature to history and philosophy. He had trouble with his colleagues because they suspected him of innovations, and he lived under the constant suspicion of the authorities of church and state, even though he was a very loyal Roman Catholic. In addition to all of his other troubles, he had a large family, and we are tempted to conclude that he was a typical university professor of his day, if not of our own. Yet in some ways he was a very notable contributor to social philosophy, and, because he left a dynamic, synthetic view of human society behind him, all subsequent social thinking is indebted to him. In this outlook, he was a pioneer, even though he had had many precursors. He set forth his views in a book, published in 1725, which he called *The Principles of a New Science*. This work was a sort of philosophy of history, or a theory of social evolution. It was revised twice before his death. Some have said that it was unknown outside of Italy for a hundred years. Nevertheless, its point of view greatly influenced the later French and English social thinkers of the eighteenth century. Vico's work is, therefore, an essential link in the chain of the development of European social philosophy.

Vico's Scientific Method

At Naples, Vico lived under the shadow of the most orthodox Roman Catholicism, and of an absolute monarchy that was, if anything, even more intolerant of free thought than was the church. We must not, therefore, be surprised that he proposed openly an alliance between reason and authority. Many before him had accepted such a method, and many have done so since. But it remained for Vico to propose it openly. It is difficult to say just what he meant by "authority." He sometimes defines it as "the common sense of mankind," but he obviously meant even more the dogmas of the church and of revealed religion. He therefore expressly excepts the history of the Jews and of the Christian Church from his interpretation of human history as a whole. Nevertheless, it is fair to say that Vico leaned toward reason as much as he dared, and at the same time accepted the authority of church and state. He had to, or else lose his job. In this again he was perhaps a typical university professor. The main thing for us to note, however, is that his method was historical or evolutionary, though his evolutionary point of view was mixed up with theology. He proposes, on the whole, to reach his theology through human history, rather than through a consideration of physical nature. He has a double aim of a natural theology on the one side, and a theory of social evolution on the other. While he holds that the affairs of our human world prove that they are directed by divine power, wisdom, and goodness, yet he does not try to explain historical events through such a theological assumption; for he holds that "the civil world has certainly been made by man.'' Therefore, he says that an understanding of history must be based upon a knowledge of human nature, which consists of three things: knowledge, will, and power. These always work together in the individual, and they also always work together in history. There is uniformity in history because there is uniformity in human nature. The life of nations is built upon these three things, as much so as is the life of individuals. Moreover, every department of life, every phase of civilization, is interdependent with every other department or phase. Hence, human history can be viewed as a unit. When such a unified view of human history is worked out, it will be a strong support to theology, as he informs his possible theological critics.

It cannot be said, of course, that Vico was wholly inductive, as he had a very definite philosophy of the universe, as well as a theory of human nature back of his social thinking. Nevertheless, he emphasized the importance of a knowledge of historical facts and processes, as Bodin had done before him, in opposition especially to the psychological theorizing of Locke and Spinoza.

Doctrine of Social Origins

Vico's view of social origins, considering his method as an alliance between reason and authority, was almost what we would expect it to be. He accepts the Old Testament legend of Adam and Eve and the Garden of Eden. Nevertheless, he holds that very early a vagrant part of humanity reverted to savagery, or to a wild, animal-like life in the woods. Vico was too well acquainted with the reports of Spanish and Italian travelers to deny that this was practically the original condition of mankind. Now this theory that the primitive cultural state was one of savagery was as much tabooed by the church of his time as any phase of the evolutionary theory has been since. However, as to the exact state of savage society, Vico is not clear. He is not clear as to whether its primitive condition was one of war or not. He holds that man is naturally social, but he agrees with Hobbes that fear is at the basis of human society; for fear gives birth to religion, and religion gives birth to virtue and morality. From the fear of the divine, therefore, sprang certain restraints upon brutal impulses. This led to the founding of independent families. Language also developed to guide and control human relations. Signs and gestures preceded words. The first speaking was an attempt to express emotions, and poetry is therefore older than prose. The independent or "monastic" family groups were organized upon the basis of fear, and religion later combined these to form neighborhoods and communities. Society is not a coming together of isolated individuals, but of independent families. In the development of society, Vico gives to the family the same constitutive function that Bodin does.

Doctrine of Social Development

Vico's social philosophy centers about his theory of social development. This theory, in brief, is that human history is a unity, and that in the course of development, all peoples pass through the same stages sooner or later. They pass from savagery to religion, to morals, to law, and to government, and so civil society becomes organized. Vico distinguishes three stages of development:

(1) *The age of the gods.* Fear, he tells us, first makes the gods. Fear and imagination, working together, gradually build up a world of the gods in which are reflected the chief features of primitive society. Primitive ideas take the form of myths. In this mythological age, everything that happens in the human world is explained as being due to gods or spirits. Law represents the will of a god or gods. The will of the ruler is supposed to be the will of the gods. Government in this stage is a theocracy. Vico presents much evidence to show that the earliest governments were formed or dominated by the priestly class, and hence were theocracies. Moreover, in this age, every other phase of civilization is dominated by mythological ideas—the family, art, industry, even language itself. At the very beginning of this age, the family is instituted. The father of the family in this age is both king and priest. He is the representative of the gods on earth, the

will of whom he seeks to ascertain by divination, auspices, and oracles. The aspects of nature themselves are conceived of as expressions of divine will.

(2) *The age of heroes, or of demigods, or of great men apotheosized.* This heroic age originates in the subjection of that portion of mankind which has remained in a savage state. The fathers of patriarchal families consequently become the rulers of considerable communities. These heads of families join together for the government of still larger communities. It is a government of strong men, of heads of families, of patriarchs, such as we find in the Senate of Rome. Government in this second stage is that of aristocracy. Slavery is developed, but some of the slaves and dependents successfully assert their rights in the long contests between patricians and plebeians. In this stage, the rudiments of theology, philosophy, and literature appear. Particularly is this the age of the heroic poets, such as Homer. Most of this philosophy and literature, however, still remain mythological. This is also shown in religious ceremonies and in judicial procedure. Scrupulous regard is paid to these ceremonies, even to particular words and formulae. The early history of the Greeks and the Romans especially illustrates this stage.

(3) *The age of men.* This is the historical age in the strict sense, and appears earlier in Greek than in Roman history. In Roman history it begins actually only with the destruction of Carthage. In this stage there is no longer a tendency to deify

men, and the happenings in human society and in physical nature are explained without the intervention of divine will. Language is reduced to writing. Civil and political rights are extended. Governments are democracies or combinations of democracies and monarchies. Religion is also humanized, and aims at the promotion of morality. Vico calls this age the "age of free government," in the sense that it is a constitutional monarchy or some form of republican government.

But the age of men contains within itself the seeds of its decay. Religions are undermined by scepticism. Society is corrupted by luxury. Strife breaks out between the rich and the poor, and governments become corrupt. The corruption of a nation may advance so far that no remedy can be found. In such a case, the nation is either subdued by a foreign enemy or sinks into barbarism. Rome particularly illustrates this decay of the human age. But after the fall of Rome, the divine age, or age of the gods, reappears in the Dark Ages, and in the Middle Ages the heroic age again comes into existence. Finally, the human age begins again in modern times.

This is the famous cyclic theory of social evolution presented by this old Italian social philosopher. It will be noted that he did not conceive of social development as going on without interruption. He conceived of reactions taking place, and then of the cycle starting all over again, but apparently on a higher plane. Vico does not say this expressly, but one has a right to infer that he conceived of each cycle as higher than the preceding one. Thus Vico gave us not only a cyclic theory of social evolution, but, by implication at least, a spiral theory. Vico taught, then, that history moves onward according to the law of cycles, each of which brings things at the end of it into a position like that in which they were at the beginning. But Vico did not mean that there is more than a general similarity between these cycles, and he apparently believed that each cycle is higher than the preceding. His belief was not inconsistent with the theory of a gradually ascending spiral movement in human history. But he drew no picture of the future, and our interpretation of his theory must be acknowledged to be only an interpretation.

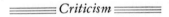

Criticism

It will be noted that Vico, in spite of theological bias and religious orthodoxy, anticipates many modern theories. His views of the unity of history, of the interdependence of all phases of civilization, of the dependence of social science upon knowledge of human nature, have been largely accepted. His dynamic view of human society would hardly be questioned by any modern social thinker. His three ages of human history, the age of the gods, the age of heroes, and the age of men, curiously anticipate Comte's law of the three states of man's intellectual conceptions. Whether there are cycles in human history in any strict sense is, however, still a matter of dispute. Vico's theories are so vague that it is hard to criticize them. We must admit his great services to social thinking, even though we cannot accept any of his theories in the form in which he gave them. Least of all can we accept his attempt to harmonize authority and reason. Reason admits of no compromise with authority. On the contrary, all human authority must base itself in the last analysis upon reason; that is, upon truth, rationally established.

CHAPTER X

Montesquieu

CHARLES LOUIS DE SECONDAT, Baron de Montesquieu, (1689–1755) was born of a noble family near the city of Bordeaux. He was educated for the law, and shortly after reaching maturity, inherited a magistracy from his uncle and became a member of the parliament of Bordeaux, which was a body of magistrates. He became disgusted with the political life of his time, sold his own office according to the custom of his age, and took up literature with something of a reformer's purpose. His first book was published in 1721 under the title of *Persian Letters*, in which he adopted the device of satirizing the social life of the eighteenth century by a series of imaginary letters written by a Persian official, supposed to be resident in France, back to his own country. The book was witty enough to please the very class he criticized, and as a result, after some opposition, he was admitted to the French Academy in 1728. In 1734, he followed this first work by a book on *Considerations on the Causes of the Greatness and Decadence of the Romans.* This book showed Montesquieu to be a careful student of history and a devotee of the historical method. He tells us, however, that even in 1728, long before the publication of this book, he had conceived the plan for his greatest work, *The Spirit of the Laws.* He went to work very systematically. As he was a man of means, he traveled extensively on the continent of Europe, especially in Germany, Austria, and Italy. Then he took up residence for two years in England, and became a great admirer of English political institutions. In the meantime, he was collecting a considerable number of books and manuscripts, and amassed an enormous library in his home. He employed a great many secretaries to aid him in his work, and perhaps there never has been a more splendid example of a wealthy man using his wealth to endow his own research. Finally, in 1748, when Montesquieu was already fifty-nine years of age, *The Spirit of the Laws* was published.

This book, *The Spirit of the Laws,* was in a certain sense the sociology of our eighteenth-century forefathers. While it must be considered primarily a work in philosophical jurisprudence, it was much broader than its title indicated, and attempted a general synthesis of scientific knowledge in its bearing upon the political problem of the age. As Professor Jaszi says: "Montesquieu may be regarded as one of the founders of modern sociology, because he had a keen sense for social reality and he endeavored to demonstrate all those complicated factors which mold and remold the forms and the content of social cooperation."

In many ways, Montesquieu was well fitted to perform this work. What he lacked in genius, he made up in industry. In addition to industry he had, however, another qualification—ability to rise above his own time and place. Though he himself was a good Roman Catholic, he shows no difficulty in appreciating Protestantism and Mohammedanism. Though a loyal subject of the French king, he was a great admirer of the English Constitution. Though an eighteenth-century French nobleman, he appreciated democracy and democratic society.

Montesquieu's problem was to determine the best laws and the best social and political organization. Yet he saw clearly that no ideal political and legal system could be sketched for all peoples and all times. He saw that political and legal forms must be relative. His very breadth introduced some confusion into his work, but it is hardly fair to say, as Voltaire did: "His work lacks method, and possesses neither plan nor order." While Montesquieu stood as an authority for more than fifty years among thoughtful people, his doctrines were not followed by the masses. If they had been, there possibly would have been no French Revolution.

One personal weakness of Montesquieu must be mentioned. He had many precursors, and drew heavily upon Bodin, Locke, and Vico in particular. While he does not mention Vico, his residence in Italy brought him into contact with Vico's ideas. However, Montesquieu acknowledged no indebtedness to his precursors. He went so far, indeed, as to place on the title page of his book the Latin motto, *Prolem sine matre natam* (Offspring born without a mother). In the world of thought, any more than in the world of nature, there is no offspring without a mother, and usually there are many mothers. Montesquieu's work was practically a synthesis of what other men had done; but we are forced to conclude that he was too petty to acknowledge this.

===== *Montesquieu's Scientific Method* =====

Professor Lichtenberger says that with Montesquieu we reach "the turning point in method," agreeing with Professor Giddings that "in *The Spirit of the Laws* the speculative methods of the social philosophers are frankly abandoned." [1] Montesquieu himself claimed that he drew his principles "from the nature of things." It must be acknowledged that, on the whole, Monesquieu's method was inductive and scientific. He amassed a great collec-

---

[1] See Lichtenberger, *Development of Social Theory,* pp. 208, 229.

tion of facts through his travel and reading, and he meant to proceed from these facts to his theory. Moreover, as we have seen, he appreciated conditions very different from those under which he lived. He made very free use of the comparative method. Like Bodin, he did not confine his attention to the civilized European peoples. He was familiar with the facts related by the French *voyageurs* and explorers. But he often used this ethnographic material uncritically. He laid equal stress on the historical method, even though he did not understand its intricacies; and like Bodin, he was learned in the history of all peoples and of all ages. Yet his method contained many defects that impaired the value of his work. We have noted Voltaire's criticism that it lacked order and system. There is much confusion at times in Montesquieu's thought. For example, he confused natural and positive law, and he often accepted the easiest explanation without subjecting his facts to critical examination.

Montesquieu's Social Philosophy

Doctrine of social origins. The fundamental thesis of Montesquieu's *The Spirit of the Laws* was that institutions are not arbitrary inventions. Laws are not the creation of the imagination, but are rooted in human nature and in the conditions of physical nature. This is shown by his definition of law in the opening chapter of the book. He says:

"Laws, in their most general sense, are the necessary relations springing from the nature of things." This definition covers, he thinks, all laws, natural or positive, physical or moral. It is a definition. easy enough to criticize, but indicates the spirit of his work. He looks to nature, rather than to convention or human agreement, for the origin of law. Although he was by implication against the contract theory as it was popularly accepted, he seems to admit that there was a presocial state, but holds that men were brought together, not through contract, but through necessity. He says that there are four laws of nature which bring men into association. The first is peace. Primitive men could not have lived in "a state of war" because they would see the danger of attacking one another. The second law is hunger and the necessity of food. While fear primitively might have induced men to shun one another, yet this fear, being reciprocal, would, together with their sense of weakness, lead them to associate to seek food. The third law of nature is sex attraction. These three laws would give rise to a fourth law, the desire to live in the society of one's fellows. Thus the necessities of human life, not contractual agreements, drew men together primitively in association. But government and laws would become necessary in such human communities on account of the conflicts that would arise between individuals, as Locke had maintained. These laws necessarily were related to the character of the people and the conditions of nature.

Laws, therefore, and institutions proceed from two facts: (1) the necessities of human nature; and (2) the conditions of the physical environment. Social institutions are expressions of the character of a people, on the one hand, and of the physical environment, on the other. But Montesquieu seemed to hold that the character 'of a people can be traced very largely to their physical environment. Therefore he emphasized the effects of climate and other physical influences on institutions and even on social changes. His views were relatively crude, but marked an advance. The influence of geographical environment is manifest in temperature, moisture, fertility of the soil, and general geographical position. People in cold countries, Montesquieu thinks, are apt to be more active; people in the tropics are apt to be more lazy. In the north again, people are more in need of stimulants, and hence they drink stronger liquor; while people in the south drink chiefly light wines. Cold climate favors political and civil liberty; warm climate favors slavery, despotism and polygyny. Europe has certain geographical advantages, such as its moderate temperature and numerous natural subdivisions. In Asia, large areas and great extremes in climate favor extensive political units and despotism. A very productive soil, such as that on the plains and in the tropics, favors idleness, and hence there is less liberty and more despotism; but where food is scarce, as in the mountains, the people are more independent and have more liberty.

In all this interpretation in terms of environment, Montesquieu is not entirely free from criticism. He evidently thought that the influence of environment acts much more directly than it does. Geographical environment acts very indirectly upon social origins and development.

Doctrine of social and political organization. Montesquieu's view of human society is, in general, static, and he confuses his general doctrine of social organization with his doctrine of the forms of government. The latter doctrine is his peculiar contribution to political and social philosophy. He looks at government from the standpoint of national psychology and attempts to get at the psychological principle back of each form of government, even though, in general, he does not make much use of psychological method. He finds that there are four fundamental forms of government: democracy, aristocracy, monarchy, and despotism. He admits that there is no logic in such a classification. Its justification is that back of each of these forms of government lies a different psychological principle that operates on the character of the people and at the same time sustains the government. Each sort of government has therefore behind it a different principle or motive in the social tradition. The principle upon which democracy rests, for example, is political virtue in the sense of love of country and love of equality. Aristocracy rests upon the same principle, but adds the principle of moderation. Just as in a democracy there must be political virtue or love of country, so in an aristocracy there must be moderation on the part of the governing classes who should rule, not for their own class, but for the welfare of all. The principle of monarchy is different; it is based upon honor in the sense of class distinction and the privileges that belong with class. Where there are class distinctions, the logical thing is to have a monarch at the top of all classes to preserve these class distinctions. Despotism, on the other hand, does not encourage classes. Its principle is fear. It is the rule of one, unrestrained, with or without law.

It is evident that Montesquieu here is trying to get at the relation of social tradition to the forms of government, a problem that no one had ever attempted to solve before. But he is also interested in the question of the duration of forms of government, and he says that this duration depends upon the principle involved. Democracy, for example, will decay with the decay of its principles, unselfish patriotism and love of equality, and will change to another form as soon as these disappear. If the people in a democracy, for example, disregard the laws that they themselves have made, it shows that the thirst for power and possessions has driven out the love for common welfare, and democracy will come to an end. Again, as soon as an aristocracy loses its sense of moderation and restraint, it will go down. As soon as the sense of class distinctions and privileges decay, monarchy will be undermined. Finally, as soon as fear disappears from a despo-

tism, it will end. Here, then, is a theory of political
revolutions, something like that which Aristotle
proposed, but yet representing a distinct advance
over Aristotle's thought.

In accordance with the emphasis that Montesquieu
places upon physical environment, it should be added
that he pointed out that forms of government were
adapted to different regions and to different-sized
territories. He says that if you want to keep the
republican form of government, you must have a
small territory, like Switzerland. A monarchy is
suited to a large, compact territory like France.
But a large territory with heterogeneous elements
in its population must be governed by despotism.
Accordingly, a government that continually seeks
expansion must prepare for despotism.

Perhaps the most notable of all Montesquieu's political doctrines, the doctrine of the separation of
the powers of government, he got from Locke. This
doctrine was embodied in the constitution of the
United States, and so has had a notable influence on
modern political development. Montesquieu says
that to secure liberty, we must have the various
powers of government separated so as to act as a
mutual check, one upon the other. These powers
are the legislative, which makes the laws; the executive, which enforces them; and the judicial, which
interprets them. The executive should have the
veto power over the legislative, and only the judicial
should have the right to interpret. These three departments of government, then, will work as checks

on one another. This is the source of the tripod form of government that we find so general in the western hemisphere. Montesquieu, at least, was the first definitely to formulate it. Because he believed in a government of checks and balances, he thought that the legislative should be composed of two chambers, each acting as a check upon the other. In a sense, his whole theory of political organization was a theory of checks and balances.

But Montesquieu was interested also in the general problem of social organization. He was a liberal, even though in a way that was very far from our more modern standards of liberalism. The liberty that he advocated for the citizen was liberty under the law. "Political liberty is security in doing whatever the law permits," he says. It is getting rid of the arbitrary power of officials. Such liberty is the opposite of despotism. England is Montesquieu's model.

Closely related to his doctrine of political liberty was his doctrine of civil liberty. This means freedom from the power and caprice of others, freedom over one's own life. Montesquieu was opposed to slavery. Prisoners of war should not be made slaves; neither should a man be permitted to become a slave by selling himself. Montesquieu says that slavery not only is not natural, but it is worse for the master class than for the slave, because it makes the master class cruel, despotic, and sensual. However, Montesquieu is not outspoken in opposition to Negro slavery, because he says, though probably ironically, that the Negro as a race seems fitted for slavery. He winds up his discussion of slavery by declaring that "men are born free and equal." In accordance with this general doctrine of civil liberty, Montesquieu is opposed also to what he calls domestic slavery, a term which he applies to polygyny. Like slavery in general, it makes the master class, that is, the males, cruel, despotic, and sensual.

In regard to economic conditions, it is to Montesquieu's credit that he brought economic factors more to the front than most preceding writers. He recognizes these as influencing the civilization of peoples. He favored the freeing of commerce and trade, because, he said, "the natural result of commerce is peace"; but he greatly feared the power of large business corporations, which, he said, must be kept inferior in power to the government, both in monarchies and in republics. Monopolies are especially to be feared because they corrupt and destroy governments. But consistently with the prejudices of his class, Montesquieu says that in a monarchy, commerce is not fitted for the ruling class, a doctrine that reminds us of the ideas of Plato and Aristotle.

Montesquieu devotes much of *The Spirit of the Laws* to the manners and morals of peoples as expressions of their nature and of the influence of physical environment. He regards manners and morals as deeper than laws, and combats the idea that law can do much to change them. Penal legislation can do little for the moral reformation of the people, because manners and morals, or the *mores,* as Sumner would have said, are deeper than political law.

According to Montesquieu, even religious institutions have a basis in natural conditions and in the character of the people. The tropics favor certain sorts of religion, and the temperate regions of Europe, other kinds. He also connects religion with the forms of government and with the principles that sustain them. Protestantism, he says, is especially fitted for democracy. Roman Catholicism, because of its hierarchies and the sense of class distinction that they imply, is especially fitted for monarchies. The ritual of Roman Catholicism also is essential to the pomp and splendor of a monarch. Finally Mohammedanism, on account of its fatalism and fanaticism, is especially suited to despotism.

Doctrine of social evolution. Montesquieu does not deal in *The Spirit of the Laws* specifically with the problem of social evolution, but in his *Considerations on the Causes of the Greatness and Decadence of the Romans,* he has some striking sentences which show that he had pondered the problem intelligently. "The world," he says, "is not ruled by fortune. There are general causes, moral and physical, which act upon every monarchy, building it up, maintaining it, or casting it down. All accidents are submitted to the control of these general causes; and if the hazard of a battle has been sufficient to ruin a state, there was a general cause which determined that such a state should perish by a

MONTESQUIEU

single battle. In a word, the principal movement of events draws with it all particular accidents.''

In general, we may say that Montesquieu's doctrine of social evolution was vague and consisted mainly in the assumption that it is controlled by natural law. Hence the course of history, he held, is determined by general, not individual, causes.

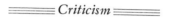 *Criticism*

Montesquieu illustrates, as Lichtenberger has well said, how, in the seventeenth and eighteenth centuries, social philosophy was imbedded in political philosophy and was often but a corollary to it.[2] His teachings appealed especially to the educated middle class, for, though in one sense a liberal, he was essentially conservative and concerned mainly with the problem of social order. In the exaltation of nature and natural law as the principle of explanation in the social sciences, Montesquieu was strictly in accord with the spirit of his age; but he showed scarcely more penetration than did his contemporaries. We can hardly agree, therefore, with the extravagant estimate of his service to social science given by Professor Giddings when he says: ''Montesquieu converted social philosophy into descriptive social science.'' Rather, he simply helped, along with many other writers, to give social philosophy an inductive and naturalistic basis.

---

[2] *Op cit.*, p. 207.

CHAPTER XI

Turgot

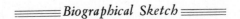

=====*Biographical Sketch*=====

ANNE ROBERT JACQUES TURGOT (1727–1781) was
born of a family that belonged to the official bureauc-
racy of France, for his father was "provost of the
merchants" of Paris. From his earliest youth he
was destined for the church, and there can be no
doubt that his early religious training had something to do with the character of his thought. He
was made a Bachelor of Theology in 1747 and was
elected a few years later to the honorary office of
Prior of the Sorbonne. The chief duty of his office
seems to have been to deliver two learned discourses.
This he did in 1750. The first was upon "The Advantages Which the Christian Religion Has Conferred upon the Human Race," and was somewhat
conventional. The second, on "A Philosophical

162

View of the Successive Advances of the Human Mind," was delivered December 11, 1750. Ever since, it has been regarded by the most discriminating minds as one of the milestones in social philosophy. Shortly after delivering these discourses, Turgot seems to have written his fragmentary notes on a *Plan for Two Discourses on Universal History.* In the meantime, however, by extensive reading in history and in the natural sciences of his time, he was led to change his mind about an ecclesiastical career, because, as he said, "he could not bear to wear a mask all his life." He entered upon the study of law and took up the work of various minor public offices with a reformer's purpose. In 1756–1760, he came in contact with Gournay and Quesnay, the founders of the French physiocratic school of economists. While not accepting all of their views, Turgot became greatly interested in the economic problems then confronting France, especially those that concerned money, taxation, and public finance. In 1761 he became Intendant at Limoges, and effected there some very notable reforms in taxation. In 1766 he wrote a short treatise entitled *Reflections upon the Formation and Distribution of Wealth,* which is usually considered one of the chief precursors of Adam Smith's *Wealth of Nations.* In 1774 he was called to Paris and became the finance minister of Louis XVI. He attempted to carry out several drastic reforms in taxation and governmental financial policy. In this way he incurred the displeasure of the nobility and even of the queen, and in 1776

he was forced to resign. He lived in retirement until his death in 1781, at the comparatively early age
of fifty-four years.

This brief sketch of Turgot's life shows that he
became eminent not only as a social philosopher, but
as a practical administrator and as one of the founders of modern economics. Perhaps we should also
add that his was one of the earliest voices within the
church to urge a return to what he well called "the
Christianity of Christ." Though he never broke
with the church openly, he refused, as we have seen,
to enter upon an ecclesiastical career, urged mutual
tolerance among religious denominations, and held
to the supreme importance of religion in civilization.

In many respects, Turgot was almost the antithesis of Montesquieu. Montesquieu did not publish his most notable work, *The Spirit of the Laws,*
until he was a man of fifty-nine, and then only after
years of laborious research. Turgot, on the other
hand, was a mere boy of but twenty-three when he
gave his celebrated discourse on "The Successive
Advances of the Human Mind." Montesquieu emphasized the problem of social order; Turgot emphasized the problem of social progress or development. Montesquieu stressed natural factors and
forces; Turgot stressed the human mind, yet was
more practical in his attitudes. Both, however, appealed to the educated classes of their day, and to
conservative rather than revolutionary methods.
Perhaps we may sum up the contrast between the
two men by saying that Montesquieu illustrated

what a man without genius could achieve through laborious research, while Turgot illustrated what the insight of genius could achieve without research.

Turgot's Scientific Method

It is difficult to say with any certainty what scientific methods Turgot employed in reaching his conclusions.   But it is certain that he had a clearer conception of the correct method in the field of the social sciences than any of his precursors.   He contrasts the method of the mathematical sciences with the methods of the concrete natural sciences.   He tells us: "The mind, in mathematics, deduces one from another a chain of propositions whose truth consists only in their mutual dependence.   The case is not the same for the other sciences, where it is no longer the comparison of ideas with one another whence springs truth, but their conformity with a train of real facts.   To discover it and show it, it suffices no longer to establish a small number of simple principles whence the mind has only to allow itself to be led on by the thread of deduction.   It is necessary to start from nature as she is."

Thus the physicist forms hypotheses by aid of the imagination "in the light of a few badly known facts."   These he tests by all the facts he can discover.   "He tries them, so to speak, on the facts, as a seal is verified by being replaced on its impression in the wax."   In this way, "Time, research, and chance accumulate observations and unveil the hidden bonds that connect phenomena."

Such passages show that Turgot understood clearly that the method of the concrete sciences was "hypothesis-testing." Indeed, he says that the sciences advance "by dint of groping, of multiplying systems, and of exhausting, so to speak, errors." Thus scientific truth is reached over the ruins of false hypotheses.

But Turgot tells us that "all the sciences lend one another mutual aid," and that therefore mathematics can be of some use in all the concrete sciences, even though these must be built upon the facts of experience. As a good follower of Locke, he holds that all the facts of experience come to us through the senses. "The senses are the sole source of ideas," he tells us; "the whole power of imagination is limited to the combining of the ideas it has received from them."

But in social philosophy, the facts of experience are the history of the race. Therefore history contains the facts by which the social philosopher must test his hypotheses. Hence Turgot appears in social philosophy as pre-eminently an advocate of the historical method. But it is the examination of the successive phases of the human mind, or the history of thought in various lines, that he emphasizes.

Nevertheless, Turgot was fully conscious of other factors in the historical process. He speaks especially of the effects of economic and geographical conditions, of human passions, of wars, and of the intermingling of peoples. In his mature life he was much influenced, as we have seen, by the physiocratic school of economists, but he did not attempt to reconcile his general social philosophy with their overemphasis upon physical nature. While he was not entirely free from their errors, it is worthy of note that he did not subscribe to their doctrine that self-interest is "the born servant of the general interest," nor to their other doctrine that free competition is "the mainspring of human perfectibility."

Turgot warns particularly against that scientific and philosophical complacency which "would restrict the limits of existing knowledge and fix these limits once for all." This sectarian spirit in philosophy and science is one of the main reasons why nations that are pioneers in philosophy and science frequently fail to advance, for it is a pride "fed on ignorance," and shuts the door to new inquiries. "The less the knowledge," Turgot tells us in one of his brilliant aphorisms, "the less the doubt."

We are forced to conclude, then, that while Turgot recognized the need of a complex method in social philosophy, his own method seems to have been mainly the exercise of scientific imagination and insight. For without extensive research and without extensive critical analysis, he seems to have achieved a well-balanced view of human affairs and a remarkable insight into human history.

===== *Turgot's Social Philosophy* =====

Doctrine of social development. It is difficult to analyze Turgot's social philosophy under conventional rubrics. His main thinking centered about the problem of social progress, but this was to be solved, according to his method, by the study of the processes of history. Turgot has no doubt that the accumulation of knowledge and the developing intelligence of man, unceasingly correcting errors and unveiling truth, has been the main factor in social development. But he does not deny "the infinite variety of circumstances" that has quickened the pace of social and cultural evolution in some nations and slowed it down in others.

At the very outset of his second discourse, Turgot points to language as the chief instrument used by man for the accumulation and diffusion of knowledge and ideas, and hence for the building of civilization. He says, "The arbitrary signs of speech and writing, by giving men the means wherewith to make sure of the possession of their ideas and to communicate them to others, have formed from individual stores of knowledge a common treasure, that one generation transmits to another, like unto a heritage continually augmented by the discoveries of each age"; and thus "all the ages of mankind are enchained one with another." Well might John Morley see in these lines "the germs of a new and most fruitful philosophy of society," for we have here an anticipation of the cultural theory of human society.

"Invention of every sort, material and non-material, springing from the accumulation and diffusion of knowledge, is the ladder on which man climbs." But inventions that enable man better to conserve and diffuse knowledge are of peculiar importance. Hence Turgot's apostrophe to the invention of writing, as marking a great turning point in the history of mankind: "Precious invention! which seemed to give the peoples that first possessed it wings to outstrip the other nations! Inestimable invention! which snatches from the power of death the memory of great men and examples of valor and integrity, unites times and places, fixes the fugitive thought and assures it lasting existence, whereby the products, the opinions, the experiences, the discoveries accumulated through all the ages serve as groundwork and as stairs on which posterity may rise ever higher." Almost of equal importance for the development of civilization was the invention of the art of printing.

But the unequal distribution of talent among mankind may also have had much to do with the unequal social development of peoples. "Nature, not impartial in the bestowal of her gifts, has given to certain minds a fullness of talent that she has refused to others; circumstances develop these talents or leave them buried in obscurity; and from the infinite variety of such circumstances springs the inequality that marks the progress of nations." The circumstances that Turgot particularly mentions as tending to bury the talent of peoples are wars, conquests, revolutions, geographic isolation, and inequalities of economic conditions and of education.

Hence the historical process in any given nation, as well as in mankind as a whole, is never a straight line. Social decay is almost as much in evidence as social progress. Progress is through errors, mistakes, and difficulties. It is not without interruption. If Turgot had used the language of our time, he would have said that it was "a trial-and-error process." He fully recognizes, then, periods of reaction and of decadence; but men learn from their mistakes and even from their calamities. Experience and the knowledge that it brings will accumulate again, and after a time progress will be resumed. Just as in the progress of science, so in all other fields of human endeavor, man learns from his mistakes. It is this possibility of learning through experience which assures social progress in the long run. Thus it is not too much to say, as many have said, that Turgot made progress "organic in human history." He believed apparently that man cannot escape from learning through experience, and that therefore history, as so many eighteenth-century thinkers asserted, is a process of the education of the race. While we must not expect uniform social progress, it is a necessary development of human history. If one group fails to progress, some other group will profit by the mistakes made by the first group and carry human achievements to a still higher level.

It is clear that Turgot considered the learning process to be back of all human progress. He does not use such a phrase, but he frequently speaks of man's learning. Men live, he says, by the aid of past experience. The history of every nation is therefore a process of self-development, and the explanation of progress is to be found in the nature of the human mind, in its capacity to learn from experience. The processes of history are processes of testing out adjustments. This testing necessarily proceeds through what we call fumbling and success. It is a process of trial and error, as we have just said, but the movement is inevitably toward a higher degree of perfection of both knowledge and practical adjustments, even though it is not without interruption.

This progress away from ignorance and error to the attainment of true knowledge is particularly illustrated by Turgot in his famous theory of the three states of man's intellectual conceptions, which anticipated Comte's law of the three states. This is found in Turgot's notes on a *Plan for Two Discourses on Universal History*. Though often quoted, it is worth quoting again:

> Before the relation between physical facts was known, there was nothing more natural than to suppose that they were produced by intelligent beings, invisible and like ourselves; for what else would they have resembled? Everything that happened without man's having had a part in it had

its god, to the worship of whom fear or hope soon gave rise; and this worship was later developed in the light of the regard paid to powerful men; for gods were only men more powerful or less perfect; according as they were the work of an age more or less enlightened as to the true perfection of mankind.

When philosophers had recognized the absurdity of these fables, without having, however, acquired true light upon natural history, they imagined they could explain the cause of phenomena by means of abstract expressions, such as essences or faculties, expressions which yet explained nothing, and in regard to which men reasoned as if they had been *beings,* new divinities substituted for the old. These analogies were followed out, and faculties were multiplied to account for each effect.

It was only later, when the mechanical action of bodies upon one another was observed, that from this mechanical relation were drawn other hypotheses that mathematicians could develop and experience verify.

Whether the above quotation applies only to the physical sciences, as some think, or whether it applies to all man's knowledge, anticipating Comte's classification of all man's conceptions into a theological, a metaphysical, and a positive or scientific stage, is of no great importance. The important thing is to see that Turgot emphasized progress away from ignorance and error, even though one error sometimes led into another. It is equally important to observe that, according to Turgot, the process is fundamentally an intellectual one. It depends upon the development of man's knowledge of his world and of himself. The active agent in all this progress is therefore the development of intelligence in man, not so much, however, in the individual, as in that accumulated experience that we call "social culture."

Doctrine of social order. Turgot's theories of social organization and social order were rather vague. In a general way he accepted the physiocrats' "system of natural liberty." Like practically all eighteenth-century social thinkers, the concepts of natural right and the law of nature dominated his mind. While he held that men are by nature intellectually unequal and are thus naturally fitted for division of labor, yet they should, he thought, find by free competition the place for which they are fitted. He was opposed, therefore, to all social institutions, such as slavery, that interfere with the natural liberty of individuals. He also favored freedom of trade and commerce and the minimum interference by government in industrial and business enterprises.

Perhaps this general attitude was inconsistent with his belief that constitutional monarchy was the best form of government for France. Perhaps it was also inconsistent with his exaltation of the family as the fundamental institution in society and his condemnation of polygyny in all of its forms. But it was consistent with his belief that justice and morality are not merely social conventions, and that a wise social order would seek to maximize and maintain justice between individuals and classes. Injustice between classes he thought to be the root of revolution. Hence he said, "Well-timed reform may avert revolution."

We have already noted Turgot's very modern ideas regarding the part that religion may play in human society. He was perhaps over-optimistic in making mutual tolerance the sufficient basis for a reunited church that would teach and exemplify "the Christianity of Christ"; but religious tolerance is certainly one of the bases necessary for church unity.

Criticism

It is hardly necessary to say in conclusion that Turgot represented eighteenth-century optimism at its very best. Perhaps a little breath of such scientific optimism is the thing most needed in the social philosophy of the present time. Turgot was not one of those who believed that "the only lesson of history is that the lessons of history are never learned." Probably he would acknowledge that some stupid ages might fail in learning them, but that sooner or later mankind must learn from its own experience. He would surely come near to agreeing with Pascal that "the whole series of human generations during the course of the ages should be regarded as one man, ever living and ever learning," though he would emphasize that the learning has proceeded with many interruptions and at times with great signs of forgetfulness.

It is also hardly necessary to point out that Turgot's social philosophy is in fundamental conflict with all crude theories of environmental determinism by natural conditions. It is in conflict, for example, with Montesquieu's exaltation of natural conditions and natural law. It is equally in conflict with the economic determinism of Karl Marx, which would reduce the intellectual conceptions of man to rationalizations of his economic condition. In brief, it is in conflict with every social philosophy that would make nature more important in historical development than the active, learning mind of man, even though this mind is so subject to errors and aberrations.

Finally, we must agree, I think, with Professor McQuilkin De Grange that "seldom has there been born into the world a greater potential sociologist than Turgot."[1] It is much to be regretted, therefore, that the chief energies of his life were spent upon the practical problems of statesmanship, in an effort to save his country from disaster. Again, all historically minded social thinkers would agree that "in the work of this youth has been found clear anticipation of the thought and perhaps of the fundamental principles on which Auguste Comte was later to erect the science to which he gave the name 'sociology.'"

---

[1] See *Turgot, On the Progress of the Human Mind,* translated by McQuilkin De Grange (The Sociological Press, Hanover, N. H., 1929).

CHAPTER XII

David Hume and Scientific Scepticism

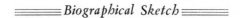

Biographical Sketch

WE NOW COME TO the great English sceptic, David Hume, who perhaps best deserves to be called the founder of orthodox scientific method, or rather, perhaps, the first philosopher to defend that method. He was born in 1711 of a prominent Scottish family, and died in 1776. He was educated in the Scottish universities, where he came in contact with the sensationalism of Locke and other philosophers. Physical science had been developing very rapidly in the two preceding centuries, and so also had psychological theories. Hume had an exceptionally keen, critical mind, which he brought to bear upon problems resulting from these new scientific theories, particularly upon the problem of how far scientific knowledge could go. Thus, because Hume

176

was interested chiefly in epistemology, or the problem of knowledge, his contribution to the social sciences has often been overlooked.

Let us note a few of the sources of his ideas. As a young man, he spent three years in France, where he came in contact with the ideas of many of the most advanced French thinkers, and where he wrote his *Treatise of Human Nature,* which was not published, however, until 1740. This was followed by *Essays Moral and Political* in 1742. In 1752, he published his *Political Discourses.* Relatively late in life, he became interested in history as a source of political and social knowledge, and wrote his well-known *History of England.* He spent the six years from 1763 to 1769 at Paris as an attaché of the British embassy, where he again came into close contact with the leading French thinkers, especially the encyclopedists. After this, he retired to Edinburgh, where he died in 1776.

Like Voltaire, Hume was essentially a child of his age. There were many differences between these two great men, but both of them went with, rather than against, the current of their time, in practically all respects. "It was an age," says one writer, "in which reason came more and more to renounce, or rather flatly deny, its creative role; more and more to resign itself to the humbler tasks of registering and analyzing the material given through the senses from without: an age of materialism, first veiled, then exultant, as regards the sources and scope of man's knowledge." In these respects, the reader will hardly fail to note, the eighteenth century was strikingly similar to the opening decades of the twentieth century. Such a social atmosphere could hardly fail to influence as sensitive a mind as that of David Hume. Indeed, he became the very voice of his age, and to a certain extent still rules the more scientific part of the world at the present time.

Such a thinker who voices the tendencies of his age is apt to be relatively superficial, and this can perhaps be said, without any unfairness, of David Hume. He was, indeed, aware of this superficiality himself, and often remarked that his various conclusions seemed mutually inconsistent; and he would add, very genially, that if anyone else could think out the problem better than he could, he would be glad to accept his conclusion.

Hume's Scientific Method

Hume was essentially a metaphysician. He accepted and developed Locke's sensationalist psychology. Sense impressions, he held, were the source of all ideas, and were also the test of their validity. The mind of man could be resolved into such sense impressions received from the external world, combined and recombined. There is therefore no such entity as "mind" that can be perceived or made the object of scientific investigation. We know of no "soul" behind the processes of thought. Likewise, we can never penetrate behind sense impressions to discover the essence of nature, or the processes of nature. Hence, we never perceive "causes" or "laws." We infer them; and as they are matters of inference, they may be doubted. Hence, Hume argued that science must limit itself strictly to mathematics and to direct experiment. It is in this sense that he set up scientific orthodoxy. Inconsistently, however, he argued that politics may be reduced to a science based on experience, and he held the same view regarding human nature. He has often been accused of holding to an egoistic and intellectualistic theory of human nature; but this is hardly correct, as his fundamental principle in interpreting all human behavior was the principle of habit. This, perhaps, was consistent with his deriving all that was in the mind from sense impressions received from the environment.

We should add that, while Hume was a keen, critical thinker, his critical attitude did not extend to such institutions as property and the British monarchy. When it came to political and social questions, he was essentially conservative. But his social and political conservatism hardly fitted in with his philosophical and religious radicalism. While sceptical regarding all religious and philosophical beliefs, his scepticism, for the most part, did not extend to the social order around him.

=====*Hume's Social Philosophy*=====

Doctrine of origins. Although Hume attacked many of the social theories of his day, he was not altogether negative in his social philosophy. He often indicated constructive views that have been largely adopted since his day. Hume doubted the easy geographical determinism advocated by Montesquieu. The characters of men, he says, do not come from air and climate, and physical causes have little to do in the making of national character, which is due almost wholly to moral causes. He throws most weight upon the social tradition and the imitative nature of the human mind. Moreover, it is wrong to ascribe too much in the social order to reason. Passions and sentiments, he says, rule mankind. But practically, he gives even greater weight to habit. Custom is the great guide of human life; and so all human institutions and social conditions should be interpreted in terms of habit and custom.

With this point of view, he naturally attacked the theory of an original contract as the base of the social and political order. This theory, which was scarcely questioned in the early eighteenth century, Hume rejects both upon historical and psychological grounds. He says that it is historically not true that the powers of government were derived from some original contract. Rather, the powers of government have come historically from force and violence and custom. The consent of the governed was not their original source. Neither does the theory of an original contract have a good foundation in psychology. The sense of social obligation arises from the necessities of human society. Fidelity, or regard for promises, is such a social necessity. Obedience to magistrates and fidelity in promises rest on the same foundation—the interests and necessities of organized human society. Civilized society, he says, could not subsist without obedience to government. While government originated in force and violence, it has been continued as a social necessity and is established by custom. There is therefore no need of assuming any contract between ruler and subject. Social necessity is the basis also of justice. Justice is absolutely necessary for the well-being of mankind, and so for the existence of human society. The same is true of most other virtues. These are not modifications of self-love, but represent perceptions of social utility.

Doctrine of social order. A measure of liberty, Hume holds, is necessary to maintain a free government. Reasonable liberty of the people is not dangerous, especially not the liberty of the press. Parties are necessary in a free government, and are rarely dangerous if given opportunity to express themselves. Hume is altogether in favor of a parliamentary government, such as he believes to be illustrated best in the constitution of Great

Britain. This will secure a government of laws with a minimum of tyranny.

While Hume is doubtful regarding the validity of religious beliefs, he sees the utility of religion in society. He says that religions are of two sorts— religions of superstition, and religions of enthusiasm. Religions of superstition are unfavorable to progress because they lodge power in a priestly class. Superstition is an enemy of civil liberty, therefore. Religions of enthusiasm, or as we would say, prophetic religions, are more favorable to progress, even though they are apt to be more violent. A religion of enthusiasm is therefore a friend of civil liberty.

Hume was a strong advocate of what we would call the theory of relativity in morals. Good and ill, both natural and moral, he held, are entirely relative to human sentiments. The virtues depend upon social conditions, and are really expressions of social and public utility. Nevertheless, society must have its conventions and customs. These may change from age to age; but as they express social interests and necessities, they have a certain relative validity.

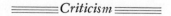

Criticism

It has been said that Hume was the embodiment of the Humanism of the eighteenth century. He was certainly the embodiment of its spirit of doubt and its sense of relativity. In many ways, his scepticism did good. To Hume, perhaps more than to any other thinker, we owe the undermining of the contract theory of the state and society. His withering scepticism left it with scarcely any vitality outside of those revolutionary parties who used it more as a weapon than as an established truth. Yet Hume's scepticism, we are beginning to see, went much too far. If it had undermined only the numerous social theories unsupported by facts, it would have been all to the good. But it extended, as we have seen, to the human mind itself; and in undermining faith in the human mind, it undermined faith in science itself.

Hume has been often likened to Voltaire, and has, indeed, been called "the Voltaire of Great Britain." But while there were similarities between the two men, they were at bottom very different, for Voltaire retained his faith in man, in the mind of man, and even in the perfectibility of man. These were faiths which David Hume never had, and we might almost say, knew nothing of.

CHAPTER XIII

French Revolutionary Thinkers

As we have seen, social crises stimulate social thinking. This was particularly true of that great crisis which we know as the French Revolution. Practically the whole literature of France in the latter part of the eighteenth century was taken up with the discussion of the social and political problems that were pressing for solution, and that finally led to the revolution. It is said that no great French writer of the eighteenth century was a supporter of the existing order. The number of revolutionary French thinkers whose names might be listed in this chapter was enormous. However, two stand out above all the others: Voltaire and Rousseau. These men were singularly unlike, and agreed only that the existing order was intolerable, and that if men were freed from their chains, human society would perfect itself. But in most other respects, they presented a strange contrast. Rousseau was a man of

184

the people; Voltaire was an aristocrat. Rousseau was an emotional; Voltaire was an intellectual; Rousseau held that civilization involved the degradation of man; Voltaire, on the other hand, believed that the development of civilization and culture was man's salvation. But the contrast between these two revolutionary thinkers is best shown by their life and work.

Voltaire

François Marie Arouet, who assumed the name of Voltaire at the age of twenty-three, was born in 1694 and died in 1778. He was the foremost literary man of Europe in the eighteenth century. He came from a middle-class family, as his father was a prosperous notary. His mother died when he was seven years old. At ten he entered the Jesuit College of Louis le Grand, where he remained until seventeen, studying mainly literature. Upon his graduation, his father wished him to study law, but he decided to make literature his profession. Through the influence of powerful friends, he was admitted to court circles. At the age of twenty-three, he was sent to the Bastille for eleven months for writing lampoons on the Regent. Upon his release, however, he was given a small pension, as he was rapidly gaining distinction for his playwriting. For a time he was attached to a French embassy at the Hague. However, directing his pen against the court, and becoming involved in a quarrel with one of the nobles, he was sent again to the Bastille. He was released at the end of two weeks, with the understanding that he should leave France and go to England. He stayed in England for three years (1726–1729), and had access to the highest literary and political circles. Here he wrote his *Letters on the English,* which were mainly a criticism of the French social and political order. When this book was published in 1733, it at once caused a storm that made it impossible for Voltaire to remain in Paris. He fled to Lorraine with a Madame du Chatelet, whom he had met in Paris, and who was one of the leading literary and intellectual women of her time. Voltaire lived with her at her chateau in Lorraine for fifteen years, returning to Paris from time to time to direct the production of his plays at various theaters. During this time he produced some of his most notable literary masterpieces. In 1746 Voltaire was made a member of the French Academy. In 1749 Madame du Chatelet died. Voltaire found it inadvisable to return to Paris to live. He had been in correspondence with Frederick II of Prussia for some time, and Frederick urged him to come to Berlin. In 1751 he went to Berlin and stayed at the court of Frederick for two years. Frederick aspired to literary eminence, and asked Voltaire to correct his poetry. The result was a quarrel between the two men. After some unpleasantness, Voltaire left Prussia, but found that he could not return to France. He settled near Geneva, finally taking a house at Ferney, about four miles from the city. Here he was in French-Swiss territory, but near the Swiss boundary line.

It was here at Ferney during his last twenty years that he entered upon the really great work of his life. From the time of his imprisonment in the Bastille, he seems to have formed the resolution to do whatever he could to free mankind from superstition and tyranny, and to spread freedom and enlightenment. It was only, however, after he took up his residence at Ferney that he entered upon the concrete work of helping the oppressed. The oppressed were particularly those who had been subjected to some injustice by the Roman Catholic Church, or by the French monarchy. It was at this point that he coined his famous phrase: *Ecrasez l'Infame.* Many have supposed that this phrase referred particularly to the Roman Catholic Church, but Voltaire seems to have meant by it the whole system or order that resulted in such injustice at that time.

It is often said that Voltaire was no revolutionary.[1] He would probably not have favored the French Revolution in the form in which it developed. Nevertheless, the above phrase shows that he was a revolutionist in the deeper sense of the word, as he was an enemy of the existing order, and no one did more than he to undermine the beliefs and conventions that supported it. Moreover, Vol-

---

[1] Cf. Hearnshaw, *The Social and Political Ideas of Some Great Thinkers of the Age of Reason,* Chapter VI.

taire was essentially a revolutionist in the sense that almost all his work was destructive. He seemed to see only the immediate task of destroying superstition and tyranny. For this reason, he, perhaps more than any other single man, prepared the way for the French Revolution.

Voltaire was visited by so many famous men at Ferney that it is often said that he made this little village the literary capital of Europe. He received many invitations to settle elsewhere. Catherine II of Russia wished him to come to St. Petersburg, but he wisely declined to accept the invitation, and instead dedicated to her his monograph on *The Philosophy of History.* In 1754 he published his chief work along historical lines, his *Essay upon the Morals and Spirit of Nations,* which was a pioneer work on the history of civilization. His works are so numerous that it is impossible to mention more than the few that immediately concern us. Besides the two which we have already noted, mention must be made of his *Philosophical Dictionary,* which was translated into English by John Quincy Adams, sixth president of the United States. This was an encyclopedic work that contained most of Voltaire's social and political, as well as his philosophical, views.

In 1777 the Edict that barred him was revoked. Early in 1778 he set out for Paris. His journey was a triumphant procession, as all France had been converted to his views. When he reached Paris, the people took the horses from his carriage and drew him through the streets. He was showered with honors and with social distinctions. But, at the age of eighty-four, his strength was not sufficient to endure the strain, and he died in the hour of his most complete triumph.

A few remarks regarding Voltaire's personal character are necessary in order to understand his work. While he had the noble aim to free mankind from everything superstitious and tyrannical and to spread freedom and enlightenment, yet at times he was petty and self-centered. He was always very careful to look after himself, and he was particularly successful in doing this in a financial way. Although his books brought him no great riches, he was continually speculating, and, unlike most professional and literary men, he speculated and won. It is estimated that, at the time of his death, he had an income in terms of our money of about $35,000 a year, which would put him in the class of near-millionaires.

Perhaps the most widespread misunderstanding of Voltaire is in regard to his religious attitude. He is often represented to have been a cynical atheist, but nothing could be farther from the truth. While we cannot say that Voltaire was Christian in his beliefs, he was one of the earliest and most enthusiastic advocates of what we might call "natural religion." He believed that all intelligent men would be naturally religious if left to themselves, and not perverted by the teachings of the church. "Superstition and atheism," he said, "are the two poles of a universe in confusion." "We are certainly the work of God, that is a truth which it may be of use for me to know; and," he added, "the evidence of it is palpable." Hence, Voltaire vigorously defended belief in God, even to the extent of offending his fellow encyclopedists. He called himself a "theist," but it is evident that his natural religion was substantially the Deism that was popular in many enlightened circles in the eighteenth century. There can be no doubt, however, that Voltaire despised the organized religion that he found in his time. He hated the Roman Catholic Church for its superstition and intellectual tyranny; and he hated the Protestant Church almost equally because of its dogmatism and moral austerity. Nevertheless, Voltaire himself built on his estate at Ferney a chapel, on which, with characteristic conceit, he put the inscription in Latin: "Voltaire built this for God."

Scientific method. It is a great mistake to look in Voltaire for any careful scientific reasoning. We must always remember above all that he was a literary man and a crusader for causes in which he believed. In Voltaire, as one critic has said, "we look in vain for anything in the nature of a serious attempt to think things through." Nevertheless, he had a method which at times approached a scientific attitude. This is evident from his attitude toward history. It may be said that his attitude was merely one of scepticism, for he said that history as it was written in his time was filled "with

events that are not very probable,'' or ''so many
fables.'' Thus he was one of the first to apply the
critical spirit to historical records, and to take the
first steps toward developing methods of historical
criticism. He favored the extension of this critical
attitude even to the Bible. The books of the Bible,
he said, should be examined ''by the same rules as
are followed in the criticism of other histories.''
Voltaire, moreover, insisted that in history we
should look behind events. He was one of the first
to make written history a history of civilization.
History to him was essentially a history of culture.
He rejected all materialistic interpretations of history as radically false. To him the forces of history were, if not ideas, at least cultural traditions.
So we must conclude that Voltaire was groping
toward a truly scientific method in the study of history.

Voltaire had a great admiration for Locke, and
hence Locke's psychology was the only psychology
that he made use of in interpreting historical events.
As this psychology was individualistic as well as
sensationalist, it gave him no adequate basis for
the understanding of human society or the interpretation of history. It was the source of much of
his superficiality.

But in Voltaire's case, it did not lead to the absolute philosophical and religious scepticism that it
produced in the case of Hume. In his essay on
The Ignorant Philosopher, Voltaire, while confess-
ing his scepticism of both substance and spirit as

treated by the philosophers of his day, said that he was obliged to acknowledge intelligence within man; and in the universe, "a supreme intelligence." "I admit that supreme intelligence," he said, "without fear that I shall ever be obliged to change my opinion." It was this philosophic certainty of a spiritual element in the universe that made Voltaire so sure of the supremacy of spiritual values in human society.

Social philosophy. Doctrine of social origins. It was chiefly in the field of social origins that Voltaire was most prolific in his speculations. Voltaire held that Providence had created different "species" or races of men in different parts of the world, and that while these races had the same fundamental human nature, they differed in many respects. In his anthropology, he was what would now be called a "polygenist." This doctrine that the human races were distinct in origin, each with different innate qualities, as we shall see, affected his social and political thinking.

Voltaire held that the original condition of mankind was brutal and savage; but he vigorously combated the theory put forth by Rousseau that man was originally solitary. "We are," he says, "in the foremost rank of animals living in herds." "All mankind live in society," he tells us, and he feels certain that there has always been some society, as human beings are bound together by natural affections. He therefore refutes the solitary theory by the same arguments that were used by

William Thompson

VOLTAIRE

Bodin, and, in all his thinking, postulates the natural sociability of man. Moreover, from this natural sociability of man have sprung the social virtues, such as benevolence, pity, and justice. These sentiments or virtues are natural to man and are the basis of human society.

Voltaire argues also for the natural rationality of man. "God has implanted in us a principle of reason that is universal," he said, "just as he has given feathers to the birds and skins to bears." So man has a natural rationality, and this natural rationality, along with his natural sociability, assures man's progress, and is the promise of the final perfectibility of human society.

Moreover, Voltaire argues that man is naturally religious. The first idea of the soul, he says, would come from dreams. The appearance in dreams of the images of deceased persons naturally gave rise to the idea of ghosts, or *manes*. From this experience came the spirit world. Among the many spirits were some that were feared and must be propitiated. Thus the pantheon of gods became organized. Gradually men rose to belief in one god, though for a long time each nation had its own divinity. It will be noted that Voltaire does not make religion the invention of priests. On the contrary, religion is natural to man. Priests have corrupted religion. If every man were left to have his own religion, then it would be natural to him. Religious toleration, therefore, is the solution of the problem of conflicting religions.

Doctrine of social development. Voltaire discriminates between what he calls two great empires, "the empire of nature" and "the empire of custom." By the empire of custom he seems to mean something very similar to that which sociologists would now call "culture." The empire of nature furnishes us the norm to which reason bids us conform; but custom is infinitely variable. It frequently varies too far from nature, and comes into conflict with nature and reason. Social development, when wholesome, will not get too far from nature. Therefore, Voltaire frequently uses nature in judging the religion and morals, the government and law, and the other institutions of human society. As we have just seen, he would have religion to be what he called natural religion. This would make it, as the same time, rational religion. Again, he would have political institutions and laws conform as nearly as possible to nature. He condemns the severe penal laws of his day, and sides with Beccaria in maintaining that excessive punishments do no good, and that the punishment should always be proportioned to the crime.

According to Voltaire, the state came into being, not by contract, but to preserve the natural rights and responsibilities of men as members of society. Therefore, to this extent, a contract is implied between rulers and subjects. When rulers fail to support natural rights, natural law, and natural religion, they pervert human relations. Then subjects have the right of revolt and of revolution to preserve their natural rights and re-establish natural and rational law.

It might seem that Voltaire, like Rousseau, advocated a return to nature; but the thought of the two men was very different. With Voltaire, "nature" is not the primitive, but a rational, coherent, and natural order to which humanity may attain by the exercise of reason. It is because customs and institutions have so often in their development departed from this order of nature that we have problems of justice and humanity in society. The problem now is how to bring customs and institutions back to this rational, natural order.

Doctrine of social organization. While Voltaire held that human nature is everywhere fundamentally the same, he also held that men differ in abilities and desires, both by nature and by training. He scouted the idea, therefore, of social equality or of a classless society. We shall always have, he tells us, the rich who command, because they are rich, and the poor who obey, because they are poor. Fundamentally, these classes rest upon the different natural abilities of men. Equal and fair opportunities should be provided for all men, but different classes or types of men should not have the same education. Education should be in accord with the abilities of individuals and with the tasks they are expected to perform.

Voltaire is therefore a vigorous defender of the institution of private property. Any society with a rational division of labor cannot exist without a large number of useful individuals possessed of no property; otherwise many types of labor would be unavailable. As against Rousseau, Voltaire defends even private property in land, though not its abuses. Like many, he argues in general for the reform, though not the abolition, of private property, for he holds that property is necessary, not only for a rational social order, but for the dignity of man. "The spirit of property doubles a man's strength," he says.

Just as Voltaire held to natural inequalities existing among individuals, so he also holds to natural inequalities among the races of man. In general, his attitude toward other peoples and races is one of tolerance and appreciation. He praises the Persians, the Indians, and especially the Chinese; but he seems to despise the Jews, and he has little good to say of "that odious, but necessary race," as he calls them. This seems to be because he regards the Jews as responsible for the existence of historical Christianity. As Voltaire was unable to appreciate the work of the Jews in religion and morals, he seemed to be unable to appreciate them in any other respect, and must be ranked among the promoters of modern anti-Semitism. We must remember also that anti-Semitism was a very prevalent attitude in the eighteenth-century Europe in which Voltaire lived.

We have already seen that Voltaire believed that the essential solution of the religious problem in the social order was through religious toleration, of which he was one of the strongest advocates in the eighteenth century. He saw clearly, however, the importance of religion as a means of preserving order in human society, especially when it was rational, natural religion. "Is it not to be feared," he said, in criticizing D'Holbach, "that in denying God men would soon abandon themselves to the most atrocious passions and most frightful crimes?"

Doctrine of social progress. Voltaire's doctrine of social progress was vague. Apparently he believed in the spontaneous perfectibility of man if emancipated and enlightened. Break from man the shackles of superstition and tyranny, and his reason will lead him to perfect himself. Voltaire also attaches great importance to great men who may act as leaders, and even to happy accidents. He emphasizes the element of accident in human history. While an admirer of Turgot, he apparently did not understand or assimilate Turgot's view of progress. Among the accidents that may delay and even abort progress is war, which he was among the first to characterize as "the greatest of all crimes." Given, then, the natural rationality of man, fairly favorable circumstances, and peaceful conditions, human society may be expected to free itself from all errors and perfect itself.

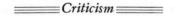

Criticism

It is easy to see and to say that Voltaire was very superficial in the understanding of human problems. We must remember, of course, that he was above all a literary man, and that on account of this, as well as on account of his time and place, he almost necessarily lacked profundity. In some respects he showed keen discriminations, as when he discriminated between the "empire of nature" and the "empire of custom." "Nature" was to him, however, essentially an abstract ideal of perfection. His reliance upon nature produced a superficial optimism that the scientific study of human problems can never endorse. Voltaire's trust, for example, in the natural rationality of man has little or no warrant either in history or human psychology. The net result of Voltaire's lack of constructive thinking was that his works were almost entirely negative and destructive. Even so, however, the social thinkers of the modern world owe him a deep debt of gratitude for his work in freeing mankind from superstition and tyranny. After all, too, we should remember that his optimism expressed a faith in human nature with which even science can hardly afford to dispense.

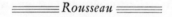

Rousseau

Jean Jacques Rousseau (1712–1778) was an altogether different man from Voltaire. As we have seen, Voltaire was an aristocrat, a highly cultivated, brilliant, polished man. Rousseau, on the other hand, came from what we would now call the proletariat. His father was a poor, eccentric watchmaker of Geneva. His mother died in giving him birth, and his father deserted him when he was ten years of age, and left him almost a mere waif upon the streets of Geneva. Though a maternal uncle assumed some care of him, he was knocked about, kicked from pillar to post, and never had any advantages. He was apprenticed first to one trade and then to another. Finally, at the age of sixteen, he ran away, and became, as we would say, a tramp. Falling in with some Roman Catholic priests, he pretended conversion to Catholicism, although his family in Geneva had been Protestants. The priests discovered that he was addicted to solitary vice, and, strangely enough, sent him to the house of a notorious Madame de Warens, who became his mistress in order to cure him of his vice. He lived with her, though occasionally wandering away, for about twelve years. Whatever education he had he seems to have owed mainly to Madame de Warens, who urged him to take up music and literature. In the meantime, he tried various positions as a house servant, tutor, and private secretary, in all of which he proved incompetent. During this early period of his life, as Professor Hearnshaw says, "He availed himself of the assistance of everyone whom he met; he begged, he stole, he told lies, he professed piety, he changed his religion; he did anything, in short, which his interests seemed to indicate, or circumstances to suggest as expedient."[2]

---

[2] *The Social and Political Ideas of Some Great Thinkers of the Age of Reason*, Chapter VII.

Finally, in 1742, he went to Paris, carrying with him letters of introduction to some of the leading intellectuals of the time, especially to Diderot and some of the other encyclopedists. They tried in vain to do something for him, but nothing permanent was accomplished, for he was unsatisfactory in every position that he tried to fill. "His vanity, his egoism, his bad manners, his loose morals, his incapacity for continuous employment, his sensitiveness, his quarrelsomeness, his irresponsibility," says Hearnshaw, "wore out the patience of all his benefactors."[3] In the meantime, he supported himself mainly by teaching music and by doing hack writing, being often on the edge of starvation. During this time he formed a mésalliance with an illiterate barmaid, Thérèse Levasseur, with whom he lived for seventeen years before marrying her. According to the statement in his *Confessions,* which we have no reason to doubt, she became the mother of five children by him, all of whom he disposed of by sending them to the public foundling hospital of Paris.

Up to 1750, Rousseau had been a failure in everything at which he had tried his hand, though many who knew him, even in this period, sensed his genius. In 1749, the Academy of Dijon offered a prize for an essay on the question "Has the Progress of the Sciences and the Arts Contributed to Corrupt or Purify Morals?" Rousseau wrote an essay in which he

---

[3] *Ibid.*

paradoxically took the negative side of the question, arguing that the progress of the arts and sciences had constantly worked for the corruption of morals. To his surprise, he won the award, and became famous almost overnight. In 1754, he undertook to carry out more systematically the thesis that he had defended in this first essay, and wrote a discourse on "The Origin of Inequality Among Men," which Voltaire termed Rousseau's "second book against the human race." This discourse is the most scientific of Rousseau's social and political writings, and comes as near to stating his social philosophy as any single one of his books. "It was, and still remains," says Professor Vaughan, "the most complete expression of revolt against human law and human convention."[4] In the meantime, he had begun the writing of plays and novels. The first of these to make a considerable impression was *The New Héloise,* published in 1761, in which he vigorously asserted the superiority of feeling to intelligence. This was one of the first free-love, sex novels of modern times, and helped to make him famous. It was followed in 1762 by a philosophical romance, entitled *Émile,* which is the story of an imaginary youth, with a detailed account of his education as Rousseau would have planned it. It was therefore virtually a treatise on education. In the same year, he published his even more famous work, *The Social Contract, or Principles of Political*

---

[4] *The Political Writings of J. J. Rousseau,* edited by C. E. Vaughan, Vol. I, p. 119.

Right, in which he attempted to set forth a practicable plan of political reconstruction. These two books created so much excitement that his friends warned him to leave France. He fled to his home city, Geneva, but he was arrested and his *Émile* was publicly burned. In 1765, Hume invited him to come to England. This was unfortunate for both men, since Rousseau was a revolutionist, while Hume's political conservatism was notorious. They soon quarreled, and in 1767 Rousseau returned to Paris, where he lived at Ermenonville, on the outskirts of the city, in a little house furnished him by one of his admirers. In 1778 he was found dead in the fields near this house. The manner of his death is still a matter of dispute. It is certain, however, that from 1765 on he manifested many signs of mental aberration, such as the fear of persecution, and delusions of various sorts. Indeed, we cannot understand Rousseau, as has often been said, without remembering the distinctly morbid element in his genius. He was the first morbid genius to get the attention of mankind. If in him the dumb millions first found a voice, it was a very unfortunate voice, because it was the voice of one who had many marks of mental abnormality, and who was at war with civilization. Nevertheless, Rousseau's thought must not be prejudged because of his mental eccentricity; for thought must stand upon its own merits regardless of the character of the man who utters it.

Scientific method. Rousseau had less scientific method than any man of ability that we have so far treated. He was an impressionist, an artist; a man of emotion, sensitivity, and of sympathetic insight; but of no controlled intellect at all. "A thinking man," he said, "is a depraved animal." Nevertheless, because he so emphasized emotion, he made a contribution to social philosophy. He believed that the feelings should be the supreme guide of life, and that instinct and feeling are more trustworthy than reason. His revolt against the rational brought into the foreground impulses, sentiments, and emotions, and these hitherto had not been taken sufficiently into account in social thinking. Through his emphasis upon these nonrational elements in human social life, Rousseau made indirectly a considerable contribution to social philosophy. But he seemed convinced that impulses, sentiments, and emotions were determined wholly by environment. As Hearnshaw says, "His wholehearted acceptance of the one-sided psychology which regards the mind of man as entirely determined by environment is one of the keys not only to his ethics, but also to his sociology."

An equally serious fault in Rousseau's method of thinking was his setting up the abstraction "natural man" as a basis of his reasoning. Rousseau himself declared that he did not suppose the "state of nature" ever to have existed, but to be simply a pure "idea of reason." Hence he says, "Let us begin by laying facts aside, as they do not affect the question." He takes "natural man" as opposed to present man, stripped of all that society has conferred upon him, a creature formed by a process of pure abstraction, and then reasons from him. Apparently, however, he throws his discourse into the form of a history of man's social development, though in reality his reasoning is wholly unhistorical, as he himself acknowledges. He therefore makes no use of scientific historical method, though he gives the reader the impression of doing so. This being his method, it is not surprising that he is continually involved in contradictions. His contemporary, Helvetius, rightly charged, "There is no proposition moral or political that M. Rousseau does not adopt and reject by turns." Surely this might be expected from a man who declared that facts do not affect the question. However, again we must remember that Rousseau was essentially of the artistic, literary type, and that if he had any knowledge of scientific methods of reasoning, he probably did not respect them.

Social philosophy. According to Rousseau, man must have begun his social life as a mere brute. He comes near to propounding the doctrine of man's animal descent; but contents himself with affirming that "it is only in degree that man differs from the brute." The origin and early development of human society must accordingly be interpreted in terms of brute nature. Nature, however, according to Rousseau, is wholly good. It is only the progress of civilization that has corrupted man. Accordingly, Rousseau considers that savage man was both good and happy, though Rousseau pictures him as solitary, speechless, without property, government, religion, or moral ideals. Nevertheless, the speechless, solitary animal was good and happy, and the primitive stage of human society was far better than any later stage thus far developed. Rousseau reverses Hobbes. Both considered that man began as a solitary, speechless savage, but according to Rousseau this condition was a happy one, while according to Hobbes it was intolerable.

"I think I have shown," Rousseau says, "that man is naturally good. What then can have depraved him to such an extent except the changes that have happened in his constitution, the advances he has made, and the knowledge he has acquired?" Again he says: "Everything is good as it comes from the hands of the Author of Nature; but everything degenerates in the hands of man."

Doctrine of social development. Logically, Rousseau should have portrayed the course of human history as a progressive degeneration of man. According to him, the Golden Age, or in Biblical phrase, "The Garden of Eden," lay in the primitive past in which man was a speechless and solitary, but happy, animal. Actually, however, Rousseau represents historical development as so many efforts and experiments made with a view to ameliorating the condition of men. But most of these experiments were mistakes and failures, according to Rousseau. In his essay on *The Origin of Inequality,* it is possible to make out four rather clearly marked stages in man's social evolution. Let us note these in some detail, quoting, when possible, direct from Rousseau.

(1) The first stage is the one that we have already described:

> In this primitive state, men had neither houses, nor huts, nor any kind of property whatever; every one lived where he could, seldom for more than a single night; the sexes united without design, as accident, opportunity or inclination brought them together, nor had they any great need of words to communicate their designs to each other; and they parted with the same indifference. . . . Let us conclude then that man in a state of nature, wandering up and down the forests, without industry, without speech, and without home, an equal stranger to war and to all ties, neither standing in need of his fellow-creatures nor having any desire to hurt them, and perhaps even not distinguishing them one from another; let us conclude, that, being self-sufficient and subject to so few passions, he could have no feelings or knowledge but such as befitted his situation; that he felt only his actual necessities, and disregarded everything he did not think himself immediately concerned to notice, and that his understanding made no greater progress than his vanity. If by accident he made any discovery, he was the less able to communicate it to others, as he did not know even his own children. Every art would necessarily perish with its inventor, where there was no kind of education among men, and generations succeeded generations without the least advance; when, all setting out from the same point, centuries must have elapsed in the barbarism of the first ages; when the race was already old, and man remained a child.

(2) The second stage began when men formed families and began to build homes and possess some

private property. In this stage, Rousseau tells us,

> They ceased to fall asleep under the first tree or
> in the first cave that afforded them shelter; they
> invented several kinds of implements of hard and
> sharp stone which they used to dig up the earth
> and to cut wood; they then made huts out of
> branches and afterwards learned to plaster them
> over with mud and clay. This was the epoch of
> a first revolution, which established families and
> introduced a kind of property, in itself the source
> of a thousand quarrels and conflicts. . . . The habit
> of living together soon gave rise to the finest feel-
> ings known to humanity, conjugal love and pa-
> ternal affection. Every family became a little so-
> ciety. The sexes, whose manner of life had been
> hitherto the same, began now to adopt different
> ways of living. Everything now begins to change
> its aspect. Men, who have up to now been roving
> in the woods, by taking to a more settled manner of
> life, come gradually together, form separate bodies,
> and at length in every country arises a distinct
> nation, united in character and manners, not by
> regulations or laws, but by uniformity of life and
> food and the common influence of climate. . . .
> Men began now to take the differences between ob-
> jects into account and to make comparisons. They
> acquired imperceptibly the ideas of beauty and
> merit, which soon gave rise to feelings of prefer-
> ence. . . . They accustomed themselves to assemble
> before their huts round a large tree; singing and
> dancing, the true offspring of love and leisure, be-
> came the amusement or rather the occupation, of
> men and women assembled together with nothing
> else to do. . . . From these first distinctions arose
> on the one side vanity and contempt and on the
> other shame and envy. . . . Hence arose the first
> obligations of civility even among savages; and
> every intended injury became an affront.

Thus began, according to Rousseau, customary law with its social rights and duties; and this law, not man's nature, was responsible for the primitive cruelties. Man was not naturally cruel, for "nothing is more gentle than man in his primitive state, as he is placed by nature at an equal distance from the stupidity of brutes and the fatal ingenuity of civilized man."

(3) The third stage was ushered in, Rousseau tells us, by the two arts of metallurgy and agriculture. Agriculture, however, played the dominant part, as it soon led to property in land. According to Rousseau, the land, like air and water, was naturally free to man, and the seizure of land was a "social theft," which accounted for many of the evils that were to follow. "The first man who, having enclosed a piece of ground, bethought himself of saying *This is mine,* and found people simple enough to believe him, was the real founder of civil society. From how many crimes, wars and murders, from how many horrors and misfortunes might not anyone have saved mankind, by pulling up the stakes, or filling up the ditch, and crying to his fellows, 'Beware of listening to this imposter.'"

"In this state of affairs," Rousseau tells us, "equality might have been sustained had the talents of individuals been equal." But as they were not equal one man could aggrandize himself at the expense of another. This soon bred dominion and slavery, or violence and rapine.

JEAN JACQUES ROUSSEAU

The wealthy had no sooner begun to taste the pleasure of command, than they disdained all others and using their old slaves to acquire new, thought of nothing but subduing and enslaving their neighbors. . . . Thus, as the most powerful or the most miserable considered their might or misery as a kind of right to the possessions of others, equivalent, in their opinion, to that of property, the destruction of equality was attended by the most terrible disorders. Usurpations by the rich, robbery by the poor, and the unbridled passions of both, suppressed the cries of natural compassion and the still feeble voice of justice, and filled men with avarice, ambition and vice. Between the title of the strongest and that of the first occupier, there arose perpetual conflicts, which never ended but in battles and bloodshed. The new-born state of society thus gave rise to a horrible state of war.

Thus, according to Rousseau, the origin of inequality among men is to be found in the institution of private property, especially private property in land. Property is justified only insofar as it is the fruit of labor. The appropriation of the natural resources of the earth by the strong leads to all sorts of social misery.

(4) According to Rousseau, this fact began to be perceived even in very early times, and led to the institution of the state, laws, and government to correct these evils. Rousseau represents this stage as a very explicit contract. The rich in particular, he says, suffered from these evils as much as the poor; "they suffered by a constant state of war, of which they bore all the expense; and in which,

though all risked their lives, they alone risked their property.'' Hence they led in the organization of government, using some such argument as this, according to Rousseau:

> Let us join . . . to guard the weak from oppression, to restrain the ambitious, and secure to every man the possession of what belongs to him: let us institute rules of justice and peace, to which all without exception may be obliged to conform; rules that may in some measure make amends for the caprices of fortune, by subjecting equally the powerful and the weak to the observance of reciprocal obligations. Let us, in a word, instead of turning our forces against ourselves, collect them in a supreme power which may govern us by wise laws, protect and defend all the members of the association, repulse their common enemies, and maintain eternal harmony among us.

But even this effort to secure social justice and establish human happiness was destined to end in failure.

> All ran headlong to their chains in hopes of securing their liberty; for they had just wit enough to perceive the advantages of political institutions, without experience enough to enable them to foresee the dangers. . . . Such was, or may well have been, the origin of society and law, which bound new fetters on the poor, and gave new powers to the rich; which irretrievably destroyed natural liberty, eternally fixed the law of property and inequality, converted clever usurpation into unalterable right, and, for the advantage of a few ambitious individuals, subjected all mankind to perpetual labour, slavery and wretchedness. It is easy to see how the establishment of one community made

that of all the rest necessary, and how, in order to make head against united forces, the rest of mankind had to unite in turn. Societies soon multiplied and spread over the face of the earth, till hardly a corner of the world was left in which man could escape the yoke, and withdraw his head from beneath the sword which he saw perpetually hanging over him by a thread.

Hence, according to Rousseau, the state and political institutions were established by a genuine contract. He says, "I regard the establishment of the political body as a real contract between the people and the chiefs chosen by them: a contract by which both parties bind themselves to observe the laws therein expressed which form the ties of their union." But as the forming of political institutions had again left man "everywhere in chains," it is now necessary to reinstitute the contract.

Doctrine of political organization. This reinstitution of the contract that forms the state Rousseau attempts in his chief work, *Le contrat social.* Logically, Rousseau should have proposed a return to the state of nature, the abolition of private property, and of government and the state. But he did not have the courage to draw the anarchistic conclusion. Instead, he proposes a reinstitution upon a new basis of the contract that formed the state, this basis being the sovereignty of the people. The institution of private property is accepted, but in the new contract, each citizen is to surrender all his rights to the whole community. "Each puts his

person and all his power under the general will of
the community.'' Sovereignty resides in the people,
and they cannot divest themselves of this sovereign
power even if they would. Rousseau agrees with
Hobbes that this sovereign power is indivisible, inalienable, and absolute; but is not above the people;
on the contrary, it resides in the general will of the
community. Individuals renounce their individual
rights in favor of the whole community, and ''the
social contract gives the body politic absolute power
over all its members.'' While the people are collectively sovereign, this sovereignty is absolute.
The state is ''a public person,'' an organism, a collective mind, a collective conscience, and therefore
has a general will that is not the same as the sum
of separate individual wills, but is directed rather
to the welfare of the entire body politic. The body
politic, taken as a whole, may be regarded, therefore, as an organized living body, resembling that
of man. The general will of this body politic is the
source of all law and all justice. It can and does
determine what is right and what is wrong. ''The
voice of the people is the voice of God.'' Hence,
''the general will is always right.''

Thus Rousseau agrees with Hobbes in making
government an absolutism, but it is an absolutism
in which the power resides in the people collectively.
Therefore, ''there is no fundamental law in the state
which cannot be revoked, not even the social contract.'' Thus the right of revolution remains with
the people and is inalienable because they are sov-

ereign. Therefore Rousseau's solution of the political problem was the substitution of a democratic absolutism for an autocratic.

Doctrine of social progress. Logically Rousseau should have ended in complete pessimism regarding civilization and human society in general. He should have advocated a complete return to primitive conditions; but he himself acknowledged that this was impossible, and, just as he proposed to reinstitute the contract at the basis of the state, so he proposed a reformed education as the most general means of ameliorating the conditions of human life. This he did in his celebrated treatise on education, *Émile.* His doctrines were, however, almost completely negative. The education that he advocated was mainly a freeing of natural impulses and tendencies. He said "Let a child have all possible freedom. Encourage its sports, its pleasures, and its instinct for happiness." "The child must be left to himself." In accordance with these general principles Rousseau advocated that from infancy to twelve years of age children should be kept in the country, wear little or no clothing, kept from contact with all institutions, taught to use their senses, and to distinguish things rather than words. Especial attention was to be given to physical training, but there was to be no introduction to books, and the whole training was a training of the senses and of the body, rather than of the mind. Of course, in this period no sort of instruction in religion or morals was to be given. Even later, Rousseau would prescribe but few studies, and those mainly along the line of the physical sciences and of trade instruction. Manual training was to be especially emphasized. Rousseau sincerely believed that this "natural" education, as he would call it, would develop the highest possibilities of man. He relied not upon instruction in knowledge nor upon education of reasoning powers, but rather upon the free development of all natural impulses and tendencies. As he believed that man is good by nature, he did not conceive that such development could be other than helpful to human society in the long run. He seems to have relied upon the natural compassion of human beings to remedy all sorts of evils, much as Voltaire relied upon man's natural rationality. It is hardly necessary to add that the educational ideals of Rousseau have had great influence upon modern systems of education, especially in the United States.

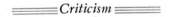

Criticism

Rousseau's teachings probably guided the French Revolution even more than did Voltaire's. Their influence today is still very great throughout western civilization. Let us notice again briefly some of his principal teachings: (1) Human nature is originally and intrinsically good. (2) Instinct and feeling are more trustworthy guides than reason. (3) Society, civilization, education, science, and art have all corrupted man. (4) Laws everywhere have been established and instituted for the oppression of the poor and the weak. (5) The fruit of civilization, in general, has been one of illusion, oppression, and crime. The remedy for the evils of society, so far as they can be cured, must be through popular democratic rule and a more "natural" education.

Western civilization has not entirely freed itself from Rousseau's errors in social thinking. There can be scarcely any doubt that much of the intellectual anarchy and social disorder of the present is rooted in his teaching. Modern education as well as modern political thinking has suffered much from the errors that he disseminated. We shall see that even such a thinker as Nietzsche is undoubtedly rooted in Rousseau's conception of the natural man. While Rousseau's anarchism and immoralism were mild when we consider the varieties that followed him, nevertheless, he undoubtedly sowed the seeds.

However, it would again be wrong to represent Rousseau's teachings as wholly negative and destructive. His emphasis upon emotion and sentiment, upon democratic ideals, and even his belief in the essential goodness of human nature, have all been constructive influences in the building of our modern world that we should not overlook or fail justly to evaluate.

CHAPTER XIV

Condorcet and Scientific Optimism

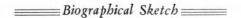

=====*Biographical Sketch*=====

A VERY DIFFERENT type of thinker from either Voltaire or Rousseau was Marie Jean Antoine Nicolas Caritat, Marquis de Condorcet, a revolutionary leader who attempted to do the constructive thinking for the French Revolution. He was born in 1743 of a noble family in Picardy, and died in 1794. He was an only child, brought up in isolation from other children by a pious mother. He was educated at the Jesuit College of Navarre in Paris, but had competent instructors in the physical sciences and mathematics. Removing from the provinces to Paris in 1762, he soon made many friends among the

---

¹ If possible, the reader should consult Professor J. S. Schapiro's excellent work, *Condorcet and the Rise of Liberalism.*

philosophical and scientific thinkers of the metrop-
olis, especially among those whom we call the "Encyclopedists." Among these friends were Turgot,
Voltaire, and the mathematician D'Alembert. He
soon shifted his interest from mathematics and the
physical sciences to political and social problems,
though he undoubtedly believed to the last that the
methods which were then proving successful in the
development of the physical sciences would be
equally successful in solving political and social
problems. Although he was a friend of Turgot
and became his biographer, he never fully assimi-
lated Turgot's point of view. With the development of the Revolution, he gradually associated
himself more and more with the Girondist party,
and came in time to be regarded as their chief spokes-
man. He abhorred the doctrines as well as the excesses of the Jacobins. Another influence in his
thinking was the success of the American Revolution, which he hailed as a harbinger of the success
of the French Revolution, and a sure token of the
perfectibility of human society.

Falling under the suspicion of the Jacobins and
proscribed by the Convention, he was hidden by one
of his friends in a garret near the Place de la Con-
corde, where the guillotine was set up and where he
could see his friends going day after day to the scaf-
fold. Nevertheless, Condorcet did not lose his faith
either in man or in the French Revolution; but in
the concealment of his garret, away from all books
and papers, composed his celebrated *Sketch of an*

Historical Picture of the Progress of the Human Mind. The reader will not fail to notice that this is almost the same title that Turgot gave to his Second Discourse. There can be scarcely any doubt, therefore, that Condorcet meant to carry out and demonstrate Turgot's scientific optimism. He did not have materials at his hand to document his book with facts and authorities. Almost necessarily, it became merely a confession of his own social faith. Its influence, however, on the development of French and English social and political thinking can scarcely be doubted. Comte acknowledged Condorcet as one of his predecessors who was specifically worthy of mention.

Condorcet's hiding place becoming suspected by his enemies, he attempted to escape, but was captured and thrown into jail. The next morning he was found dead in his cell, and it is believed that he committed suicide by taking poison concealed in a ring on his finger. Thus he died before the age of fifty-one.

Condorcet's Scientific Method

In general, the point of view of Condorcet was that of physical science. He believed that the methods which were being developed in physical science could be transferred without essential change to the social sciences. Especially did he believe that the mathematics of probability would be the key to the social sciences. Condorcet, therefore, must be regarded as one of the first of those thinkers who encouraged the transfer of the point of view and methods of the natural sciences to the social sciences. He probably did this innocently enough. He was apparently not so much of a critical thinker as an enthusiast. But he also gave a large place to observation and the historical method. He believed that by studying past world history we could foresee future events, just as in the physical sciences prevision had been demonstrated to be possible. Undoubtedly, Condorcet's view of human history and of social evolution was much simpler than the facts warrant or than any theory that we could now accept. He was carried away with his unbounded enthusiasm for scientific method, as he understood it, as applied to human society. His faith in science, indeed, became his religion. Whether he was an atheist, or a deist of Voltairian type, has often been discussed. While his general philosophical attitude seems to warrant the conclusion that he was essentially, like Diderot, an atheist, yet it is necessary to remember that above all he was a humanist, with an enthusiasm for humanity unequaled by any of his contemporaries save possibly Herder in Germany. It is this enthusiasm for humanity which has given to his work lasting value and which was the basis of his scientific optimism.

It should be added that Condorcet was a firm believer in Locke's sensationalist psychology and in Voltaire's theory of the natural rationality of man.

This theory was largely the basis of his social optimism.

Condorcet's Social Philosophy

The purpose of Condorcet's famous *Sketch,* to use his own language, was "to show from reasoning and from facts that no bounds have been fixed to the improvement of the human faculty; that the perfectibility of man is absolutely indefinite; that the progress of this perfectibility has no other limit than the duration of the globe upon which nature has placed us." The whole book, therefore, is taken up with an attempt to delineate the evolution of civilization in the past and to sketch the probable social progress of the future. It is a social dynamics on the one side, and on the other an attempt to picture the future. The book is midway, we would say, between historical sociology and prophecy.

Doctrine of social origins and evolution. Condorcet's view of primitive human society differed materially from that of Rousseau. He assumed that man from the beginning was a social and speaking animal, living in family groups. Of the origin of man, he says nothing, but notes that the only difference between man and the brutes is that man makes and uses tools. Like Bodin, he finds the social bond in the primitive family groups to have been essentially one of affection. This affection spread gradually to the kinship group and gave rise to the social sentiments. Thus the life of primitive man laid the foundations of social and cultural evolution.

Condorcet divided man's history into nine epochs, or stages. The first of these was the one that we have just described, when man lived by hunting and fishing, though occasionally cultivating plants around his camp. In this stage, human groups developed two superstitions that have inflicted untold calamities on humanity. These were (1) the belief in the survival of the soul after death; and (2) belief in gods, whom the imagination created in man's own image. Sorcerers and medicine men, a primitive priesthood, also arose, forming the first professional class.

The second epoch is that of the domestication of animals and the development of the pastoral industry. The domestication of animals gave man a new control over his food supply and encouraged the increase of population. Agriculture in the true sense arose toward the end of this period. War, also, which began in the first period, became now an institution, and war prisoners were saved and made slaves. Thus social classes and authoritarian institutions began to make their appearance.

The third epoch was that of settled agriculture. Property rights now became definite, because each parcel of land had its owner. Condorcet accepts Rousseau's idea that land ownership is the foundation of civil society. Society now became divided into rich and poor. Manufactures were established, and commerce developed. This third epoch in Condorcet vaguely covers the whole development of civilization until classical antiquity.

The fourth epoch was that of Greece. It is notable that Condorcet does not stop to treat specifically of the earlier peoples, especially the Jews. But he was greatly enamored of the Greeks. From them has come the art, the philosophy, and the science of the modern world. But their ideas, according to Condorcet, fell short of establishing the true social and political philosophy, because their political system was based upon slavery.

The fifth epoch was essentially that of Rome, but it is indefinitely defined by Condorcet as stretching from the beginning of Roman supremacy to the beginning of the early Middle Ages. To the Romans, he acknowledges, we owe our systems of law and government, but he regards their culture as merely a variation of Greek decadence. Philosophy and art he declared were "foreign to the soil of Rome." Nor did he think highly of the political ability of the Romans who, he declared, were the "sport of their tyrants." In addition to the Roman system of law, the Roman Empire was important because it gave opportunity for the spread of Christianity. The oppressed humanity of the Roman Empire welcomed a religion in which all were made "equal in slavery." The triumph of Christianity, according to Condorcet, signalized "the complete breakdown of science and philosophy."

The sixth epoch was from the fall of Rome to the

Crusades. Condorcet sees little of value in these early Middle Ages. "Barely did a glimmer of the light of talent or of human goodness and greatness," according to Condorcet, "pierce the profound darkness. . . . Theological moonshine and superstitious illusions were then the only characteristics of human genius, and religious intolerance was then the only morality."

The seventh epoch extended from the Crusades to the invention of printing. Essentially the age of feudalism, the people suffered under the triple tyranny of the King, the Warrior, and the Priest. According to Condorcet, the only good that issued from these Middle Ages was (1) scholasticism, which sharpened the wits of its practitioners and made possible philosophical analysis; (2) serfdom, which substituted for slavery a local bondage of the common people to the soil; and (3) gunpowder, which revolutionized the art of warfare, created equality between the knight and the common soldier, and resulted in destroying the superiority of the feudal nobles over the common people.

The eighth epoch covers the period from the invention of printing to Descartes. Its principal occurrence was the invention of printing, as a result of which a universal diffusion of knowledge became possible. In the opinion of Condorcet, this invention was the most revolutionary event in the history of the human mind. Printing not only made the destruction of books impossible, but, through the diffusion of knowledge, progress was now made safe.

The result was a great development of science in the sixteenth and seventeenth centuries, with the work of such men as Copernicus, Galileo, Kepler, and Bacon. The Renaissance became the scientific rebirth of civilization. The freedom of thought encouraged the Protestant Reformation. As Protestants based their position upon freedom of thought, they could not restrict the right of examination of any dogma, though, according to Condorcet, they gave this freedom of thought not to men generally, but only to Christians. Hence "the chain was not broken, but it was less heavy."

The ninth epoch covers the period from Descartes to the French Revolution. In this age, according to Condorcet, Newton established the true system of the universe, Locke disclosed the true theory of human nature, and Rousseau analyzed human society. To Locke's sensationalist psychology he credits a method of finding truth in the social sciences as certain as that in the natural sciences. This ninth epoch culminates in the Age of Reason, which pointed out the possibility of the perfectibility of man and of human society.

Ahead, according to Condorcet, is the tenth epoch ushered in by the French Revolution. This is to become the age of the perfectibility of man, in which man's aspirations for social justice and individual development, physical, moral, and intellectual, will be realized.

This classification of the stages of development of civilization is notable because it was one of the first that was attempted. While it has little to commend it from the point of view of either history or logic, it became a basis for further attempts in this direction. The various epochs that Condorcet pointed out, it is hardly necessary to add, frequently lacked connection and were not divided from one another by any consistent principle, as the logic of a good classification would require.

Doctrine of social progress. The French Revolution, according to Condorcet, marked the beginning of a new era, the era of the perfectibility of man and of human society. Accordingly, he devoted the last chapter of his book to sketching the probable progress of mankind in the future. In this chapter Condorcet takes the rôle of a prophet, and predicts three lines along which perfectibility will develop.

(1) First of all, he prophesies the destruction of inequality between nations as regards freedom. All nations, he says, are bound to become perfect in freedom. Being equally free, they will enjoy equal rights as nations. Small nations will have their rights respected equally with great ones. Nations will cease to exploit one another, and their differences will be settled on the basis of reason in a Council of Nations in which all will be represented. Thus, Condorcet anticipates the organization of a League of Nations.

(2) Condorcet prophesies the destruction of inequality between classes. This will come about in two ways: first, there will be destruction of inequality between classes as regards education; and second,

there will be destruction of inequality as regards wealth. Equal opportunities for instruction are bound to become the right of all classes of men. This equality of instruction or education will give them substantial equality of opportunity as regards all the rewards of effort. Equality of education will open up to every individual the place that he is best fitted for in society. No artificial impediments will be placed in the way of the progress of the individual. Therefore, there will be no impediments to his accumulation of the rewards of labor. This will not result, to be sure, in any absolute equality of wealth. There will still be differences in the amount of wealth that individuals will accumulate, but, as all will have equal opportunity, the differences will be much less than at present. Exploitation of one class by another will come to an end. Every individual will receive the just reward for his labor, whether it is that of hand or brain. In effect, Condorcet said, "Free men, break their shackles, and you will destroy the inequality which has grown up between social classes."

(3) Condorcet prophesies the indefinite perfectibility of man as an individual. Man, as an individual, will become more and more perfect: first, he will develop intellectually. This will result from the increase and relatively equal diffusion of knowledge through equality of education. Knowledge of every sort is bound to accumulate more and more as civilization advances, and through equality of educational opportunities, it will be open to everyone.

Moreover, everyone will have equal opportunity to train and develop his intellectual powers. Hence, the individual man will progress indefinitely, both as regards knowledge and his intellectual ability. Condorcet thinks that there may be also some inheritance of the effects of generations of education and training, and thus future generations will be born with better capacities to learn and to think than earlier generations.

Man as an individual will also become more perfect morally. More and more the experience of mankind will teach men the need and the nature of the moral virtues. More and more men will acquire knowledge of the right in human relations. Thus knowledge of moral conditions will lead to the practice of virtue. Again, Condorcet suggests that the practice of the virtues may result in the inheritance of better moral characters by individuals.

Man as an individual is bound to become more perfect physically. Knowledge of the body will increase and be more and more diffused. Condorcet prophesies the elimination of all preventable and contagious diseases. Disease will gradually be overcome. Moreover, physical training and education of the masses will result in the prevention and elimination of many bodily defects. All this, Condorcet says, will lead to the prolongation of life, its indefinite prolongation. Moreover, he thinks that there is a possibility that by the prevention of disease and physical education, each generation may be born slightly stronger physically than its immediate predecessors. Thus human life will be indefinitely prolonged and death indefinitely postponed. "Man will not become immortal," Condorcet says, but he does not hesitate to prophesy that "A period must one day arrive when death will be nothing more than the effect either of extraordinary accidents or of the slow and gradual decay of the vital powers."

Criticism

There can hardly be any doubt that Condorcet's scientific optimism can no longer be justified. He did not take into sufficient account the limitations of mankind that cannot be overcome by science. There is, of course, no scientific basis as yet for believing in the improvement of mental and moral traits or of bodily strength through the inheritance of acquired traits. To be sure, Condorcet did not definitely endorse this Lamarckian principle, and all must acknowledge that Lamarckism is not yet dead or finally disproved. But the very fact that nature seems to have set very definite limitations upon the bodily strength and mental and moral capacities of human beings negatives a great deal of the scientific weight of Condorcet's argument. On the other hand, there is no scientific reason why we should not work for the equality of nations, for the relative equality of classes, both in regard to education and wealth, and for the elimination of disease and physical defects among mankind. Therefore, something of Condorcet's scientific optimism may still animate social scientists and humanitarian workers. Indeed, something of Condorcet's faith is indispensable for the continual development of the social sciences. We need not believe unqualifiedly in the "natural rationality" of mankind, as did both Voltaire and Condorcet. But there is no reason why we should not believe in the continued success of science in eliminating both individual and social defects. The perfectibility of mankind was therefore not an idle dream of the French philosophers of the nineteenth century. It is still the animating principle of all social science capable of giving guidance to mankind, and, as Professor Schapiro says, "of social and political liberalism." The spirit of Condorcet thus continues to lead us upward and on.

CHAPTER XV

Eighteenth-Century German Social Philosophy

GERMAN THINKERS WERE relatively late in developing a well-worked-out and coherent social philosophy. The Cameralists attempted this in the late seventeenth and early eighteenth centuries. But their influence upon the social thinking of western Europe was not great. It was not until the very last decades of the eighteenth century that German social thought began to show signs of maturity. It did this particularly in two writers: Immanuel Kant and J. G. Herder.

 *Immanuel Kant*

Biographical sketch. Immanuel Kant (1724–1804) was born at Königsberg, East Prussia, and was partly of Scottish descent. He was, however,

IMMANUEL KANT

typically German in his culture, and never in all his life was more than twenty miles away from his native city. As a boy, he was very poor, and had great difficulties in obtaining his education. Moreover, he seems to have been for a time relatively unsettled in his own mind; for at the University of Königsberg he studied physics and theology before he studied philosophy. He was troubled with very delicate health, and was very slow in maturing. He did not become a private-docent in the University until he was thirty-one, and did not secure his professorship until he was forty-six. His great masterpiece, *The Critique of Pure Reason,* was not produced until he was a man of fifty-seven. However, he had earlier produced some interesting monographs that were characterized by original thinking; such was his *Theory of the Heavens* (1755), which anticipated Laplace's nebular hypothesis. Shortly after, he seems to have written his notes on *Anthropology,* suggesting the evolution of man from some lower animal form, though these notes were not published until 1798.

Kant's *Critique of Pure Reason* became the foundation, not only of the so-called critical philosophy, but practically of all modern philosophical thought. Its influence upon philosophical thinking, therefore, has been enormous. Its chief problems were in the theory of knowledge, or epistemology. Its conclusions were sceptical; namely, that we cannot know universal or absolute truth through pure reason. In practice, however, Kant was very far from being

agnostic, and in 1788 he followed his masterpiece
with a *Critique of Practical Reason,* which attempted
to show that we can reach absolute or universal
truth on a pragmatic basis. In 1790, he published
his *Critique of Judgment,* and in 1796, a work on
the *Theory of Law.* Earlier, he had published a
monograph on *The Natural Principle of Political
Order in Connection with the Idea of a Universal
History from a Cosmo-Political Point of View.* It
is chiefly in this monograph that we find Kant's ideas
on social and political development. He was undoubtedly primarily metaphysical in his thinking.
But the political disturbances of the later years of
the eighteenth century greatly stimulated his social
thinking. In 1793, he published a monograph on
Religion within the Limits of Pure Reason, and in
1795, a pamphlet on *Eternal Peace.* The last two
publications greatly disturbed the authorities of the
Prussian state. An official letter was sent him by
the Council of the King, rebuking him for his views,
particularly in the field of religion. This greatly
humiliated Kant, and he soon ceased to teach. He
died in 1804.[1]

Scientific method. From what has already been
said, it is evident that Kant's mind was encyclopedic.
Yet there can be no doubt that his method was chiefly
the Platonic one of the criticism of concepts. Locke
and Hume were the chief philosophical adversaries

---

[1] A good summary of Kant's philosophy, including his social and
political doctrines, can be found in Durant's *Story of Philosophy,* pp.
285–317.

whom he sought to overthrow. Locke had said: "There is nothing in the intellect except what was first in the senses." Kant agreed with Leibnitz's criticism when he said: "nothing, except the intellect itself." Kant's chief service to philosophy was to show that while the specific content of our ideas comes from experience, yet the form of our ideas comes from our own inner make-up. Truths derive their necessary character from the inherent structure of our minds, from the inevitable manner in which our minds must operate. The mind of man, then, according to Kant, is not a passive wax tablet, as Locke thought, upon which experience and sensation write anything they please. The mind of man is an active organ that molds and co-ordinates experience into ideas, wishes, and standards. Space and time, for example, Kant said, are not simply things we see, but necessary modes of perception.

Accordingly, Kant believed that objects of sense conform to our conceptions, rather than that our conceptions conform to objects. We cannot know things as they really are, in themselves. The human mind determines the way we perceive things. It is self-determining and free. This inner determination, or autonomy, lifts the mind of the individual in its moral and social decisions above the determinism of the physical world. Hence, Kant starts from the postulate of the freedom and purposeful determination of human actions.

=====*Kant's Social Philosophy*=====

Kant's social philosophy centered in his doctrine of social and political evolution especially, as set forth in his monograph on *The Idea of a Universal History from a Cosmo-Political Point of View.*[2] He held that human history is a realm of teleological law. Individual behavior taken by itself may seem incoherent and lawless, but individual men pursuing their own contradictory purposes are unconsciously promoting a historical process that has a goal and obeys law. The problem of the philosopher is to discover a meaning in this senseless current of human action. Though Kant wrote before Condorcet, his general position is similar. He affirms that nothing can be known about the course of civilization until the laws of its movement have been discovered. This is a matter for scientific investigation. He admitted that these laws are not yet known, but thought that some future genius may do for social and historical phenomena what Kepler and Newton did for astronomical phenomena.

Kant maintained in the monograph which we have just mentioned that conflict in human society was one of the main stimuli to its development. Man is

---

[2] This was translated by Thomas DeQuincey and has been published by the Sociological Press (Hanover, N. H., 1927), under the title *The Idea of a Universal History on a Cosmo-Political Plan.* The author has tried to simplify and condense this essay in the pages that follow.

not completely social; there is also an unsocial, self-assertive side of his nature. These two qualities exist side by side in every human being, and give rise to what Kant called "the unsocial sociableness of man," so that the experience of man is that he cannot live at peace with his fellow men, and yet, at the same time, without them he cannot live at all. Now these natural tendencies of man give a clue to the inevitable course of human history; for Kant lays it down that all the tendencies to which any creature is predisposed by his nature must finally reach a complete and appropriate development. Those predispositions in man that lead to the use of reason are therefore destined to be fully developed. But they can be fully developed only in the species; not in the individual. Each man would require an inordinate length of time to develop perfectly his rational faculties. The means that nature employs to develop these faculties and all natural tendencies is opposition in the social state. A constant conflict exists in society between man's gregarious and his antigregarious tendencies. His antigregarious nature expresses itself in the desire to force all things to comply with his own wishes. If it were not for these antisocial propensities of man, a social life of perfect harmony and mutual love would easily be possible; but it would suffocate and stifle all talent in its very germs. For reason is developed through conflict, a conflict that ranges all the way from the conflict of ideas to the conflict of institutions. According to Kant, "man wishes concord; but nature knows better what is good for the species.'' Kant, however, did not draw the conclusion that war was desirable. On the contrary, these conflicting tendencies of man simply set the problem of the establishment of a civil society in which peace and justice shall reign. The establishment of such a society is the indispensable task of reason; for happiness can be established in human society only when there is a universal civil society founded on social and political justice. The establishment of such a society, therefore, is the highest problem of the human species.

Kant believed that such a perfect civil society could be established only when there was due consideration both of international relations and of the relations of individuals and groups within the state. For the international relations, Kant advocated as the political goal a confederation of free states in which the utmost possible freedom should be united with rigorous limits upon aggression. In other words, he advocated the establishment of a constitution over all the nations, or what we would now call ''a league of nations.'' He believed that such a cosmo-political organization of mankind would finally be necessitated through the conflicts between nations. The struggle for existence, then, is not altogether an evil; but men must soon perceive that it must be restricted within certain limits, so that any one state might expect the same sort of regulation by international law that individuals now expect through the civil law. It follows that the history of mankind reveals a hidden plan of nature to perfect a civil constitution for a universal human society, since such a universal society is the indispensable condition for realizing justice in human relations, or a reign of reason in which all men, obeying the moral law, shall mutually treat each other as ends in themselves.

Thus it is evident that Kant held that the whole meaning and movement of human history is in the direction of the greater restriction of pugnacity and violence and the continuous enlargement of the area of peace. Hostile conflict and violence are characteristic of the wild state of nature, and the cessation of war is made more and more necessary by the development of civilization. This idea Kant developed in his essay, *Eternal Peace.*

Doctrine of social and political organization. In the essay just mentioned, Kant takes a very firm stand for a republican organization of the government and the state. He declared that peace could never be secured until the mass of the people had the deciding vote about war or peace. Absolute monarchs and princes could not be trusted to decide such a matter, as usually they had little danger of suffering personally by war. In general, then, Kant favored a democratic and liberal social order. He was opposed to slavery and to all forms of human exploitation. While he sympathized with the French Revolution, he did not accept its ideal of absolute equality among men, but strongly advocated equality of opportunity. All hereditary privi-

leges and prerogatives of birth and class were therefore to be done away with. Naturally these views
did not bring Kant into favor with the Prussian
authorities.

Ethics and religion. A word must be said about
Kant's ethics and religion, as they are the key to
his social philosophy. He held it to be an uncon-
ditional command of conscience that we should always so act that the maxim of our action could be
made a universal law for all individuals acting in
similar conditions. This Kant held to be a necessary postulate of morality. From it necessarily
followed his other ethical axiom, that we should always so act as to treat humanity, whether in our
own person or in that of another, as an end, and
never as a means. In other words, human beings
are always to be treated as ends in themselves, and
never used as mere means. This was Kant's reformulation of the golden rule. Morality consists
in the conforming of all action to these two moral
imperatives, which alone can render possible a kingdom of ends (a morally perfect human society).

Thus it is evident that Kant's conception of morality was pre-eminently social, but not in the sense
in which Hobbes or Hegel conceived morality to be
social. According to Kant, a human individual can
never be considered a mere cog in the social machin-
ery; he is always an end in himself. Perhaps it
would be fair to say that no one since Jesus of
Nazareth so exalted the supreme worth of persons
as did Immanuel Kant. Moreover, it followed that

human society could not be founded upon mere relations of might, but must always be based upon
considerations of right and justice.   Hence it is only
through following the imperatives of our ethical
nature that we can create an ideal human society.
We must seek a moral basis for all human institutions, and this basis is found in the supreme worth
of individuals.

Religion itself must be based upon ethics, and is
to be judged by its value for morality.   Creed and
ritual have little value in themselves, and should
never take the place of the good life.   Religion is
essentially the perception of our duties as divine
commands.   Its end is, therefore, not only the salvation of the individual soul, but the moral regeneration of human society.

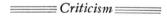

Criticism

However much we may admire Kant's conclusions, there is hardly any doubt that his method
is not to be commended.   He carried the criticsm of
categories, or of the concepts employed in reasoning, too far.   He had too much faith in this criticism as a method of discovering truth.   It is no
doubt a useful and necessary part of a sound scientific and philosophical method; but it centers the
problems of philosophy too much in the theory of
knowledge.   Moreover, Kant's idealism, like Plato's,
almost reverses the method of modern science.

Finally, it is to be doubted whether any such antithesis exists between the pure reason and the practical reason as Kant made the very basis of his philosophical system. It introduces into the human mind a dichotomy that probably does not exist. To assume such may be dangerous in practice and lead to anti-intellectualism. This we may see even in Kant himself; for he held that we cannot know with the pure reason anything about God, freedom, or immortality. These, he said, were simply necessary postulates of the practical reason. The danger in such a position the reader can readily see. However, it is surely absurd to explain the Great War, as some have attempted to do, through this dualism, sponsored by Kant, in theoretical and practical thinking.

===== *J. G. Herder* =====

Johann Gottfried von Herder was the great eighteenth-century German precursor of sociology. He was born in 1744, twenty years after Kant, and a year after Condorcet. He died in 1803. Herder's name is a very notable one in German thought and literature, and his contribution to social philosophy was only one of many achievements. He was born of very poor parents, and was barely able to attend the University of Königsberg. He studied there for two years under Kant, but his poverty prevented him from finishing his course. He was first interested in medicine, but later turned to philosophy and theology. He was ordained, and preached fairly successfully at Riga, Strasburg, and other places. After a short period of travel in Holland and France, he reached Strasburg, and there met Goethe, the German poet. They became fast friends. Through Goethe's influence, somewhat later, he was appointed court preacher at Weimar and superintendent of the clergy of that little duchy. Among his duties, however, were the superintendency of the schools and of poor relief. As Herder was very active in literature, as well as in science and philosophy, it is evident that he was a many-sided man. He became noted as a philologist of considerable ability. He was a student of comparative religion, comparative mythology, and popular songs and ballads. At the same time, he maintained his interest in theological matters, and was counted one of the leaders of the liberal German theologians of his time. He was also a leader and pioneer in Biblical criticism. But his main interest, perhaps, was in human history, in human society, in humanity, in anthropology, and in sociology, although the last two were not then known by those names. Now, all of Herder's work really hangs together. His mind was synthetic and his spirit humanitarian. His moto was "Love, Life, Light," and it is said that on his deathbed he exclaimed: "If I could only get a new idea, I think I could live." Thus Herder was one of the great leaders of thought in the eighteenth century, particularly in Germany.

Scientific method. Herder repudiated the criticism of the categories of thought, the method of his teacher, Kant. He was objective and sought to avoid *a priori* considerations and speculations. Kant had opposed human life to nature by giving to man an absolute free will, rational and independent. But Herder, like Montesquieu, considered human life continuous with nature. He regarded history as a natural science and proposed to study the whole of human life by evolutionary, genetic methods. This is all the more remarkable because his training and life work were primarily philosophical and theological. Like Montesquieu, also, he studied widely the history, literature, and customs of all peoples, so far as known to his time. He advocated the genetic, comparative method in the study of all these phenomena. He was no mere empiricist, but was a synthetic, if not a profound, thinker. But like Montesquieu, again, his catholicity and liberality of mind made up for much of his lack of profundity. His difficulty was that he tried to cover too many fields, and the result was that he was somewhat amateurish and superficial. Kant criticized his work rather severely for this reason, and he, in turn, criticized Kant and Kant's methods. He claimed that if philosophy were any good, it should come down to earth and interpret human life and history. On account of his naturalism, some of his contemporaries accused him of being a materialist; and he was monistic in his approach to human problems, but this was consistent with his theological pantheism. His main work, *Ideas Toward a Philosophy of the History of Mankind,* in four volumes (1784–1791), accordingly was unlike all preceding philosophies of history. It sought to base the philosophy of history on antecedent scientific knowledge. Therefore, it approached a sociology. But Herder was, after all, too much of a humanitarian and a mystic to construct a scientific sociology, even though he is said to have had a positive hatred of metaphysics.

═══ *Herder's Social Philosophy* ═══

Herder's aim was to explain human development as a consequence of the nature of man and of man's physical environment. Human society is therefore viewed as a part of nature, and the different forms of human culture as strictly natural processes. Man is considered as an animal among animals. Herder stresses the erect posture of man as explaining his development of culture. He also, however, emphasizes that man has innately a capacity for reasoning that none of the brutes possess, is organized with finer instincts, and is formed for "humanity and religion."[3] He takes a strictly evolutional view of man as only preparation, "the bud of a future flower."[4] Everything in human

---

[3] See Herder's *Outline of the Philosophy of the History of Man,* Book IV.

[4] *Ibid.,* Book V.

history must be viewed, therefore, as a process of development. From one point of view, language plays a chief role in this process, as it is the special means of learning and of improving culture. Moreover, the arts and sciences of mankind have been invented and diffused through imitation, reason, and language. Language he regards as the chief vehicle of tradition and as the means by which the past acts upon individuals in the present. But imitation is also a means for diffusing ideas and inventions throughout mankind.

However, like Montesquieu, Herder falls back upon geographical conditions to explain the differences in culture and institutions of different peoples. He even believed that geographical conditions were the main factors to be used in explaining the physical, mental, and moral differences among peoples. Thus they gave the explanation of the differences in traditions and social institutions that we find among the various peoples. Yet it must be said, in fairness to Herder, that he was careful to say that these geographical conditions do not compel, but that rather they incline to certain developments. This he says explicitly regarding climate, and he seems to apply this principle to all the other geographical factors. Hence, it was possible for him to emphasize other elements than geography in human history and in human society.

The most striking contribution that Herder makes to social theory is probably his doctrine of the nature of human society, that it is an organic unity. He emphasizes that men are not isolated individuals, but are connected with and dependent upon one another; and that this interdependence stretches through all the generations of mankind. He thus breaks with eighteenth-century individualism and comes very near to formulating an organismic theory of human society. But his organismic conception of society is implied rather than explicitly expressed.

An outcome of his emphasis on the interdependence of the generations is his acceptance of the idea of Turgot and of Lessing that history is the process of the education of the human species. Lessing had given this idea a more or less theological connotation, but Herder puts it upon a naturalistic basis. Even though he says that there is no such entity as nature, he practically personifies nature and says that the development of humanity has been brought about through the course of instruction that nature affords. This explains the accumulation of experience in tradition and the differing traditions of different peoples. It ultimately explains also the different types of personality produced by different cultural traditions. "The history of mankind is a whole," Herder tells us, "that is, a chain of sociability and tradition, from the first link to the last. There is an education, therefore, of the human species; since everyone becomes human only by means of education, and the whole species lives largely in the chain of individuals." Even in his terminology, Herder emphasizes this conception of the education of humanity, because he speaks of the infancy, childhood, manhood, and old age of nations and of humanity as a whole. Unlike Augustine, however, he does not mark out definite boundaries between these stages. Moreover, he does not have the idea that history has a definite goal of perfection and development. On the contrary, each stage in the development of humanity or of a nation's life is an end in itself. The earlier generations do not live for the sake of the later ones. Each generation, through its experience, finds the good that is peculiar to itself and suitable for itself. Therefore the process of development, whether of a people or of humanity as a whole, presents itself as a series of separate segments, each containing its own meaning and justification. There are no cycles, as Vico thought, and there is no spiral in human development.

But while Herder held that the history of mankind can and should be viewed as a whole, he was firm in his conviction that the vehicle of every concrete culture was a distinct *Volk* or *Nation,* with its distinct language and traditions.[5] Every people should, therefore, have its own national culture and cherish its own national traditions. The culture of every nation, if original, and spontaneous, has a special mission to perform and a distinct contribution to make in the building of the total culture

---

[5] Cf. Ergang, R. R., *Herder and German Nationalism* (No. 341 of Columbia University *Studies in History, Economics, and Public Law*).

of mankind. Moreover, it buds, flowers, and fades according to natural laws of growth.

Herder was a firm believer in progress. He perhaps did not believe in progress in Condorcet's way. He believed that there was a progressive realization of the good in human history. That realization he expressed by the vague phrase that the end of humanity is in itself. "Humanity," he tells us repeatedly, "is the end of human nature." The realization of a developed humanity seems to have been his idea of progress. Humanity, according to Herder, is only in the germ, in almost the earliest stage of its development. He says: "The flower of humanity will blossom out one day into the true form of man like unto God, in a state of which no terrestrial man can imagine the greatness and the majesty."

Nevertheless, Herder believes that all of man's development has taken place in accordance with natural law. He makes bold to formulate four laws of nature [6] that he says hold for all of human history and all of social development. The first law is, "Whatever can take place among mankind within the sphere of given circumstances of time, place, and nation actually does take place." Herder is fond of repeating that everything earthly and human is governed by time and place, and every particular nation by its character. This is Herder's

---

[6] These laws are found in Book XIII of Herder's *Philosophy of History* under "General Reflections on the History of Greece" (Chapter VII).

grand law of social determinism. He does not admit any possibility of departure from this law, though inconsistently he emphasizes the moral freedom of man. However, this law is consistent with Herder's naturalistic monism, even though he finds it impossible consistently to adhere to it himself.

His second principle, or natural law, is, "What holds for one people, holds also for the union of several peoples taken together; they stand together as time and place unite them; they interact as the combination of their active powers brings it about." This law is simply a further carrying out of the first law so far as groups and combinations of people are concerned.

Herder's third law is, "The culture of a people is the flower of its existence; its display is pleasing indeed, but transitory." Herder means, of course, the literary and artistic culture. Here he brings out his more or less concealed organismic conception of society. The implication is that there is an analogy between the life of a people and the life of a flower or plant. This, indeed, Herder repeatedly implies in several places.

Herder's fourth law of history and of social development is, "The health and duration of a nation rest not on the point of its highest culture, but on a wise or fortunate equilibrium of its active powers. The deeper in its life energy lies its center of gravity, the more firm and durable it is." Here again, Herder implies an analogy between the life of a state or nation and the life of an organism, let us say, of a tree.

Doctrine of social progress. Consistently, or inconsistently, Herder, in Book Fifteen, outlines a philosophy of social progress in five propositions.[7]

I. The end of human nature is humanity; and that they may realise their end, God has put into the hands of men their own fate.

II. All the destructive powers in nature must not only yield in time to the preservative powers, but must ultimately be subservient to the perfection of the whole.

III. The human race is destined to proceed through various degrees of civilisation, in various revolutions, but its abiding welfare rests solely and essentially on reason and justice.

IV. From the very nature of the human mind, reason and justice will inevitably gain more footing among men in the course of time.

V. A wise goodness disposes the fate of mankind, and therefore there is no nobler merit, no purer or more abiding happiness, than to cooperate with its designs.

Religion and ethics. It is evident from these quotations that Herder's social philosophy is pri-

-----
[7] *Op. cit.*, Book XV.

marily ethical and religious, even though to some this may seem inconsistent with his naturalistic monism. Although an enthusiastic advocate of Spinoza's pantheism, Herder nevertheless was one of the founders of modern religious humanism. One might also say, indeed, that an ideal humanity is his divinity. He had a blind faith in nature, but even more of a blind faith in man and in the ultimate development of reason and justice in human society. His religious faith was clearly akin to that of the philsophers of the French Enlightenment; however, as has often been pointed out, it was not hedonistic, but as we would say now, more of a faith in man's inevitable evolution into a being dominated by reason and justice.

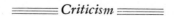
Criticism

It is evident that Herder shared, in general, the optimism of the eighteenth century. We must rank him very high as a humanitarian and a prophet, but it is impossible to give him a high rank from the scientific point of view. He was far from clear in his thinking and writing. It is not clear, for example, what he means when he proclaims that the end of human development is humanity (*Humanität*), and that the measure of all development is humanity. Again, his laws of history are hardly worthy to be called laws. At best they are rather questionable generalizations, springing in the main from Herder's naturalistic conception of human society. While we cannot rank Herder high as a scientist, we must rank him high as a leader of later eighteenth-century thought, especially in Germany. In Germany, he represented very well the movement which Condorcet represented in France. As a liberal, as a humanitarian, and above all, as one of the founders of the religion of humanity, he deserves to be remembered in the history of social thought.

CHAPTER XVI

Later Eighteenth-Century British Social Philosophy

WE HAVE ALREADY SEEN how the sceptical philosophy of Hume came to dominate English social thinking in the later half of the eighteenth century. We have also seen that Hume's social philosophy was not wholly negative, but that it laid the foundation for a further development of social theory in such principles as habit, sentiment, and self-interest. It was natural, therefore, that two of Hume's friends should have carried out the implications of his social philosophy through reflection upon the working of these principles in human society. These two friends were Adam Smith and Adam Ferguson.

 *Adam Smith*

Biographical sketch. Adam Smith was born at Kirkcaldy, Scotland, in 1723. He was educated at the University of Glasgow and at Oxford. In 1751 he became Professor of Logic in the University of Glasgow, and the next year was made Professor of Moral Philosphy. In 1764 he resigned his professorship, and, while a tutor in a noble family, lived for nearly two years in France. Here he came into contact with Quesnay, the leader of the physiocrats, and with Turgot. In 1759, while Professor of Moral Philosophy at Glasgow, he had already published a notable treatise on the *Theory of Moral Sentiments.* In this work he rather consistently carried out some of the implications of Hume's philosophy. In France, however, he was greatly affected by the theories of the physiocrats and the economic ideas of Turgot. Apparently, while still in France, he set to work to write his *Inquiry into the Nature and Causes of the Wealth of Nations,* which was not published, however, until 1776. This book at once received almost unprecedented attention, and had a world-wide influence through a century or more, probably because it fitted in so well with the tendencies of the time. The later years of Smith's life were passed in writing and in public service. He died in 1790.

Scientific method. As Professor of Moral Philosophy in the University of Glasgow, Smith gave courses in natural theology, ethics, jurisprudence, and political economy. He seemed to have considered that his lectures in political economy were a part of moral philosophy. Indeed, his whole system of thinking centered in his ethics, as he found the roots of religion in moral obligation, and made jurisprudence and political economy essentially applications of ethical principles. It is needless to say that this attitude of Smith's was often overlooked by the students of his *Wealth of Nations*.

Expressed in other language, Smith assumed that there was a natural moral order, a law of nature that was at the same time a divine law. Hence, his thinking contained a very large element of deduction from what he assumed to be natural law. Yet it is only fair to say that Smith used a great deal of induction to fill in the framework that he considered to be natural law. *The Wealth of Nations* was said to be the result of nearly ten years of careful investigation and research. It certainly abounds with facts and observations. Smith himself believed that his standpoint was that of "a dispassionate observer," but he certainly had many unproved or *a priori* assumptions. Perhaps the chief two of these were his assumptions of the beneficence of "the obvious and simple system of natural liberty," especially in the economic life, and of the inevitable harmony of self-interest and public welfare in the long run. Both of these assumptions seem to have come mainly from the political and economic atmosphere in which he lived. To some extent, as we have already seen, they were the assumptions of the physiocrats in France.

However, Smith probably did more injury to social thinking by his abstraction of the economic life from the total social life, and by setting up an "economic man" actuated by purely selfish motives, working uniformly in the direction of private gain. He did not carry this abstraction as far as many of his successors. Nevertheless, it is entirely fair to say that the conception of an "economic man," concerning whom legitimate scientific deduction might be made, reveals Smith as essentially an individualist in his social thinking.

Smith's Social Philosophy

The significance of Smith's social thought lies largely in the fact that he sensed the rising importance of economic factors in western civilization. With him, social philosophy definitely turned from its political phase to its economic phase. For a century or more, the economic factors had been growing in importance, and the whole framework of modern capitalistic society was emerging. Smith made it his task to describe this framework and to point out the presuppositions of capitalistic enterprise.

In *The Wealth of Nations,* Professor House says, "Economics first came of age as a distinct and systematic science."[1] If taken in a broad sense, this statement is true. Nevertheless, as Professor Small emphasized, *The Wealth of Nations* was essentially a work in social or moral philosophy.[2] There are

---

[1] House, *Development of Sociology,* p. 71.
[2] Small, *Adam Smith and Modern Sociology,* Introduction.

abundant evidences in the book that Smith so considered it himself.

As Professor Small further remarked, "The fact remains that Smith set a new standard of inquiry into the economic section of the conditions of life, while life presented itself to him as, on the whole, a moral affair, in which the economic process is logically a detail."[3] However, we must not attribute to Smith too much philosophical consistency or clear thinking. On the contrary, his writings appear to have been relatively unsystematized. Buckle suggested that Smith's two main books, *The Theory of Moral Sentiments* and *The Wealth of Nations,* together constituted a complete treatise on social philosophy: the former describing the working of benevolent impulses and sentiments in society, while the latter traced out the working of self-interest. There is no evidence that Smith so intended them. It simply so happened that in one work he dealt mainly with social sympathy, and in the other with self-interest. It is plain, however, that he did not find in self-interest an adequate explanation of human society. It is therefore unfair to attribute the interpretation of human society exclusively in terms of self-interest, which so commonly prevailed in the nineteenth century, as due to the influence of Adam Smith. *The Wealth of Nations* undoubtedly had an influence in this direction, but Smith's less-read *Theory of Moral Sentiments* emphasized the other aspect of human relations.

---

[3] *Op. cit.,* p. 235.

The distinguishing doctrine in Smith's *Theory of Moral Sentiments* is that the social and moral life of mankind is based essentially upon fellow feeling, or sympathy. Justice, he finds, is the most important moral virtue, and human society has therefore essentially a moral basis. "Society," he says, "cannot subsist among those who are at all times ready to hurt and injure one another."[4] Therefore, back of justice and all the other virtues lies social sympathy. This expresses itself particularly in seeking the approbation of others. That approbation of ourselves which we call the moral sense is brought about by our placing ourselves imaginatively in the place of others—seeing ourselves as others see us. The moral life is therefore based upon the subjective process of self-approbation in terms of our approbation of others; but this itself springs from the social process that we call sympathy. As Professor Small says, "Society, according to this account, would seem to be a collection of images reflecting one another back and forth in a group of mental mirrors."[5] Moreover, according to Smith, this social imagination is what makes both society and morality possible. "Sympathy, or fellow feeling," he tells us, "are two synonymous words expressing our tendency to enter into the situation of other men," and as "fellow feeling between different persons is always agreeable to

---

[4] Smith, *Theory of Moral Sentiments*, Part II, Section II, Chapter III.

[5] Small, *op. cit.*, p. 50.

both,'' it is the basis of social congeniality and of comradeship.

This doctrine of sympathy, or fellow feeling, being the basis of human society, obviously foreshadows the doctrine of Professor Franklin H. Giddings that society is based upon the consciousness of kind or of resemblance. This, Professor Giddings amply recognized. But Smith did not develop his thought. Indeed he left it in a totally individualistic state, and admitted apparently no basis for either human social life or moral judgments outside of the mental states of individuals. His philosophy of society remained essentially subjective. Nevertheless, Smith claimed that his explanation of the origin of the moral sense and of the moral basis of human relations left the rules of justice settled once for all. Small therefore sarcastically remarks that Smith could feel perfectly secure in leaving the rules of justice to take care of themselves, while he turned his attention to the rules of prudence. In other words, Smith, in his *Wealth of Nations,* undertook to discuss especially the political regulations over industry that are founded not so much upon the principles of justice as upon those of expediency, and that are calculated to increase the riches and prosperity of a state.

The political regulations over industry under the mercantile system Smith found to be altogether unwise. He believed that the riches and prosperity of the state would be enormously increased if practically all of these regulations were abolished. He advocated, therefore, for commerce and industry a system of *laissez faire,* or nonintervention, by government. He certainly made out without difficulty a good case for *laissez faire* for the strong and the rich. He forgot that the very system which would increase the profits of strong and wealthy business men might be bad for the weaker type of business man and for the laboring man. Smith's advocacy of *laissez faire* had the greatest effect upon the political and industrial life of the nineteenth century.

Undoubtedly a further reason for Smith's advocacy of nonintervention in industry on the part of governments was his belief in the natural and divine harmony between self-interest and public interest. "The obvious and simple system of liberty" seemed to him certain to work out in the long run for the public good. Speaking of this natural harmony between individual and public interest in one connection, he says: "The individual intends only his own gain, and he is in this, as in many other cases, led by an invisible hand to promote an end which was no part of his intention."[6] Thus in economic matters self-interest might safely be left to take its course.

However, Smith agrees with Rousseau that inequalities in private property are the main source of inequality in human society; for, he says, "Wherever there is great property there is great inequality. For one very rich man there must be at

<hr>

[6] Smith, *The Wealth of Nations.* Book IV, Chapter II.

least five hundred poor and the affluence of the few supposes the indigence of the many.''

Moreover, Smith recognized that such inequality was a source of evil in human society; for in another memorable passage he says: ''No society can surely be flourishing and happy, of which the far greater part of the members are poor and miserable. It is but equity that they who feed, clothe, and lodge the whole body of the people, should have such a share of the produce of their own labour as to be themselves tolerably well fed, clothed, and lodged.'' In other words, Smith's doctrine of expediency in economic matters breaks down, and the doctrine of social justice comes in; but Smith does not recognize his own inconsistency at this point. However, it is only fair to say that he did recognize that the accumulation of wealth was not wholly a matter of ability, wisdom, and virtue, but also largely a matter of fortunate circumstances and fortunate birth. It seems to have been his sole purpose, however, to discuss the means by which a nation might be made rich and prosperous. Nowhere in *The Wealth of Nations* does Smith attempt to correlate and to harmonize what he says about the means of becoming prosperous with what he says in his *Theory of Moral Sentiments* about justice. Thus Smith's own social teaching was so unsystematized that it led to great discrepancies among his followers.

Doctrine of social progress. Smith found that economic prosperity depended upon increasing the productive power of labor, and that this productive power depended upon increase in the division of labor. He strongly implies that the increase of prosperity and wealth in a nation would lead to progress. He nowhere discusses the specific problem of progress, but seems rather to imply that progress would automatically result from the increase of prosperity. He seems to have assumed rather uncritically that progress in the increase of wealth would result in general social progress.

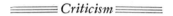

Criticism

As we have already seen, Smith's social philosophy was so unsystematized and desultory that it is impossible to give it any very high rank in the development of social thought. Nevertheless, his influence was very great, especially on the economic side, and modern nations have scarcely transcended that influence even today. It would be unfair to attribute to Smith the social philosophy that we call ''economic determinism'' or ''historical materialism.'' Nevertheless, the trend of his chief work was undoubtedly to furnish a foundation for such a one-sided social philosophy. Both modern capitalism and modern socialism go back, therefore, in a certain sense, to Smith's *Wealth of Nations*. His other work was largely forgotten in the overwhelming popularity of this masterpiece.

It is hardly necesary to add that Smith's assumption of a natural harmony between self-interest and public welfare has not been substantiated by the course of human affairs since he wrote. Modern social conditions, moreover, no longer justify his praise of "the simple and obvious system of natural liberty."

===== *Adam Ferguson* =====

Biographical sketch. A very different type of thinker was a close friend of Adam Smith, Adam Ferguson. Unlike Smith, his influence upon the English-speaking world was almost negligible, and even now he is just coming to be recognized as one of the leading precursors of modern sociology. Ludwig Gumplowicz goes even so far as to call him "the father of modern sociology." Ferguson was born in Perthshire, Scotland, in 1723, and died at St. Andrews in 1816. He was educated at Aberdeen and at Edinburgh. He prepared for Holy Orders, and was for a time chaplain for the Black Watch Regiment. It is said that he fought with that regiment at the Battle of Fontenoy. He became dissatisfied with the clerical calling, however, and obtained a librarianship in Edinburgh. Owing partly to the influence of Hume, he was appointed first to the Chair of Natural Philosophy in the University of Edinburgh in 1759, and then to the Chair of Moral Philosophy in 1764. In 1767 he published *An Essay on the History of Civil Society,* which immediately secured for him recognition on the Continent. In 1772 he published his *Institutes of Moral Philosophy,* which was revised and enlarged and republished in 1793 under the title of *Principles of Moral and Political Science.* As Professor Lehmann points out, this book covered the whole range of his lectures in anthropology, psychology, economics, politics, sociology, and ethics. On account of ill-health, Ferguson retired from his professorship in 1785, but continued to live to the advanced age of ninety-three.

Scientific method. Ferguson's use of scientific methods certainly represents an advance upon anything that we have found in his predecessors. Like Montesquieu, his effort was to integrate the phenomena of human society with those of nature. But his naturalistic conception represented a great advance over those who had preceded him.[7] He discards all fixed conceptions of the "natural." For Ferguson, whatever is, is natural. "All of the actions of men," he says, "are equally the result of nature." Art and science are therefore equally natural with the simplest forms of human behavior. This may seem so to broaden the conception as to obliterate all distinctions. Nevertheless, it must be remembered that Ferguson was a professor of natural philosophy before he was a professor of moral phi-

---

[7] See Professor W. C. Lehmann's *Adam Ferguson and the Beginnings of Modern Sociology* (Columbia University *Studies in History, Economics, and Public Law,* No. 328). Very few eighteenth-century social philosophers have had their systems as carefully summarized.

losophy. His approach to the facts of human history and society is therefore undoubtedly naturalistic. Just as the object of physical science is fact and reality, so in the moral and political sciences theories cannot be sustained that do not rest upon known facts or upon some known existing law of nature.

First of all, Ferguson would emphasize knowledge of the facts of human history. "History," he says, "consists in the detail of particulars, while science consists in the knowledge of general principles and their application." He draws not only upon a wide and critical knowledge of history, but also upon his knowledge of human nature for the understanding of historic events and processes. His method here is not wholly inductive, but is in part deductive from what he believes to be principles of nature, axioms, and self-evident definitions. While at times he is guilty of basing conclusions on too few data, yet he recognizes that all the inductions and deductions from history must be checked by critically established facts.

Ferguson also, perhaps, makes better use than any of his predecessors of ethnographical knowledge. He points out that observations of peoples living in the simplest condition may greatly help in the understanding of present society. He goes even so far as to say that the American Indian may furnish us a sort of mirror of the features of our progenitors, and that from a study of them we may draw conclusions with respect to the influences of situations in which we believe our forefathers were placed.

Again, Ferguson shows a wide knowledge of contemporary human society. He was a keen observer, and as frequently drew upon his observations of social conditions and events around him as upon human history. He was therefore basically empirical in his method, even though he sometimes joins a deductive with an inductive procedure.

Finally, Ferguson's conception of human society was essentially psychological. He did not have, of course, the psychological systems of the present to draw upon, but he considers man to be essentially a creature of animal impulses and acquired habits, and fitted by nature for intelligence and reason. There is, however, a difference between man and other animals in that man has not only greater intelligence, but also greater variability. Uniformity characterizes animals of the same species, but variety characterizes man. Instinct, which he defines as "a natural propensity," in the brutes leads to the use of means, while in man it results in the selection of ends, more or less intelligently. Man, Ferguson says, is fundamentally a creature of habit, and it is habit that makes the difference between individuals, communities, and nations. Therefore, human society must be interpreted mainly in terms of habit.

Professor Lehmann rightly points out that Ferguson did not limit these methods to the study of individuals in their social relationships, but applied them also to the study of group behavior, of social institutions, and of society as such. To this extent Ferguson had a truly sociological point of view.

Social philosophy. Ferguson held that the state of nature of Hobbes and Rousseau is a mere abstraction, and that certainly there is no evidence that the original state of man was a state of war. On the contrary, all observations go to show that "to be in society is the physical state of the species." Argument for the naturalness of society is therefore superfluous. Man is a naturally associating or gregarious animal. "Man is made for society and for the attainments of reason." Instinct and habit, however, not reason and calculation, create the forms of human society. Out of the efforts of groups to safeguard their interests, institutions take shape. The first of these institutions is the family, which is the basis not only of society in general, but even of empires. Ferguson stresses here the long duration of human infancy, the naturalness of altruism, especially in the family and in intimate groups, and how instinctive attachments grow into habits and give rise to sentiments of kinship.

Nevertheless, political forms did not grow out of the family, but rather out of the use of force in human society. Political constitutions, in their earliest beginnings, at least, do not rest upon consent, though the consensual element may greatly increase with the development of civilization. Originally, the basis of the state was in force. Here Ferguson, like Bodin, seems to distinguish between society and the state; but the force that is the background of the state comes to pervade also the natural groups of men. However, it is relatively late as a basis of society.

Ferguson holds that "progress is natural to man." Because speech is peculiar to man, inventions will be diffused throughout human society by communication. He anticipates the debate among anthropologists as to the relative weight of original invention and of borrowing. While he recognizes that much of civilization is the result of borrowing, yet he also holds that inventions can take place independently. The invention of writing, he says, has been often repeated, and so have many other inventions. It is evident that Ferguson approaches a cultural conception of human society; but while he seems to regard social progress as a result of the increase and of the diffusion of inventions, he also holds that man has natural propensities, or instincts, which lead him into the direction of progress. He goes even so far as to say that ambition is a peculiar human instinct that works for progress, defining ambition as "the desire for something better than is possessed at present." He also speaks of man as "by nature an artist."

Ferguson holds, like Kant, that opposition and strife among men are on the whole beneficent. Out of such opposition and strife arise institutions that safeguard the welfare of individuals. As the state is necessarily based upon force, its power should be limited, and the rights of individuals safeguarded.

Ferguson seems, therefore, to endorse something like Locke's conception of the state as limited in its powers to keeping internal order and protecting its citizens against external enemies. With Adam Smith, too, he seems to hold that there is a harmony between self-interest and public welfare, but unlike Smith he does not hold consistently to the application of the principle of *laissez faire,* or noninterference by government. On the contrary, the state may even, to a certain extent, consistently limit the increase of excessive private fortunes and prevent the ruin of modest ones.

Criticism

This brief and inadequate sketch of Ferguson's teachings shows that he came near to outlining the principles of a scientific system of sociology. He failed, however, to point out clearly the principles that make human society distinct from animal associations and cause human history to be altogether *sui generis.* On the contrary, Ferguson's effort to make man merely a part of the system of nature, "a variety in the system of life," leads him to overlook many human factors and especially to minimize the part that intelligent purposes have played in human society. His attack upon the intellectualistic interpretations of many of his predecessors, and his emphasis upon the role of instinct, habit, and sentiment in human society, were undoubtedly wholesome.

But he carried it too far. On the whole, therefore, Ferguson's social philosophy must be regarded as a development from that of David Hume. It failed to give a place sufficiently large to distinctively human factors. On the contrary, it seemed to make social progress itself something that is brought about automatically by the forces of nature. It is hardly necessary to add that Ferguson's analysis is also very incomplete. In blending moral and political science, he was not, after all, rendering a service to clear and critical social thinking. His moral philosophy and his natural philosophy thus present a strange blend, which the more critical thinking of our time regards as merely an odd mixture.

PART II

ONE-SIDED SOCIAL PHILOSOPHERS

CHAPTER XVII

The Ideological Social Philosophers

AFTER THE WRITINGS OF such men as Condorcet, Herder, and Ferguson, it is difficult to understand why sociology did not develop at once in the later eighteenth and early nineteenth centuries. One reason was doubtless the great disturbance due to the Napoleonic Wars. While these should not be compared with the last World War in extent and destructiveness, yet they did absorb a very large part of the intellectual energies of Europe. They created a crisis in European culture that needed thought; but men could think only along one line—how to bring the war to an end—and so broader questions had to be left untouched. But another reason why sociology did not develop at once after the writings of Herder, Condorcet, and Ferguson is the proneness of the human mind to see only one aspect of truth, to see things only from one side. One of the weaknesses even of the best-trained minds is to accept some single clue as sufficient for the discovery of truth. The result has been that in the development of scientific thought many minds have gone off on certain sidelines and have not taken a general view of their subject in a perfectly level-headed way. We still have with us such one-sided views, unilateral conceptions, of social evolution and of human society. One-sided views characterize the early development of all sciences, but they have been particularly evident in the social sciences because of the complexity of the subject matter with which these sciences deal. Hence we have intellectualistic theories of society, geographical theories, biological theories, psychological theories, economic theories, and even political and religious theories. Carried to an extreme, these develop merely into so many determinisms in social philosophy. Sociologists have to a certain extent shared in these one-sided views, and have often endorsed particularistic determinisms; but the great majority of scientifically trained sociologists are beginning to recognize that such one-sided views of human society are inadequate, and are really marks of immaturity in social thinking.

The first of these one-sided movements in social thinking which we wish to consider is that which throws the whole stress upon ideas. We have seen that this movement began with Plato, and, in a certain sense, those who have continued this method of social thinking may be regarded as representing a Platonic method of approach to social reality. They are perhaps best represented by the so-called German idealists. These were a school of thinkers who took their departure from Kant, but who developed essentially Platonic methods. They thought, in other words, that human society could be understood in terms of ideas and of the logic of ideas. We shall call this school the Ideological School, though the word "ideology" is sometimes now used in a different sense. As they held to the interpretation of human society and of human history in terms of a logic of ideas, they were ideologists in the strict, literal sense of the term. The two thinkers that we shall take to represent this movement are J. G. Fichte and G. W. F. Hegel.

===== *J. G. Fichte* =====

Biographical sketch. One of the best representatives of the ideological interpretation of human society is J. G. Fichte, who was born in 1762 and died in 1814. He was trained as a theologian, but became interested in philosophy, and in 1794 became Associate Professor of Philosophy at the University of Jena. In 1799 he lost this position because he was accused of atheism, having denied that God could be considered a person. He moved to Berlin, where he took a leading part in establishing the University of Berlin. In 1810 he became the first Rector of the University of Berlin and its first Professor of Philosophy. He died in 1814 during the German war for independence from the French.

Fichte lived in troubled times and developed an extreme nationalistic spirit. He felt it incumbent upon himself to awaken the confidence of the German people in themselves. He threw, therefore, his whole emphasis upon the inner life, upon ideals, upon the self. It is not unfair to say that his philosophy was one of enthusiasm for self-expression and self-development. But as Fichte was an ardent patriot, his philosophy took a nationalistic turn. We are not so much concerned with his general works in philosophy, but rather with three works which contain his political and social theories. The first of these is *The Closed Commercial State,* published in 1800, in which he advocates what is now known as "economic nationalism." The second, *Characteristics of the Present Age,* published in 1804, contains a loosely thought-out philosophy of history. The last, his *Addresses to the German People,* delivered while the French still occupied Berlin, and published in 1808, expresses his enthusiastic nationalism and Germanism.

Scientific method. Fichte's interpretation of history was almost wholly in terms of the logic of ideas. His method was the *a priori* or the speculative method carried to the extreme. In a certain sense, he outdid Plato. Like Plato, he would separate social philosophy and all philosophy from experience— from facts. "The philosopher," he tells us, "must deduce from the unity of his presupposed principle all the possible phenomena of experience."[1]   In an-

---

[1] See House, *Development of Sociology,* p. 90.

other place he says: "The philosopher follows the *a priori* thread of the world-plan which is clear to him without any history; and if he makes use of history, it is not to prove anything, since his theses are already proven independent of all history." [2] In other words, all man has to do to discover truth about human society is to turn to his inner consciousness, and from it he can deduce everything that has happened or can happen in the world outside. This is Fichte's subjective idealism, or rather, we might say, "ideaism."

Therefore Fichte says our own self, our own ego, is the only thing that we really know, and he lays down the maxim, "the self alone is real." This is what is now called "solipsism" in philosophy, though Fichte would probably deny that he was a solipsist. The ego, he says, "posits" itself, that is, affirms itself, presents itself to consciousness. But as the ego can be conscious of itself only through contrast with that which is not itself, it must posit or bring to consciousness the nonego, or the objective world. In this way it gives itself a limitation, but this limitation is not imposed from without. It is a limitation that the ego gives itself, and can therefore be changed. The ego of the individual is a manifestation of the eternal universal reason. Although we cannot know anything beyond ourselves, we can know everything from self-knowledge, because we are expressions of the eternal universal reason.

---

[2] Quoted by Bury, *The Idea of Progress*, p. 253.

It is almost needless to remark that Fichte's method is the absolute antithesis of modern science. Science does not try to deduce how the planets have evolved, or how life has developed, from some pre-supposed principle. It tries to find out the facts through human experience, and from these facts to generalize truth.

Social philosophy. Fichte's social philosophy need not detain us long. It is important chiefly because it foreshadows the social philosophy of Hegel. According to Fichte, the process of human history is the realization of the freedom of the human mind. Freedom, Fichte says, is not only a means to truth, but in one sense is the highest truth. There are various stages of this freedom. First of all, there is the instinctive stage, in which reason rules as blind instinct. But it is not free because it is not conscious of the implications and consequences of action. Then, second, there is the age of authority, in which reason rules through authoritarian institutions and creeds that demand blind assent from individuals. The third, his own age, is the age of indifference to truth and right. In it, reason is rejected as both instinct and authority, without being accepted in any higher form. The fourth stage, still ahead, is the age of science, in which truth is generalized from the facts of experience. Finally, there is a stage still farther ahead, in which truth and right will be intuitively perceived as beauty. In this stage, reason will exercise perfect freedom, and truth and right will be realized as beauty.

Fichte's doctrine of social organization seems far removed from this lofty doctrine of human evolution, representing so many stages in the realization of freedom. It is a modification of Rousseau's social contract, except that the contract is between the classes of society rather than among individuals. Such classes as the farmers, the artisans, and the merchants must each agree to their place and function in the community. Only thus can they realize free activities and function properly in the community. The resulting picture of an ideal society is somewhat similar to Plato's *Republic*. With Plato, Fichte agrees that government, if wise and efficient, can never be democratic, but must be entrusted to all-wise philosophers. Unlike Plato, he presents no detailed scheme of securing these all-wise philosophers for the administration of government. Nevertheless, Plato's influence is again discernible in Fichte's thinking. Fichte's exaltation of the mission of the Germans is perhaps again to be likened to Plato's Greek ethnocentrism, although as we have seen, it sprang directly from his patriotism and the crisis through which Germany passed during the Napoleonic Wars.

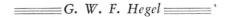

G. W. F. Hegel

Biographical sketch. Hegel, the greatest of the German ideologists, was born in 1770 and died in 1831. His philosophy marks the culmination of this school of thought. In many ways, he was greater as a thinker than either Kant or Fichte, for his mind was more synthetic and he had a broader culture. He was educated at the University of Tübingen, where he received his Doctor's degree in 1793. He tutored for a time and became interested in philosophy, especially in the writings of Kant and Fichte. He became a lecturer at the University of Jena in 1801, and an Associate Professor in 1805. On account of the disastrous consequences of the Battle of Jena, he was forced to discontinue his work there in 1806. In 1808 he was called to Nuremberg to become Rector of the Gymnasium. Here he remained until 1816, publishing his most fundamental work, *The Science of Logic,* which appeared in three volumes from 1812 to 1816. In 1817 he was called to the chair of philosophy in the University of Heidelberg, where he published his *Encyclopedia of the Philosophical Sciences,* containing a summary of his system of philosophy. In 1818 he was called to the University of Berlin to occupy Fichte's chair. In 1821 he published his *Outlines of a Philosophy of Law,* which brought him into close relations with the Prussian government, as it expressed very nearly the Prussian state philosophy. It has been also called "a sociology dominated by the idea of the state." Hegel died of cholera in 1831. After his death, his students brought together his notes on the philosophy of history, which were published in 1831 under the title, *The Philosophy of History.*

Scientific method. Hegel's method represents a step in advance from Fichte, who said that the ego —the self—alone is real. Hegel asked, What is the ego or self? He answered, that it is simply an idea. Hence he converted Fichte's subjective idealism into an objective idealism. Thought alone, Hegel said, is real. Thought is at the bottom of all things. Pure thought is synonymous with reason. Hence reason or intelligence is at the heart of all things, the center and core of all knowledge. All things can be understood in terms of thought. Hegel, therefore, like Fichte, proposed to interpret everything in terms of the logic of ideas. He found three great levels of the expression of thought. (1) The movement of thought or reason within itself, expressing itself in philosophy. The foundation of philosophy is logic, which, if rightly developed, becomes "a genealogy of ideas." (2) The movement of thought or reason in the objective world, through physical nature. This movement is expressed in the physical sciences, of which physics is the chief, revealing the constitution of material things. (3) The movement of thought in human history and society. Thought becomes embodied in human institutions, of which the state is the culmination—the final embodiment of reason. What logic is to philosophy, and what physics is to the physical sciences, political science or philosophy is to the world of human society. It is fundamental for the understanding of human society.

It is the work of science and philosophy to trace

the movement of thought or reason in these three realms. But the foundation of all is thought about thought itself. In other words, the foundation of all science and philosophy is logic; and it becomes necessary briefly to explain Hegel's logic in order to understand his dialectical method. All thought, he said, is necessarily about "being," which is the fundamental category. But "being" unqualified is the same as "nonbeing." All forms of being are necessarily defined by their contradiction, some form of nonbeing. Being is therefore the thesis, nonbeing the antithesis. Neither being nor nonbeing is real. The synthesis that produces reality is the movement from being into nonbeing and from nonbeing into being. Reality, therefore, is to be found in the process of "becoming." If we are to understand the real world, we must understand the processes of "becoming"—within the mind, within physical nature, and finally, within society. Reality is a process. It is the process of becoming. This process is, however, always a logical process. It consists in the logical movement from something that exists to its opposite. Therefore, according to Hegel, the principle of contradiction that Aristotle set up in his formal logic must be ignored if we are to understand reality. Moreover, because all movements in nature and society are logical, it follows that "the real is the rational and the rational is the real." This methodological conclusion, as we shall see, had the utmost influence upon Hegel's practical social philosophy.

Before leaving Hegel's method, let us note that

modern thought owes much to his stress upon the idea that all reality consists of processes, of movements. Perhaps more than anyone else at the beginning of the nineteenth century, he popularized the evolutionary point of view in a broad sense, viewing everything as a process of development. Indirectly, therefore, he did much to introduce the historical spirit and method into the social sciences.

===== *Hegel's Social Philosophy* =====

Doctrine of social origins and development. According to Hegel, human history is a development of *Geist*. This is a German word hard to translate. Perhaps the expression "pure intelligence" would come nearest to conveying its meaning, but it is usually translated by the English word "spirit." Hegel defines it for us. He says it is the opposite of matter. The essence of matter, he says, is gravity. Therefore the essence of *Geist,* or spirit, is freedom, and the process of history will be a process in which spirit realizes its essential nature, which is freedom. Human history can be nothing more than a growth of the consciousness of the essence of spirit, of the consciousness of freedom. The final cause of human history is therefore that the mind of man may know itself as free. Concrete human history is nothing more than the stages of this growth. If the law of gravitation will reveal all the mysteries of the physical world (which was a popular idea in the physical science of Hegel's time), then the law of the growth of the consciousness of freedom will help us to understand all the mysteries of the human world.

It is obvious that freedom with Hegel means the freedom of the mind, of pure intelligence, though he does not hesitate to find its expression in political institutions as well. Taking freedom in this very broad sense, he finds that there are three universal stages in the development of the consciousness of freedom: (1) The Oriental stage, in which spirit slumbers, ignorant and unconscious of that freedom which is its very essence, patiently submitting to despotism. In this stage there is only one free personality, only one who is conscious of his freedom, and that is the despot. (2) The Graeco-Roman stage, in which the spirit develops a partial consciousness of freedom as its true nature. This stage is first attained by the Greeks, among whom free individualities first developed. Intellectual freedom, Hegel says, is born at a very definite time in human history, and that is in the age of Pericles. Yet only a few are free; the masses are still slaves. (3) The final stage is the modern, or Germanic, in which the spirit knows itself for what it is, free by its very nature. It knows that all men have the inherent right to freedom. Free society has its first advent with the modern world. It is most of all embodied in Germany, though Hegel includes France and England also in this free, or Germanic, stage.[3]

---

[3] These stages are described in Hegel's *Philosophy of History*, Sibree's Translation, pp. 18, 19.

The spirit of the French Revolution seems to have deeply impressed itself upon Hegel's way of thinking, in that he makes freedom the very end of development. However, he considers apparently that the final stage of social development has already been reached by the nations of western Europe. He does not speak of any stage beyond the Germanic. We shall see, however, that Hegel in his theory of social and political organization is very far from endorsing the radical ideas of the French Revolution.

Doctrine of political and social organization. Hegel's *Philosophy of History* seems to point to philosophical anarchism as the logical conclusion of the process of development. But we find a very different theory in his *Outlines of a Philosophy of Law,* published in 1821, which, as we have already said, someone has characterized as "a sociology dominated by the idea of the State." Hegel has already told us that historical movements must be logical, must pass from a conception to its negation, or from a negation to a conception. He has also told us that there must be a subject in which this movement manifests itself. This subject may be either the human mind or human history. But human history is the objective process in which this movement takes place. The will of the individual is not strictly will in the most objective sense of the word. Will is not an attribute merely of the individual. That was the mistake of Rousseau and Fichte. Will is equally an attribute of society. By this we mean the customs, laws, and institutions that society has worked out for the good of its members. The supreme reason is embodied in these customs, laws, and institutions. The three fundamental institutions are the family, civil society, and the state. In submitting to these, the individual becomes free, for the will is truly free only when it is in accordance with the universe. Freedom is found in the harmony of the particular and the universal. The objective will of society alone is truly free; for the mass of institutions are rational. In submitting to them, the individual finds his harmony with the universal. Morality has no universal except the will of society. Hence, according to Hegel, morality is simply the legality of the heart, the reflection of the laws of social order in individual conscience and will.

Of the three fundamental institutions, the state is the most complete embodiment of the rational will of society. Hegel held that the state is the realization of the social, ethical ideal.[4] It is "perfected rationality." It is of the eternal and necessary essence of spirit. The individual realizes his highest possibilities, his highest freedom, his greatest perfection, when he merges his life with this almost divine institution. As Professor Dunning said: "With Hegel the glorification of the state became a sort of Bacchic frenzy. . . . Having brought forth the idea of the state, he set no limit to the adulation of his offspring; it is the absolute spirit, consciously realizing itself in the world; its existence has no

---

4 Cf. Dunning, *Political Theories*, Vol. III, pp. 154–169, especially 159 f.

other explanation than that God so wills; it is God.''

Just as Thomas Aquinas became the great philosopher of the absolute authority of the church, so Hegel became in the nineteenth century the great philosopher of the absolute authority of the state. He reaches the same conclusion as does Thomas Hobbes, that the authority of the state approaches the divine will as near as is humanly possible. But Hegel does more than reinstate Hobbes's absolutism. By implication, at least, he reinstates the Machiavellian conception of the state, that there is no moral law above it. The state, Hegel says, is final. The individual has no appeal above or beyond the state. There are accordingly no moral principles that should govern international politics, for there is no law of nations. Ordinary morality does not, and cannot, apply to nations. It can only apply within the state. Christian morality is a beautiful thing and should apply in the relations between individuals within the state, but it has no application outside of the state.

As Hegel does not believe in a moral law above the nations, he does not talk about a family or community of nations, as did Dante and Kant. There may be ''etiquette'' between nations, but not morality. It is impossible, therefore, for the state to commit any crime. Moreover, states, in order to define themselves, must have their opposites, that is, their enemies. War must therefore be expected. A war of defense may take place without waiting till the enemy attacks. It is still a war of defense if there is probability of attack. Hegel also does not forbid

or condemn conquests or annexations.   The strongest and best organized states are those that should
survive.   War and conquest must remain; and Hegel
believed, to put it mildly, that they are not wholly
maleficent.

======= *Criticism* =======

We shall not concern ourselves with other aspects
of Hegel's philosophy, as it is his philosophy of the
state as an absolute end and the realization of reason
that has had most influence in the modern world.
Those who have criticized Hegel as a mere word-
juggler have missed the main basis for criticizing
his social philosophy.   Perhaps the deepest criticism that can be made of Hegel's social philosophy
is that he confounded the real and the rational.
This led him to justify the political and social order
which he found already established.   That order on
the continent of Europe was one of absolute states.
Hegel saw that as a matter of fact the behavior of
states and nations did not conform in any degree to
idealistic morality.   On the basis of his logic, he set
out to rationalize this fact.   He did so by making
the state the embodiment of morality and reason.
What he did, as has often been remarked, was simply
to state and formalize the practical philosophy that
had already guided and ruled the Prussian state for
several generations.   The culture history basis for
Hegel's social philosophy goes, of course, still

deeper. The state in Hegel's time had become the largest "in-group," to use Sumner's phrase. It recognized no morality in dealing with other state groups, exactly as primitive groups had recognized no morality in dealing with "out-groups."

It is remarkable that only a few scholars during the late World War recognized that it was not so much the philosophy of von Treitschke that was the basis of the policies of imperial Germany as the philosophy of Hegel. Von Treitschke merely echoed Hegel's social and political philosophy. It has been more generally recognized that the policies of Prince Bismarck were based largely upon Hegel's philosophy. It is not difficult to recognize the outlines of Hegel's political and social philosophy today in the policies of the "Nazis." Hence Hegel, like Machiavelli, lives again in "the Authoritarian Volk State" that Hitler and his followers have set up.

It may seem very inconsistent to say that Marxian socialism is rooted in the same tradition. But we shall see when we come to consider Marxianism that it not only makes use of the Hegelian dialectic, but sets the economic class in the place of the political state, and at bottom holds that no moral principles stand above the relations of classes any more than they stand above the relations of nations.

Ideological social philosophy started with an absolute metaphysical individualism; but it ended with an absolute metaphysical "statism." Interpretation of human social life in terms of a pure logic of ideas may turn out, therefore, to be quite as dangerous to higher social values as interpretation in terms of materialistic forces. It is also evident that the confusion of the state with society and of political philosophy with sociology may lead to very dangerous unilateral views.

CHAPTER XVIII

The Individualistic Social Philosophers

FICHTE SAID, AS WE have already seen, that the self alone is real. This is extreme philosophical individualism, the doctrine that the human individual is a self-determined and self-determining whole. In a broader sense, individualism is the doctrine that the human individual is an independent, self-determining entity, both in the universe and in human society. It assumes not only that the individual self is the center of experience, a view to which all would agree, but also that there are no values outside of the individual. There have been many such individualists in the history of social thought. Epicurus in ancient times, for example, with his doctrine that there is no such thing as human society, but only an aggregate of individuals, was an individualist. Hobbes, with his doctrine of the social contract between independent individuals, was an individualist. Rousseau, with his exaggerated emphasis upon the rights of the individual, was an individualist. Indeed, it has often been said by historians that the crest of individualism reached its height with Rousseau. But many more extreme individualists than Rousseau lived in the nineteenth century. It is impossible for us to give more than a single example. Leaving aside the whole school of philosophical anarchists, we shall take Friedrich Wilhelm Nietzsche as our example of extreme nineteenth-century individualism. If in him individualism seems pushed to an absurd extreme, it is only because he carried out with relentless logic the implications of this one-sided social thinking.

===== *F. W. Nietzsche*[1] =====

Biographical sketch. Nietzsche was born in 1844. His father, of remote Polish descent, was a cultured Lutheran clergyman. Nietzsche's mother, however, was German, and as his whole culture was so thoroughly German, nothing should be attributed to his Polish blood. He was a very precocious child, learning to read the Greek and Latin classics at the early age of five or six years. Thus he became very early steeped in the lore of Greece and Rome, and, as in the case of Machiavelli, these countries awakened his admiration; but his admiration was rather for early Greece than for Rome. Nevertheless, young

---

[1] An excellent sketch of Nietzche's social philosophy will be found in Chapter IX of Durant's *Story of Philosophy.*

Nietzsche was destined for the ministry, and went to study at the University of Bonn with this intention. Soon, however, he gave up theology for classical philology, following his professor in the latter subject to the University of Leipzig. At the same time he became a great admirer of the German pessimistic philosopher, Schopenhauer. Upon the recommendation of his teachers, Nietzsche became at the early age of twenty-five a professor of classical philology in the University of Basle, Switzerland. There he formed a close friendship with Richard Wagner, the great German composer, who was living at Triebschen, near Lucerne. Nietzsche had long admired Wagner, and now found in him an exponent of Teutonic paganism, which again became one of his ideals. On account of ill-health, Nietzsche gave up teaching in 1876, and was finally put on the pension list of his university in 1879. In the meantime he had discovered that his idol, Wagner, had feet of clay. This produced in Nietzsche a very intense emotional reaction, and may have had something to do with the unbalancing of his mind.

From 1872, when Nietzsche produced his first considerable book on *The Birth of Tragedy,* until 1889, when he was declared hopelessly insane, Nietzsche was continually busy producing, one after another, a series of volumes in revolt against modern ideals of life. Here a word must be said about the nature of Nietzsche's illness. According to reliable medical authorities, during all this period, Nietzsche was suffering from the gradual onset of paresis, a form of neurosyphilis. On this account, it has often been said that no attention should be paid to Nietzsche's thought. However, thought stands upon its own basis, whether uttered by sane or insane, sick or well. We cannot dismiss a man's thinking, for example, because we know he has tuberculosis. All arguments against Nietzsche's philosophy on account of his physical condition fall short of their mark. Morbid geniuses are comparatively common in the history of thought, especially in modern times. Perhaps we may rightly say that it requires a certain degree of mental unbalance to carry out with relentless logic the implications of certain mental and social attitudes. Moreover, we are bound to take Nietzsche into account because his followers in western civilization have been so numerous, whether directly acquainted with his writings or not.

The chief reason, however, for calling attention to Nietzsche's illness is the undoubted fact that it affected very greatly his thinking. His glorification of health, brute strength, and power was undoubtedly in part a reaction from his physical condition. Thus his chronic invalidism had much to do not only with the form, but with the content of his thinking. It is carrying the matter much too far, however, to attribute the quality of his thought wholly or even chiefly to his invalidism. Nietzsche himself said that he was but carrying out the social implications of the doctrines of Charles Darwin. He claimed that he merely took over from Darwin the idea that the individual struggle for existence and supremacy was the whole content of the human social process. Nietzsche was probably mistaken in this, but we cannot deny that a crude sort of social Darwinism was in the air at the time that Nietzsche wrote. But beyond Darwinism was the individualism of the nineteenth century, and its general emphasis upon a crude naturalism in its social thinking. If, as Dr. Durant says, Nietzsche was not "the last great scion of the lineage of Rousseau," he was certainly at least a direct descendant. Both Rousseau's naturalism and individualism stand out in Nietzsche in an exaggerated degree.

Nietzsche's chief works are *Human, All Too Human* (1876), *The Dawn of Day* (1881), *Thus Spake Zarathustra* (1883), *Beyond Good and Evil* (1886), *The Genealogy of Morals* (1887), *Antichrist* (1889), and *The Will to Power* (1896). Of these, probably *The Will to Power* is the best introduction to Nietzsche's essential ideas, though it is a fragmentary work, written in periods of lucidity after he was declared hopelessly insane in 1889.

Nietzsche's method. Nietzsche had no scientific method. One is inclined to say that he had no scientific mind at all; for he threw logic out of the window. One of his mottoes was, "Let the truth perish, let there be life." As Durant says, he does not prove, he announces and reveals. Yet Nietzsche had certain points of view from which he proceeded. One was his exaltation of instinct against thought; another, of the individual against society. Like Rousseau, he held that "instinct is the most intelligent of all kinds of intelligence.'' Like Rousseau, too, he emphasized that all values must be found in the feelings and emotions of individuals; but of all instincts and emotions, ''the will to power'' is the strongest and most fundamental. It is not simply the will to live, but the will to power and to over-power that explains all life and therefore all human society.

It must be remembered that, above all, Nietzsche was a literary man, a poet and an artist. As a literary artist he was, moreover, an impressionist, and so fitted in with a strong tendency of his time. Perhaps, however, all this is inadequate to explain the vogue of his writings in the early years of the twentieth century. Two additional explanations of his vogue should be given. First of all, Nietzsche's writings became popular because they were in harmony with a certain spirit of the times that depreciated Christianity and humanitarianism. They harmonized with the *Zeitgeist,* particularly in Germany. But another reason for the vogue of Nietzsche's writings was his style. Nietzsche knew something about the psychology of the human mind. He knew that it took short, catchy sentences to appeal to the popular mind. He disregarded, even shattered, the traditional periodic style in which German, previous to his time, had been written. To this extent he was perhaps right in saying that in the future the history of the world would be divided into the time previous to his writing and the time after his writing.

===== *Nietzsche's Social Philosophy* =====

Doctrine of social origins and development. According to Nietzsche, man is simply an animal among animals, stronger, more energetic, more cunning, and with a greater will to power than other animals. The origin of human society was accordingly in the act of a horde of strong individuals who established themselves as masters over weaker individuals and reduced them to slavery. Society is merely a means for the enhancement of the power and personality of individuals; the group is not a reality nor an end in itself. All this is particularly illustrated, Nietzsche says, by the overrunning of Europe by Teutonic tribesmen. These men were not burdened with morals. They "were free from every social restraint; in the innocence of their wild beast conscience they returned as exultant monsters from a horrible train of murder, incendiarism, rapine, torture, with an arrogance and compromise as if nothing but a student's freak had been perpetrated." These men, "a herd of blond beasts of prey, a race of conquerors and masters, with military organization, with a power to organize," supplied the ruling classes for Germany, Scandinavia, France, England, Italy, and Russia. Very similarly, in pre-Socratic Greece, the barbarous Hellenes, coming down from the north, established ruling classes in the Greek city-states and set up the worship of Dionysus, the pagan god of life, enjoyment, music, dancing, and all that goes with the revelry of power.

It was especially the pre-Socratic Greeks, with their childlike love of life and enjoyment, whom Nietzsche seemed to regard as the social ideal. From pre-Socratic Greece down to the present, Nietzsche seemed to hold, there had been progressive degeneration. This degeneration began with the teaching of Socrates, Plato, and Aristotle, whom Nietzsche regarded not as true Greeks, but as aberrations from the pagan ideal. This movement was continued by the Epicureans and the Stoics. It made its conquest of western civilization, however, through the Jews and the Christian movement. The Jews, as a conquered race, had developed what Nietzsche called "a slave's morality." Through the Christian church, they were able to foist this slave's morality upon the world. While the Romans at their best had a master morality, this was undermined through the influence of the Christian movement, and Rome fell because it was emasculated and feminized by Jewish-Christian ethics. Gradually the Christian church, which Nietzsche called "the greatest of all imaginable corruptions," gained power and set up in the medieval world this slave morality as its ideal. The Renaissance, if it had been allowed to pursue its course, would have restored the master morality of the early Greeks and Romans and of the early Teutonic tribesmen. But just when the modern world was pursuing its course back to Greece and Rome through the influence of the Renaissance, Luther and the other Protestant reformers pulled it back again to the ridiculous slave morality of the Jews.

The triumph of the Jewish-Christian ethics resulted in the rise of the modern democratic movement. The democratic movement gave birth to humanitarianism, and then to socialism and feminism, all of which represent progressive degeneration from master morality. Nietzsche thinks, however, that there is still some hope of the revival of paganism. The will to power still manifests itself beneath all of these attempts to smother it by the Christian and democratic movements. In Napoleon, Nietzsche sees a true manifestation of his ideal of the superman. Moreover, Christianity as a theology is dead. It is only Christian ethics that survives, an ethics that is responsible for all of our evils, and is cowardly and weak. We need only return to the pre-Socratic Greeks, with their joy in life and power and beauty, to restore health to the modern world.

Doctrine of social organization. Nietzsche's doctrine of social organization is vague and inconsistent. It may, perhaps, be characterized as aristocratic anarchism. First of all he insists, however, that there must be gradations of rank. The common people must not be allowed to drag down the exceptional, superior individual. The whole process of civilization should be such as to produce these superior individuals. The masses, the common people, Nietzsche says in a vigorous metaphor, are nothing but the manure to fertilize the genius of the transcendent great. Society should be organized so as to make possible the exploitation of the inferior by the superior. It should be a true aristocracy with just enough organization not to hinder or hamper the development of the strong man. Moreover, life for all is to be an adventure. Its motto should be, "Live dangerously." Instead of war being discredited, all war should be regarded as good. "A good war," Nietzsche tells us, "halloweth any cause." Revolution is good if it does not lead to the supremacy of the masses. "Live in a state of war," Nietzsche says.

However, the ideal society will be divided into rulers, officials, and producers. The last two are to be the servants of the first class. The rulers will be men of refinement, as well as of courage and strength. They will be united by courtesy and *esprit de corps,* rather than by formal government; for Nietzsche regards the state in its present form as another manifestation of social degeneration. These aristocratic supermen will constitute a caste that will not contaminate and weaken its blood by marrying rich vulgarians. No equality will be permitted between classes or between men and women. The whole organization of society is to be such as to exploit the masses for the benefit of the superior few. Aristocracy is the key to ideal social organization.

Nietzsche's ethics. It is hardly worth while to discuss Nietzsche's conception of social progress. So far as he had one, it seems to have been a return to the paganism that we have already sketched, plus the eugenic breeding of "supermen." It is the ethics of strength, of power, however, rather than eugenics, politics, industrial organization, or anything else, which Nietzsche regards as the foundation for the establishment of an ideal human society. He tells us that there are two kinds of morality in nature—the morality of the lamb and the morality of the eagle. The morality of the eagle produced the master morality of the pagan world, the egoism that did not hesitate to take what it wanted, keep it, and take all that it could get. The morality of the lamb was developed into Jewish-Christian ethics, and has resulted in such manifestations of degeneracy as democracy, socialism, and feminism. Hence, Nietzsche sets up a program to restore human society to a normal, natural condition in which the biological forces of struggle and selection that have produced man can again function: (1) All obstacles to the individual's development are to be removed, so that the superman may be produced. (2) The only obligations that are to be recognized as binding on the individual are those of enlightened egoism. (3) All institutions and ideals connected with the doctrine of altruism are to be done away with.

The vigorous application of these rules, Nietzsche believes, will restore human society to a natural condition and will result in the further evolution of man, in the production of the superman. Finally, it should be noted that Nietzsche's superman is to be "a blond beast." But why "blond"? This seems to show that Nietzsche was also infected by the "Nordicism" which was rising in the later half of the nineteenth century, and which held that the north-European blond is alone capable of the highest civilization.

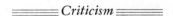

Criticism

It seems idle to use space to criticize such ideas. Yet millions of people in western civilization, most of whom have never heard of Nietzsche, have acted in whole or in part upon these principles. After all, they are simply the principles of a crude naturalism and of an extreme individualism. Nietzsche pretended that his doctrines were the logical outcome of Darwin's teachings, and a whole school of social Darwinians endorsed, in part, such principles. But it is hardly necessary to say that there is no support given these ideas in modern biology. Although Darwin may have made the mistake of considering the struggle for existence a purely individual one, his successors have long since corrected that idea. The paganism that Nietzsche preached, instead of bringing forth a new and superior race of men, would probably result in human degeneration, if not in human extinction. There is every reason to believe that the movement to interpret human social life in crude biological terms would result in something like Nietzsche's social philosophy.

But it must be pointed out that other influences

than the biological tradition had to do with the shaping of Nietzsche's philosophy. After Machiavelli had declared that moral principles had no application in political life, and after Rousseau had exalted savage man above civilized man, it was quite easy for Nietzsche's diseased mind to come to the conclusions that he did. Moreover, the worship of pagan antiquity, the approach to its ideals on hands and knees, again led Nietzsche easily to the conclusions he reached.

Finally, we must remember that the undermining of the philosophical foundations of the Christian movement almost inevitably led, considering the circumstances which we have just mentioned, to an attack upon Christian or humanitarian ethics. It was Nietzsche's distinction that he did not deign to discuss Christian theology, but openly attacked Christian ethics, the last stronghold, so to speak, of the Christian movement. Whether Nietzsche is only an aberrant social thinker or whether he is the herald of a new civilization based upon pagan ideals of life, only time can decide.

CHAPTER XIX

Racial Social Philosophers

WE HAVE ALREADY SEEN that Nietzsche's biological view of human society and human history tended to a glorification of the blond race. If one takes the biological view of human society as an individualistic view, it issues logically into something like Nietzsche's philosophy. But if one takes the biological view from the standpoint of race, it issues in a racial view of human society and human history. It is the latter view that is ordinarily thought of as the biological theory of society. It is the theory that blood, race, and heredity account for all social and cultural differences among human groups. The theory is very old, having roots again in classic antiquity, but the development of biological science in the nineteenth century, and especially the scientific theories of heredity of that century, gave the racial view new vitality. To some extent, the eugenics movement also worked in the same direction. But

304

the fact that racial problems and interracial struggles came to the front in the nineteenth century probably had even more to do with the recrudescence of racial theories. Racial sociological theories, at any rate, gave birth to an enormous sociological literature in the latter half of the nineteenth century and in the early decades of the twentieth. The foremost advocate of these theories, or, at any rate, the first modern thinker to put them into definite form, was a Frenchman, Count Arthur de Gobineau.

===== *Arthur de Gobineau* =====

Biographical sketch. Count Arthur de Gobineau was born in 1816 and died in 1882. He came from a French family of some standing, which claimed descent on one side from the old Norsemen who had founded Normandy. He entered political life, and soon after was transferred to the French diplomatic service. He served on French embassies in South America, in Greece, in Persia, and in several other countries. It was through this experience in diplomatic service that he came to the idea that racial problems were fundamental in human history and human society. His interests, however, were largely literary and historical, rather than scientific. As an historian, he distinguished himself with his *History of Persia* and with some historical sketches on *The Renaissance.* But he is remembered chiefly for his *Essay upon the Inequality of the Human Races,* published in four volumes, 1853–1855. While this work received at first but little attention in France, it was published at a strategic time when racial questions were uppermost in a number of countries. It immediately attracted attention in our South, where the slavery question was rapidly approaching a culmination and where the defenders of slavery as an institution were eagerly searching for confirmation of their belief that the Negro race was essentially inferior and incapable of civilization. Chiefly through the influence of Richard Wagner, the work also attracted attention in Germany, where the so-called "Aryan question" was beginning to come to public consciousness. Strangely enough, this work remained untranslated into English until 1915, when the first volume only was translated by Adrian Collins, with an introduction by Oscar Levy, the editor of the English version of Nietzsche's works.[1] The book cannot be considered in any sense scientific, but it was written in a literary style that, though paradoxical, made it understandable and popular.

Gobineau's method. Again we must say, as we said of Nietzsche, that Gobineau seems quite innocent of any scientific method in the strict sense of that phrase. He was, as we have seen, essentially a diplomat and a literary man. He had, however, considerable knowledge of the history of various peoples, and his extensive travels gave him a basis

---

[1] *The Inequality of Human Races*, by Arthur de Gobineau, translated by Adrian Collins (New York, 1915). See especially the author's dedication.

for making social and cultural comparisons. On the whole, what he did was to generalize his impressions and, possibly we should add, his own prejudices.

Gobineau's social philosophy. Gobineau's attempt was essentially to present a philosophy of history in terms of race that would explain the rise and fall of nations and civilizations. He finds the explanation in what he calls "a kind of historical chemistry," the chemistry of races. He tells us in the dedication of his book that, as he pursued his studies, he was "gradually penetrated by the conviction that the racial question overshadows all other problems of history, that it holds the key to them all, and that the inequality of the races from whose fusion a people is formed is enough to explain the whole course of its destiny." [2] But Gobineau is not content to recognize race as merely one factor in human society. He finds it to be the one and only adequate explaining factor. He says: "I convinced myself at last that everything great, noble, and fruitful in the works of man on this earth, in science, art, and civilization derives from a single starting point." In other words, Gobineau goes the full length of racial determinism. He divides mankind into three great races: the white or European; the yellow or Asiatic; and the black or African. These he further divides into secondary and tertiary types. Among the types of the white race he finds the north-European blond, or, as we would now say, the Nordic type, to show the greatest capacity for creative civiliza-

---

[2] *Ibid.,* p. xiv.

tion. He identifies the blond north-European with
the Aryans and says: ''There is no true civilization
among the European peoples where the Aryan
branch is not predominant.''   As regards the Negro,
he tells us, ''No Negro race is seen as the initiator
of a civilization.   Only when it is mixed with some
other can it even be initiated into one.''   Furthermore, ''No spontaneous civilization is to be found
among the yellow races.''   Whatever civilization
they have developed is due to Aryan intermixture,
and stagnation supervenes as soon as Aryan blood
is exhausted.

Thus it is clear, according to Gobineau, that culture or civilization is wholly a product of race.   His
argument seems to be somewhat as follows: The
way people think depends upon their nervous structure, which in turn is dependent upon heredity, or
upon the purity of breed.   Purity of breed results in
unity of thought and action.   It follows, first, that
so long as a race is pure, the way of thinking of all
of its members will remain essentially the same; second, people will think differently where there is mixture of blood, and antagonisms will develop; for
manifoldness of blood produces manifoldness of
ideas; third, the white race alone in human history
has shown itself capable of high civilization, and
where the white race is purest, as in northern
Europe, you will have the highest and best civilization.

At this point, Gobineau develops a new definition
of social degeneracy.   He says: ''Societies perish

because they are degenerate and for no other reason." But the word "degenerate" means that the race has deteriorated. This deterioration comes essentially through intermixture of blood. When a nation no longer has the same blood in its veins, because of continual adulteration through intermixture, it can no longer maintain its original qualities, and its civilization decays. Unity of action and ideas is now no longer possible. Conflicts break out and finally revolutions occur. Thus revolutions are an indirect result from mixture of blood, as South American countries already show. "Peoples degenerate only in consequence of the various admixtures of blood which they undergo," and "their degeneration corresponds exactly to the quantity and the quality of the new blood."

Gobineau then argues that human institutions are simply an expression of racial qualities, and that institutions are powerless, therefore, to stop or prevent the decay of a people. The institutions of law, government, religion, and morality, he says, have no influence upon civilization. Even physical environment has no direct influence. Only the purity or mixture of its blood has any significance for the history of a people.

As regards the qualities of the three races, Gobineau finds the black race represents passion, the yellow, mediocrity in everything, and the white, godlike reason. He finds that the white is endowed not only with reason, but with energy, generosity, and physical beauty. The supreme subrace in the white is the Aryan, of which the Germans are the purest modern representatives. Gobineau sets forth the theory that all the other civilizations of the world have sprung from the conquest of weaker peoples by Aryans. Thus the civilization of Egypt was produced by Aryans, but when they mingled with the natives, Egyptian civilization declined. In both China and India, a similar process took place. As for the future, Gobineau thought that for America there is little hope, for there all nations are intermingling. In southern Europe and western Asia, the white race is rapidly losing its purity. He thought that for northern and western Europe, civilization might be secure yet for a few centuries. Thus his conclusion regarding western civilization was pessimistic, because the purity of its blood was rapidly being lost.

===== *Criticism* =====

There is, of course, no scientific evidence that civilization is dependent upon racial heredity. Civilization, or culture, seems to be wholly an acquired trait. It consists of the accumulation of inventions that have been diffused through a process of teaching and learning. The most that racial heredity can do is to give a bias in certain directions. All of the evidence from history and experience fails to justify Gobineau's theories. On the contrary, all the races of mankind seem to be capable of taking up the essentials of both material and spiritual civilization. Differences of racial temperament and endowment may result in different peoples developing their civilization in different directions. To acknowledge this, however, is very different from acknowledging Gobineau's strictly biological, racial theory. We are not justified in taking Buckle's position that race counts for nothing. But, on the other hand, we cannot agree with Gobineau that race accounts for everything. Modern biology no longer upholds Gobineau's position of the all-might of racial heredity.

The political dangers of such one-sided social philosophy as Gobineau's are well shown in present-day Germany. Here the racialism of Gobineau was popularized by Houston Stewart Chamberlain, who, though the son of a British admiral, became a German citizen, and in his *Foundations of the Nineteenth Century* preached the superiority of the Nordic type. Chamberlain's book became, in Germany, a sort of Nordic bible, and in spite of the boasted culture and scientific achievements of the German people, their whole national policy under Hitler has been based upon this one-sided social philosophy, resulting not only in the persecution of the Jews and other non-Nordic elements in Germany, but also in arousing throughout the world racial antagonism to an extent scarcely known in previous generations. The inadequacies and dangers of one-sided social philosophies, when converted into practical political policies, were never better illustrated.

CHAPTER XX

Geographical Social Philosophers

WE HAVE ALREADY SEEN in Bodin, Montesquieu, and Herder the tendency to attribute great social influence to the geographic environment. All of these writers, however, recognized other elements in human social development than geographical forces and conditions. Practically, it is impossible to find pure geographical determinists. All the so-called geographical determinists have felt compelled to modify geographical determinism by the recognition of other factors. The pure geographical determinists should, of course, say that "man is a child of the earth," and that therefore everything that he achieves is "earthy," in the sense that it is determined by geographical conditions. Perhaps no one would deny that all human societies show some conditioning by geographical factors. But hardly anyone any longer seeks for adequate interpretation of human social life through geographical conditions. We are forced, therefore, to select an author who is only in part a geographical determinist. Perhaps we cannot do better than take Henry Thomas Buckle, because he first brought this way of looking at human affairs into prominence in the nineteenth century.

Henry Thomas Buckle

Biographical sketch. Buckle was born in 1821 and died in 1862 at the early age of forty-one. He was a sickly child and did not attend any university, but as his parents were wealthy, he had excellent tutors, and very early developed scholarly tastes and habits. He traveled a good deal, and thus became interested in the history of all European and many non-European countries. Returning home, he amassed an enormous library that is said to have included sixty thousand volumes. He was an omnivorous reader, but read especially in the fields of physical science, economics, and history. He decided that all history hitherto written had been nonscientific, and he set out to write a history of civilization that should be in accord with the principles of inductive science as he understood them. Hence, he undertook to write his *History of Civilization in England.* He lived, however, to complete only two volumes of this work, the first volume of which was published in 1857 and the second in 1861. What we have of his history of civilization is therefore a mere fragment; but it is sufficient to show his method and his leading ideas.   It is a book that every student of social thinking is bound to take into account because of its wide popularity for over fifty years and because of its influence upon all subsequent writing in history and the social sciences.

Scientific method.   Buckle's purpose was to produce an inductive science of human history.   Nevertheless, it is fair to say that he had no very clear or carefully thought-out method.   As we have seen, he was essentially a self-educated man.   Through his reading in the physical sciences, he had gained a strong materialistic bias, and attempted what we should now call a materialistic interpretation of history.   He was particularly opposed to the doctrine of human free will, and sought to bring all human actions under the determinism of laws as fixed as those of the physical world.   It is doubtful whether he clearly understood what was meant by free will or by fixed laws.   But he made use of statistics to show that all human behavior is governed by fixed laws.   He used also the arguments of the classical economists to support his materialistic interpretation.   But strangely enough, he appealed to human intelligence to explain what could not be explained by geographical forces or by economic laws.   Thus more than one historian of social thought has classified Buckle among the ideological theorists.   This inconsistency is one reason why we can say that he had no very clear method.   It is perhaps not unfair to add that, while he professed scientific impartiality, he showed most of the prejudices of the average Englishman of mid-Victorian times, especially in regard to political and economic matters. He was decidedly a child of his age.

Buckle's Social Philosophy

Buckle attempts primarily an interpretation of human society in terms of its physical environment. He lays it down at the very beginning that there must be an intimate connection between civilization and physical laws;[1] for all that man has done has been a result of the interaction of his mind and physical conditions, especially geographic conditions. "Civilization," he tells us, "begins only where conditions make it possible to produce a surplus, where supplies of food are regular and reliable, and a leisure class is made possible." Only in lands where man can live and accumulate surplus wealth does civilization develop. Buckle discounts the possibility of race or heredity being much of a factor. In general, he holds that we have no right to believe that race and heredity have any influence upon mentality or culture. So far as we know, all races have about the same endowment, and their social differences must therefore be due to the differences of their geographic environment.

---

[1] See Chapter II of Buckle's *History of Civilization in England.*

Doctrine of social development. Rejecting all other factors, Buckle divides the factors of social development into geographical and intellectual. He classifies the geographical factors that produce social differences among peoples under four heads: climate, food, soil, and the general aspects of nature. Climate, soil, and food influence the social life of peoples, Buckle says, mainly through the accumulation of wealth, because some accumulation of wealth is necessary for leisure, and there can be no high development of knowledge without leisure. It is the surplus resulting from an excess of production over consumption that makes the accumulation of wealth and the existence of intellectual classes possible. Therefore the fertility of the soil and the conditions of climate are "the great physical causes by which the creation of wealth is governed." As all civilization is based upon the economic factor, it follows that ultimately it is based upon these geographic factors. Especially in the early stages will the development of civilization be found to depend entirely upon soil and climate.

After the accumulation of wealth, comes the matter of its distribution. As soon as any degree of wealth is accumulated, the population divides into two classes, the employers and the employed. Accepting Ricardo's iron law of wages, namely, that wages paid will, in the long run, amount to only that which is sufficient to maintain the laborer and his family and allow him to reproduce, Buckle says that the price paid for labor will depend largely upon the cheapness or dearness of food. Agreeing with Malthus that food is the most important factor affecting the growth of population, Buckle says that where food is most abundant the increase in population will be greater than where food is scarce and difficult to secure. Now it is obvious that in warm and fertile countries food is more abundant than in cold and barren countries and is more easily secured. In such countries, therefore, there is a greater tendency toward an increase in population, and as labor may be regarded as a commodity, it cheapens the price of labor and lowers wages. Therefore, Buckle said, "There is a strong and constant tendency in hot countries for wages to be low, and in cold countries for them to be high." The increase of population decreases wages and the average wealth of the laborers; that is to say, it is the main factor responsible for the poverty of the masses. This poverty weakens the laboring classes and gives greater power into the hands of the wealthy. The result is the subjection of the lower classes, politically as well as economically. Hence, both in hot countries and on fertile plains democracy and free government do not easily flourish. Only under conditions of life where food is scarce, wages high, and the great accumulation of wealth practically impossible, do we find the natural conditions under which free governments and free societies can flourish. Other conditions give rise to classes and the poverty and degradation of the masses.

Another geographical factor that greatly affects

the social development of peoples is the general aspects of nature. If natural phenomena are such as to inspire feelings of terror or of great wonder, or powerfully inflame the imagination, then man, contrasting himself with the forces and majesty of nature, becomes painfully conscious of his own insignificance. His sense of inferiority inhibits his will to achieve. On the other hand, where the works of nature are small and feeble, man regains confidence, comes to understand, and finally to harness natural forces, and so his mind has a chance to act. Cool intelligence and reason have no chance to develop when the aspects of nature are overpowering. To illustrate, Buckle contrasts the civilization of India, where the works of nature are of startling magnitude, with that of Greece, where they are smaller, feebler, and less threatening to man.   Practically all of the countries outside of Europe discourage all attempts on the part of man to subdue nature. Consequently, "Looking at the history of the world as a whole, the tendency has been, in Europe, to subordinate nature to man; out of Europe to subordinate man to nature."

Hence, Buckle says, the fundamental division of human history, to be made if it is written scientifically, is the division between the civilization of Europe and the civilization that is non-European. In European civilizations, geographical conditions have favored the development of that critical scientific spirit upon which all social progress must depend. Hence, European civilization is what it is fundamentally because in Europe man is stronger than nature. Europe is the only continent where this is true. In other continents, nature is stronger than man. In Europe the human mind is not overawed by nature. The mind can work and can overcome nature. Moreover, climate and soil, as we have seen, are favorable to a balanced economic development. Consequently, if we are to understand the history of European countries, we must make the growth of knowledge and of intelligence our principal study. "The advance of European civilization is characterized by diminishing influence of physical laws and an increasing influence of mental laws." Consequently, "These mental laws, when ascertained, will be the ultimate basis of the history of Europe"; that is, if the history is written scientifically.

Only in Europe then, Buckle thinks, has the human intellect a fair chance to function, and four laws of the functioning of the intellect in social development and progress become evident: (1) The first of these laws is the law of the exclusion of other factors than the intellect, such as race or moral qualities. The progress of mankind, Buckle says, depends upon the success with which the laws of phenomena are investigated and the knowledge of these laws diffused. Moral qualities are relatively static and have no bearing upon progress. It is knowledge alone which counts. (2) The native faculties of men do not improve, Buckle tells us, but civilization rests solely upon intellectual progress, upon the increase of knowledge. There is no evidence, he tells us, that the hereditary qualities of mankind, either physical or mental, have improved. These qualities are static. The accumulation and diffusion of knowledge is therefore the only dynamic factor. (3) It follows from the first two laws that scepticism in every department of thought has been invariably a preliminary to social progress, because it has led to the examination of old beliefs and to the search for new knowledge. To get a basis for social progress we must have the critical attitude of mind. Even destructive criticism is necessary for the progress of truth. (4) Again it follows that the great enemy of civilization—the great enemy of human progress—is "the protective spirit," by which Buckle means the church teaching men what to believe and the state teaching them what to do. If church and state would leave men to determine their own beliefs and actions, social progress would be more rapid. Thus Buckle, like Nietzsche, takes his stand for a *laissez-faire* individualism.

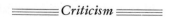

Criticism

The two parts of Buckle's social philosophy, the geographical and the intellectual, hardly harmonize. The geographical part of his social philosophy is the logical basis of all materialistic conceptions of human history. There is, however, not much evidence to sustain even as much geographical determinism as Buckle seeks to establish. Indeed, he himself was forced to admit that the evidence was better for primitive society than for present civilization. Buckle's division of human history into European and non-European upon the basis of the determinism of geographical factors seems to us now almost ludicrous. Naturally, this idea of Buckle's was not well received in America. The idea itself was a manifestation of European ethnocentrism.

Not much more can be said to support Buckle's four so-called "mental laws." Hardly any trained social thinker today would make the progress of mankind depend upon the accumulation and diffusion of scientific knowledge. We now know too much about human nature and the mind of man. It is evident that knowledge as knowledge cannot function alone. After all, the question of progress, no matter what sense we may attach to the term, depends upon the human will. And the human will depends upon impulses and emotions quite as much as upon knowledge. Social progress, therefore, depends upon the diffusion of altruism and good will not less than upon the diffusion of knowledge and intelligence. It is not correct to say, as Buckle said, that social progress has not been affected by moral qualities.

Buckle's law of the function of scepticism in social progress is almost taken for granted today and seems harmless enough, though at the time it was put forth by Buckle, it caused a great storm of protest. It is true that we must have the critical attitude of mind in order to improve or progress. But it is also true that destructive criticism may be carried so far that it results in confusion and in a loss of ability to take constructive attitudes. Destructive criticism may become a mere intellectual bad habit productive of nothing except the destruction of old values. Again, Buckle's *laissez-faire* individualism, if carried to an extreme, could hardly result in social progress. Buckle fails to see the church and the state as great cultural agencies, maintaining civilized traditions and standards. If Buckle's *laissez-faire* individualism were to be carried out, the state could scarcely carry on education for good citizenship. His attitude, and this seemed to be his personal belief, was that the schools and education should be private concerns. We have given up that attitude for very good reasons. Moreover, we know that all human beings need guidance in the development of their ideals and standards. It is the business of the church to teach men ideals and standards that will function in the direction of social progress. It is equally the business of the state to enforce minimum standards of conduct that will enable human communities to live at peace within themselves and to build for future progress. There are, of course, dangers in what Buckle calls "the protective spirit," but no human community has been able to build a high civilization without some use of this protective spirit; and there is no reason to think that the protective spirit necessarily makes men either moral weaklings or intellectual slaves. We are forced to conclude, therefore, that the crude naturalism of the nineteenth century led Buckle into error, both in the direction of geographical determinism and in the direction of *laissez-faire* individualism.

It is only fair to add that geographical influences in human society have been treated more sanely and hence more adequately by a great number of other writers. For example, Friedrich Ratzel, the great German geographer of the nineteenth century, did this in his work on *Anthropo-geographie*. His pupil, Miss Ellen C. Semple, did so in her work on *Influences of Geographic Environment*. These authors are not altogether free from criticism, but in general they did not make the crude errors of Buckle. The most modern school of geographers, which recognizes to the full the influences of culture in determining the social behavior of man, has made available many studies of the influence of geographical factors that are unobjectionable.

CHAPTER XXI

Economic Social Philosophers

CLOSELY CONNECTED WITH the geographical philosophy of human society is what is called "the economic interpretation of history," "the materialistic conception of history," or, still more accurately, "economic determinism." It is the theory that seeks to interpret human society in terms of the production and distribution of material goods. We have already seen that Adam Smith's *Wealth of Nations* tended to develop an economic philosophy of human relations. The development of economics after Adam Smith produced many economic thinkers who took a predominantly economic view of human society. They almost succeeded in converting the scientific world to their point of view. Most economists, however, gave an exceedingly conservative trend to their economic social philosophy. It remained for social revolutionists to perceive that this materialistic conception of social evolution might be turned in a radical direction and made to support their revolutionary program. The man who did this above all others was Karl Marx, and naturally we select him to illustrate this unilateral social theory.

 *Karl Marx*

Biographical sketch. Marx was born in 1818 and died in 1883. He came of a Jewish family who had gone over to Christianity shortly after his birth. This was something for which Marx could never forgive them. As an only son, they planned for him an academic career. He attended the universities of Bonn and Berlin and finally received his Doctor's degree in 1841 at the University of Jena. At Berlin he had come into contact with the so-called "young Hegelians," who, while accepting the Hegelian dialectic, had given it a materialistic turn. Their influence did much to shape Marx's thought and career. He had become much too radical to have any chance of obtaining a professorship in a German university of his time. Accordingly, in 1842 he started a radical newspaper at Cologne, the *Rheinische Zeitung,* which was suppressed the next year by the Prussian government. He then went to Paris, where he was thrown into radical and revolutionary circles, and where he met Proudhon, the leading philosophical anarchist of the day. Proudhon had written a book called *The Philosophy of*

Poverty, and Marx replied to him in a book with the sarcastic title *The Poverty of Philosophy.* The revolution of 1848 was coming on, and Marx went back to Germany, where, in collaboration with Friedrich Engels, he issued his famous *Communist Manifesto.* He also attempted to start another paper, the *Neue Rheinische Zeitung,* which was promptly suppressed by the German authorities. Marx wished to return to Paris, but finding that he could not, he finally made his way to London. Here he became a correspondent of the New York *Tribune,* then edited by Horace Greeley, a Fourierite socialist. Out of this work and various other hack work, Marx got a bare pittance. We may remark here that, all of his life, Marx continued to write and think in German. All of his articles and books had to be translated into English with the help of others. In 1859, Marx published his first considerable work, entitled *A Critique of Political Economy.* It is in this book that we first find a full and clear statement of his social philosophy, though it was adumbrated in the *Communist Manifesto.* In 1869, Marx published the first volume of *Das Kapital,* the second and third volumes of which were published from his manuscript and notes after his death.

Throughout his life, Marx remained closely associated with revolutionary movements and revolutionary organizations. He was, in fact, the actual leader of the revolutionary party among socialist thinkers. In 1864, he helped to organize the first International Working Men's Association. As he was decidedly in opposition to the ideas of the philosophical anarchists, in 1872 he took a hand in expelling Bakunin, the Russian anarchist, from the organization. This led finally to the second International Working Men's Association, organized in 1889.

At the same time, Marx devoted himself to a studious collection of all facts and theories that would support his revolutionist position. Although he wrote from the standpoint of a controversialist, no one can deny his capacity as a student and that he collected an immense number of facts on the economic side of human social life. Neither can anyone deny that Marx lived all of his life long a simple and heroic life. He was a great revolutionary leader and the only question that can be raised is, Was he a great social thinker? Marx died in abject poverty in London in 1883.

Scientific method. Marx looked at human history and at human social life, then, from the standpoint of a revolutionist. He found that the Hegelian dialectic confirmed him in his belief that the evolutionary process proceeded in human society through the conflict of opposites. At the time of his education, 1835–1841, the Hegelian method of thinking was at its height. Marx retained it fully in his own thinking, but, as we have seen, he belonged to the materialistic wing of Hegel's followers. He found the causes of all social movements to be materialistic. Thus, in a sense, he reversed Hegel's logic as a logic of ideas, but rediscovered it, so to speak, in the materialistic processes of nature. Economic life of the nineteenth century, he thought, especially illustrated the Hegelian dialectic. Labor was the thesis, and capital the antithesis. The synthesis was to be manifest in the socialist state. Marx, therefore, read the dialectical method into the real movement of facts. As Edward Bernstein, one of the fairest and most liberal of his critics, says: "In Marx, speculation triumphs over science." [1] But we cannot deny that Marx saw perhaps more clearly than any of his predecessors the part that the agencies of production and distribution played in human social evolution. Although Marx was primarily a revolutionist, and his conclusion was a preconceived idea, nevertheless, it is fair to regard him as an enthusiast who had discovered a new and fruitful clue to the understanding of human history and human relations. We may eliminate from Marx's thinking the dialectical method and it still remains true that his point of view has remained a very fruitful one in social science and philosophy.

Marx's Social Philosophy

We shall not concern ourselves with the economic teachings of Karl Marx, although undoubtedly his economics played the leading part not only in his social philosophy, but in his practical attitudes.

---

[1] See Bernstein, *Evolutionary Socialism.*

While his economics was built upon the familiar ideas of Locke, Smith, and Ricardo, it was constructed to bolster up a revolutionary social philosophy. Briefly, Marx's economics may be summed up as the theory that labor is the source of all economic value, and that, according to Ricardo's iron law of wages, the laborer obtains from the value that he creates merely a subsistence wage, the surplus being appropriated by exploiting capitalists. The capitalists were therefore pictured by Marx as the tyrants of the economic system, oppressing the wage earners. If we take all of Marx's writings into account, it is quite ludicrous to say with Spargo that Marx compelled the revolutionary proletariat "to regard the capitalist system as a great and splendid epoch." On the contrary, Marx argued that the capitalist system is necessarily and inevitably the fountainhead of all social inequality and of all class exploitation. Nevertheless, all this was inevitable, through the very method by which human history proceeded, the struggle and the conflict of opposites. But this struggle for human beings was fundamentally and primarily an economic struggle. Hence, the three leading doctrines of Marx's social philosophy; namely, economic determinism, the class-struggle theory of human history, and the theory that social evolution necessarily proceeds by revolution.

Theory of economic determinism. In the *Communist Manifesto,* Marx and Engels had already made plain their materialistic conception of history. But in the preface to Marx's *Critique of Political Econ-*

omy we find perhaps the clearest statement, as follows:

> In the social production which men carry on they enter into definite relations that are indispensable and independent of their will; these relations of production correspond to a definite stage of development of their material powers of production. The sum total of these relations of production constitutes the economic structure of society—the real foundation, on which rise legal and political superstructures and to which correspond definite forms of social consciousness. The mode of production in material life determines the general character of the social, political and spiritual processes of life. It is not the consciousness of men that determines their existence, but, on the contrary, their social existence determines their consciousness. At a certain stage of their development, the material forces of production in society come in conflict with the existing relations of production, or what is but a legal expression for the same thing—with the property relations within which they had been at work before. From forms of development of the forces of production these relations turn into their fetters. Then comes the period of social revolution.

This long quotation makes it evident that Marx believed that human ideas, beliefs, values, and even institutions, were largely reflexes of economic conditions. He did not, it should be noticed, deny the power of ideas and beliefs, but he regarded them principally as rationalizations from the economic situation. It is clear, therefore, that Marx himself held to a doctrine of economic determinism, however much he may have qualified this doctrine in certain of his later utterances. I see no reason for changing the statement that I made in 1911: "There can be no doubt that Marx's theory of social evolution is that the biological and psychological factors in human social life are all mediated and ultimately determined in their expression by economic processes. The theory is, therefore, in spite of the objection of recent apologists of Marx to the term, essentially a theory of economic determinism." [2] It is indeed upon this theory essentially that the followers of Marx base their claim that Marx should be considered the Darwin of the social sciences. The reformulation of the theory by Marx's colleague and co-worker, Friedrich Engels, does not sufficiently modify it to justify any other characterization. Engels summarized Marx's doctrine as follows:

> In every historical epoch, the prevailing mode of economic production and exchange, and the social organization necessarily following from it, form the basis upon which is built up, and from which alone can be explained, the political and intellectual history of that epoch, consequently the whole history of mankind (since the dissolution of primitive tribal society, holding land in common ownership) has been a history of class struggles, contests between exploiting and exploited, ruling and oppressed classes.

The class-struggle theory of human history. The quotation just given from Engels states clearly enough Marx's conflict theory of human society. In the words of the *Communist Manifesto,* "the history of all hitherto existing society is the history of class

---

[2] *American Journal of Sociology,* Vol. XVII, July, 1911, p. 38.

struggle.'' The middle class, or bourgeoisie, wrested political power from the privileged feudal classes. The battling classes are no longer the nobility and the bourgeoisie. They are now the bourgeoisie and the manual workers. The way in which each class has been overthrown has been by the oppressed class rising in revolution. The tyrannic class is now the capitalists, and they will be overthrown by the oppressed and exploited proletariat. Present economic conditions tend to absorb all minor social classes into one or the other of these two principal classes. Thus the professional class tends to be absorbed by the capitalist. While class struggle has gone on throughout human history, yet, when the proletariat rise and overthrow the capitalist, a classless society will be produced. The wresting of all capital from the bourgeoisie will result in the regeneration of society and in the ownership and management of all the instruments of production by the workers themselves. Exploitation will cease. There will be no classes to continue class struggle, and even warring nations will forget their antagonisms.

Marx believed that this class-struggle theory of human history was strictly harmonious with the Darwinian theory of evolution by struggle and selection. He argued that the Darwinian theory had made his own theory ''absolutely impregnable.'' However, Marx had his theory, as the *Communist Manifesto* shows, before he had any knowledge of Darwin's work. In his mind, it was a case of the Hegelian dialectic, the proletariat standing for the thesis and the capitalist for the antithesis. The dialectical movement of human history would resolve this contradiction by bringing about the establishment of the socialist state.

The dualism between the proletariat and the capitalist in the doctrines of Marx, it may be added, was quite as important and as absolute as the dualism in St. Augustine between the saved and the unsaved. Anyone who comes from the capitalist class, or who is suspected of being friendly to capitalism, is to be looked upon with suspicion. On the other hand, proletarian ideals, art, and politics, are all to be favored. The end of class war can come only with the supremacy of the workers both socially and politically. By this supremacy, the proletariat will abolish all classes in human society, and society will become an association in which the free development of each individual is the condition for the free development of all.

Social evolution through revolution. Although Marx presented his theory of social evolution as an inevitable movement, yet he was constantly occupied throughout his life in promoting practical movements for the overthrow of the existing social order. He was not content, as has often been remarked, to let any automatic process of evolution take its course. While he believed that the present order of society, owing to the exploitation of the workers, would result in a series of economic crises, because the workers would not have sufficient income to aid adequately in the consumption of what they produce, nevertheless, Marx seemed to hold that this inevitable and automatic process could be shortened by a revolutionary movement to put the ownership and management of all productive industry in the hands of the wage-earning masses. This revolutionary movement, he acknowledged, might come peacefully in Great Britain and in America. But he saw no prospect of its occurring without violence in the countries on the continent of Europe. There, if not everywhere, bourgeois tyranny would have to be overthrown by violence. The proletariat would arise, seize business and industry, and manage them in its own interest, which would be the interest of society as a whole.

Because of his belief in the dialectical nature of the historical process, Marx believed that only through such revolution could social evolution take place. Long after his death, Marxians found in the mutation theory of organic evolution, propounded by Hugo DeVries, another theoretical basis for Marx's theory of social evolution through revolution. It cannot be doubted, however, that the theory was more deeply grounded in a general-conflict view of human society. The Hegelian dialectic and the mutation theory in organic evolution were both used as supports for a revolutionary philosophy. They were not the original bases of the theory. The basis for the theory was in the revolutionary wishes of Marx and his co-workers.

These three theories, therefore—economic determinism, class struggle, and social evolution through revolution—and not his economics, are the very essence of Marx's social philosophy.

 *Criticism*

Professor Albion W. Small, in the later years of his life, declared, "Marx will have a place in social science analogous with that of Galileo in physical science."[3] This astounding declaration, by a teacher of sociology who had repeatedly stated that the economic process was only a detail in the general social process, challenges attention. Over and again the followers of Marx have also claimed that Marx was the Darwin of sociology.[4] What reaction is critical social intelligence to give to such thinking? It would seem to the present writer that the only reaction of critical social intelligence must be that such judgments are without adequate scientific foundation. In the first place, do we find any evidence to prove that the ideas and beliefs of men are mere rationalizations from their economic conditions? Such evidence would have to include scientific ideas and beliefs, as well as all other kinds. Is the Copernican theory of the universe, for example, a rationalization of the economic conditions under which Copernicus lived? Is it in any sense an outcome of economic processes or interests? Yet, this

---

[3] Quoted by Lichtenberger in *Development of Social Theory,* p. 302.
[4] Spargo, *Karl Marx,* p. 323.

theory had very great influence upon human society. Again, is the Darwinian theory of evolution by natural selection to be explained by the competition and struggle that we find in the economic life of the nineteenth century? If so, it and all the biology based upon it will pass away with that competitive order. No doubt, the reader may say that Marxians have never carried their economic determinism or historical materialism so far. But logically they should do so. Even if we take religious beliefs, we find no evidence that they keep step with, or even in the long run are determined by, economic conditions and interests. The Jews, for example, developed a monotheistic religion while they were still in the pastoral stage, or just emerging from it. They should not have done so, according to the economic interpreters. They should have remained ancestor worshippers. On the other hand, the Chinese remained ancestor worshippers after they had left the pastoral stage of industry behind for over two thousand years. Practically all anthropologists have concluded that there is no such close integration or harmony between the various traditions and institutions of human society as Marxian economic determinism presupposes. There may be a "strain" for consistency among institutions and traditions, but hardly enough to produce any such social determinism. The most general view among sociologists and anthropologists today is that human culture is a complex structure made up of many traditions and institutions, each of which may have more or less independent develop-

KARL MARX

ment by itself. Like the other one-sided theorists, Marx made here the mistake of a monistic interpretation of human society, when realistic science points clearly to a pluralistic interpretation.

As I said in 1911:

> There is, therefore, no scientific warrant for an "economic interpretation of history" except as that interpretation is but a phase of a larger interpretation which will make due allowance for other factors in social evolution. The historical process is not fundamentally an economic process, but is rather a socio-psychological, that is, a sociological process. The economic interpretation of that process *does* [changed from "may"] throw a useful side-light upon social evolution, but it can never offer an adequate theory of society, because it is attempting to interpret the whole in terms of what is merely a part.[5]

As to the class-conflict theory of human society and history that Marx offers, it has, of course, all of the objections to it that could be brought against any conflict theory of society. Hostile conflict is always dissolving of social bonds. No social organization could long exist that was permeated by the hostile conflict of either individuals or classes. We cannot deny, of course, the reality of class conflict, but in any sane view of human society, it is exceptional, rather than the usual and predominant mode of behavior. Human societies exist only through the co-ordination and co-operation of their members.

---

[5] "Marx's 'Economic Determinism' in the Light of Modern Psychology," *American Journal of Sociology*, Vol. XVII, July, 1911, p. 45.

Hostile conflict is always something relatively abnormal within a human group. Marx's conflict view of society is, of course, wholly an outcome of his economic determinism of individual and class behavior. As a sociological theory, it stands or falls with economic determinism.

Wrapped up with Marx's class-struggle theory of society is the theory that social evolution normally proceeds by revolution. Again we cannot deny that many of the great changes in human society have been brought about by violent revolutionary movements. To acknowledge this, however, is quite different from saying that social evolution normally proceeds by revolution. There is almost no evidence to show that this has been the normal process of change or development in human society. Careful study of social changes and the movements of history in the past shows that these movements and changes have been brought about through gradual processes of learning and adjustment. Every invention, every new idea, for example, has become diffused and generalized in human society through processes of intercommunication and learning. Only when there has been abnormal resistance to normal processes of change have these processes been accompanied by violence. Every custom and every institution represents a learned adjustment on the part of human groups. Force and violence may have in some cases helped to establish this adjustment. The usual experience, however, has been, particularly in the higher stages of culture, that

force and violence are ineffective in establishing lasting adjustments and harmonious relations between
either classes or individuals. For this reason nearly
every revolution effected by violence has been followed by a reaction. The general conclusion of
practically all scientific sociologists is that revolution is the most costly way to bring about rational
changes in human society.

It is hardly necessary to say that the mutation
theory in biology gives no support to the theory that
social evolution proceeds by revolution. We cannot
reason in social sciences by biological analogies.
Even if organic evolution proceeds by mutation, this
fact offers no evidence that social evolution proceeds
in the same way. On the contrary, as we have just
said, all the evidence goes to show that social evolution normally proceeds through learning processes;
and these processes are usually step-by-step processes.

It is also needless to add that Hegelian dialectics
is a very weak prop for a cataclysmic theory of social
evolution. No psychological or sociological writer
has succeeded in showing that there is any dialectical
process in human history. Any such interpretation
of history can be made only by forcing facts to fit a
theory.

Finally, the Russian Revolution, with its bloody
and brutal excesses, demonstrates once for all the
danger of such a one-sided and inadequate social philosophy as that of Karl Marx. It is a commentary
upon the sociological ignorance of our time that

many who see the danger to society of such one-sided social philosophies as those of Hegel, Nietzsche, and Gobineau fail to see the equal danger in a one-sided economic social philosophy. The social philosophy of Marx, if it is to be judged by its results, is equally threatening with the social philosophies of Nietzsche and Gobineau. Yet Marxism is continually preached from the housetops as the only possible scheme of social salvation. Very recently some of the younger Marxians in the United States have started a new periodical to be devoted to the exposition of the social philosophy of Karl Marx, asserting that as yet there has been no adequate consideration of his sociological theory. It is surely just to reply that for over a half a century economists and sociologists have paid more attention to the theories of Karl Marx than to any other social thinker in western civilization. If they have not replied adequately to his sociological theories, it is because our present age has been so dominated by economic motives, so pervaded by class conflicts, and so indoctrinated by theories of force, violence, and war, that Marxian doctrines have a seeming plausibility that they do not merit. We must, if our civilization is to go on in the pathway of progress, get rid of these doctrines, but even more we must get rid of the social conditions that have bred them.

═══*Conclusion—One-Sided Social Philosophies*═══

The reader may say that the author's treatment of these one-sided social philosophies is something like that which Catherine de Medici is reputed to have recommended for the Huguenots—"Kill them all, the Lord will know his own." It is possible, of course, that the writer has been unfair in judging these one-sided social philosophies. It is true that all sciences have advanced at times through one-sided theories; but it is also true that one-sided theories have prevented a balanced view of realities, and so have stood in the way of the true progress of science. The writer is forced to conclude that one-sided social thinking not only stands in the way of the development of the social sciences and of social philosophy, but is the source of most of the conflicts between classes, nations, and races in the modern world. One-sided social philosophies, no doubt, do us a service in calling attention to social maladjustments; but, as in the cases of Russia, Germany, and some other nations, they are just now offering insuperable impediments to intelligent adjustments.

At bottom, these one-sided social philosophies are rooted in ignorance, and in the proneness of the human mind to accept an oversimplified theory of social situations. Professor Small, in commenting upon these unilateral thinkers, offered, in effect, five conclusions, with which we must surely cordially agree:[6] (1) People have attempted to make a little knowledge go a long way in reaching world-wide social generalizations; (2) People have tried to create the general truths of human social life out of philosophical assumptions, instead of building them up out of facts; (3) People have had very crude conceptions about the complexity of human social life; (4) We need a method that shall be an improvement over the method of these one-sided social thinkers; and (5) The chief service of these one-sided thinkers has been to bequeath to the social sciences the perception of a complex problem, namely, to discover when, how, and in what proportion these factors emphasized by one-sided thinkers have been at work in human affairs.

It would be foolish to claim that sociologists have altogether avoided the pitfalls of particularism or of one-sided social thinking. Some sociologists, so-called, have been quite as one-sided in their social thinking as any of the thinkers that we have used to illustrate unilateral views. Even yet the sociological movement has not freed itself from this proneness to see but one aspect of reality. However, it may be claimed for the sociological movement that it started as a protest against one-sided views of human social life, particularly against the "fractionalism" of economics and other social sciences. It is also just to claim for the sociological movement

---

[6] Small, *General Sociology*, Chapters IV and V, especially pp. 46, 47.

an attempt to develop an adequate scientific method for the study of social problems. Oftentimes, sociologists have seen the methods of the physical sciences as adequate for the study of social problems; but in general this has not been true. Moreover, sociologists have, as a group, set up more programs for social investigation and research that will conform to the best canons of scientific method than any other set of men. They may have differed at times as to these programs of research, and sociologists have not yet all emerged into that maturity that welcomes any means of discovering the truth, any means of throwing light upon social reality. The twentieth century, however, is beginning to show signs of more mature thinking and research in the social sciences. Therefore, the sociological viewpoint, the movement to obtain an adequate understanding of all the processes and developments of human society is worthy of careful consideration. In the remaining chapters we shall try to survey this movement among leading western peoples down to about the year 1900.

PART III

THE SOCIOLOGICAL MOVEMENT

CHAPTER XXII

Saint-Simon,
Sociology's Immediate Precursor

IN THE BROAD SENSE of the term, the sociological movement has existed ever since Greek philosophy, but the attempt to construct a definite science of sociology begins with Auguste Comte. However, many of Comte's ideas were derived from his teacher, Claude Henri, Comte de Saint-Simon. Saint-Simon is important in the history of social thought because he is the connecting link between Comte and the French philosophers of the eighteenth century.

===== *Biographical Sketch* =====

Claude-Henri, Comte de Saint-Simon, was born in 1760 of a noble family that claimed descent from Charlemagne. He was brought up in the lap of luxury, but early in his life revolted against aristocratic ideas and the prejudices of his class. His whole life was a contradiction of any narrow theory of environmental determinism. Some of his ideas, however, were probably derived from his tutors, among whom were many prominent scientific and literary men, especially D'Alembert, the friend of Condorcet. His adventuresome and pioneering spirit led him to come to America, where he fought under Washington for American independence. He was present at the battle of Yorktown, and was later decorated for his bravery. On his way home, he was captured by the British, and did not get back to France until it was virtually on the verge of revolution. He joined the revolutionary movement and in his own commune voted for the abolition of the titles of nobility and the confiscation of the estates of the nobles. However, he had become critical of military and political methods of achieving progress. He took, therefore, no direct part in the revolution, but instead devoted himself to speculation in the confiscated lands of the clergy and the nobles, making a considerable fortune. He now began to realize, however, his own limitations and deficiencies in education. He was apparently ashamed to enroll in the university, so he did the next best thing. In 1798, after he was thirty-eight years of age, he settled down in the Latin quarter of Paris near the university. Here he opened his house to the professors in the Sorbonne, the École Polytechnique, and other famous schools, and established, as the French would say, a salon. Thus he got his

science from the discussions of the professors and
literary men whom he gathered about him. It was
really only a smattering of knowledge that he gathered; but Saint-Simon's mind was very fertile, and
he began to elaborate hypotheses upon the basis of
what he believed to be adequate scientific knowledge.
Materialism was in the air, and hence Saint-Simon's
attempt was to reduce all knowledge to the fundamental principles established by physical science.
In 1808 he published a book entitled *An Introduction
to the Scientific Works of the Nineteenth Century.*
This was followed by his *Memoir upon the Science of
Man,* published in 1813. In 1814 he wrote a *Treatise
on Universal Gravitation.* It was popular at that
time to attempt to reduce all the laws of science down
to the operation of one force, gravitation; and for a
time Saint-Simon was enamored with this idea, al-
thought he soon discarded it. In 1816, after the overthrow of Napoleon, he published a monograph on *The
Reconstruction of European Society.* In 1817 he
published a work on *Industry,* which contains his
main socialistic ideas. In the meantime, Saint-
Simon had gotten rid of practically all of his property, and, after 1816, he gathered around him a
body of students through whose tutoring he was able
to eke out a scanty existence. Among these students
there came to him in 1818 young Auguste Comte,
who remained more or less as his student and secretary for six years. A quarrel then developed between the two men, which was never healed and
which we shall note again in discussing Comte. The

last book of Saint-Simon, *New Christianity,* was published in 1825, the year of his death. This is generally regarded as his greatest work, and foreshadowed both the Christian socialism and the social gospel of the nineteenth century.

Saint-Simon's Method

Enough has been said already to indicate that Saint-Simon's method was that of an amateur. It should be added, however, that he did very much more than exalt the method of the physical sciences in the study of human society. He was one of the first to insist that society must be studied as a whole, that all social phenomena are interrelated, and that therefore even the course of human history has a certain unity. In general, his position, however, was that of a monistic materialist. He himself called it *physicism.* He held that physiology, broadly conceived, included not only the understanding both of the body and the mind of the individual, but also the understanding of human history. History was a function, according to Saint-Simon, of human physiology. Politics, education, and religion, therefore, should be regarded as applications of the physiology of man. All the sciences should be made certain or "positive" by following the methods of observation, experiment, and generalization employed in the physical sciences. Imagination should be subordinated strictly to observation and experiment. In this way the social sciences were to become as exact and as capable of prevision as the physical sciences themselves.[1]

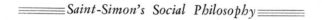

Saint-Simon's Social Philosophy

Doctrine of social development. Saint-Simon uses two principles to explain social development. The first is the continual extension of the principle of association, from the smallest human groups to the ultimate group, humanity itself. His second principle is the progress of knowledge, from that of the simplest culture to the highest civilization. He assumes that, in accordance with these two principles, there is a succession of forms of human society, from the simplest and most primitive to the most recent and advanced. From the lowest savages to the most highly civilized human society there is a series of social and cultural forms depending upon the inclusiveness of association and the progress of knowledge. A third principle is also used by Saint-Simon to judge social development. The lowest societies, he believes, are characterized by the exploitation of the weak by the strong; but there is a gradual mitigation of this exploitation as we ascend toward the higher civilizations. This exploitation of the weak is roughly represented by the conditions of slavery, serfdom, and the wage system. The wage system is

---

[1] See Flint, *History of the Philosophy of History in France*, pp. 395–408; also Bury, *The Idea of Progress*, pp. 282–289.

the last form of exploitation, and is destined to be replaced by co-operation.

Moreover, there is a parallel in development between the individual and society. We have already seen that this idea was common in the eighteenth century. Saint-Simon attempts to work out the parallelism, especially on the side of thinking. The mind in its thinking proceeds by two methods: analysis and synthesis. He says that it is the same with societies. At times, prevalent thought in human societies is analytical, and hence critical. At other times it is synthetic, and hence constructive, or "organic." Thus Saint-Simon distinguishes between what he calls "organic" and "critical" periods in human history. Greece, for example, was in the organic period until the time of Socrates, when it went over into a critical period that lasted throughout classical antiquity to the invasion of the barbarians. From the time of Charlemagne to the Reformation, medieval Europe was in a constructive, or "organic," period. It was a great mistake for Condorcet, Saint-Simon thought, to say that the Middle Ages contributed little or nothing to the progress of civilization. On the contrary, they were organic, and made a great contribution to the relation of the spiritual and the temporal. From the Reformation onward, Europe has been again passing through a critical or disruptive period. Apparently Saint-Simon hoped, like Condorcet, that the French Revolution would mark the beginning of another organic or constructive period.

All of this social development has been accompanied by a progress in knowledge that illustrates again the parallelism between social development and the development of the mind of the individual. In his thinking, an individual's mind is at first content with theological or conjectural explanations. But as the individual mind develops, it becomes more and more matter-of-fact, and so "positive," or scientific. It is exactly the same with the development of culture. All the sciences pass gradually from a conjectural or theological stage into a matter-of-fact, "positive," scientific stage. The first science to do this was mathematics; then astronomy followed, then physics, and then chemistry. Last of all, the bodies of knowledge that concern human society will go through a similar development. Physiology, the science of the human individual, is now leaving its conjectural, or theological, stage and is entering the positive, or scientific, stage. The applications of physiology in politics, education, industry, ethics, and religion will follow a similar development. All will, in time, become scientific, or "positive." This means that society as a whole will pass from the stage in which it was organized on a theological or conjectural basis to become organized upon a positive, or scientific, basis. This is true even of religion; for, according to Saint-Simon, religion is merely science clothed in a form suitable to satisfy the highest emotional needs. Thus Saint-Simon anticipates Comte's doctrine of the law of the three states, or stages. Saint-Simon, like Comte, lays it down that this doctrine is the law of social progress.

Doctrine of social and political organization.
Saint-Simon is usually reckoned among the founders
of socialism; but his socialism is so mild that it would
hardly be recognized by the Marxians as socialism
at all. Saint-Simon is opposed to any use of violence to bring about social transformations. But he
believes that industry ought to be organized on a co-
operative basis. Industry is the chief concern of
civilized human society. The main function of government is to help in the proper development of industry; and industry will be properly developed only
when it is organized on such a basis. Government
ought to assist the working classes in forming free
co-operative associations to carry on industry.
Only in this way can a proper standard of living be
realized by the working classes. As a preliminary,
however, the right of inheritance of property should
be abolished. While Saint-Simon does not believe
that men were created equal, he believes that the inheritance of property is the source of most of the un-
desirable inequalities that we find in human society.

It follows directly from all this that government
should be in the hands of useful or producing classes.
These are not to be limited, however, to the manual
workers, but include equally men of science, artists,
and captains of industry. Nonproducers (idlers)
and destroyers (soldiers) should have no part in
government, and should, therefore, be disfranchised.
Thus a new social order would be established through
the recognition of the supreme significance of pro-

ductive industry and through political leadership and control by the useful classes, the men of science, art and industry. Saint-Simon does not make very clear the organization of such a government. He proposes, however, that the legislature should consist of three houses: a house of invention, made up of engineers and artists; a house of examination, made up of mathematicians and physical scientists; and a house of execution, composed of the heads of the free co-operative associations. The house of invention is to propose laws, the house of examination is to pass upon their wisdom, and the house of execution is to enact them and put them into effect.

Ethics and religion. Saint-Simon's social and political system can scarcely be understood apart from his religion and ethics. In his old age, as we have already seen, he published his final work, his *New Christianity.* This is a bitter attack on both the Catholic and Protestant churches for their neglect of the fundamental teachings of Christ. The essence of Christ's teaching, according to Saint-Simon, is that men should regard each other as brothers. Therefore, human society should be organized upon a basis of love and sympathy quite as much as upon a basis of scientific knowledge. Christian theology is dead, and it is a mistake to emphasize the theological elements in Christianity. But all should unite in preserving Christian ethics, with its doctrine of a universal inclusive love. From this doctrine it follows directly that "all should labor for the material, moral, and intellectual development of the class the poorest and most numerous"; in other words for the workers.

This book is the more remarkable because it was produced by a man who started out with a crude materialistic monism. Because of this book, Saint-Simon is usually counted among the founders of Christian socialism; but equally he must be regarded as one of the precursors of the so-called social gospel, or social application of Christianity, which was developed among English-speaking peoples in the later decades of the nineteenth century. It is almost needless to remark that the book was not favorably received at the time of its publication, either by Roman Catholics or by Protestants.

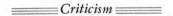

Criticism

Saint-Simon was so much of an amateur in his social thinking that criticism seems hardly worth while. Yet we must recognize that his fertile mind produced many of the seed-thoughts that were destined to germinate and flourish in the nineteenth century. Not only do we find many of Saint-Simon's ideas again in the writings of Auguste Comte, but also in the writings of many other thinkers of the nineteenth century. Many of his doctrines, however, were so twisted and perverted by his followers that they would scarcely have been recognized by Saint-Simon himself. Thus, some of his followers developed doctrines of communism and free love. Hence, the necessity for the distinction between Saint-Simon and Saint-Simonism. Nevertheless, the failure to recognize Saint-Simon as one of the precursors of modern sociological thinking, and especially of some of the doctrines of Auguste Comte, is unpardonable.

CHAPTER XXIII

Auguste Comte, the Founder of Sociology [1]

AUGUSTE COMTE IS THE central figure in the history of social thought, just as Darwin is the central figure in biological thought. A greater than Comte may arise, but none has arisen as yet; for Comte did for science what Jesus did for religion—he socialized it. This does not mean that Jesus did not have many precursors, nor that Comte did not have many. Nor does it mean that Jesus was successful in converting the religious world to his point of view; or that Comte was successful in converting the scientific world to his point of view. Probably four out of

---

[1] Fortunately, the English-speaking student who wishes a clear idea of the philosophy of Auguste Comte, does not need to read his long and somewhat involved works. *The Philosophy of Auguste Comte*, by Professor Lucian Levy-Bruhl, makes Comte's philosophical system clearer than he made it himself. The author desires to express his indebtedness to this work. See also F. S. Marvin's *Comte, The Founder of Sociology.*

five scientific men, even today, would deny, or denounce, the idea of humanizing and socializing science. But here the parallelism between Comte and Jesus of Nazareth stops, for Jesus had a personality that was remarkably in harmony with his teaching. He was, himself, the embodiment of all that he taught men to be or to do. Comte, on the other hand, had many intellectual and moral faults. He was a petty individual in many ways, and an unsocialized, disgruntled individual in other ways. We must distinguish between the man and his work. That is what we have to do with many of the thinkers that we have already considered. However, a man's thought, as we have seen, cannot be understood wholly apart from his character or from his private biographical experiences. We shall, therefore, need to sketch rather carefully the life of Auguste Comte.

Biographical Sketch

Comte was born in 1798 in the city of Montpellier, southern France, of Catholic and Royalist parents, who did everything in their power to make him both a Catholic and a Royalist. Whether because of heredity or environment, he early showed an independent spirit and an ability to think for himself. It is said that, at the age of thirteen, he had become an enthusiastic Republican and was sceptical of the doctrines of Catholicism. He was educated at the local "college" and lyceum of Montpellier, distinguishing himself for his ability in mathematics. At the age of sixteen, he went to Paris to attend the École Polytechnique and to study to be an engineer. In his school life, Comte showed not only an independent but also an insubordinate spirit. He was very critical of one of the professors, and got up a petition to have him dismissed, obtaining numerous signatures from his fellow students. The result, however, was that Comte and his fellow students were expelled. He returned home to Montpellier, but could not endure the religious and royalist atmosphere of his home. He determined to return to Paris and start out independently for himself. He was moderately successful in so doing, because he took up the work of tutoring students who had difficulties with mathematics. Two years after he had returned to Paris, he became attached to the little circle of advanced thinkers who had gathered around Saint-Simon. Comte's meeting and association with Saint-Simon had the greatest influence upon him. Saint-Simon, as we have seen, was a brilliant, original, erratic and suggestive thinker. Comte's mind was almost the opposite of Saint-Simon's. He had the careful, systematic, synthetic mind of the trained scientific man. Hence, he was able to systematize and synthesize the ideas he received from Saint-Simon. Thus Saint-Simon proved to be the fertilizing principle for Comte's genius. He soon discovered Comte's ability, and set him at various tasks of writing. We may say that Comte got a postgraduate course with Saint-Simon. In 1822 he completed for Saint-Simon a remarkable monograph on "The Scientific Labors Necessary for the Reorganization of Society," which in 1824 was published by Saint-Simon under another title. This early essay contained nearly all of Comte's later ideas. We are sorry to record that a quarrel developed between the two men. Comte accused Saint-Simon of publishing and using some of his ideas without giving him due credit. Saint-Simon replied, perhaps justly, that the ideas had originally come from himself. It is regrettable that the two men never became reconciled. Comte terminated his association in 1824, and Saint-Simon died in 1825. It is still more regrettable to record that, all his life, Comte was never willing to acknowledge his great debt to Saint-Simon. In part, perhaps, this was due to the fact that the Saint-Simonians fell into such discredit after the death of their leader. Moreover, Comte dissented from Saint-Simon's socialism.

Comte continued to teach during all of this time, and was fairly successful in getting pupils and in making a living, but in 1825 he made a misstep that hampered him practically the rest of his life. He married a woman who was far beneath him; in fact, her name was among the registered prostitutes of Paris.[2] Comte apparently married her with the hope of reforming her. But the marriage was unhappy from the beginning, and all of his biographers, without exception, speak of it as a great mistake.

---

[2] See F. J. Gould's *Auguste Comte*, Chapter II, especially pp. 15–23.

He intended to return to Montpellier to live, but when he arrived at his parents' home with his wife, he was very coldly received. Comte and his wife, after a few weeks, returned to Paris, where he undertook a very ambitious work in the whole field of the sciences. Comte had already received some recognition among the intellectuals of Paris, and in 1826 he undertook a course of lectures to cover all of the established sciences, beginning with mathematics, and ending with biology and the social sciences. These lectures attracted a number of eminent men, among them Alexander von Humboldt. But after the second lecture, Comte experienced a mental breakdown and was in a state of mental alienation for over a year, during which time he attempted to commit suicide by throwing himself in the River Seine.

The circumstances of Comte's mental breakdown deserve a word of explanation. To prepare his lectures, he had to give up most of his work of tutoring, and he and his wife were confronted with very great privations. It is said that Madame Comte suggested to him that if she could receive the attentions of a certain young lawyer friend, the income of the family might be considerably increased. Comte indignantly drove her from his house. In addition, there was the break with his parents and his quarrel with Saint-Simon. There might also have been a neuropathic strain in his heredity. At any rate, these mental conflicts and tensions upset his balance. He was taken to a large public hospital for the insane. Whatever we may think of Madame Comte, it is to her credit that she went to this institution, brought him home, cared for him, and gradually nursed him back to health. While he was in this condition, his mother appeared on the scene and insisted that, as his marriage had only been a civil one, it should now be solemnized by the church.

In 1829, Comte again took up his work upon his lectures. The first volume of the lectures was published in 1830 under the title *A Course of Positive Philosophy*. The lectures were continued and five more volumes were published, the last one in 1842. For a time, Comte now enjoyed comparative prosperity. His old school, the École Polytechnique, made him a tutor in mathematics and appointed him examiner for the candidates applying for admission to the school outside of Paris. This was in 1833. For this work, the school paid him a yearly salary of 5,000 francs. He was also earning about 5,000 francs from outside tutoring and teaching; while all of this was the equivalent of only about $2,000, it had more than double the purchasing power it would have today.

But this prosperity did not continue. No children were born to Comte and his wife, and his domestic troubles began to increase. Their mutual incompatability became more manifest. Madame Comte was uneducated and had no understanding of, or sympathy with, his work. After a number of quarrels, they finally separated in 1842, and it is said that Comte never saw Madame Comte after that date, but he continued to send to her one half of his income as long as he lived. Comte never asked for a divorce. Madame Comte died in 1877, twenty years after Comte, and during the later years of her life was given, as Comte's widow, a small pension by the French government.

In the meantime, another disaster overtook Comte. He was never a discreet man; his office as examiner for the École Polytechnique for the provinces outside of Paris brought him into contact with the school system of France. This he did not hesitate to criticize. In addition, he criticized one of the prominent professors in the École Polytechnique. The result was that he was put out of his position in 1844. At the same time, he lost another teaching position, and had other troubles and reverses. His income was so reduced that he told John Stuart Mill of his difficulties. Comte had early attracted the attention not only of Mill, but of other English thinkers. When he learned of Comte's troubles, Mill, with the aid of Grote, the historian, raised about 20,000 francs for Comte and sent it to him that he might continue his study and publish his books. But after five years Comte was in as great financial straits as ever. The money was meant purely as a gift, but Comte had taken it as a pension, and asked for the continuance of the pension from his English friends, which, of course, necessitated a break.

About this time, in 1844, Comte met at the house of a pupil an intellectual woman named Madame Clotilde de Vaux, who was separated from her hus-

band. She was a woman of considerable intellectual
development, and of a kindly, sympathetic nature
that qualified her to enter into Comte's life both on
the side of his aspirations and on the side of his difficulties. Apparently, Comte had never before met
a woman who could command his whole-hearted respect, enthusiasm, and affection. Hence, this was
an entirely new experience for him, although he was
a man of forty-seven years of age. He fell deeply
in love with Madame de Vaux. Both had already
been married, and both were separated from their
mates. Neither believed in divorce. There was apparently never any thought of marriage between
them, and we have every reason to believe that the
relations between them were pure. What would
have been the outcome had Madame de Vaux continued to live, we can only imagine, but unfortunately, within six months after he made her acquaintance, she became a victim of a rapid tuberculosis. In another six months, she was dead.
Comte now came to worship her as almost superhuman. This experience had the greatest influence
upon Comte's personality, because he now discovered that he had human sympathies; and he saw that
the world could not be saved simply by science and
reason. It would have to be saved by love also. *The
Positive Philosophy,* written before he met Madame
de Vaux, represented the cold, intellectual side of his
social philosophy; now he undertook and wrote a
four-volume work entitled *A System of Positive Polity, A Treatise in Applied Sociology,* which he dedi-

cated to Madame de Vaux.   In it a new emphasis was given to social philosophy; the cold intellectualism was displaced by warm humanitarianism.   It was published from 1851 to 1854.

There has been much debate among the admirers of Comte as to the relative merit of these two works, *The Course of Positive Philosophy* and *The System of Positive Polity*.   The scientific world almost universally regards *The Positive Philosophy* as Comte's greatest work; and perhaps, from the intellectual standpoint, it was his greatest work.   *The Positive Polity,* however, was a much more mature work, emphasizing as it did the whole nature of man and correcting many of the errors in the earlier work.[3]   It is manifestly unfair to judge Comte by *The Positive Philosophy*.   *The Positive Polity* is more truly representative of both his completed social philosophy and of the man himself.   Moreover, *The Positive Philosophy* is a philosophy of the sciences, while *The Positive Polity* is more strictly limited to the field of social philosophy.   Comte's final views, moreover, are confirmed in two other briefer treatises: the *General View of Positivism,* published in 1848, and the *Subjective Synthesis,* published in 1856.

During the later years of his life, Comte's friends and disciples rallied about him and furnished him with sufficient funds to end his days in comparative

---

[3] This is shown, for example, by the correction of errors in terminology that abound in *The Positive Philosophy*.   Thus, throughout the latter work, the word ''religious'' signifies ''theological''; but this is corrected in *The Positive Polity*.

comfort. For the last two years of his life, he was especially occupied with instituting his "Religion of Humanity." It is generally agreed by both friends and critics that these were years of mysticism. Comte died of cancer in 1857.

The Sources of Comte's Thought

In the case of a synthetic thinker like Comte, it is important that we recognize so far as possible the principal sources of his thought. We have detailed the biographical features of Comte's life, and their influence will be manifest. It would not be unfair to say that practically all the social thinkers whom we have considered, and who lived previous to the nineteenth century, had a share in shaping Comte's thought, either positively or negatively. However, Comte recognized only three predecessors in the founding of a scientific social philosophy: Aristotle, Montesquieu, and Condorcet. But the truth is that Comte's encyclopedic mind had taken thoughts from many predecessors. Let us note some of the principal of these:

(1) The first was the French Revolution, with its many doctrines. By the time Comte began to write, the Bourbons had been restored to the throne, but nearly everyone realized that this reaction was only temporary. Comte cannot be understood unless the background of the French Revolution and Bourbon Restoration are kept steadily in mind. He was

thinking, as so many others have thought, with reference to a crisis. He saw that progress out of the crisis could be made only through scientific guidance. The stimulus to his thinking was the Revolution. The material was the scientific knowledge that had been accumulated down to his time.

(2) Another source of Comte's thought was eighteenth-century French philosophy, especially the philosophy of the French Encyclopedists. This philosophy, as we have seen, was sensationalist in its psychology, materialistic in its metaphysics, and agnostic in its religious attitude. Comte broke away from some of these positions, but he had absorbed this philosophy as a student, and, in general, accepted its fundamental attitudes. He was especially influenced by Condorcet, as he acknowledged, though he corrected him at numerous points.

(3) Strange as it may seem, another source of Comte's thought was the reactionary school of theocratic thinkers, especially De Maistre and De Bonald. These were Roman Catholic thinkers who pointed back to the Middle Ages as an organic period that offered the best solution of social problems. Under the influence of Saint-Simon, Comte read their works, and, strangely enough, was influenced by them. Like Saint-Simon, he borrowed from them the idea that a spiritual power must be established alongside of the state.

(4) A final source of Comte's thought was the rising school of socialistic thinkers, Saint-Simon above all. Comte was in close contact with these early

French socialists; like them, he would, on the one hand, make science social, and, on the other hand, he would make social life scientific. Comte's attitude was to a certain extent a reaction from this school; but he remained essentially a collectivist, for he would establish a collective control in society, and wished this control to be on a scientific basis.

Perhaps we should also mention, as having a negative influence upon Comte's thought, his practice of what he called *cerebral hygiene*. This was his custom in the later years of his life of refraining from reading the books of other social thinkers. The result was that Comte's thinking, both along scientific and philosophical lines, was not always up-to-date, even in his own time.

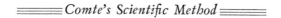

Comte's Scientific Method

Comte's greatest contribution to the establishment of a science of sociology was undoubtedly on the side of method. His *Positive Philosophy* is essentially a philosophy of the sciences, and is taken up largely with a discussion of scientific methods. Comte holds that science is at bottom nothing more than "a simple methodical extension of common good sense to all the subjects accessible to human reason." While he does not always adhere consistently to this simple conception of science, yet it underlies most of what he has to say about methods of thinking and investigation. It may be justly claimed, therefore, that he headed the social sciences in the right direction. That is, right in general; but, as we shall see, not in detail. He made some mistakes, but he advanced scientific method in the social sciences much further than it had been before.

We shall indicate frankly what we consider his mistakes by dividing his contributions to scientific method into negative and positive contributions. Let us begin with his negative contributions.

(1)   In the first place, Comte neglected and belittled logic. He was familiar with the physical sciences, and he saw that logic, as ordinarily understood, was of little use to them. He saw that their main method of verifying their conclusions was through measurement and mathematical analysis. Now, because Comte himself was a highly trained mathematician, he set up the claim that mathematics is the logic, or the fundamental reasoning method, of all science. Since the physical sciences had found in mathematics a sufficiently standardizing discipline, so also would the social sciences. Comte himself, in his social thinking, did not adhere to this position. He had to fall back upon qualitative reasoning. He could do nothing else when it came to the interpretation of historical phenomena, the phenomena that he claimed to be most important for the understanding of human society.

(2)   Comte held, with eighteenth-century philosophy, that only phenomena, or sense impressions, can be known. His objection to logic rested upon the dogma that we cannot know anything behind phenom-

ena. We cannot infer from phenomena anything that lies back of them. This "phenomenalism" led, of course, to general philosophical agnosticism, and to the denial of the validity of all metaphysical speculation. It led also to Comte's narrowing very strictly the use of hypothesis in science. He denied, for example, that we can know anything about cause and effect. He opposed the use of such theories as the hypothesis of a luminiferous ether in physics, and the hypothesis of the transformation of species in biology. He held that such hypotheses were outside of the realm of science, which must be limited strictly to verified knowledge; that is, verified by the senses, not by logical reasoning.

(3) It followed that Comte denied the scientific value of introspection or self-examination. Introspection, he said, could not give us verifiable scientific knowledge. For this reason Comte is sometimes counted among the founders of behaviorism in psychology. However, he does not consistently adhere to the dogma that only objective observations are valuable for science. On the contrary, he continually appeals to human nature, and in his *Positive Polity* raises the subjective method to equal validity with the objective.

Let us now take up Comte's main positive contributions to scientific method in the social sciences:

(1) Comte freed social philosophy and the social sciences from overspeculation. He did it in part through these very negations that we have just noticed; but largely he did it through insisting that

hyptheses should always be subordinated to the actual facts of experience. He saw, in other words, the limitation of the *a priori* speculative methods that some of the people of his time, particularly the German ideologists, were using. Comte did not deny the value of hypotheses in science, but he insisted that they be subordinated to observed facts.

(2) Comte insisted, in general, that the social sciences should be built up by inductive methods. He emphasized observation as the basis of all science. As we advance toward positive science, he tells us, imagination is more and more subordinated to observation. This does not mean that there should be no use of imagination, or that science should become merely factual. The empiricism that would interdict the use of theory is irreconcilable with the spirit of science. Moreover, Comte admitted that observation of phenomena must be directed by some theory, and that phenomena can be interpreted only by properly formed theories.

(3) Comte believed that the method of experiment was applicable, to a limited extent, in the social sciences:

> We must remember that there are two kinds of experimentation, the direct and the indirect: and that it is not necessary to the philosophical character of this method that the circumstances of the phenomenon in question should be, as is vulgarly supposed in the learned world, artificially instituted. Whether the case be natural or factitious, experimentation takes place whenever the regular course of the phenomenon is interfered with in any

determinate manner. The spontaneous nature of
the alteration has no effect on the scientific value
of the case, if the elements are known. It is in
this sense that experimentation is possible in Sociology.[4]

Perhaps we should now say that this indirect experimentation is simply a part of historical observation.

(4) Comte dwelt much on the value of the comparative method in sociology. This method, he
points out, had been most fruitful in biology, and
there is every reason to believe that it will be fruitful in sociology. We should not disdain even the
comparison between human society and the social
state of the lower animals. However, it is the comparison of coexistent states in different human societies, ranging all the way from Fuegian savages
to the most advanced nations of western Europe, if
used with sufficient caution, that will yield valuable
scientific results. Let us note, however, that Comte
did not go to the extreme of making the comparative
method the chief method in sociology, as Herbert
Spencer did later.

(5) It is, however, the historical method that is
the chief and final mode of the art of observing in
the social sciences. Comte calls this historical
method the comparative method applied to the con-
secutive states of humanity. It is the method that
thoroughly distinguishes the social sciences from

---

[4] See *The Positive Philosophy,* translated by Harriet Martineau,
Book VI, Chapter III.

biology, since man is the only animal that has language and history.　The positive study of humanity, Comte thinks, must appear a simple prolongation of the natural history of man; but as soon as we can trace the influence of human generations upon one another, we shall have an altogether different sort of science from that which the natural history of the animals below man yields.　The preponderant use of the historical method will give a philosophical character to sociology.　Without this method, it is impossible to constitute sociology.　Sociology is the chief of the social sciences, and history the chief of its methods, Comte concludes.

(6)　Mathematical methods and measurements should be employed wherever possible in the social sciences.[5]　At first Comte believed that the statistical method would yield very valuable results to sociology.　Later, however, he himself became sceptical of the value of a statistical approach to social problems.

(7)　Comte held that sociology must, by its very nature, bring together and utilize all the valid results of the preliminary sciences.　While sociology, like all science, is fundamentally inductive, nevertheless, it should utilize the results of other sciences. Thus Comte made a place for deduction in the social sciences.　He especially believed that valuable use might be made of deductions from biology; but at

---

[5] But Comte adds, *op. cit.*, Chapter IV, "As for any application of number and of a mathematical law to sociological problems, if such a method is inadmissible in biology, it must be yet more decisively so here." (That is, in sociology.)

first he had little use for deductions from psychology. At first, indeed, he made no place for psychology as an independent science antecedent to sociology, and he professed not to believe in the method of psychological analysis, although, actually, he used it more or less, even in *The Positive Philosophy.* We have already seen that this was because psychology in Comte's time was made the justification for the *a priori* speculations of the German ideologists and their French disciple, Victor Cousin. Later in his life, however, when he came to write his *Positive Polity,* Comte insisted that sociology rested upon "true mental science," and made very free use of psychological deductions.

(8) Comte would limit sociology, like all science, to demonstration. He proposed that the method of demonstration in sociology should be through checking up induction by deduction. An induction from human history, for example, should be capable of being checked up through our knowledge of human nature. If human history points to certain conclusions, and if our knowledge of human nature points in the same direction, then, according to Comte, we have demonstration. For example, in demonstrating his famous "law of the three stages," Comte says that, as we go back in human history, we find more and more of the anthropomorphic, or mythological, way of looking at things; and also that, as we go back to the childhood of the individual, we find the same tendency. Therefore, the law of the three stages is demonstrated.

Whether this method of demonstration in the social sciences is valid or not, the reader can scarcely fail to note that Comte is making a considerable use of logic and of deduction from psychology in proposing such a method of demonstration. But possibly this is as close as we can approach to demonstration in the social sciences; and we certainly owe something to Comte for emphasizing that both induction and deduction must play a part in scientific demonstration.

Criticism. Many criticisms might be directed toward Comte's contribution to the scientific method of the social sciences. We have to note, first of all, that Comte rendered formal allegiance to the standards of scientific orthodoxy set up by Hume and the French philosophers of the eighteenth century. But of course, in practice, he could not adhere to such methodological orthodoxy. Certainly today we can no longer justify Comte's "phenomenalism" as a presupposition of all sound scientific method. Even the physical sciences have got beyond that standpoint. In a certain sense, the work of all science aims at getting back of phenomena, or mere appearances. Comte's negative attitude toward qualitative reasoning, toward metaphysical speculation, and toward carefully used introspection, is not in accord with the soundest scientific practices today. On the other hand, his insistence that the social sciences should be built upon inductions from the facts of experience, upon the paramount importance of the historical method, and upon the need of synthesis in the

social sciences of all scientific knowledge seems to
the writer in accord with the soundest and best social
thinking of the present. Perhaps Professor House
has summed up as well as anyone all of the criticisms
that might be made of Comte's scientific methodol-
ogy. Professor House has said of Comte, "His general concept of positive science, based on observation
and experiment rather than on speculation, came to
have great prestige; indeed, the question arises
whether it did not have an exaggerated and unfortunate prestige, to the prejudice of the proper use of
trained imagination in science." [6]

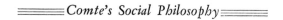

Comte's Social Philosophy

Comte divides sociology into two parts: social
statics and social dynamics. By *social statics,* he
tells us, he means the investigation of the laws of
action and reaction of the different parts of the social system. This, he says, is naturally the beginning of sociological science, but it is not the most important part of sociology. The most important part
of sociology is *social dynamics,* which he defines as
the theory of the natural progress or development
of human society. Social dynamics is thus a science of history, and so supersedes the old speculative
philosophy of history. This division of sociology
into two parts, however, does not make it two sepa-

---

[6] House, *The Development of Sociology,* p. 119.

rate sciences. While social statics, or the study of human society in cross section, affords the most elementary approach to sociology, yet social order can never be understood except as it is understood as the result of social development. There can be, therefore, no proper understanding of social problems without the dynamic, or historical, approach.

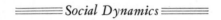

Social Dynamics

Social dynamics, then, affords the key to the understanding of human society. As we have seen, Comte makes it the theory of the natural development of human society. He does not discuss the problem of human social origins; for he holds that all questions concerning origin are beyond the scope of science. He concedes the existence of animal societies, and, as we have seen, recognizes even the value of the comparison of human society with animal associations. But he does not admit the validity of deriving the human from the subhuman. He holds that Lamarck's doctrine of the transformation of species is not and cannot be proved. Therefore, he will not derive human society from animal association. However, he holds that, within human society, there is a continual gradation of steps in social development. Indeed, for methodological convenience, he considers the continuous succession of phases of human social development as if humanity were one. The general movement of human society, however, has not been in a straight line, but subject to oscillations caused by race, climate, and political action, especially political mistakes. If these oscillations are ignored, there has been a continuous social development that Comte believes is governed by a general law. Let us note here, too, that Comte does not doubt progress. He shares in the general optimism of the thinkers of the eighteenth century. He says,

> To me it appears that amelioration is as unquestionable as the development from which it proceeds, provided we regard it as subject, like the development itself, to limits general and special, which science will be found to prescribe. The chimerical notion of unlimited perfectability is thus at once excluded. . . . There is no need to dwell upon the improvement in the conditions of human existence, both by the increasing action of man on his environment, through the advancement of the sciences and arts, and by the constant amelioration of his customs and manners; and again by the gradual improvement in social organization.

What, then, is the general law that governs human social development, and so human progress? Comte says it must be sought in that which differentiates man from the other animals, and that no one doubts that this is the higher development of man's intelligence. Hence the law of the development of human society will be the law of the development of man's intelligence. This Comte finds to be the law of the three states, or stages, of man's intellectual conceptions. Comte says that this law is that each of our chief conceptions, each branch of our knowledge, passes successively through three different theoretical states: the theological, or fictitious; the metaphysical, or abstract; and the scientific, or positive. Thus, according to Comte, human history consists essentially in the growth of the human mind, and, therefore, the chief law of sociology will be the law of the development of man's intelligence. It follows that abstract ideas are, in the last analysis, the determining factor in human social behavior. Thus, Comte takes the opposite view from that of Karl Marx. It would be a mistake, however, to characterize his social philosophy as another ideological or intellectualistic system. As we shall see, it takes in the whole mind of man, the development of religion, morals, government, industry, and feeling and emotion, as well as intellectual conceptions. These develop, according to Comte, as one organic whole, but center around man's intellectual conceptions.

(1) *The law of the three stages.* This is the law of the development of man's intelligence, and applies not only to the development of the race, but also to the development of the individual. It is the generalization that the fundamental conceptions of each branch of our knowledge pass successively through three theoretical states: the theological, or fictitious; the metaphysical, or abstract; and the scientific, or positive. Within each of these general stages are found subordinate stages. Thus, the theological stage presents three subordinate stages: fetishism, polytheism, and monotheism. Fetishism is the word that

Comte uses to describe the most complete anthropomorphic way of looking at things. It is the view of savages and children, who think that things are moved by an indwelling spirit or will—a god, you might say. Everything that happens is explained through the action of some intelligent will. This is the stage that students of the evolution of religion have called "animism," or "animatism." In human history, it is found in the stage usually called savagery, in which men still live practically an animal existence, and think of things much as children would think of them. Everything is interpreted in terms of fictions.

Fetishism is succeeded by the stage of polytheism, which arises through the work of the imagination in reducing the number of imaginary beings, or spirits, who rule over the forces of nature. Instead of every blade of grass and every tree and every other object of nature having an indwelling spirit, there will be a god of the grass, a god of the trees, and so forth. Great gods arise, each of whom rules over a whole class of objects or events. Polytheism characterizes especially the stage in human history that is known as barbarism.

But the inevitable end of this process of abstraction is to reduce all of the intelligences or wills at work in nature to one. Hence arises monotheism, in which stage a single personal deity is found to be sufficient to explain all that occurs in the universe. The theological, or anthropomorphic, way of thinking of occurrences in nature comes to an end with monotheism, which Comte regards simply as the last stage of primitive animism.

The metaphysical stage or way of thinking develops through the further working of the principle of abstraction. As it is discovered more and more that the anthropomorphic way of looking at events in nature will not work, the human mind takes refuge in abstract principles that are used to explain things. By the metaphysical stage, Comte means an attempt to get behind phenomena to certain principles like matter and mind, which are used abstractly to explain concrete phenomena. This is a transitional stage, for, according to Comte, such explanations in terms of abstract logical principles really explain nothing. Dialectical argumentation is mistaken for positive knowledge.

The human mind finally comes to a positive, matter-of-fact, or scientific way of looking at experience. In this positive, or scientific, stage, phenomena will no longer be explained either by abstract principles back of them or by personal wills. We will simply formulate the sequences and coexistences of phenomena; we will give up the idea of penetrating behind phenomena, and simply say that we can know nothing beyond the sequences and coexistences of phenomena. These sequences and coexistences, when generalized, will give us the laws of nature. Just as the theological way of interpreting nature stretches indefinitely into the past, so the positive, or scientific, way will be indefinitely prolonged in the future; and this positive, or scientific, way of looking at phenomena will be characterized by agnostic attitudes toward everything that is alleged to be behind or beyond phenomena. Moreover, just as the theological and metaphysical stages are characterized by certain peculiar institutions and general social development, so the positive, or scientific, stage will be characterized by institutions based upon scientific knowledge and by a general scientific social development.

This law of the development of man's intelligence is undoubtedly the fundamental law in Comte's whole social philosophy. It may seem that in it Comte has himself exceeded what he has declared to be the limits of positive science. However, it should be noticed that he claims not to have exceeded the facts of human experience. The more we go back in history, the more we find the anthropomorphic, or mythological, way of thinking. We are justified therefore, in concluding that this way of thinking increases as we go toward the beginnings of human history; and we are confirmed in this by observing how it prevails in the earliest years of childhood. Therefore, Comte says that the law of the three stages is demonstrated both inductively and deductively.

Criticism. Probably the best psychological criticism of Comte's law of the three stages is that given by the late Professor L. T. Hobhouse. Hobhouse says that it seems to be true that children and savages accept easily a "fictitious" way of explaining things.[7] In this stage of mental development, based upon uncritical credulity, opinions and judgments

---

[7] *The Sociological Review,* July, 1908. Cited by F. S. Marvin in *Comte, The Founder of Sociology,* p. 107.

are fictitious. Later, argumentation of a dialectial sort is brought to bear upon these fictitious opinions, and by such criticism abstract principles are developed as means of explanation. Still later, if the growth of mind continues, there is more and more correction of conceptions by reference to experience, and hence the correlation and interpretation of the facts of experience become the final method of human intelligence. Professor Robert Flint suggested another criticism that seems to the writer also to hold good.[8] In effect, he says that Comte was mistaken regarding human psychology—that he mistook three ways of looking at reality for three successive stages of mental development. Flint says that the human mind never entirely abandons the theological or animistic view of nature; nor does it ever adandon its effort to penetrate behind phenomena to ultimate principles. But we learn more and more to use the matter-of-fact, scientific way of thinking as we find it most fruitful in practical life. Accordingly, Flint says man will never outgrow the theological and metaphysical ways of looking at things, but will probably come to employ more and more the matter-of-fact, scientific way of thinking. Thus, in effect, Comte was substantially right in claiming that general social development and human institutions are bound to be more and more influenced by demonstrated scientific knowledge. Comte's law does not mean that the re-

---

[8] See Flint, *History of the Philosophy of History in France*, p. 611.

ligious and philosophical way of thinking is destined
to disappear, but rather that religion and philosophy
are both destined to become more and more scientific,
that is, based upon tested knowledge and the facts of
experience.

(2) *The law of the hierarchy of the sciences.*
The sciences do not all emerge into the scientific or
positive stage together.   Often, in the same individual mind, we find a scientific way of thinking about
physical phenomena, but a theological way of thinking about social phenomena.   This is due to the different degrees of complexity of the different sciences,
and suggests at once that there is an order in human
knowledge.   This order results from the mutual dependence of the sciences, a dependence that springs
from that of the corresponding phenomena.   Hence,
there is a necessary order in human knowledge that
is determined by the dependence of scientific studies
and by the simplicity of those studies, or, what comes
to the same thing, by the degree of the generality of
their phenomena.   The sciences emerge into the scientific stage in the order of the simplicity or generality of their conceptions, or in the reverse order of
their complexity.   In Comte's words, "our conceptions reach the positive or scientific stage in the order
of their dependence on each other, which is that of
decreasing generality and increasing complexity."
This is Comte's law of the hierarchy of the sciences.
Hence, the first science to become truly scientific or
positive is the science of mathematics, which deals
with such simple general phenomena as number, ex-

tension, and measurement. Mathematics was the first science to become truly scientific, but it has now become, because it was the original positive science, a sort of standardizing discipline, as we have already seen, for all other sciences. Then comes next, astronomy, or celestial physics, dealing with the relatively simple phenomena of the movements of heavenly bodies; then comes terrestrial, or molar physics; then chemistry, or atomic physics; then biology, or organic physics; and finally sociology, or social physics. This is the order not only of the dependence of the great abstract general sciences, but also of their emergence into the positive or scientific stage. Theological and metaphysical thinking are only slowly crowded out of the more complex sciences, like biology and sociology, because those are the sciences whose laws can least easily be brought to the test of positive facts. Biology, however, has now emerged, Comte says, into the positive, or scientific, stage, and sociology is bound to emerge next. ▶ In *The Positive Philosophy,* Comte said that the phenomena of all of these sciences were "homogeneous," and differed only in complexity. Therefore, he made no place for psychology, but treated individual psychology as a branch of physiology, a sort of cerebral physics. Social psychology, dealing with human relations and the behavior of human groups, he regarded as a part of sociology. However, in his *Positive Polity,* Comte makes a separate place for mental science because of its importance. Thus, he includes psychology as a relatively independent sci-

ence between biology and sociology. At the same
time, he protests against the reduction of the higher
sciences to the lower, although, in *The Positive Philosophy,* he had suggested that all of the concrete
sciences might be regarded as branches of physics.
Moreover, in *The Positive Polity,* he recognizes a
science beyond sociology, the science of moral standards or ethics, although he implies that this is not a
science of the same order as the others in the
hierarchy.

Criticism. If Comte's hierarchy of the sciences be
taken as simply a statement of the filiation of the
great general sciences, or of their natural order of
dependence, there can be little objection to it. Comte
did not mean it to be a classification of all the sciences, but simply a statement of the order of dependence of the great general sciences. There can be no
doubt that, if the sciences are ever to be integrated,
the more complex sciences will depend on the simpler
sciences. This will be true even if we do not accept
Comte's earlier view that their phenomena are all
homogeneous. To take Comte's hierarchy of the
sciences as simply divisions, distinguished by increasing complexity, in one universal science of physics,
is, of course, to convert it into a metaphysical system. Comte did not steer clear of this danger in his
Positive Philosophy. However, he vigorously re-
futed the idea in his *Positive Polity.* Comte's own
mature thinking does not, therefore, support criticism
of this sort. It is evident that he did not intend it
to be either a complete classification of the sciences

or a metaphysical theory of the relations of the various branches of knowledge, but only a generalization of the historical emergence of the various sciences into the scientific stage, with the logical reasons for the order of their emergence.

(3) *The law of the correlation of practical activities.* Comte was certain that there was an affinity or natural connection between the theological way of thinking and militarism. The dogmatic, anthropomorphic way of thinking, he argued, led to the attempt to settle all questions by force. Conquest became the aim of primitive societies in their relations one with another. Industry existed in such primitive society only for the production of necessities, and to aid in carrying on warfare. The natural results of conquest and the subjugation of one society by another, in the theological stage, were various forms of slavery for the workers. Government in such a stage was almost necessarily theocratic and, therefore, autocratic. As societies in this stage were organized for warfare, Comte held that it corresponded roughly to aggressive warfare, and that all human institutions and relations of the period were determined by this fact.

In the metaphysical stage, there is a gradual amelioration. As the metaphysical stage is one that is characterized by abstractions, legalistic principles now come to be the basis of social organization and human relations. Freedom has a certain development, and the slavery of the workers is mitigated in various ways, especially by the development of forms of serfdom. There is a growth of industry, not only to support militarism, but to maintain the luxury of the ruling classes. Societies in this metaphysical stage, Comte says, are characterized by defensive warfare. There is still the trust in force, but it does not go to the extent of making conquest the principal aim of society.

The legalistic metaphysical stage is only transitional to the positive, or scientific, stage, in which industry will become the dominant activity of society, and the chief factor in determining human relations. This Comte holds to be the natural outcome of the development of positive science. Warfare, therefore, is destined to disappear with the development of science and industry. Comte even made the mistake of predicting that the Napoleonic wars would be the last of the great European wars. The practical activities of industry, trade, and commerce, Comte argued, tend to unite and humanize the nations. The positive scientific stage will usher in, therefore, an era of peace and good will. To quote at length from Comte:

> By the highest and truest test that we can apply —the gradual ascendancy of the faculties of humanity over those of animality—the substitution of the industrial for the military life has raised the primitive type of social Man. The use of the understanding in practical matters is more marked in the industrial life of the moderns than in the military life of the ancients. Industrial pursuit is suitable to the intellectual mediocrity of the vast mass of the race, which best deal with clear, concrete, limited questions, requiring steady but easy

attention, admitting of a direct or proximate solution . . . and bringing after them a pretty certain
reward of ease and independence, in return for
sense and industry. . . . It also favours a universal goodwill, because every man's daily toil may
be regarded as concerning others quite as much
as himself; whereas the military life encouraged
the most malignant passions in the midst of the
noblest devotedness. . . .[8]

(4) *The law of the correlation of the feelings.*
Comte held that human society can be unified only
through feeling. There has been, however, in human history, a progressive expansion of social sentiment, which corresponds roughly to the stages of
development in man's intellectual conceptions. Corresponding to the theological stage was the limited
social sentiment and sympathy of remote antiquity,
limited to the local community or the city-state. In
the Middle Ages, social sentiments became expanded
and attached themselves to Christendom. This corresponded roughly to the metaphysical stage. But
in the positive or scientific stage, social sympathy is
going to become universal. Altruism or good will
will extend to all. Again, Comte argues that the
scientific attitude of mind is favorable to the development of good will and universalization of social
sympathy.

Criticism. Comte set out to demonstrate that invariable natural laws governed human social evolution; but the critic may well say that the laws that he
states are nothing but rough generalizations that

---

[8] Comte, *op. cit.*, Book VI, Chapter XI.

may be questioned. No social scientist today would call them "laws" at all. We have already criticized the law of the three stages, and the hierarchy of the sciences. Still less can be said in defense of the so-called law of practical activities, and of the development of social feeling. These generalizations seem almost to be wishful conclusions rather than scientific laws. The social scientist may hope that they will prove to be true, and there are many historical facts that seem to indicate that the trend has been in the direction that Comte indicates. But there are also historical facts that do not support his generalizations. Whether there is any psychological connection between the theological, or anthropomorphic, way of thinking, and the tendency to warfare, may be questioned. An entirely different phychological argument could be constructed at this point from good historical evidence; for example, it is probably true that the most primitive human minds are anthropomorphic in their way of thinking. But it is also true that the most primitive human societies are relatively peaceful, certainly nonwarlike. Even in the metaphysical stage, it seems logically absurd to characterize this stage as one of defensive warfare rather than offensive warfare. Finally, it may be questioned whether there is any psychological connection between science and industrial development on the one hand, and peace and good will on the other. The most scientifically advanced and most industrialized nations in the modern world have often, at the same time, been exceedingly militaris-

tic. The physical sciences have aided rather than
hindered the development of warfare. The same
may be said of industrial and commercial development. Perhaps, however, the development of the
social sciences may tend to help the cause of peace
and good will in human society. Perhaps this was
what Comte was thinking of, but he failed to express
it clearly. In any case, we may still hope that there
is an element of truth in these last two laws of social
evolution, as stated by Comte.

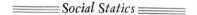

Social Statics

By "social statics," Comte meant the theory of
the natural order of human society.[9] This division
of sociology occupies a distinctly subordinate place
in Comte's social philosophy, even though it is the
more elementary aspect of sociology. Its function
is to investigate the laws of action and reaction of
the different parts of the social system. While in
social dynamics we look at human society from the
standpoint of sequences or social evolution, in social
statics we look at it from the standpoint of coexistences, or social order. Just as in the discussion of
Comte's social dynamics we divided it for convenience into four laws, so let us divide the social statics
for convenience into four doctrines: that of the individual, the family, society, and the state.

---

[9] *Op. cit.*, Book VI, Chapter V.

(1) *The doctrine of the individual.* Comte rec-ognizes that a theory of individual human nature is indispensable in sociology. Comte does not call this psychology, as he should have done. There is a seeming inconsistency in his doctrine of individual human nature. In many places, he tells us that hu-man nature is not an irreducible element in society. The individual that we know is always the represent-ative of a group. When you take away from the indi-vidual everything that his group has given him—in-tellectual, moral and social qualities—you have only the physical body and its physical energy left. The individual that we know is a product of his group life, and as he is a product of society, he cannot be the unit out of which society has developed. This doctrine seems to imply something like Locke's theory of human nature. But in other places Comte pictures for us a very different individual, one with recognizable innate dispositions and tendencies given by his biological nature. Comte derives this theory of the individual from Gall, the founder of phrenology. While Comte rejects Gall's localiza-tion of faculties, he holds very strongly to the gen-eral doctrine of innate tendencies and dispositions. Besides innate capacities, Comte recognizes what he calls "instincts." He defines "instinct" as "a spon-taneous impulse in a determinate direction" [10]—a definition that comes very close to that of many mod-ern psychologists. Comte goes on, moreover, to say

---

[10] *Op. cit.*, Book V, Chapter VI.

that man has as many, if not more, instincts than any other animal. This conception of a complex instinctive nature in man was emphasized by William James, but so far as the author knows, without giving any credit to Auguste Comte. Comte, moreover, divided man's instincts or innate impulses into two main classes: the egoistic and the altruistic. The altruistic he held to be much weaker than the egoistic. Therefore, the whole organization and teaching of human society should be such as to aid the individual in the development of his altruistic impulses, and to repress and control his egoistic tendencies. Moreover, Comte held, as we might expect, from this doctrine, that "our social affections are inferior in strength and steadiness to the personal." [11]   Again, Comte held very strongly, especially in the latter part of his life, to the preponderance of the affective over the intellectual faculties. From all of this it follows that "man is most in need of precisely the kind of activity for which he is naturally the least fit." [12]   He needs constantly to employ his intelligence in order to control his natural impulses and emotions, and to give a preponderance to altruistic social sentiments over egoistic personal ones. Nevertheless, Comte held that this natural unfitness of man for the higher requirements of society and civilization could be modified by education and by wise social arrangements. One must say that this doctrine is very different from the Lockian psychol-

---

[11] *Op. cit.*, Book VI, Chapter V.
[12] *Ibid.*

ogy which, in other places, Comte apparently en-
dorses. It is needless to add that this latter doctrine is much more in accord with modern biology
than the first.

(2) *The doctrine of the family.* According to
Comte, "the true social unit is the family." [13] It is
the unit out of which society grows. It is a small
group that is created by instinct and by natural affection, and that is capable of perpetuating and multiplying itself. It is comparable in society, therefore, to the cell in the biological organism. Marriage, according to Comte, is the spontaneous union
of the sexes brought about by instinct and natural
affection. It is normally monogamous, because human nature tends in that direction. The family, as
the smallest social unit, furnishes the medium
through which we learn to live with others. It is
the chief medium, therefore, for developing personality. Hence, the family is the basis of the social
spirit, and furnishes a bridge between the natural
egoism of the individual and the altruism that social
life demands. The family should be kept stable,
therefore, because otherwise it will lose its power to
stimulate altruism and self-sacrifice. Serious as-
saults upon the family are symptoms of social disor-
ganization. Nevertheless, marriage, like other human institutions, undergoes modification as human
development proceeds. These modifications should
be guided by scientific knowledge, and should not be

---

[13] *Ibid.*

the expression of arbitrary impulses and sentiments. The family's capacity to generate altruism and self-sacrifice should be guarded at all costs; therefore, for no reason would Comte permit divorce with re-marriage, because it would introduce into the family a germ of selfishness, and would make the family life lacking in altruism.

Here we may briefly note Comte's doctrine as to the nature of woman.[14] Each sex, he says, has special and permanent functions that it must fulfill in the natural economy of the family. The preponderance of the affective faculties in women especially fits them for the functions of wifehood and motherhood. Women are, in general, superior to men in the spontaneous expression of sympathy, but inferior to men in understanding and reason. Their function in the economy of the family, and consequently of society, must be to supply this element of social sympathy and affection in which the male is so often deficient. Women, therefore, are socially superior to men, but inferior in their intellectual powers; and this fact must be constantly borne in mind in the organization of the family and of society.

(3) *The doctrine of society.* The family is not society, according to Comte. Society is a larger unit made up of many interdependent families. More-over, the family is a union based on natural instincts and affections. Society, on the other hand, is a co-operation based upon the division of labor.[15] The

---

14 *Ibid.*
15 *Ibid.*

division of labor can never be very marked in the family, because its members are few, but it becomes marked in any larger co-operation in which there is necessity of many interdependent employments or occupations. The intelligence of man, by inventing things, makes a division of labor possible, but this specialization of functions leads to co-operation and interdependence. To this extent, Comte acknowledges that the basis of society is economic. It is a development from the function of carrying on interdependent occupations. The mark of human society, then, is interdependence in function. Comte holds that this interdependence that results from the specializing of functions is closer in human society than it is in the biological organism. Therefore, he accepts the analogy between a society and a biological organism. But he is careful not to push this analogy too far. He says that society, in a general way, is like an organism, but he specifically repudiates in various places the idea that society is like a plant or animal organism. The organic analogy in Comte, therefore, receives only a very limited development.

If society is a functional interdependence of individuals and families that have more or less common aims, what are the limits of the social organism or society? Comte says that there are no limits except humanity itself. All parts of humanity are gradually becoming more and more interdependent. Humanity itself, therefore, may be considered a vast organism, not only in space, but projected in time. The nation, or even the civilization, is an incomplete society. Therefore, through this conception of social interdependence based upon the division of labor, we come to the ultimate conception of society itself, which is that society is humanity viewed from the standpoint of its reciprocal relations.

We might sum up Comte's doctrine of society in three brief statements: (1) society is a co-operation, or interdependence, based not on instincts and natural affection, but on the division of labor; (2) it is like an organism in the most general sense; (3) the limits of society are humanity itself.[16]

(4) *The doctrine of the state and of the relations between church and state.* Comte is careful to keep the state separate from society. Thus he does not make the mistake of Hobbes or Hegel in identifying the state with society. On the contrary, the state is a special form of association, or social organization. It is organized to secure unity in the national group. The division of labor, which Comte regards in one sense as the foundation of society, tends to tear society apart. Different employments and occupations give individuals and classes different interests, and in this way they become separated. There is need, therefore, of some institution to keep up the idea of the whole, and the feeling of common interdependence. The state is the institution that undertakes this work. Its function is, first of all, to preserve social unity throughout the political group. Thus government is a social necessity. All social

---

16 Cf. Levy-Bruhl, *The Philosophy of Comte,* Book IV, Chapter III.

groups have a spontaneous tendency to set up governments to preserve their unity.[17] The state and government, therefore, are natural developments of human society, but, according to Comte, their function is mainly with the material and external aspects of social life, and first of all, in that connection, to regulate property, industry, and all of the external relations of life as they affect the unity of the group. Thus Comte would retain private property and private industry, but would have them supervised and regulated by the political government. Except for this, he leans strongly toward the socialism of Saint-Simon. We may cite here Comte's own words:

> Capitalists, as the administrators of the common fund of wealth, must so regulate the distribution of wages, that women will be released from wage-earning; and they must see that the proper remuneration also, is given for intellectual labor. . . . The institution of property can be maintained no longer upon the untenable ground of personal right. . . . Modern industrial society is radically devoid of systematic morality. Among producers and consumers, and above all, between the employers and workers, it seems agreed that everybody should be solely absorbed in his personal interest.[18]

To put an end to this unmoral state of modern industrial life, Comte would introduce much government regulation, including profit sharing, but, above all, he would introduce moral education of all classes. He says, "The two great requirements of the work-

---

[17] Comte, *Positive Philosophy*, Book VI, Chapter V.
[18] Cf. Gould, *Auguste Comte*, p. 79.

ing classes are the organization of education and the organization of labor." Again, "Universal education is eminently calculated, without encouraging disorderly ambitions, to place each person in a station suited to his principal qualities, no matter in what class he was born."

Alongside of the state, therefore, there should exist in every society "a spiritual power" to look after the mental and moral welfare of citizens. This idea Comte borrowed from Saint-Simon, and from the theocratic school of the Jesuits, who pointed to the Middle Ages as furnishing a pattern for social order. This spiritual power, which was to look after the moral and intellectual interests of society, Comte called "the church." Comte's church differs from any ecclesiastical organization that we find in human history, because it is to be made up of scientific men who are to train the young for the service of society, to supervise education, and to develop science. Perhaps we can get a correct idea of Comte's church if we liken it to the modern state university, adding the function of moral training, and diffusing its works through every community. The work of this scientific church is not only to train character and instill right beliefs in the young, but also to prosecute research and to diffuse knowledge. The freedom of thought of its teachers is not to be infringed upon by the state. It is, however, to be supported by the state. In this way, Comte would constitute a spiritual power within each state that was entirely free in the work of intellectual and moral guidance.

======*Comte's Ethics and Religion* [19] ======

Comte's social philosophy can hardly be understood without a consideration of his ethics and his
religion. As Comte believed that human institutions rest upon morals, and that morals rest upon
beliefs, ethics occupies a central place in his social
philosophy. As we have already seen in his *Positive Polity,* he makes it the capstone of the pyramid
of the sciences.[20] Comte, however, attempted no
new system of ethics. He was altogether preoccupied with preserving "Christian ethics," if we understand that phrase to mean "the ethical teachings
of Christ." Here, he said, is the ethical system by
which human society must live, if it is not to perish
through its own conflicts. Science should rally to its
defense and save it. Following Saint-Simon, Comte
would sum up this ethics in a single phrase, "Live
for others." "Act from affection," he says, "and
think in order to act." Again, "Love is our principle, order our basis, and progress our end." Thus,
it is evident that Comte wholeheartedly endorsed
the love ethics taught by Jesus of Nazareth. Comte,
therefore, remained essentially a Christian in his
ethical point of view. The life of the individual was

---

[19] See Levy-Bruhl, *op. cit.,* Book IV.

[20] For detailed study of Comte's religion, the student should refer
to *The System of Positive Polity*, the secondary title of which is *A
Treatise of Sociology, Instituting the Religion of Humanity,* especially
Volume IV.

to become a service of humanity. Comte contended, however, that the theological basis upon which this ethics had been placed was a mistake. It should be the concern of the scientific world to furnish new scientific support for this ethics upon which the welfare of human society depended, and to detach it from theology. It will be noted that Comte proposed no hedonistic basis for his ethical system, but rather made it an ethics of universal order and progress. Many of the details of his ethical ideals we would now consider austere and even highly Puritanical.

Comte's religion reveals even more clearly his general social philosophy. It is the religion that we now call "Humanism," but, to connect it with his theory of knowledge, Comte called it "Positivism." Comte defined religion as the "state of complete harmony peculiar to human life, in its collective as well as its individual form, when all the parts of life are ordered in their natural relations to each other." But Comte does not leave his new religion in the state of mere vague generalities. After experiencing his affection for Madame De Vaux, he saw that human society could never be reorganized through the work of science alone. It would also need something to control the moods of men, and to bring harmony in the relations between them. This sense of personal and social harmony must be sought in the realm of the affections or the emotions, and especially in the attitude and emotion of love. Har-

mony and unity among human beings he saw to be
more a work of feeling than of intellectual perceptions.

Now this work of bringing the feelings, the sentiments, the emotions into harmony with life and with
all the relations in human society, Comte was sen-
sible enough to see, had been the essential work of
religion. Hence, after Madame De Vaux's death,
he set about to institute a "Religion of Humanity,"
based upon science. As Comte had spent a great
deal of his time in denouncing the God-concept and
other concepts of current theology, we may imagine
some of his difficulties. Nevertheless, he was hon-
est enough to admit that all developed religions are
characterized by three doctrines: A doctrine of God,
a doctrine of sin and salvation, and a doctrine of immortality. How could these three doctrines be reconciled with a purely positive scientific basis for
religion? How could they be put upon the basis of
observed phenomena? Comte answered that there
is a supreme reality to which all other human realities are subject, and that that supreme reality is
humanity. Humanity must, therefore, become the
object of worship, the god, of a positive scientific religion. We may regard humanity as an object of investigation and study for science. But we may also
regard humanity as an object of love, adoration, and
service. Thus humanity becomes "a relative absolute," the only absolute that a positive scientific religion can know. From humanity, all of our bene-

fits have come; therefore, it should be the supreme object of our adoration and love. We should worship the best in humanity.

But Comte said that all individuals were not permanently a part of humanity. There is a selection going on—a selection in which there is a rejection of those who live selfish, brutal lives. There is a rejection of these from the permanent life of humanity, and incorporation of those who serve in the developing life of humanity. Hence, Comte's doctrine of sin and salvation is clear. Sin becomes essentially selfishness, and salvation consists in freeing the individual from sin or selfishness. Hence, too, Comte's doctrine of a relative immortality. It is an immortality of those who serve and truly love their kind. All that is best in such individuals shall continue to live on forever in the relatively immortal life of humanity. While there is no objective immortality of the soul, there is a subjective immortality of all who live for others. Moreover, it is an immortality for which we can live and yearn, even more than is the objective immortality that the Christian church has taught. For there can be no selfishness in the yearning for such an immortality of helpful influence. Moreover, death itself becomes something no longer to be feared. Death is the purifier. The evil in our lives is rejected. The good in them is taken up by this immortality of influence. Death, then, is something that the server of mankind may look forward to as a release from labor. His individual life may end, but his good works will go on forever.

Comte spent much time during the last two years of his life working on a suitable ritual for his new Religion of Humanity. Perhaps the less said about this phase of his religion the better; though it hardly deserved to be characterized by Huxley as "Catholicism Minus Christianity." The religious positivism of Comte, however, did not spread as widely after his death as he had anticipated. Its adherents succeeded in organizing only a few congregations in France and Great Britain, and still fewer in the two Americas. Its influence lives on, however, in modern religious Humanism, though modern Humanism is often not characterized by the strict adherence to Christian ethics that Comte advocated.

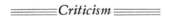

Criticism

Comte's work, like that of all pioneers, was characterized by many defects. First of all it may be said that, although he advocated making sociology a positive science, he left it in the realm of social philosophy. Even so, however, sociology owes him a great debt of gratitude for pointing out the necessity of the use of inductive scientific methods in sociology. He made grave mistakes in his early phenomenalism and objectivism; but this should not blind us to the value of his positive contributions to a scientific method adequate for the establishment of sociology. Again, the sociologist of the present, who is anxious to establish sociology as a science, may see little or nothing in Comte's social dynamics and social statics. Yet, surely, Comte was right in insisting that human history was essentially a record of the development of the human mind, especially of its intelligence. He was right again in showing that sociology and social philosophy depended upon all the knowledge gathered by the less complex antecedent sciences. We may hope that he was right in predicting that the development of science would ultimately lead to the peaceful development of industry and the abolition of war. The whole task of the social sciences becomes futile unless this generalization is true. Again, we have grounds for agreeing with Comte that, historically, there has been an expansion of social sympathy, keeping pace, though haltingly, with the development of social intelligence. Unless, again, this generalization is true, the future of humanity is dark indeed.

Turning, now, to Comte's doctrines in his social statics, we must surely agree that the individual is not an irreducible element in society; that individual personality is itself largely a product of group culture; but that this doctrine does not preclude the recognition of certain general inherited dispositions.

It is all very well for the modern mind to say that the unit of society is now the human individual, and is no longer the family group. Yet, if Cooley's doctrine of the importance of primary groups as the bearers of social life, especially the family, is true, it would seem that sociology would have to reinstate something like Comte's doctrine of the family as the original social unit. Again, Comte's idea that interdependence in function is the essential mark of society, and that this interdependence is an expanding process, which must make the ultimate society identical with humanity, is surely a generalization from which social philosophy, and possibly even scientific sociology, cannot escape. Finally, Comte's conception of the state as concerned with the integration of society and the regulation of its material interests, while the church concerns itself more with the personal and the spiritual, furnishes at least a beginning for a sane doctrine of the functions and the relations of both of these.

We may add a word of criticism of Comte's beautiful and noble Religion of Humanity. We have already seen that it did not appeal to the masses. Yet, surely, Comte was entirely right in thinking that man cannot get along without religion any more than science can get along without hypotheses. There has been much misunderstanding of Comte's religion, and many unfair criticisms, among which we must reckon Huxley's jibe, that he would as soon worship a wilderness of apes as worship humanity. Such a remark shows a total misunderstanding of Comte's conception; for Comte meant that it was the best and noblest in humanity that should be worshipped; and, from a strictly psychological point of view, it must be acknowledged that this is what the more highly developed ethical religions have always worshipped. Yet, even in making the best and noblest in humanity the God of positivism, Comte showed little understanding of human nature. As Edward Caird pointed out, humanity cannot deliberately and consciously worship itself.[21] Religion demands objectivity not less than science, and it demands wholeness in its viewpoint. Humanity, after all, is a part of nature, and, if we are to have any vital religion, it must extend to nature as well as to man. This is shown by the fact that throughout all history man has been a nature worshipper, and, although the projection of his higher and personal social values into nature may be without adequate scientific basis or justification, yet even a vital religion of humanity requires such a belief. It is for this reason that the idea of God has taken a central place in the developed religious consciousness of man; and we have every reason to believe that man will always remain, in some sense, a theist.

----

[21] See Caird, *The Social Philosophy of Comte.*

CHAPTER XXIV

The French Reaction to Comte's Sociology

IF COMTE'S SOCIOLOGICAL successors had taken him as the pioneer of sociology—taken what he had to give, not as a dogma, but as something upon which they could build—the development of sociology might have been much more rapid. Certainly there was reason to attempt to make sociology much more scientific than Comte had made it. But we can hardly construe the reaction to Comte's sociology, even in France, as simply an attempt to get a better scientific foundation for sociology. On the contrary, religious conservatives, almost at once, denounced Comte's sociology as "the diabolical science," while socialists and revolutionary radicals saw little or nothing in Comte's teaching except an attempt to bolster up the existing order. In part, the reaction against Comte's sociology was due to his own dogmatism and lack of open-mindedness, which stimulated an exceedingly dogmatic reaction against

409

him. Moreover, the very boldness of Comte's generalizations not only disturbed conservatives, but led devotees of pure science to seek other methods and aims in sociology than those that Comte advocated. We shall take, as the three names that typify the French reaction to Comte's sociology, those of Le Play, Tarde, and Durkheim.

═══════*Frédéric Le Play*═══════

Biographical sketch. Frédéric Le Play was born in 1806 of a pious Roman Catholic family.   In 1825, he entered the École Polytechnique to study to be an engineer, and, in 1827, he entered the École des Mines, from which he was graduated in 1832.   Here we may point out that it is remarkable how many of the early sociologists were educated as engineers, or, at least, were trained in the physical sciences.   Le Play made a brilliant record as a student, and, in 1840, after some travel in a few European countries, including Russia, he was made Professor of Metallurgy in the School of Mines.   From his travels, his professional experience, and governmental work, he gathered much information concerning laborers in various parts of Europe, especially those engaged in mining.   Very early he seems to have formed the idea of putting the social sciences upon a definite inductive basis through the minute study of laboring families.   In 1855, accordingly, he published a large work in six volumes entitled *European Working*

Men, which gave the results of the detailed study of thirty-six families.   In 1864, he published two volumes on *Social Reform in France,* which were largely an interpretation of his previous study. This work met with the favor of the French Government, and Le Play was promoted to various positions of honor and responsibility, becoming in 1867 a senator of the French Parliament.   In 1881, he published a summary of his views, entitled *The Essential Constitution of Humanity.*   His death occurred in 1882.

Le Play is important in the history of sociology, not only as the founder of the social-survey method, but also as representing the Roman Catholic reaction to Comte's social philosophy.   His training in the physical sciences and his deep religious nature fitted him to typify in his own person both the natural science and the Roman Catholic reaction to Comte.

Le Play has had a multitude of followers, both in France and in the English-speaking world.   Perhaps it will be sufficient to mention for the English-speaking reader Professor Patrick Geddes and Mr. Victor Branford, both of whom, however, sought a synthesis of Le Play's contributions with those of Comte.

Scientific method.   Le Play is usually counted as the founder of the social-survey method; but he was even more the founder of detailed, minute, monographic studies of family groups.   Perhaps it would be correct to say that, in the nineteenth century, he was the leader of the attempt to find a concrete method for the investigation of social facts that should furnish a secure inductive basis for the scientific study of human society. Agreeing with Comte that the family was the elementary and basic social unit, he sought his concrete inductive basis in the study of family life. As a practical man, family income and family budget appealed to him as the basic elements in both the life of the family and of society at large. Morals, religion, and general culture of the family were not to be overlooked, but Le Play considered that the economic life of the family was more fundamental. He began his study, therefore, with a minute study of the income and expenditures of the families of workingmen. Although he believed that the work and income of the family were fundamental in the understanding of its life and social status, his travels had taught him that the geographic environment of the family also plays a part, being basic to the work and economic organization of the family. The method that he proposed, therefore, in substance, was that of detailed study of the income, expenditures, and geographical location of individual families, as well as their religious, moral, and social condition. His plan for the study of family budgets has practically remained standard among economists, even down to the present time.

Le Play's followers, who were numerous, were not content with this modest program of social research. Headed by such men as de Tourville, and Demolins, the Le Play method of social investigation was expanded and modified until it became practically a social-survey method in the broad sense, although the family still remained the starting point.[1] Starting with the place of the family, its work, its property, its intellectual culture and its religion, the method was enlarged to include the city and the state in which the family was located, and even its contacts with foreign societies. Perhaps no better method of cross-section analysis of social conditions has yet been devised. Moreover, in the hands of such followers as Demolins, extensive correlations were made between the condition of the family, the forms of property and labor, and geographical location. Thus the method of the Le Play school became, in effect, a careful study of the relations between geographical conditions and social conditions. In this way it laid the foundations for the regional sociology of the present.

But another methodological assumption runs through the whole of the Le Play method and through much of the social-survey method that was developed upon the basis of his work. And that is the assumption that it is not the business of social science or sociology to seek for any new fundamental principles of social organization or of social progress. The assumption of this pious Roman Catholic French engineer was that the Christian religion had already given to us these fundamental principles. In a striking passage in his work on *Social Reform in France* he said:

---

[1] Cf. Sorokin, *Contemporary Sociological Theories,* pp. 65 f.

Since the revelation of the Ten Commandments and their sublime interpretation by Christ, the human mind has not discovered more useful principles. Nations which practice these principles are progressing and those which are not, declining. . . . Solution of the social problem does not require an invention of new principles. . . . An innumerable number of the thinkers who have analyzed the virtues and vices of man did not add anything new to the decalogues of Moses and to the teachings of Christ.[2]

Thus it is evident that Le Play himself took very nearly the same attitude that St. Augustine did when he affirmed the superiority of the revelation of the Scriptures to any human knowledge. We have already commented upon this attitude in discussing Augustine, and it is unnecessary to say anything further.

Social philosophy. Le Play's contribution was almost wholly to sociological method. His contributions to social philosophy were almost negligible. Indeed, down to the present, the contributions of his school have been, to say the least, superficial. Demolins, for example, says that the geographical routes of migration have created the social and racial types. He also lays stress upon the particularistic family, found more especially in the English-speaking nations. Le Play had earlier upheld a modified form of the patriarchal family as best for the welfare of both children and society. He especially condemned the unstable family, which was already be-

---

2 Quoted by Sorokin, *op. cit.*, p. 91.

ginning to develop at this time. So far as possible, the patriarchal family should be restored. In accordance with this idea, Le Play was opposed to the government regulation of industry. Such regulation should be brought about by co-operative agreements between managers and workingmen. In all of this, the assumption of Le Play seems to be that Christian moral ideals would be strong enough to establish justice in human relations and even to bring about reasonable conditions in industry. As Professor Sorokin has said, "Instead of advocating class hatred, Le Play pleaded for class solidarity; instead of atheism and materialism, religion; instead of revolution, reform; instead of egotism, altruism; instead of profit, sacrifice; instead of rights and privileges, he stressed more duty; instead of destruction of the existing institutions, their slow and careful remodeling." [3]

The Le Play school went much further than Le Play himself in the attempt to get fundamental interpretations of social conditions. Their chief stress, as we have already said, was upon geographic conditions. Many of their generalizations concerning the connection between geographic and social conditions have shown keen insight, but they failed to state that these correlations held only for a given cultural state.

---

[3] *Ibid.*, p. 92.

═══*Criticism*═══

As we have already seen, the criticism of Le Play's concrete, inductive method of social investigation began with the Le Play school itself; for example, P. De Rousiers, a member of the Le Play school, said that the monographic method of Le Play "did not grasp society as a whole; it allowed facts of great importance to escape, so that a conscientious disciple could perform his task with exactness and yet fail to see the underlying causes of the prosperity or the wretchedness of the country where his observations were made."[4]   But practically the same criticism must be made of the social-survey method in general, and with less force perhaps, even of the regional survey.   In the United States, for example, it is estimated that over 30,000 local social surveys have been made of one sort or another during the last generation.   In a sense, all were inspired by Le Play's passion for inductive social research.   It is difficult to say what contribution, if any, these surveys have made to the social sciences.   Certainly not more than a dozen of them have made any outstanding contribution.   For the most part, they have been devices to support local programs of social improvement, and to that extent have been worthy, although

---

[4] Quoted by Sorokin, *op. cit.*, p. 49.

many of them have undoubtedly been devices to secure degrees for graduate students who could not do
original constructive thinking.   It must even be said
that such vast regional surveys as are afforded in
the data of the United States Census and the various
state statistical bureaus have not added greatly to
the development of the social sciences.   However, it
must be acknowledged that such concrete inductive
social research has served a useful function, and will
probably help greatly in the development of the social sciences and the social philosophy of the future.

Gabriel Tarde

Biographical sketch.   A very different type of reaction to Comte's sociology is found in the work of
Gabriel Tarde.   Tarde was born in 1843, and was
educated for the law at Toulouse and Paris.   At the
age of twenty-six, he became a judge in one of the
lower courts of his native town; and at thirty-two
he became a judge of one of the higher criminal
courts, a position that he held for over eighteen
years.   It was while he was a judge of this criminal
court that he became convinced that Lombroso's attempt to explain criminality in terms of biological
conditions and forces was a mistake.   Tarde was
convinced that crime was essentially a matter of social conditions, even though biological conditions at
times might play a part.   He set forth these views

in a book entitled *Criminality*, published in 1886; and elaborated them more fully in his *Penal Philosophy*, published in 1890.

Undoubtedly, Tarde's leading sociological ideas were derived from his experience as a criminal judge.   He saw how crime was so often the result of contagion and association.   Such a social philosophy as that of Comte appealed to him as very remote.   He did find, however, something to sustain his views in one of Comte's most interesting contemporaries, Augustin Cournot, whom he termed "an Auguste Comte, purified, condensed, and refined." [5] The essence of Cournot's social philosophy was that imitation creates the specific qualities of individuals.   Walter Bagehot, an English writer, had set forth the same view in his *Physics and Politics*, published in 1869, but probably Tarde had no direct personal acquaintance with this book.

Convinced of the correctness of his views, Tarde began to set them forth in a series of remarkable books.   The first was the *Laws of Imitation*, published in 1890; then followed his *Social Logic*, in 1895; then, his *Universal Opposition*, published in 1897; and finally, his *Social Laws*, in 1898, a little book that summarized his entire system of sociological thought.   In 1900, Tarde was made Professor of Modern Philosophy in the College of France, and died in that position in 1904.

Scientific method.   Tarde undertook to interpret

---

[5] Cf. Lichtenberger, *Development of Social Theories*, p. 404.

social phenomena in terms of the interaction of individuals. His approach to every social problem, therefore, was individualistic and through individual psychology. Instead of ignoring individual psychology, as Comte had done, and as Durkheim did later, Tarde made individual psychology the basis of sociology; or rather, he made the psychology of individual interaction the whole of sociology. His sociology was in essence a social psychology. It was, therefore, welcomed by psychologists generally. William James declared the *Laws of Imitation* to be a work of genius; James Mark Baldwin[6] found in Tarde's analyses of social processes a confirmation of his own, and elaborated a point of view not greatly differing from Tarde's. It seemed for a time that Comte had been corrected, and that the social sciences might find a new and firm basis in Tarde's social psychology.

Although it cannot be claimed that Tarde developed any painstaking method of inductive social research, such as was advocated by the Le Play school, and while he may be characterized, therefore, as "a social philosopher, rather than an accurate scientific scholar," yet his thinking was backed up by many years of concrete practical experience. Hence, for a time, Tarde's ideas exerted an enormous influence in sociology, and they are still not without influence on contemporary social thought.

---

[6] See his *Social and Ethical Interpretations in Mental Development, A Study in Social Psychology;* also the author's article on "The Social Philosophy of James Mark Baldwin," in *Journal of Social Philosophy,* October, 1936.

Tarde insisted that all truly social phenomena are psychical in their nature. They consist of the interaction of the individual minds. Where such mental interaction is found, there also is found society, and where there is no such interaction of individual minds, there is no society. There is no such collective entity as a social mind. What we see in society is the mental, or intercerebral, interaction of individuals. This takes the form of repetition or imitation, adaptation or invention, and opposition. Now science, by its very nature, is limited to repetition; unless phenomena are repeated, they cannot be observed and do not lend themselves to generalization. All resemblance, Tarde held, is due to repetition. All resemblances in the physical world are caused and explained by periodic or vibratory motions. All resemblances in the world of life result from hereditary transmission. All resemblances in mental life are due to the repetitions of habit. Finally, all resemblances in society, custom, fashion, sympathy, obedience, and so forth, are due to the various forms of imitation. Sociology will become a science only when it abandons mass interpretation and studies the minute interactions between individuals. Therefore, according to Tarde, "the general laws of imitative repetition are to sociology what the laws of habit and heredity are to biology, the laws of gravitation to astronomy, and the laws of vibration to physics." The sociologist must seek his data in the processes of interaction between individuals, even in the relations existing between two persons, one of whom exerts a mental influence upon the other; in other words, in the intermental processes that go on between individuals.

Although Tarde represented imitation as the central feature of the process of social interaction, yet he maintained that what was imitated in human society was essentially desires and beliefs, which, he asserted, are the forces underlying all social life. It is, therefore, evident that Tarde used "imitation" in a much broader sense than "imitative action," or the copying of the action of one person by another. In the second edition of his *Laws of Imitation,* he went so far as to say, "By imitation I mean every impression of an interpsychical photography, so to speak, willed, or unwilled, passive or active." Thus it is evident that his concept of imitation was very vague, and, as Professor House says, was more of a sociological than a psychological concept. Nevertheless, he offered this concept as "the key to the social mystery." He undertook to explain, in other words, all the changes and movements in human society through the suggestion-imitation process. Imitation, he held, is "the elementary social phenomenon," "the fundamental social fact," and is the criterion of the social phenomenon. "The unvarying characteristic of every social fact whatsoever," Tarde tells us, "is that it is imitative. And this characteristic belongs exclusively to social facts."

Social philosophy. It is evident that Tarde saw clearly that most of the phenomena of human society are socially acquired and socially transmitted. In other words, he was groping his way toward a cultural theory of human society, but he never succeeded in stating it clearly. Social origins, he held, were to be found in primitive inventions, and not in hereditary or instinctive reactions. The diffusion of these primitive inventions, and not natural selection, accounted for social development. All this process of diffusion takes place through the suggestion-imitation process. He tells us, "The minute interagreement of minds and wills which we find in a human group is not due to organic heredity; it is rather the effect of that suggestion-imitation process which, starting from one primitive creature possessed of a single idea or act, passed this copy on to one of its neighbors, then to another, and so on." In a sweeping statement, Tarde declares, "There is not a word that you say which is not the reproduction, now unconscious, but formerly conscious and voluntary, of verbal articulations reaching back to the most distant past, with some special accent due to your immediate surroundings . . . even your very originality itself is made up of accumulated commonplaces, and aspires to become commonplace in its turn."

Thus Tarde laid the foundations for that school of cultural anthropologists who have held that the development of culture depends entirely upon the diffusion of invention; that invention is rare; and that copying, or imitation, is common. Like the diffusionist school of anthropologists, Tarde did not explain the origin of primitive invention. Social changes originate in inventions, but inventions are a problem more for the psychologist than for the sociologist. However, Trade held that most inventions are the result of social causes, especially of the adaptation or adjustment that takes place between differing imitations. Invention in the main is the union of two harmonious imitations, while social conflict is the result of the interference of two dissimilar waves of imitation.

Tarde's general theory of social development, therefore, is clear. Social evolution, he says, is not like organic evolution, or like biological growth. It is more like a ladder, where the rungs represent successive inventions inserted in the process of development. Thus the great man, the genius who makes socially valuable inventions, is an indispensable element for the understanding of the process of human social development. Social development, then, in general, becomes a result of the cumulative effect of inventions and of the diffusion of these inventions. Every invention tends to be diffused, unless it meets with obstacles, in a geometrical progression, just as a stone thrown into the water produces waves that slowly and then more rapidly spread until they meet other waves. The imitation of an invention, therefore, tends to spread in geometrical progression from its initial center. But Tarde admitted that the physical or racial conditions of a population might check an invention's successful diffusion by imitation. Therefore, a second law of the development of society by imitation is that "imitations are refracted by their social media." A third law is that imitation usually proceeds, under the influence of prestige, from the socially superior to the socially inferior. A fourth law is that inner imitation in the mind usually precedes an overt imitation in practice. Thus a fashion in thinking spreads before a fashion of acting.

This process of imitation, Tarde held to be not only the process by which inventions, and consequently civilization, have been spread, but it is also the process by which the individual is socialized and the group unified. The process may be modified by a number of factors, but Tarde believed that he had discovered and stated the essential laws of imitation, and so the essential laws of social development and social organization. In his enthusiasm he even declared, "Society is imitation." There are all sorts of imitation in a human group—custom imitation, fashion imitation, sympathy imitation, precept imitation, unconscious imitation, and deliberate, or rational, imitation. Sociology will become a pure science when it stops dealing with mass phenomena and analyzes these social phenomena on the basis of the initial processes by which they are constituted; and these processes are those of the repetition, opposition, and adaptation of actions, beliefs, and desires. If sociology will recognize the part that is played in human society by all of these different phases of imitation, it will be possible to have intelligent progress that almost necessarily consists in the deliberate, rational imitation of certain social patterns that society finds advantageous. This will result in evolutionary, rather than revolutionary, progress. Tarde believed that this evolutionary progress would in time result in the disappearance of war, and even in the disappearance of the grosser forms of competition. "Like war," he tells us, "competition proceeds from the small to the great, and from very numerous instances of the very small to very infrequent instances of the very great." Thus the development of human social life through the imitative process, especially when it becomes rational, becomes meliorated in the long run.

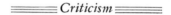

Criticism

Tarde represented the individualistic psychological reaction to Comte's social philosophy. Such a reaction was to have been expected, and served the useful purpose of calling scientific sociology back to the study of the minute social interactions of individuals, and to their interpretation through psychology. Even if Tarde's use of the term "imitation" was very vague and hardly acceptable to the modern psychologist, yet the very fact that his idea of the diffusion of inventions by the process of imitation has proved fruitful in cultural anthropology shows that it was not without scientific value. Tarde's emphasis, too, upon the diffusion of ideas, beliefs, desires, and other inner experiences as important for understanding the human social progress is important for sociology. But his whole analysis was too simple and too mechanical. We cannot explain cultural development in human society adequately through the process of suggestion-imitation. We particularly cannot explain adequately through that process the appearance of the new elements in cultural development. Like all interaction theories in sociology, Tarde's intercerebral process tends to become too formal and too simple to explain adequately the behavior of human groups. Even though Tarde demanded for sociology a psychological basis consisting of only one central process of interaction, he produced a sociology almost as one-sided as the recognized unilateral thinkers themselves.

Émile Durkheim

Biographical sketch. In the writings of Professor Émile Durkheim, the reaction of the pure scientists of France to Comte's social philosophy expressed itself even more than in those of Le Play and Tarde. Many of Durkheim's writings fall within the twentieth century, but it is impossible to understand the present condition of social philosophy, either in Europe or in the United States, without taking Durkheim's influence fully into account.

Durkheim was born in 1858 of a cultured French-Jewish family. It may be that his Jewish descent had something to do with his reaction to value judgments in sociology in the fields of ethics, politics, and religion, such as Comte proposed. At any rate, he set to work to make sociology a pure science with very definite limitations. He did not want it to be even a social philosophy. Durkheim did not take his Doctor's degree at the Sorbonne in Paris until 1892. His Doctor's dissertation was *On the Division of Social Labor,* and was published in 1893. His typical attitudes in sociology, however, did not come out until he published his *Rules of Sociological Method,* in 1895. This was followed by two notable monographs that were written to illustrate his sociological method, one on *Suicide,* published in 1897, and the other on *The Elementary Forms of the Religious Life,* published in 1912. In the meantime, he had been called to a chair in the University of Bordeaux, where he taught sociology and pedagogy. In 1903 he was called back to the Sorbonne to teach the same subjects. He died in 1917 in the midst of the Great War.

Scientific method. Like many others before him, Durkheim sought to make sociology follow the same methods that the natural sciences followed. The natural sciences, he believed, had been built up by the careful and exact observation of "things." A "thing" he defined as anything that could be observed. Social phenomena, he said, must be treated as "things," if sociology was to be made a science. However, he admitted that such social "things" could not be observed as exactly as the physical scientist observes phenomena. They could, however, be experienced and inferred from very exact observations. Moreover, there is a very definite line between the vital and the psychological, and the social. Social facts are characterized by certain marks to set them off from psychological and vital facts. The two marks that Durkheim finally decided upon are "exteriority" and "constraint." He admitted that social facts—as, for example, traditions, customs, and institutions—are in one sense psychic, but that they are always exterior to any given individual. Also, they always exert pressure, control, or constraint upon the individual, as traditions, customs, and institutions always do. It follows that the social is a realm by itself, not to be confused with the biological or psychological. It is wrong, therefore, to base sociology upon individual psychology, and even more so upon biology. Social phenomena should be studied as unique facts in a realm by themselves.

Here it may be remarked that Durkheim is usually represented as a continuer of Comte's point of view. Like Comte, he ignored individual psychology, or rather, professed to do so. Like Comte, too, and unlike Tarde, he started with mass phenomena rather than individual social interactions; but the resemblance stops here. Unquestionably, Durkheim represents a reaction to Comte's social philosophy, rather than a continuance of his point of view.

As Durkheim disavowed the idea that we could find the explanation of social phenomena in individual psychology, he advocated the careful study of these phenomena by comparative historical and statistical methods. He did not, however, go to the extreme of external behaviorism. What should be studied are the ideas, beliefs, opinions, attitudes, and actions of people; in brief, their traditions, customs, and institutions. Sociology, he held, is not yet ready to become a general science of social phenomena. It must investigate these phenomena piecemeal, and construct scientific monographs upon them. Durkheim recognized that there were various phases or departments of these social phenomena, such, for example, as the domestic, the economic, the political, the artistic, the moral, and the religious. All the traditions and institutions connected with these various phases of human society were to be studied by this monographic method. Thus Durkheim laid it down, like Le Play, that, before a science of sociology could be achieved, an inductive basis of social facts must be secured through long and patient investigation; but he did not give the same central position to the life and work of the family. On the contrary, he apparently took as his unit of investigation the cultural group, or, at least, groups that afforded different types of social facts. It is noticeable, however, that, unlike Tarde, he did not start with the individual, but restored the social group to the central place in social research. In the latter years of his life, Durkheim held very strictly that sociology, at the time, was not able to offer any value judgments concerning cultural and social phenomena. It must keep to the point of view of pure science and not become mixed with social philosophy.

Social philosophy. Nevertheless, the very premises of Durkheim's sociological thinking necessitate that we speak of his social philosophy. For he assumes that, just as the sensations and perceptions of the individual mind are compounded into concepts and individual representations, so the ideas of individuals get compounded into what he calls "collective representations." These may be ideas, opinions, beliefs, or values current in the social group—in brief, its traditions. These are still psychic, though objective to the individual. Instead of being made by the individual mind, they are mainly what make the content of the individual mind. Thus, in a certain sense, there is a social mind, though there is no social brain. The study of this social mind in all of its phases will account not only for the behavior of the group, but largely for the great mass of individuals that compose it. Let Durkheim describe this social, or group, mind himself, and then perhaps we shall be able to understand it.

> The totality of the beliefs and sentiments common to the average members of a social group form a definite system which has its own life. One can call it the *collective consciousness.* To be sure, it does not have a unique organ for its substratum, for it is by definition diffused throughout the extent of the society, but nevertheless it has specific characters which make it distinct reality. It is independent of the particular conditions in which individuals happen to be placed; they pass, it remains. Likewise, it does not change with each generation, but on the contrary, unites them. It

is then something different from individual consciousness although it is realized only through individuals.[7]

The present-day sociologist might well exclaim, ''But this is culture on its subjective or mental side!'' Yes, Durkheim was feeling his way toward a cultural sociology, from a different point of view from that of Tarde; but he was never able to state it quite clearly. If we substitute some such phrase as the mental or immaterial culture of the group, we can understand his doctrine of the social, or group, mind. We will understand him, for example, when he tells us:

> Society is not at all the illogical or a-logical, incoherent and fantastic being which it has too often been considered. Quite on the contrary, the collective consciousness is the highest form of the psychic life, since it is the consciousness of consciousness. Being placed *outside of* and *above* individual and local contingencies, it sees things only in their permanent and essential aspects, which it crystallizes into communicable ideas. . . . Society sees farther and better, than individuals.[8]

On account of this stressing of the reality of a social mind and of the independence of social phenomena, Professor P. A. Sorokin charges Durkheim with ''sociologism.'' That this charge is substantially correct, we shall see as we proceed; for

---

[7] Quoted by Bristol, *Social Adaptation,* p. 139, from Durkheim's *De la Division du Travail Social,* p. 84.

[8] Durkheim, *The Elementary Forms of Religious Life,* p. 444; quoted by Sorokin, *Contemporary Sociological Theories,* p. 465.

Durkheim makes tradition, or the mental side of culture, not only determinative of a group's behavior, but determinative of the very language and concepts employed in communication between the members of a group. In other words, Durkheim's system is a system of social determinism that leaves little or no place for the creativity of the human individual. This is well illustrated in his celebrated monograph, *The Elementary Forms of the Religious Life.* Durkheim does not appeal to the individual mind to explain religion; on the contrary, religion is to be explained purely as a social product. The source of religion is to be found in the experiences of the group itself. Religious conceptions are nothing but symbols of social values. The concept of God, for example, is a symbol of society personified; and the social function of religion is the creation and maintenance of social solidarity. For this reason, religion has played a great role in human society as an integrating or conserving force. Thus Durkheim's theory of the origin and development of religion is purely sociological. "The religious life," he says, "is the concentrated expression of the whole collective life. . . . The idea of society is the soul of religion. Religious forces are therefore human forces, moral forces. . . . Religion, far from ignoring the real society and making abstraction of it, is in its image; it reflects all its aspects, even the most vulgar and the most repulsive." [9]

---

[9] Quoted by Sorokin, *op. cit.*, p. 474.

Durkheim attempts to carry his social determinism even to such general concepts of the human mind as time, space, and causality. He argues, in effect, that all of these are simply products of culture, or social products. He forgets the part that individual biological factors and individual psychological factors have played in the elaboration of such concepts. Social tradition, after all, cannot change the nature of things or the nature of the human mind. Neither of these are social creations in the strict sense.

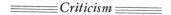

Criticism

Durkheim's extreme social realism led him astray. It led him to ignore the psychological individual, who, at bottom, is both the creator and the carrier of culture. Durkheim was right in restoring the group and group behavior to the central place in sociological research, but he was wrong in not taking psychology into account. In characterizing prevalent social ideas, beliefs, opinions, and traditions as "collective representations," it is doubtful if he advanced the cause of scientific understanding of such phenomena. On the contrary, his objectivism became tainted with a subjectivism that bordered on mysticism. When he went still further and attempted to construe as purely social products such prevalent social concepts as space and time, he bordered upon the absurd, and ran squarely into the face of scientific biology and scientific psychology.

Finally, Durkheim's extreme devotion to the attitudes and methods of natural science also betrayed him into believing that the social sciences could be devoid of value judgments. Perhaps such sciences are possible; but they are incomplete and abortive, and far from the type of knowledge that is desired or desirable about human society.

We are, therefore, compelled to conclude that these French successors to Auguste Comte fell short of doing for social philosophy as much as Comte attempted. Indeed, on the very points upon which they attempted to correct Comte, they made, for the most part, worse mistakes than Comte. Even the scientific world has not agreed to recognize their attempts at a scientific sociology as productive of anything more than social philosophy. Sociology might have developed more rapidly if their attitude toward Comte's social philosophy, while critical, had also been constructive.

CHAPTER XXV

Herbert Spencer

FOR SOME REASON hard to divine, the English-speaking world produced no first-rate social philosopher during the first half of the nineteenth century —none, indeed, after Adam Ferguson. Perhaps this was due to the fact that its social thinkers were occupied almost entirely with the development of the science of economics. This science received its incentive to develop from the expanding industrial and commercial life of the English-speaking peoples, especially of Great Britain. For the mass of Englishmen, economics was the only social science, and the only one possible. Only a few in the English-speaking world were affected by Continental currents of thought that presented a different view. It is not unfair to say that such currents came into that world largely through the influence of the writings of Auguste Comte, but their chief embodiment was in the writings of Herbert Spencer. It is also not unfair to say that Spencer's writings were responsible almost entirely for the popularization of sociology throughout the English-speaking world during the latter part of the nineteenth century. Hence, in the way of popularizing social philosophy, Spencer did for the English-speaking world what Comte did for the French-speaking world. Let us notice briefly the salient points in his life.

===== *Biographical Sketch* =====

Herbert Spencer was born in Derby, England, in 1820. He was an only child and was somewhat sickly and pampered. He did not, therefore, attend regular schools, but was educated by his father, who was an English schoolmaster, somewhat radical in his views. He educated young Herbert almost exclusively in the physical sciences and mathematics. His uncle, who was a liberal English clergyman, wanted to send him to Cambridge University, but young Herbert was interested in physical science and wanted to be an engineer, for which Cambridge afforded but meager training at that time. Hence, he did not go to a university at all, but, at the age of seventeen, actively undertook surveying and other engineering work for one of the early English railways. He was exclusively engaged in this civil engineering for four years, and practiced it more or less for eleven years, during which time, like Comte, he showed great proficiency in mathe-

matics. But, at the age of twenty-two, he became
interested in social problems, and began to write
papers on social and political subjects for *The Non-
conformist,* in which he advocated that government
should be limited to police administration and the
preservation of social order. At the age of twenty-
eight, he became an associate editor of *The Economist,* a periodical with similar social and political
views. He now gave up engineering and devoted
himself to writing. Through the intellectuals associated with *The Economist,* he became acquainted
with George Eliot and her husband, George Henry
Lewes. Both of these had already accepted not only
Comte's scientific point of view but, in good degree,
his religious positivism. They undoubtedly had a
great influence over the young Herbert Spencer.
In 1850, he published his first book, *Social Statics.*
This was a treatise on the function of the state, in
which he again advocated confining the state to
police functions and to defense against foreign
enemies. He now began to write more along lines
of general philosophy and social philosophy, and
contributed articles to many journals. In 1852, for
example, he wrote a paper on ''The Development
Hypothesis,'' in which he set forth a general theory
of evolution. In 1855, he published a work on *Principles of Psychology,* which was an effort to break
new ground. The book attempted to cling to the old
associational, or sensationalist, psychology and still
to develop psychology upon a new, evolutionary,
mechanistic basis. This book built up Spencer's

reputation at once. Through the influence of Lamarck, Alfred Russel Wallace, and Darwin, the idea
of evolution was now in the air, and, in 1857, Spencer
published his famous essay on "Progress, Its Law
and Cause," which contained a rough statement
of his theory of universal evolution.

In 1859, Darwin published his *Origin of Species*.
Spencer saw, even before this, that he must get
busy or Darwin would rob him of his fame as the
formulator of the evolution hypothesis. Already,
in 1858, he had prepared a rough draft of his theory
of universal evolution and had embodied it in the
prospectus of an ambitious work in ten volumes,
to be entitled *Synthetic Philosophy*. The first volume of this series came out in 1862, and was entitled
First Principles. This volume is of peculiar interest to the student of Spencer's thought, because he
states in it most of the principles that he elaborated
in the later volumes of the *Synthetic Philosophy*. By
"first principles," Spencer meant the first principles of scientific knowledge, which he finds to be
matter, motion, and force. In 1864, he published
the first volume of his *Principles of Biology*, and,
in 1867, the second volume. In 1870–1872, he expanded his *Principles of Psychology* into two volumes, and included the two in his *Synthetic Philosophy*. Meanwhile, he issued a monograph on *The
Study of Sociology*, which, while a study of the scientific methods that should be used in sociology, was
one of the best of his books, though not included in
the ten volumes of the *Synthetic Philosophy*. He

did not publish the first volume of his *Principles of Sociology* until 1876, and the second and third volumes did not appear until 1879 and 1896. In the meantime, in order to write the two volumes of his *Principles of Ethics,* he laid aside the completion of the third volume of his *Sociology,* as he had become alarmed at the signs of moral disintegration that were beginning to appear. Volume I of the *Principles of Ethics* appeared in 1892, and Volume II was completed in 1893. He then resumed his work upon the *Principles of Sociology,* the final volume of which appeared, as we have already seen, in 1896. Thus he lived to complete his *Synthetic Philosophy* in ten large volumes. In the meantime he had written several minor works, and supervised the publication of eight large atlases, entitled *Descriptive Sociology.* These were, however, almost entirely the work of his secretaries, and he simply supervised the gathering and the publication of the material, which aimed to set forth in a descriptive way the customs and institutions of the principal peoples of the world. Spencer died in 1903 at the age of eighty-three years.

Spencer lived alone all of his life. He never married, and was practically a hermit philosopher. We can perhaps ascribe certain things in his social thinking to his solitary and isolated life. Moreover, most of his life he was an invalid, and had a very precarious income. It was only within the last years of his life that he received much revenue from the publication of his books. At first he put more into them than he got out; for he usually employed amanuenses to write them. Even in the later years of his life, the publication of his *Descriptive Sociology* took from him a large part of his earnings. Considering his ill-health and his slender resources, his achievements in the way of writing and publication were remarkable. All of these facts and many more Spencer set forth for the general public in his *Autobiography*, published after his death.

The Origins of Spencer's Thought

In general, Spencer's thinking is pretty much rooted in that of the middle-class Englishman of mid-Victorian times. Like the English middle class of that day, he was entirely given to *laissez faire* individualism. But an equally important influence upon his thinking was the rise of the evolutionary hypothesis. The public, indeed, tended to think that Spencer's work was rooted in Darwin's. But Spencer stoutly maintained that he had had the idea of evolution long before Darwin published it. He claimed that he got the idea chiefly from three works: Von Baer's *History of the Development of Animals,* published in 1828; Laplace's *Celestial Mechanics*; and Lyell's *Principles of Geology.* Certainly, Spencer's doctrine of evolution was very different from Darwin's. Much of it was rooted in Laplace's nebular hypothesis, and some of it in Lamarck's theory of evolution by adaptation, a view that Spencer defended to the end of his days. Spencer also claimed that he got a great many of his ideas from his father; and that was probably true of his social and political theories. But it is entirely reasonable to say also that Spencer got much from Auguste Comte—indeed, the very outline and some of the central positions of his *Synthetic Philosophy* were derived from him. But Spencer would never acknowledge his indebtedness to Comte, as Comte would never acknowledge his indebtedness to Saint-Simon. Professor House's contention that "Spencer would have written his works substantially as he did if Comte had never lived," can scarcely be defended. Assuredly, if there had been no Comte, there would have been no Spencer. The *Synthetic Philosophy* and the *Positive Philosophy* have too many resemblances, even though Spencer at first did not know Comte's writings in the original. He used many of the terms that Comte used, and he followed, in the main, Comte's hierarchy of the sciences, though he criticized it. Finally, as we have already seen, Spencer's mature life was in close contact with the English Positivists and others who were under Comte's influence.

Spencer seems to have been hardly conscious of the part that general social tradition plays in influencing thinking. He almost invariably denied that his thinking had been influenced by anyone whose works he had not read. This was not only the case with Comte, but he seems also to have been quite unaware of the great influence that Thomas

Hobbes had upon his thinking. Spencer took so many of the same positions that Hobbes did, and there is so much parallelism between their lives and thought, that we may perhaps justly call Spencer "the Hobbes of nineteenth-century England." In general, Professor Royce's remark concerning Spencer seems amply justified: "He never learned how to regard human philosophical thought itself as an evolutionary process in which his own thinking had an organic place."

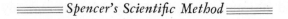

Spencer's Scientific Method

All of Spencer's social philosophy is based upon the assumption that human society is a purely natural phenomenon. Like Hobbes in the seventeenth century, he set himself the task of taking over to the social sphere the ideas, methods, and principles of the physical sciences. He did this with the pretense that the methods of strictly inductive science were to be respected. Nevertheless, he himself recognized that, from one point of view, his method was deductive. In his later years he styled his method as "deduction fortified by induction." Professor Albion W. Small characterized Spencer's method, perhaps not altogether unfairly, as "speculation fortified by illustration." The justification for such a characterization is that Spencer started with a very narrow theory of universal evolution that he sought to apply to all realms of phenomena

—physical, organic, mental, and social. This theory he expressed in his final definition of evolution, thus: "Evolution is an integration of matter and concomitant dissipation of motion; during which the matter passes from an indefinite incoherent homogeneity to a definite coherent heterogeneity; and during which the retained motion undergoes a parallel transformation."[1] This formula was to explain everything from the development of the earth and solar system to the way in which a simple society of primitive men grows into the complex structure of modern civilization. Quite evidently, Spencer's method was not that of multiple-working hypotheses, but that of a pet theory that he sought to support by selecting instances in its favor.

When we analyze this famous definition of evolution, we find that it reduces itself to a purely physical science formula, the redistribution of matter and energy. Evolution is a change, but it is that particular change that we call the integration of matter, and, at the same time, the dissipation of energy. Spencer's formula seems to point, therefore, to a materialistic metaphysics. This, however, he always denied; but, in some of his later writings, he had to acknowledge that his formula, apparently, did not cover all phenomena.

The charge of materialism brought against Spencer is corroborated by the fact that, in his *First Principles,* he spoke confidently of interpreting the phe-

---

[1] See Spencer, *First Principles*, Part II, Chapter XVII.

nomena of life and mind in society in terms of matter, motion, and force. While acknowledging that there will remain an ultimate mystery, he held that the task of science is "to formulate all phenomena in terms of matter, motion, and force." He added, "The highest achievement of science is the interpretation of all orders of phenomena, as differently conditioned manifestations of this one kind of effect under differently conditioned modes of this one kind of uniformity," [2] the "one kind of uniformity" being that which we class together under the names of matter, motion, and force. Such an interpretation, Spencer held, is not necessarily materialistic because it is relative. All of the knowledge of man, he said, is simply a knowledge of relations. We cannot know reality itself.

Spencer called his system "Synthetic Philosophy." He held, however, that "Synthetic Philosophy" did not attempt to deal with ultimate reality. Philosophy, in his use of the term, was only "knowledge of the highest degree of generality." "Knowledge of the lowest kind," he said, "is *un-unified* knowledge; science is *partially unified* knowledge; philosophy is *completely unified* knowledge." [3] Both science and philosophy, therefore, deal with the relative or conditioned, the visible and comprehensible, the objects of sense perception. Ultimate reality is therefore *Unknowable*. To this *Unknowable,* Spencer would consign both religion and metaphysics.

---

[2] *Op. cit.*, Part II, Chapter XXIV.
[3] *Op. cit.*, Part II, Chapter I.

Therefore, his position is one of religious and philosophical agnosticism. The reader will not fail to see the close similarity of this position to that of Comte, who held to phenomenalism, and said that any attempt to solve metaphysical problems was futile. Like Comte, too, Spencer paid only formal deference to logic and made no practical use of it, not even to the extent of a careful definition of the terms and concepts that he made use of.

If Spencer's definition of evolution had been broad enough to include all forms of humanly experienced reality, there would have been little objection to his method. The deductive method is not unsafe if the premises cover all the facts. But Spencer's premises did not cover all the facts, and his whole conception of evolution seems today very narrow and fragmentary. Even in the organic field he did not approach Darwin's conception. Rather, Spencer's theory of organic evolution rested upon Lamarck's theory of the inheritance of useful adaptations. This was more in accord with his general formula for evolution; for it will be noticed that Spencer's formula says nothing about natural selection. Spencer's conception of evolution seems to have been that it was a process in a relatively straight line toward increasing definiteness, coherence, and heterogeneity. The linear conception of evolution as a straight-upward trend toward greater complexity and better adjustment, which became popularized in the nineteenth century, seems to have sprung largely from Spencer.

Even on the physical-science side, Spencer's conception of evolution is very inadequate, according to modern physics. He does not make any room for unchanging elements in the universe. He starts the universe with chaos. But modern physical science discovers no evidence to support such a hypothesis.

Spencer's evolutionary method goes to such an extreme that it leads him to neglect the facts of present society and to depend too much upon the use of anthropological and ethnological materials. Some sociologists and anthropologists would still classify Spencer's *Principles of Sociology* as a work in cultural anthropology. In his *Study of Sociology*, Spencer does lip service to the historical method; but there is very little intelligent use of the historical method in his work, and still less use of Le Play's method of inductive observation of present social conditions. Had Spencer made more use of Le Play's method and combined it with Comte's historical method, he might have advanced sociology much further than he did.

Because Spencer's sociology was so preoccupied with the problem of social origins and early social development, he seems to assume that evolution can establish the social and moral validity of what we find in human relations. Now, it cannot be denied that genesis does throw some light on the social and moral validity of human institutions. But this use of the evolutionary method, if carried far, is misleading, since genesis does not show us the social value of anything at the present time. It is like the wrong use of the historical method. History, as we have seen, cannot show the social validity of an institution, like slavery or war, at the present day; neither can past social development or evolution.

Finally, in his sociology, Spencer's formula of universal evolution, which he was going to use as a key to all social mysteries, inevitably led him to stress mechanical and biological processes and forces much more than psychological. If we want to find his principles of sociological interpretation, we must turn not so much to his *Principles of Psychology* as to his *First Principles,* where he deals with the laws of redistribution of matter and energy; and to his *Principles of Biology,* where he deals with unconscious adaptation, the increase of numbers, and the survival of the fittest. The result is that Spencer seems to imply that social evolution is an automatic process in which conscious intelligent purposes play, and can play, very little part. As Professor Small says, Spencer left the impression upon the multitude of his readers that social evolution was a sort of mechanically determined redistribution of matter and energy that thought could neither accelerate nor retard. Spencer's sociology, therefore, was a determined effort to bring the social sciences within the conception of a mechanistically determined universe.

===== *Spencer's Social Philosophy* =====

Spencer, like Comte, divides social philosophy into social statics and social dynamics, the former treating of the equilibration of a perfect society, and the latter of the forces by which society is advanced toward perfection. He makes these divisions of sociology, however, much broader than Comte; for in social statics he would include the problem of what laws we must obey for the attainment of complete happiness, and in social dynamics he would include the problem of analyzing the influences that are making us competent to obey these laws. This, at least, is the conception of sociology that he sets forth in his first treatise, *Social Statics*. In his later works, however, the division is less practical, and aims only at scientific understanding, for Spencer is bent upon reducing everything to invariable natural laws. He, therefore, assumes at the very beginning that "the course of civilization could not have been other than it has been." [4]

Doctrine of social origins. Spencer is, above all, the sociologist who emphasized origins. But his doctrine of social origins is not very satisfactory, because it rests, not on a Darwinian, but on a Lamarckian foundation. He makes practically no use of animal societies. He holds that animal groups

---

[4] Spencer, *Social Statics*, p. 233; quoted by Lichtenberger, *Development of Social Theory*, p. 315.

HERBERT SPENCER

are not true societies, but are genetic aggregations, or "families." Therefore, he proceeds at once to his doctrine of primitive man. He has a lot of hypotheses regarding primitive man for which he offers little proof. He makes primitive man incapable of abstract thought, of foresight, or of power of analysis. Moreover, primitive man was dominated by fear, and Spencer's social philosophy makes almost the same use of fear that Hobbes' did in the seventeenth century. There are two principal kinds of fear, Spencer says, which dominated primitive man. The first is the fear of the dead, which Spencer regards as the root of religion; and the second is the fear of the living, which is the root of government and law.[5] The primitive fear that men have for one another must have led, Spencer argues, much as Hobbes did, to a state of actual or potential war. Aboriginal man, Spencer claims, must have had a desire to kill; "for it is the law of animal life that to every needful act must attach a gratification, the desire for which may serve as a stimulus."[6] In other words, primitive man was a predatory animal. This led to war and the conquest of one human group by another. But "the conquest of one people over another has been in the main the conquest of the social man over the anti-social man; or, strictly speaking, of the more-adapted over the less-adapted."[7] Therefore, Spencer assumes that the

---

[5] Spencer, *Principles of Sociology*, Vol. I, Part I, Chapter XXVII, p. 426.

[6] *Social Statics*, p. 234; quoted by Lichtenberger, *op. cit.*, p. 315.

[7] See Lichtenberger, *op. cit.*, p. 316.

struggle for existence results in the survival of the superior in a majority of cases; and that through struggle and survival we can sufficiently account for the rise of the level of civilization and of the type of human society. Through struggle, adaptation, and selection, equilibration is secured, and also the elimination of the nonadapted.

Spencer makes much of primitive religion, the root of which he finds in the fear of the dead. Human society arises out of the primordial ideas and emotions that primitive man developed. Primitive man, on account of his inability to think abstractedly, could not differentiate clearly between the subjective and the objective, and, hence, could not differentiate clearly between his waking life and his dream life. In dreams and in other abnormal mental states, primitive man saw departed comrades, and many other objects. He was not able to distinguish these objects of his dreams from real objects. Moreover, his observation of the world around him confirmed him in the belief that all sorts of changes are possible in objects, and especially in plants and animals. His experience with shadows, reflections, and echoes also gave rise to the conception of the duality of things. Therefore, primitive man came to believe from all of these experiences that there was a soul independent of the body, and that all objects were endowed with doubles, or "spirits." From this primitive dualism, which Spencer presents as essentially an error of the primitive mind, sprang religious and metaphysical beliefs. Coupled with the emotion of fear, these gave rise to religion and to the various systems of superstitious beliefs. Chief among these was ancestor worship, in the sense of the fear and veneration of the dead. Spencer concludes that ancestor worship is the root of every religion." [8]

Spencer held that the beginning of human institutions and of human society was to be found in such ideas, beliefs, and emotions of primitive man. These original intrinsic factors, as he called them, conditioned by the original extrinsic factors of climate, flora, fauna, and soil, including physical and racial traits, were the basis of all later social development. That development was almost entirely a process of unconscious gradual adjustment brought about by the interaction between these original social factors, both inner and outer.

Doctrine of social development. Spencer's original doctrine of social development, or evolution, is to be found, not in the *Principles of Sociology,* but in certain paragraphs of his *First Principles.* In these paragraphs, he attempts to apply his famous formula of evolution to the problems of social development. In other words, he attempts to make social evolution a phase of the redistribution of matter and energy. He argues that societies show increasing definiteness of arrangement, and therefore proceed from the indefinite to the definite. He also holds that societies pass from a homogeneous state to a heterogeneous state, and, therefore, illustrate the laws of differenti-

---

[8] Spencer, *Principles of Sociology,* Part I, Chapter XXV, p. 411.

ation and of segregation.   Finally, he holds that societies, like physical aggregates, pass from stages of less coherence to stages of more coherence.   This he calls the law of integration.

In his *Principles of Sociology,* however, Spencer does not attempt to carry out this interpretation in terms of the redistribution of matter and the equilibration of energy.   Rather, he resorts to the biological principle of the survival of the fit, and to the Lamarckian principle of the inheritance of useful adaptations.   A single example will suffice for our purposes.   In accordance with his general method, he holds that, primitively, all forms of family life and of sex relation existed in confusion, but that gradually, by the elimination of inferior forms of the family (such as promiscuity, polyandry, and polygyny), monogamy in its present form was evolved and became prevalent.   Monogamy, he believes, is becoming "innate" in man, and, with this touch of Lamarckism he concludes his discussion of the family.[9]

It should be added that Spencer holds that this biological interpretation of social evolution is entirely in harmony with the mechanistic.   In any case, the process is automatic and takes place through the great forces of nature.   He makes no place, for example, for the learning of individuals or of society.   In other words, he does not conceive of social development as fundamentally a psychological process.   Even mental adaptations are the result of the equili-

---

[9] Spencer, *Principles of Sociology,* Part III, Chapters XII and VIII, especially pp. 673 and 745.

bration of energy that lies at the bottom of all processes of development. Back of all mental and social processes, he believes, lie physical processes that can be interpreted mechanistically.

This might be further illustrated by Spencer's famous contrast between the militant and industrial types of society. He accepts Comte's idea that the militant type of society was primitive, and that it was destined to be superseded by a peaceful industrial type that is now just beginning to come into existence. Originally, man was predatory and warlike, but militancy required that the individual be ordered and controlled in a hard and fast way, that he live constantly under compulsion. The militant stage, accordingly, was characterized by lack of freedom on the part of the individual, and industry, as we know it, scarcely existed. Government was necessarily autocratic. But this militant stage of human society is destined to be succeeded by the development of the industrial stage through man gradually learning to control nature and to make things through his labor. Industry depends not upon compulsory co-operation, but upon voluntary co-operation. It is no longer necessary for the government to control the individual. Instead, it releases its control over the individual and lets him do what seems best to him. So the industrial stage gradually undermines the traditions of authority and caste that grew up under militarism. The whole organization of society under the industrial regime will be characterized by the least possible control by external authority, since everyone, in seeking his own interest, will be seeking, at the same time, the interests of society. All of this development Spencer calls a transition from status to contract, from slavery to freedom. The causes of war will be removed, and industry will firmly establish democracy and peace in human relations.[10]

But this development of the survival of the more peaceful types of individuals and societies, and the growing tendency to peaceful work and voluntary co-operation among men, Spencer believes, were brought about by essentially automatic forces, such as the elimination of the militant on the one hand, and the growing inheritance of tendencies toward peaceful labor and voluntary co-operation on the other hand. Even if thought could accelerate or retard this process, the evolution from the militant type to the industrial type was natural and inevitable.

Doctrine of social organization. In striking contrast to Spencer's doctrine of social development toward a state of absolute freedom and voluntary co-operation is his doctrine of social organization. For Spencer holds to the organismic theory of society. He holds that society is an organism, or rather, a superorganism. It is impossible to know exactly what he means by society, but he seems to imply that a society is a national group. He tells us that society is a real entity, and, therefore, places himself with the social realists, even though he is at the same time an individualist.

---

[10] See *Principles of Sociology*, Part V, Chapters XVII and XVIII.

He gives four analogies between a society and a biological organism. Both a human society and a biological organism exhibit in their development (1) continuous growth; (2) increasing complexity of parts; (3) increasing dependence of parts; and (4) possible independent life of organism and individual part. But Spencer also finds these differences between a society and a biological organism: (1) a society lacks specific external form; (2) its units are discrete and dispersed, instead of being in contact; (3) it has greater mobility of parts; and (4) each individual of a society is a center of feeling and intelligence. He concludes that the similarities are more important than the differences, and that we may be justified in calling society an organism, or, at least, a superorganism.[11]

Spencer goes on to develop this biological analogy. He finds that every society has a sustaining system, a distributing system, and a regulating system, corresponding to systems of nutrition, circulation, and regulation in the biological organism. The sustaining system includes all the productive industries that are concerned in the making of the material goods necessary to the life of society. The distributing system includes all means of traffic, transportation, and communication. The regulating system includes all the organs of government, not only those connected with the political state, but those developed for the regulation and control of individuals en-

---

[11] *Op. cit.*, Part II, Chapter II.

gaged in private enterprises, of one sort or another.[12]

One would expect that, with such an organic analogy, Spencer would have declared himself in favor of state socialism, or, at least, in favor of an autocratic government, as he likened the central nervous system in its functioning to the central political government. But he does nothing of the sort. When it comes to actual political, economic, and social practice, his bias in favor of *laissez-faire* individualism, acquired from early Victorian English politics, leads him to cast aside both evolution and the organic analogy. He does this on the basis of the differentiation and segregation that we find in the social organism in contrast with a biological organism. "In the one," he tells us, "consciousness is concentrated in a small part of the aggregate. In the other, it is diffused throughout the aggregate; all the units possess the capacity for happiness and misery, if not in equal degrees, still in degrees that are approximate." [13] Because human society is such a "discrete" organism, its government rests with its units, with its separate adult individuals. The classification of governments as monarchical, aristocratic, and democratic is superficial. Government, as we know it, is almost wholly a development of the military stage of human society. With the passing of militancy, it will tend to disappear. Its sole functions have been to preserve order and discipline within the society and to protect against external

---

[12] *Ibid.*, Chapters VII, VIII, IX.
[13] *Ibid.*, p. 449.

enemies. With the passing of militancy, these functions will be reduced to a minimum, if they do not
altogether disappear; for the compulsory co-operation of militarism will be replaced by the voluntary
co-operation of industry. Militarism molds social organization into fitness for habitual warfare. Hence,
under militarism, government is necessary. Industry, on the other hand, molds social organization into
fitness for peaceful co-operative living; under it,
therefore, government will tend to disappear, or to
take on the character of voluntary co-operation,[14] for
the economic life of developed industry is too complicated to submit to governmental regulation by a
centralized political authority. Any attempt at governmental regulation of industry will end in disaster
and should be discouraged. A system of natural
liberty in industry is best suited to bring about social
and economic progress. The government that governs least is best. Thus Spencer ends his discussion
of the functions of government with a near approach
to the position of the philosophical anarchist.

But Spencer is not satisfied with the setting up of
a *laissez-faire* philosophy simply for government and
industry. He carries it more or less consistently
through every phase of social life. He would not
have an established church, and he strongly implies
that he is not in favor of organized religion at all.
He would not have any state poor relief, but would
limit charity to the spontaneous acts of helpfulness

[14] *Op cit.*, Part V, Chapter XIX.

between friends and acquaintances. He would not have any social legislation to protect the weak, because he says that the net result of such legislation is "to fill the world with fools." He seemed quite unconscious of the brutal exploitation of the laboring classes and even of children, which early British industry had introduced. He would have no state-supported education, but education only through private agencies, as he held that education was a matter that should be controlled entirely by parents, and that it was a fallacy to place the state in the place of the parent. Finally, he would have no public sanitation, as this was an expense that did not properly belong to the government. Absurd as it may seem to us, he was opposed even to a state post office, and thought that private agencies could carry and distribute the mails better than the government.

Thus Spencer stood for a system of natural liberty, not only in industry, but in the moral and social realms as well; and probably no more consistent exponent of all-round *laissez-faire* principles is to be found among modern thinkers, with the possible exception of the philosophical anarchists. The reader should notice that all of these positions of Spencer are rooted in his extreme naturalistic philosophy of human society, and especially in his belief that the natural forces of evolution tend to bring about a stage of perfection.

Doctrine of social progress. Spencer is justly accused of confusing evolution with progress, and of popularizing the idea that the forces of nature make human progress inevitable. He tried to deny that he had ever advocated such a doctrine, but there are too many passages in his works that support this idea. He says, for example, "Evolution can end only in the establishment of the greatest perfection and the most complete happiness." Let us remember that by evolution he means the integration of matter and the equilibration of energy. Again, he tells us, "The ultimate development of the ideal man is logically certain—as certain as any conclusion in which we place the most implicit faith." One is inclined to say that Spencer shares the social optimism of Condorcet, but it is an optimism upon an altogether different basis. Condorcet's optimism was based upon the inevitableness of the increase and diffusion of knowledge. Spencer's optimism is based upon the nature of the cosmic process as an equilibration of energy. Evolution inevitably moves in the direction of such equilibration, and will inevitably establish it for human society; with it will come that perfect adaptation of man to the conditions of his life that will bring about complete happiness. But such progress, through natural evolution, is conditioned, Spencer argued, upon noninterference with the natural process. The natural process of adjustment through natural selection and unconscious adaptation will bring about, in the long run, better results than any that can be secured by human intelligence. Evolution, therefore, virtually assures progress. Hence also, Spencer's extreme advocacy of the doctrine of natural liberty and *laissez faire.*

===== *Spencer's Ethics* =====

Spencer cannot be understood as a social thinker unless we pay attention to his ethics. He himself tells us that his ultimate purpose in all of his social philosophy was to find the principles of right and wrong. We have already seen how he laid aside the completion of the *Principles of Sociology* because, he said, "Now that moral injunctions are losing the authority given by their supposed sacred origin, the secularization of morals is becoming imperative." Again, he tells us, "Few things can happen more disastrous than the decay and death of a regulative system no longer fit, before another fitter regulative system has grown up to replace it." Hence, in a certain sense, Spencer's whole life work may be viewed as an attempt to find a scientific basis for ethics. But, unlike Comte, he was not content to take over his system of ethics from the teachings of the Christian church, and to attempt simply to find a scientific basis for the ethics of love that the church had taught when at its best. On the contrary, Spencer attempts to find new sanctions for conduct in natural conditions. Just as Voltaire had advocated "natural religion," so Spencer became the great advocate in the nineteenth century of "natural morality." He tells us that this new morality must be built upon the science of biology. It will be evolutionary, but as perfect adaptation leads not only to survival, but also to happiness,

Spencer espouses hedonism upon an evolutionary basis. He lays it down as a fundamental principle that "sentient existence can evolve only on condition that pleasure-giving acts are life-sustaining acts." Right conduct will therefore favor not only adjustment and survival, but also the increase of happiness. Progress, he implies, may be viewed as an increase of happiness, a thought that Lester F. Ward was to take up later. But right conduct is at bottom a social matter. It is a matter that concerns the interrelations of men, the establishment of justice in human relations. Hence, ethics brings in again every phase of the problem of human relations. It is simply an extension of psychology and sociology to define and ascertain the principles of right and wrong conduct.

In the field of ethics, as in the field of politics and industry, Spencer is confident that his principle of natural liberty should be the guiding principle. Every man should be free, he tells us, to do that which he will, provided he infringes not the equal freedom of any other man. Upon the basis of this natural right, Spencer defends practically the whole system of natural rights, including life, liberty, and the pursuit of happiness, as these were understood in his day. For the same reason, he defends private property as an absolute right, and from it springs the right of bequest or inheritance without limitation by the state.

Even more strongly than Comte, Spencer is the champion of social order, and the defense of the individual in his private rights. All aggressions of individuals upon one another, upon each other's rights, he severely condemns. He particularly, therefore, condemns all acts of aggression between nations. He calls war ''wholesale cannibalism,'' and argues more strongly for international peace than perhaps any other English-speaking writer of the nineteenth century. He tells us ''The possibility of a high social state fundamentally depends upon the cessation of war.'' But the cessation of war depends upon the establishment of the industrial stage of society with its voluntary co-operation. The end of war will not come merely through moral conversion to the ideal of peace. It can come only through the development of peaceful industry. However, Spencer believed, even to the very last, that this development was at bottom a matter of evolution through the equilibration of energy. Thus, in the very last years of his life, we find him saying, ''The change from militarism to industrialism depends upon the extent of the equilibrium of energy between any given society and its neighboring societies, between the societies of any given race and those of other races, between society in general and its physical environment. Peaceful industrialism cannot finally be established until the equilibrium of nations and of races is established.''

Hence, Spencer looked forward to the spread of the voluntary co-operative movement as the chief practical solution of the problems and perplexities of our time. Socialism he identified with the militant type of social organization. It was another attempt at the "regimentation" of society, bound to end in lack of freedom, and ultimately in social disaster. We may add, therefore, that Spencer looked forward in the later years of his life with great apprehension to the rise of labor parties in politics, and to the possible establishment of a labor government. He regarded such a possibility with apprehension because he believed that it would result in the reversion of human society to the military stage of social organization.

Yet we must remember that, with all of his advocacy of natural liberty and *laissez faire,* Spencer was not championing the cause of any class, but believed himself to be the champion of the true cause of humanity. This is shown clearly enough throughout his work, but perhaps nowhere more clearly than in those memorable paragraphs with which he closes his *Principles of Ethics:*

> There exist a few who . . . look forward through unceasing changes, now progressive, now retrogressive, to the evolution of a Humanity adjusted to the requirements of its life. And along with this belief there arises, in an increasing number, the desire to further the development. . . . Hereafter, the highest ambition of the beneficent will be to have a share—even though an utterly inappreciable and unknown share—in "the making of Man." Experience occasionally shows that there may arise extreme interest in pursuing entirely unselfish ends; and, as time goes on, there will be more and more of those whose unselfish end will be the further evolution of Humanity.[15]

[15] Spencer, *Principles of Ethics,* Vol. II, Part VI, Chapter X, p. 433.

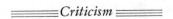

Spencer's social philosophy was a product of the extreme naturalism and individualism of the nineteenth century. His naturalism, indeed, verged upon a mechanistic materialism, though at the same time it was optimistic. The optimism of Condorcet was replaced in Spencer by an optimism that rested upon faith in blind nature. It represented the complacency of the natural science of his time. Closely connected with his naturalistic optimism was Spencer's *laissez-faire* individualism, which, we may say, represented the complacency of nineteenth-century political England. However, as we have seen, in Spencer, individualism triumphed over his mechanistic naturalism. When it came to practical issues, Spencer did not hesitate to lay aside his mechanistic determinism and his organic analogy. His modified ethical hedonism was undoubtedly more rooted in his social and political prejudices than in his biological theories.

In all of these matters, Spencer was a child of his age. He rarely rose above the influence of his social environment. Still more rarely was he critical of his own thinking. He failed almost completely to get any cultural view of human society, in spite of his liberal use of the comparative, or ethnographic, method. He seemed to think of human society as a sort of a machine of the gods that we could describe but could hardly attempt safely to control. As Ward said, there is hardly a trace of "anthropo-teleology" in Spencer's writings. If he considered the purposes of man at all, they were considered as the outcome of essentially automatic processes.

Yet Spencer did more than any other man in the nineteenth century to popularize sociology in the English-speaking world. He had the good sense to see that fractional social sciences could never take the place of a synthetic social philosophy. Moreover, in Spencer's hands, as has been well said, "Comte's promise began to assume something of the aspect of a definite program of scientific activity." Particularly was Spencer's influence great in the United States. His emphasis upon the difficulties, both subjective and objective, of the development of social science was a wholesome influence, even though he was unable to appreciate the difficulties in his own mind. The total effect of his work was therefore to forward greatly the sociological movement in the English-speaking world. Nevertheless, we cannot agree with Dr. Durant that, "No man, not even Comte, has done so much for sociology." We should more nearly agree, however, with the estimate of another critic, with which we may fittingly close our study of Spencer:

It is all very well to say that Spencer's sociology is out of date. That is true only in a little larger degree than would be the assertion that the astronomy of Copernicus, or the physics of Galileo, is out of date. Spencer's sociology is one of the rungs on the ladder by which his successors have been able to climb. As no science can be completely mastered apart from its history, the student of sociology must thoroughly study the works of its two great fore-runners—Comte and Spencer.[16]

---

[16] Lewis, *An Introduction to Sociology*, p. 88; quoted by Lichtenberger, *Development of Social Theory*, p. 350.

CHAPTER XXVI

The Organismic School of Sociology

IT IS DIFFICULT TO say just what the connection was between Herbert Spencer and other advocates of the organic analogy in social philosophy. The connection was probably indirect rather than direct. We should remember that Spencer had published much in the way of occasional papers before he published his *Principles of Sociology*. These occasional writings of Spencer seeped through to the German-speaking world. We should remember also that Professor Ernst Haeckel, the German biologist, was a friend of both Darwin and Spencer. In the case of Lilienfeld, there is no question as to Haeckel's influence. We should remember finally that the organic analogy was in the air—that it had been stated in very vague terms by Auguste Comte and several other writers. While in Spencer the organic analogy was not a necessary part of his system of thought, it was made the principal part of their systems by several social

467

thinkers on the Continent.   The chief of these was
a Russian, Paul von Lilienfeld.

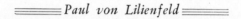

Biographical sketch.   Lilienfeld was a descendant
of a noble Swedish family that had settled in Russia
and become a part of the Russian autocracy.   He was
born in 1829 and died in 1903.   He held a number of
official positions under the Russian government, especially as governor of the Russian province of Kur-
land.   From 1873 to 1881 he published a five-volume
work entitled *Thoughts About the Social Science of
the Future.*   It will be noted that a part of his work
was published before Spencer's *Principles of Sociology.*   Lilienfeld is probably the most extreme
representative of the analogical school.   Let us note
briefly, therefore, his method and the content of his
social philosophy.[1]

Scientific method.   One is inclined to say that
Lilienfeld's method could by no means be called scientific, for it consisted in tracing minute analogies
between a biological organism and a human society.
One of his mottoes was, "No one is a sociologist, unless he is a biologist"; but he meant by this that the
sociologist must have enough knowledge of biological
organisms to trace similarities between them and hu-

------

[1] A fuller account of Lilienfeld's social philosophy can be found
in Professor F. W. Coker's *Organismic Theories of the State,* pp. 139–
153.   (No. 101 of Columbia University *Studies in History, Economics,
and Public Law.*)

man social groups. Apparently the social group that Lilienfeld called a "society" was the autonomous nation-state. One may more than suspect that a principal reason for Lilienfeld's use of the analogical method was that it gave him an opportunity to defend the Russian autocracy and its institutions.

Social philosophy. The first volume of Lilienfeld's *Thoughts About the Social Science of the Future* was entitled "Human Society as a Real Organism." Lilienfeld was not only a social realist, but a "real organicist." He calls society a "real organism," not an entity like an organism, or a "super-organism," as Spencer had said. Human societies are real organisms, but of a different class than biological organisms. He goes on to enumerate many likenesses between a human society and a biological organism. The individuals in a human society correspond to the cells in the biological organism. Just as the brain rules over the body, so in the social organism there must be a central portion that rules over the rest. In Russia, this is the autocracy. Russia, therefore, represents not a low stage of social evolution, but a high stage of social development. Thus Lilienfeld turns the organic analogy into an instrument for the defense of the Russian autocracy. All societies must be governed by an elite, and the governing elite represents in society what the brain and the nervous system represent in the biological organism; that is, the indispensable means of social integration and social control.

Lilienfeld makes little use of Spencer's mechanistic principles of evolution, but he holds, nevertheless, that the social organism goes through essentially the same stages of development and organization that a biological organism goes through.   There is for societies, as for biological organisms, an organic cycle of growth and decay, an inner unity of life, a correlation of forces working out in purposeful action, a trend toward perfection, and a storing up and transmission of surplus energy.   The last two, however, are especially characteristic of human personalities and human societies.   They show that social organisms are not a low form of organic life, but are the highest form.   They are especially marked off from animal groups by the storing up and transmission of energy in all of its forms, which Lilienfeld terms a process of "capitalization."

A further similarity of human societies and biological organisms is that both are subject to diseases. Probably it is right to say that Comte and Spencer paid but little attention to problems of social maladjustment, and that here Lilienfeld introduces a new note.   In 1896, he published a work entitled *Social Pathology,* in which he sought to show how disease may affect society in the same way that it affects a highly developed biological organism.   Social maladies correspond roughly to nervous diseases.   Disturbances in industry he likened to insanity; disturbances in the administration of justice, to delirium; and disturbances in political administration, to paralysis.   He surely should have added that the policemen of civil society are like the phagocytes in the

blood; they exist to protect the social body from enemies and intruders of all sorts!

These biological analogies of Lilienfeld seem more
amusing than informing to us. Comte had warned
the social thinkers of his time not to press the biological analogy too far; but if Lilienfeld knew of Comte's
warning, he did not heed it. The development, or
evolution, of society, he thought, was also like that of
a biological organism. Human societies start in a
sort of amoeba state, and, through evolution, develop
their perfected forms. Just as the biological world
is filled with survivals from past stages of organic
evolution, so the social world is also filled with survivals from past stages of social evolution. Even
within any particular national group can be found co-
existing all the types of culture traversed by man in
his ascent from savagery to civilization. This may
be true; but, as Professor Ross says, Lilienfeld
scarcely gave the right explanation of these survivals.[2] With Lilienfeld, this law of recapitulation
of the forms of culture was taken over from Haeckel's
law of individual recapitulation, according to which
the individual person recapitulates in his development the culture periods of racial history.

We need hardly say that Lilienfeld's use of the organic analogy was not particularly illuminating for
the processes of human society. The analogy became in his hands, however, as indeed it was to some
extent in Spencer's, a means of justifying an extreme

[2] Ross, *The Foundations of Sociology*, p. 48.

social and political conservatism. Everything in human society was a product of nature. Like Topsy, it "just growed." But as nature was beneficent, the growth was conceived to be toward perfection. Any interference on the part of man in this process of natural development would be unwise, even if it did not result in disaster. Quite evidently, the organic analogy was, in some degree, a natural reaction to the contract theory of society with its radical, if not revolutionary, implications. It seems probable, too, that the extreme realistic development of the organic analogy by such thinkers as Lilienfeld had much to do with its demise.

Albert Schaeffle

Biographical sketch. A very different use of the biological analogy was made by Albert Schaeffle, a German economist and sociologist of liberal and progressive ideas. Schaeffle was born in 1831 and died in 1903, the same year as Spencer and Lilienfeld. He was primarily an economist. For many years he was a professor of economics at the University of Tübingen. Later he was a professor at the University of Vienna, and for one year was the Austrian Minister of Commerce. He wrote a number of books along economic lines. He was usually reckoned among the "socialists of the chair," although in 1875 he published a book entitled *The Quintessence of Socialism,* criticizing the socialist movement, which largely

alienated the German Social-Democratic party.
Schaeffle's main interest all along seems to have been
in sociology, and in 1875–1878 he published a large
work in four volumes entitled *The Structure and Life
of the Social Body.* In the German-speaking world,
this was one of the epoch-making treatises in sociology. He condensed this work into two volumes, and
published the revised edition in 1896. Usually this
work is thought of as an elaboration and variation of
Spencer's organismic theory of society. The reader
will note, however, that the first edition was published
in part before Spencer's *Principles of Sociology* appeared. It seems probable that Spencer's influence
upon Schaeffle was, therefore, indirect rather than
direct. It is worthy of note, too, that Schaeffle always held that the organic analogy was not necessary
to his sociology. He, therefore, prepared an outline
of his theory minus the organic analogy, entitled *Outline of Sociology,* which was not published until 1906,
three years after his death.

Scientific method. We have already seen that
Schaeffle was a trained economist. He was one of
the first to lead the revolt against Spencer's anthropological, or ethnographical, method. He says, in
effect, Why should we turn to the study of primitive
and barbarous peoples when we see social facts right
before our eyes? He argues for the use of analysis
of the social process in contemporary social life, "a
process now going on before our very eyes." The
structure and functioning of society as it is at present
has greater value for the sociologist than the analysis

of primitive and barbarous society. However, Schaeffle did not neglect the anthopological approach to social facts and theories. In all of this, Schaeffle was inductive and modern. Moreover, he was sociological in his approach to social facts because he advocated the group approach, first through the study of the family, then the community, then the "Volk." Accepting the struggle for existence as a determiner of social conditions, he held that the unit of struggle is always the group.

Nevertheless, in his chief work, *The Structure and Life of the Social Body,* Schaeffle is held by the organic analogy. He believed firmly that this analogy could furnish great clews to sociological truth. Accordingly, he divides his work on the basis of the organic analogy into (1) social physiology and morphology, (2) social psychology, or the study of the psychic facts of social life, and (3) social pathology, or the study of the evils of society. It is very evident that these names, in a certain sense, are misnomers. Yet they have stuck to sociology and are still used. Schaeffle was one of the first to use the term social psychology, not in the sense of the study of the social behavior of the individual, but in the sense of the study of the mental facts of social life.

Schaeffle's conception of general sociology was that it was an organization or philosophy of the results of the special social sciences. This has been a favorite conception of sociology by some economists, and has been endorsed by some sociologists, especially by the late Professor Small of the University of Chicago.[3]

Social philosophy. Unlike Spencer, Schaeffle throws his emphasis upon co-operation, or mutual aid, as the constitutive principle of human social life. Consequently, he also emphasizes social processes of growth and development. He starts, to be sure, with the mutual aid found in animal groups, but he holds that organic evolution has issued in the still higher form of co-operation that we find in human society. In the opening paragraph of his chief work he tells us,

> At the very summit of the phenomena of life on our earth stands human society,—the social body and its private and national institutions. Built up out of matter, and impelled by forces of the inorganic and organic world, it is nevertheless a living body of a peculiar kind. Human or civil society, a far higher structure than the societies of animals, is a purely spiritual result, an indivisible social life of organized individuals wrought out through the force of ideas and achievements of art.

It is evident that Schaeffle seeks to emphasize the spiritual and purposive character of human society. Human society, he says, is a fact that concerns men's minds. The social groups of men represent life purposes, and function to achieve life ends. The life of an autonomous human group is, therefore, a spiritual

---

[3] A simplification of Schaeffle's fundamental positions and methods can be found in Small and Vincent, *Introduction to the Study of Society* (1894), one of the first elementary textbooks in sociology to come into general use in the United States.

unity.   However, Schaeffle says that every mental or spiritual unity of which we have knowledge has an organic basis.   Human society represents not only an interrelation of minds, but of life processes.   Accordingly, society can be likened to an organism. The organic theory in Spencer, says Small, is mechanical or physical; but in Schaeffle it becomes functional, and so it is more of a spiritual analogy.[4] Moreover, Schaeffle does not push this analogy to the extreme that we have noticed in Lilienfeld.

Schaeffle makes much of struggle and adaptation in human society.   The struggle is not so much for existence, however, as for a kind of existence.   It becomes a struggle of interests, which characterizes the co-operative labor of human society, and which brings about the transformation of civilization in the line of the greatest possible perfectionment.   Struggle thus creates persons, institutions, and parties best adapted for social competition and social conflict. Those persons, institutions, and parties that are relatively fittest for this struggle survive, while enemies and rivals that are unadapted are forced to a lower level of existence.   The best adapted, therefore, attain supremacy and development.

In his doctrine of social organization, Schaeffle traces out the general arrangements of human society and likens them to the tissues of the animal body.   Some tissues are protective, some are concerned with nutrition, and some concerned with reg-

---

[4] Small, *General Sociology*, p. 167.   Chapters X and XI of this work contain a brief résumé of Schaeffle's social philosophy.

ulation. Like Lilienfeld and Spencer, Schaeffle connects government in human society with the brain and nerve tissues of the animal body. But the function of government, according to Schaeffle, is not merely protection against external enemies, and the preservation of internal order; its function is like that of the mind of the individual—to improve the welfare of the whole organism. Hence Schaeffle agrees with Lorenz von Stein that, practically, the function of the government is not only to stand above contending classes and parties as an umpire, but also to improve the condition of the backward members of the social body so as to make them fit members, and to organize the whole social life for social efficiency and well-being.

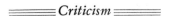

Criticism

In Schaeffle's hands, the organic analogy became not an instrument of conservatism, but a mildly progressive philosophy of social control and social betterment. However, analogical reasoning can never furnish valid science. Schaeffle himself apparently perceived this before his death. It is doubtful, moreover, if the organic analogy furnishes, as Schaeffle earlier thought, any great clew to the solution of social problems. Schaeffle himself stressed not so much the analogical method as the study of the social processes "going on before our eyes." This was the clew that later German sociologists took instead of following the organic analogy with Schaeffle.   If we study the social process "going on before our eyes," we do not need to neglect the historical process of development; but, in such a case, sociology becomes not merely a philosophy of the results of the special sciences, but, even more, the fundamental science of human association.

CHAPTER XXVII

The Conflict School of Sociology

WHETHER CONSERVATIVE OR mildly progressive, the likening of a human social group to an organism was bound to provoke reaction. The unity and harmony between the individuals in a human society, which seem to be implied by the use of the organic analogy, simply provoked laughter in cynically minded and "hard-boiled" social thinkers. Some, like Nietzsche, saw about as much unity and harmony in a human social group as they did in a dog fight. More sane-minded thinkers contented themselves with asserting that struggle and competition, either between groups or between individuals, were the very essence of the social process; that there was no unity in human social groups, except that which resulted from a "balance of egoisms." Thus, as a reaction to the organismic theory, there grew up the conflict school of sociologists.

Many of these conflict sociologists, because they

emphasized struggle and natural selection as the essential factors in the development of human society, were called "social Darwinists." These social Darwinists were a very numerous body of writers in western civilization, being well represented in England, France, and Germany.[1] Some were essentially followers of Nietzsche; but others took the group, or sociological, point of view, and, while they repudiated a social philosophy of individual struggle and individual egoism, they claimed that a social philosophy of group struggle and group egoism fitted the facts of human history and contemporary society. Chief among these social Darwinists, or conflict sociologists, in the nineteenth century was Ludwig Gumplowicz.

Ludwig Gumplowicz

Biographical sketch. Ludwig Gumplowicz was born in 1838 in the city of Cracow, in the extreme north of Austria. His parents were Polish Jews. He was educated at the Universities of Cracow and Vienna. In 1875 he became a docent in the University of Graz. In 1882 he was made an associate professor of law, and in 1893 he was raised to the rank of full professor. In studying the origin and evolution of law, he became interested in general sociology. In 1883 he published his fundamental work, *Race Con-*

---

[1] See House, *The Development of Sociology*, Chapter XIV.

flict (*Der Rassenkampf*), a book that we shall mainly cite, because Gumplowicz himself considered it the most important of his works. In 1885 he published his *Outline of Sociology,* which is also important for understanding his system of thought. Finally, in 1906, he published *An Outline of Social Philosophy,* in which he presents a revision of his views greatly moderated; but this was after he had come under the influence of Lester F. Ward. In 1909, finding that he was afflicted with an incurable cancer of the tongue, he and his wife, who had been an invalid for a number of years, entered into a suicide pact, and took their lives at the same time.

Scientific method. Of all the social thinkers that we have considered, Gumplowicz held most rigidly to a strictly mechanistic conception of nature. This mechanistic conception, which he took over from Spencer, he believed held absolutely for the human mind and human society. "Modern natural science," he says, "has successfully demonstrated that every human mind is subject to physical laws, that the phenomena of the individual mind are emanations from matter."[2] The same is true for human societies; they are subject to physical laws, the laws of physical science. Hence, Gumplowicz, without reservation or equivocation, may be counted as a materialist. "Eternal iron laws" (the phrase is Gumplowicz's) determine all processes both in the physical and in the social worlds. "The alpha and omega

---

[2] *Outlines of Sociology* (Moore's translation, p. 74); quoted by Bristol in *Social Adaptation,* p. 162.

of sociology," he tells us, "its highest perception and final word is: human history is a natural process." [3] He calls his book, *Der Rassenkampf*, "a natural history of mankind." He accepts Spencer's theory of mechanistic evolution as an equilibration of energy, but criticizes Spencer for giving any place whatever to value judgments; for "sociology must refrain from all criticism of nature," and it is absurd to set up value judgments in a rigidly deterministic system. Whatever is, is nature; and the only effort of the sociologist should be to understand and describe natural processes. He also criticizes Spencer for taking the individual unit as his standard instead of the primitive horde. Sociology is concerned with the behavior of groups, with intergroup relations. The sociologist as such has no business to raise the question of the origin of these groups. Social origins, in this sense, are a problem with which sociology has nothing to do. It is not concerned with genesis, but with "becoming." Sociology begins with the countless different groups of which mankind is constituted. Primitively, these groups were made up of heterogeneous ethnic elements. Originally, Gumplowicz believes, these groups were different races, and he argues that this is supported by both logic and historical observation.

Gumplowicz leaves no place for the creative individual. He does not altogether despise psychology; but he lays it down that:

---

[3] *Ibid.*, p. 453.

The great error of individualistic psychology is the supposition that man thinks. . . . It is not man himself who thinks, but his social community; the source of his thoughts is in the social medium in which he lives, the social atmosphere which he breathes, and he cannot think aught else than what the influences of his social environment concentrating upon his brain necessitate. . . . What we think is a necessary result of the mental influences to which we have been subjected since childhood. . . . Man is not self-made mentally any more than he is physically. His mind and thoughts are the product of his social medium, of the social element whence he arose, in which he lives.[4]

It follows, therefore, that a scientific interpretation of human society is possible only if we posit man as "a non-free part of nature." Even if we cannot prove this assumption for individuals, it is easily provable for the behavior of social groups. They are absolutely governed in their relations to each other by rigid inflexible laws, as definite as those that govern the planets in their orbits, or the development of an organism. These laws are not deducible from the qualities of individuals, according to Gumplowicz. Therefore, social phenomena constitute a unique group of phenomena, separate from the physical and mental even though it is rooted in them. The sociologist must study the interaction of human groups, or the interrelations of human groups as they are disclosed by history and by present society. The unit of his study is the group, not the individual.

---

[4] *Outlines of Sociology*, pp. 156–160; quoted by Lichtenberger, *Development of Sociology*, p. 449.

Social philosophy. Originally, as we have seen, there were a number of small groups of men, each with its own language, morals, religion, each with great similarity among its individual members, but each unlike other groups, and with a hatred of every other horde or group. How these groups originated, Gumplowicz does not take time to consider, but they were unlike, each with its own hereditary traits, and each group living for itself. Gumplowicz's argument for this view of human social origins is that, the farther we go back into history,[5] the greater number of different ethnic stocks we find, and also the greater number of languages and religions. Races, languages, and religions have tended to diminish in number during the period of history. Mixed hordes or groups have resulted, but each, manifesting the extreme of herd feeling, considers itself "the chosen people." Other groups are fit only to be eaten or to be despoiled. Hence arises a second stage, and that is the struggle of these unlike groups to conquer each other.

History, Gumplowicz tells us, is a process of the assimilation of the heterogeneous. The primitive groups hated one another and entered into struggle with one another. Warfare developed with the increase of population, and, by the union of groups fairly equal in strength, tribes were formed to crush other groups. This led to triple and quadruple alliances, but always with the purpose of war. Gumplowicz agrees with Hobbes that the original condi-

---

[5] Cf. Lichtenberger, pp. 446–447.

tion of mankind was one of actual or potential war. Hostility and exploitation were primitive. Human societies are not expanded families based on natural affection. They are made up of heterogeneous groups held together by military force.

The state takes its rise, therefore, through the consolidation of such fighting groups. The mutual assimilation or alliance of such groups forms the nations or the state. The state, in other words, is always the result of some conquering group imposing its sovereignty upon conquered groups. The government of the state is always that of a minority who represent this conquering group. With all other classes enslaved or held in rigid subjection, the conquering group develops leisure; and higher forms of culture, as well as new social classes, begin to arise. Originally, social classes were formed on the basis of race, but, with the rise of the state, they begin to be formed on the basis of economic status. After the conquest of some new group, the sovereign, or ruling, class frees a part or all of its slaves. These freed slaves form a middle class without the full rights of the ruling class, and, like the ruling class, devote themselves to the exploitation of weaker classes. This the middle class does mainly through trade and industry, both of which are but forms of exploitation. All political states are, therefore, founded upon inequality of classes and the lack of freedom of some classes. All political states are characterized by the rule of minorities who strive to hold their positions and privileges.

But a further stage of social development now begins to manifest itself. In order to get a greater share of the good things of life, the oppressed classes arise in the name of such ideals as human rights, freedom, and equality. This is really a struggle between the "ins" and the "outs," and an attempt of the lower classes to scramble to the top. It is the stage in which we are now living.

As regards social organization, Gumplowicz holds that all stratifications of classes in society had their beginnings in conquest and in the clashing of racial and group interests. They are perpetuated by this process of class struggle, each class or caste endeavoring to keep the other in its place by seeking its own advantage through the exploitation of the others. Some mollifying factors are discernible in language and religion. The conquerors usually impose their language upon the conquered and proclaim their gods as superior, admitting the gods of conquered people to inferior rank. This is a great aid to the conquerors in maintaining their power, and, at the same time, these two agencies foster the solidarity of the state and make possible the development of a common economic, political, and national life. Under such circumstances, hatred and antagonism are now directed toward other peoples, and growing, developing states seek other states to conquer. There is, therefore, no trend toward international peace among nations.

Certain things in this conflict sociology of Gumplowicz now come out. This struggle of races and classes is the essential content of human history.

The process widens, but it never changes its character. Because of the eternal similarity of the moving forces in history, it can never cease. What has been, always will be. Gumplowicz tells us that sociology has nothing to do with the philosophy of history; but he has a philosophy of history of the most startling sort. Race and class opposition are the eternal moving forces of history. They are the sole factors in the human social process. They make the actions, reactions, and interactions of groups. The struggle does not change in its character. The struggle between modern states and between classes in the state is still essentially like the struggle of savage hordes. There is no limit but that which is imposed by force. Man is still essentially the same savage that he has always been. He assumes new forms of behavior, but remains essentially the same. He appropriates more of the goods of life, adds the veneer of civilization, but still remains at heart the same egoistic savage. It is not the egoism of individuals, however, but of groups. The individual is altruistic regarding his group. It is the group that is egoistic, and this egoistic spirit of groups, whether of classes, nations, or races, is, so far as we can learn, unlimited.

Gumplowicz tells us that "ideals have no power in human history." The belief that they do have is all an illusion. Social ideals, such as human rights, justice, freedom, and equality, are simply shibboleths of groups that are seeking power. They are symbols, or rather weapons, of groups that are seeking advantages. If such groups rise to power, they continue the exploitation initiated by early conquering groups. Moreover, there is no such thing as the general social progress of humanity. Nor is there hope of such progress. Social progress, or amelioration, if it occurs, is always partial, local, and limited in time. ''We can form no conception of the evolution of mankind as a unitary whole, because we have no comprehensive conception of mankind.'' All that sociology can do is to describe the fluctuations that occur among different peoples through the struggle of races and of classes:

> Even though, short-sighted and captivated by traditional views of human freedom and self-determination, one should believe that this knowledge derogates from morals and undermines them, yet it is, on the contrary, the crown of all human morals, because it preaches most impressively man's renunciatory subordination to the laws of nature which alone rule history. By contributing to the knowledge of these laws sociology lays the foundation for the morals of reasonable resignation, morals higher than those resting on the imaginary freedom and self-determination of the individual.[6]

Out of the understanding of the human social process, according to Gumplowicz, can come one good thing—resignation. Gumplowicz, for this reason, has been called a Stoic, but he was rather Buddhistic in his religious and moral views.

---

[6] *Outlines of Sociology*, p. 210; quoted by Lichtenberger, *op. cit.*, p. 452.

===== *Criticism* =====

Gumplowicz deserves to be classified among the one-sided social philosophers, perhaps quite as much as any of the theorists we mentioned under that section. He exaggerated the factors of conflict and of race to such a degree that all other factors are obscured. Even his contemporary, Ratzenhofer, in a veiled reference, spoke of his contribution as "wild fruit on the tree of science." In extenuation, it may be said that Gumplowicz was a member of a subject minority group in that curious conglomeration of twenty-seven different ethnic groups that were held together by force in the old Austro-Hungarian Empire. This social fact undoubtedly accounts for most of the theories in *Der Rassenkampf*. In further extenuation, it should again be mentioned that, after Lester F. Ward paid him a famous visit in 1903, Gumplowicz greatly modified his views in a melioristic direction.

===== *Gustav Ratzenhofer* =====

Biographical sketch. A very different type of conflict theorist was Gustav Ratzenhofer, a member of the dominant German element in the Austro-Hungarian Empire, and a high military officer. In Ratzenhofer's hands, the conflict theory took a mild form, favorable not only to the conservation of essential social values, but even to the attainment of permanent peace. Just as Lilienfeld and Schaeffle illustrate the extremes of the organismic theory, so Gumplowicz and Ratzenhofer illustrate the extremes of the conflict theory. It is doubtful, indeed, whether we should speak of Ratzenhofer as a social Darwinist.

Gustav Ratzenhofer was born in Vienna in 1842. His father was a watchmaker who died in his early youth, leaving the family in poor circumstances. At the age of sixteen, Gustav enlisted as a private in the Austro-Hungarian army. He served at the battle of Königgrätz, and, seeing the weakness of the Austrian army, he decided upon a military career, entering the Governmental Military Academy in 1868. By 1889 he had risen to the rank of colonel, and in 1898 was given the high rank of Lieutenant Field Marshal of the Austro-Hungarian army. At the same time, he was made president of the military supreme court in Vienna. In 1901, however, he retired on account of his health. In 1904 he visited the United States to deliver an address before the Congress of Arts and Sciences, held during the St. Louis Exposition. On his return voyage he died on board steamship.

Ratzenhofer was a self-educated man, and it is very remarkable that he escaped as much as he did from the class in which he was born and to which he belonged. In fact, it is remarkable that he should have been a sociologist at all. He seemed to have received his impetus from reading the works of Spencer and

Comte. He also must have been influenced by an earlier Austrian political thinker, Lorenz von Stein. He acknowledged, too, that he was influenced by Gumplowicz. His first books were along military lines, but in 1893 he published a three-volume work, *The Essence and Purpose of Politics* (*Wesen und Zweck der Politik*), a work which pleased Professor Small so much that he declared that in it "sociology attained its majority." This was followed in 1898 by a volume entitled *Sociological Knowledge* (*Sociologische Erkenntniss*). In 1908 his son edited and published a summary of his father's views in a volume entitled *Sociology*.

Scientific method. Like Spencer and Ward and many other social philosophers, Ratzenhofer makes his system of sociology a part of his system of general philosophy. This general philosophy he calls "positive monism," a system that is not unlike that of Spinoza. In his address at St. Louis he frankly said,

> Sociology is a *philosophical discipline*, not on a *basis of pure reasoning* merely, but rather on the basis of all real and intellectual facts correlated by the causality of all phenomena. Social life can be scientifically understood only on the basis of this monistic view of the world; that is, in the light of a philosophy which *subordinates all phenomena to a unifying principle.* . . .[7]

Ratzenhofer's philosophical system starts with

---

[7] From Ratzenhofer's address before the International Congress of Arts and Sciences, held in connection with the St. Louis Exposition in 1904; in *American Journal of Sociology*, Vol. X, pp. 177–88.

the assumption of an *Urkraft,* or *primal interest.* "Every form of phenomena from heavenly body to atom," he tells us, "and every organism is a part of the primal force with an interest appropriate to its particular development."[8] It follows that there are two kinds of consciousness in the universe: the consciousness of the undifferentiated primal force as it exists in every creature, and the consciousness of the differentiated primal force that has come up through the evolutionary process to that self-consciousness that has its highest expression in the adult civilized man. This endeavor on the part of the primal force to come to the largest and fullest experience of life is the cause of the differences between species. The primal force and the inborn interest of the individual are the two principles of creation working together to try out all possible conditions of successful living. The inborn interest in the individual is the prime factor in his attention, association, purpose, and will, conditioned, of course, by his organic structure and the influences of environment. The individual impelled by his interest constantly struggles to come to completion, and in this way builds up his own individuality and modifies the conditions of life. But selection, heredity, and the struggle for existence constantly determine the forms of individual and group life that survive, in the human species as well as in other species.

From this frank statement of his philosophical

---

[8] For an epitome of Ratzenhofer's theories, see Small's *General Sociology,* Chapters XII–XXVII.

premises it will be seen that Ratzenhofer's background is mainly biological. However, his biology seems to foreshadow the theories of emergent evolution, and his psychology that of a self-active creative self. His psychology, unlike Gumplowicz's, gives a large place to the individual. The individual is the product of his own "inherent interest-capacity," and even the "social interest" exists only in the individual. As has been well said, "Ratzenhofer made of his individual more than an automaton and gave the tyrant group some constitutional limitations." This is just the opposite of Gumplowicz, who made the individual but a puppet of the group life. However, Ratzenhofer agrees with Gumplowicz that the social process is the subject matter of sociology. He defines sociology as "the science of the reciprocal relationships of human beings"; but, while Gumplowicz wishes to study only the interaction of groups, Ratzenhofer is concerned chiefly with the social and political process going on within groups. Unlike the formal German school in sociology, Ratzenhofer's sociology is profoundly evolutionary, and, at the same time, value-discovering. The task of sociology, as he conceived it, is "to discover the fundamental tendencies of social evolution, and the conditions of the general welfare of human beings."

Social philosophy. The original social forces are to be found, according to Ratzenhofer, in the differentiations of the *Urkraft,* or primal interest. The first of these is *the racial interest,* which has its roots in the physiological impulses of sex. It is the basis of those social structures that are expressed in the family and the race. The second interest is *the physiological,* which is rooted in the activities concerned with nutrition. It expresses itself in the food quest, and becomes a foundation for the economic life. The third interest is *the individual.* It impels the individual toward individualistic gratifications, and expresses itself socially in "individualization." The fourth interest is *the social,* which, while originally physiological, becomes a group interest through the relations of consanguinity that it establishes. Through it, selfish individual interests are subordinated to group welfare, and the process of "socialization" arises. The fifth and final interest Ratzenhofer calls *the transcendental.* It takes the form of a sense of dependence upon the unseen, and expresses itself in religion.

Professor Small was so enthusiastic over this analysis of Ratzenhofer's that, in his *General Sociology,* he said, "The latest word of sociology is that human experience yields the most and deepest meaning when read from first to last in terms of the evolution, expression, and accommodation of interests." [9] Again he says, "Our knowledge of sociology will be measured by the extent of our ability to interpret all human society in terms of effective interests." [10] Finally, "The social process is a continual formation of groups around interests, and a continual exertion of reciprocal influences by means of group

---

[9] Small, *General Sociology,* p. 282.
[10] *Ibid.,* p. 442.

action." [11] All these statements are undoubtedly exactly expressive of Ratzenhofer's views. The working of individual and group interests, according to Ratzenhofer, is the essence of the group-making process. Interests are real forces in individual and group action. But they are not simply conscious feelings. An unrealized need produces a feeling of discomfort and unrest. Subjectively, the interests are motives, but objectively, they are the possible satisfactions that lie in the physical and social environments. Social evolution, according to Ratzenhofer, is a process of grouping and regrouping men about ever-changing human interests. In this process, there is a necessary struggle or competition between interests. Groups as well as individuals come to represent interests; but the struggle for the satisfaction of interests tends to realize higher and higher goods, and therefore it tends to be a progressive competition that ends in an equilibrium, or harmony, of interests. The conflict theory thus points to progress, and, eventually, to social harmony.

From each of these fundamental interests Ratzenhofer derives a series of human motives that function in individual human behavior. There is *the material motive,* corresponding to the physiological interest, which functions in the struggle for subsistence. There is *the egoistic motive,* corresponding to the individual interest, which functions to satisfy the self-interest of individuals in the struggle for existence. There is *the intellectual motive,* which

---

[11] *Ibid.,* p. 209.

deals with ideas, and functions in the search for knowledge and truth. There are *moral motives,* corresponding to the social and transcendental interests, which guard the interests of society at large. The social, political, and economic life is a constant struggle to satisfy these interests. As individuals differ in innate mental capacities and in will power, their achievements will be unequal. Races, too, differ in these innate qualities. Hence, in social organization, there is inevitably a subordination of the weak to the strong. Hence, too, strong personalities formulate the social policies and purposes accepted by groups, and hence these strong personalities have much to do with molding the group will.

Unlike Gumplowicz, Ratzenhofer recognizes that his sociology constitutes a philosophy of history, and he outlines six stages in human development down to the present time. The *first* stage is that of *the origin of the human species* out of the primates in the Tertiary period. Unlike Gumplowicz, Ratzenhofer assumes the monogenetic origin of mankind. Man was characterized from the first by sociality and co-operation in the struggle against physical conditions and wild animals. This earliest period marks the separation and migration of the various races of mankind, and their characterization by environmental conditions according to the law of adaptation. The *second* stage is that of *primitive culture,* under which term Ratzenhofer groups not only the hunting and fishing peoples, but also those practicing very primitive agriculture and herding. Institutions begin to get formed in this stage. The *third* stage is that of *barbaric culture,* in which, owing to the increase of numbers, robbery and warfare begin to take place frequently among human groups. The institution of slavery now has its rise with developed agriculture. The *fourth* stage is *the stage of warfare,* characterized by the general practice of living by plunder and war, and by the development of social institutions adapted to militant life. This stage sees also the development of property rights, especially in land. The *fifth* stage is that of a *conflict of classes,* in which we have ruling classes struggling for the possession of the earth, and subject classes struggling for better conditions of life. This stage overlaps the sixth stage, the *spread of capitalism,* in which we are now living. This is a stage of scientific discovery and invention, and of bloody conflicts between culture groups for the possession of the earth. It involves the exploitation of new lands and the extension of the capitalistic system, and leads to further conflicts between the capitalistic and laboring classes. But it is also accompanied by the development and spread of higher civilization.

The present struggle between classes and peoples, Ratzenhofer thinks, must eventually come to an end and result in an age of settled social life, characterized by harmonious relations between classes and peoples. Every country will devote its land to the support of its own people. Each country will produce the commodities for which it is best adapted, and the whole world will be organized on a basis of free international exchange, but with the continued dominance of the weaker peoples by the stronger races.

This classification of the stages of social evolution by Ratzenhofer is much more satisfactory than Gumplowicz's views. It will be noted that Ratzenhofer's conception of the social process as a progressive competition of interests leads to meliorism, and to the hope of possible harmonization of conflicting interests of various groups in the distant, if not the near, future. His formulation of the social process in terms of conflict is, therefore, only relative, since he points to the existence of tendencies or forces that progressively tend to limit and mitigate conflict.

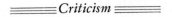

Criticism

If ever there was a social philosophy based upon a metaphysical assumption, Ratzenhofer's social philosophy would have to be so characterized, as it is based upon the assumption of a primal force with an inherent interest that gives rise to all the subsequent forms of its evolution. Ratzenhofer's positive monism is perhaps quite as objectionable to sound scientific method as Spencer's "matter, motion, and force." If social philosophy is going to proceed according to the spirit of scientific method, it cannot have any such philosophical assumption, even though it may be argued that the assumption appeals to common sense. Social philosophy must build itself out of the facts and experiences of life, and not proceed by deduction from *a priori* assumptions. On this account, Ratzenhofer's system has had a very limited acceptance, although Professor Small came, in the latter years of his life, to base his sociological system upon Ratzenhofer's. Again, the conflict theory of society, even in the mild form in which we find it in Ratzenhofer, is open to many objections. Conflict between groups and between interests within groups has always been a large factor in human social life; but this fact should not obscure the even more important fact that the reciprocal relations between human beings, especially those living within an autonomous group, have always been predominantly co-operative. If this had not been the case, no such thing as an enduring group culture could have been built up.

It is curious, by the way, that neither Gumplowicz nor Ratzenhofer perceived clearly the importance of group culture in determining group behavior. Gumplowicz sensed this fact in pointing out and emphasizing the determination of the individual's behavior by his group. But with neither writer is culture a determining factor. The determining factors are still the blind forces of nature, or, at most, interests that move individuals as though they were the puppets of blind forces.

CHAPTER XXVIII

William Graham Sumner and Laissez Faire

SOCIAL PHILOSOPHY IN the United States has followed, in general, the patterns of European social philosophy. There is scarcely one of the European social thinkers we have mentioned who has not his echo in some American thinker. This is, of course, what we should expect, if general social culture controls to the extent that we believe individual thinking; for the culture of America has been essentially European culture.

Only in Lester F. Ward, Charles Horton Cooley, and a few other thinkers do we find a tendency to break away from the various European schools of social philosophy. For the most part, and with only slight variations, American thinkers have echoed, as as we have just said, the attitudes of European thinkers. We shall see that this is true even of one

500

of the most original American social thinkers, William Graham Sumner.

═════ *Biographical Sketch* ═════

Sumner was born in 1840, of English immigrant parents who had recently settled in the United States. He was graduated from Yale College in 1863. He intended to enter the Christian ministry, and went to Germany, and then to Oxford, England, to study theology. In 1866 he returned and became a tutor at Yale in mathematics and Greek. He was ordained a deacon in the Episcopal Church in 1867, and was raised to its priesthood in 1869. For two years, from 1870 to 1872, he was rector of the Episcopal Church at Morristown, New Jersey. In 1872 he was called back to Yale as Professor of Political Science, his actual teaching, however, covering courses in economics and sociology as well as political science. In 1874 he became involved in a controversy with the college authorities for using Spencer's *Study of Sociology* as a textbook. Spencer bore the reputation of being an atheist, but Sumner refused to give up the use of his text and won the support of the faculty in his uncompromising attitude.

It was in 1873–1874 that Sumner formed the first class in sociology at Yale, which some suppose to be the first class in sociology in any American institution of learning. He became more and more interested in sociology, or, as he preferred to call it, "the sci-

ence of society." On account of the humanitarian
implications that had become attached to the word
"sociology" in the United States, through its use by
nineteenth-century social reformers and philanthro-
pists, Sumner remained somewhat unwilling to employ it, even up to his death. He proposed at one
time the word "societology" instead of sociology,
but this was never generally adopted. He was more
successful in introducing the word "societal" to take
the place of the word "social," which also, he feared,
had some taint of altruism attached to it. However,
Sumner's courses at Yale can scarcely be called anything else than sociology or social philosophy. They
were attempts to understand the laws and forces
that have made human society what it is. Sumner
continued to teach sociological courses until his retirement in 1909. In 1907 he had published an epoch-
making book in sociological theory, entitled *Folkways*. During his latter years, he was at work upon
a comprehensive *Science of Society,* but, dying in
1910, he left this work in a very incomplete condition.
It was, however, completed, quite as Sumner had
planned it, by his disciple and successor, Professor
Albert Galloway Keller. Much earlier, in fact in
1883, he had published a little controversial book to
uphold the philosophy of *laissez faire,* entitled *What
Social Classes Owe to Each Other.*

Numerous events in Sumner's somewhat stormy
career must have greatly influenced his social thinking. He passed from one battle to another in defense
of his views. His courageous stand for freedom of

teaching at Yale made him a defender of academic freedom for the rest of his life. As a defender of *laissez faire* and the system of natural liberty, he became deeply involved in the political and economic controversies of his time, especially as an advocate of free trade. Possibly on account of some religious experience, he seems to have had a deep reaction against many of the conventional religious attitudes of his time. Perhaps no social scientist was ever more completely emancipated from the religious bias. He maintained his priesthood in the Episcopal Church to the end of his days, and continued regularly to make his reports as a priest. But he never suffered his religious sentiments to influence his social philosophy, unless, indeed, we except the final chapter of *What Social Classes Owe to Each Other.* This chapter was entitled "Wherefore We Should Love One Another," but the love that was advocated was purely personal and individual, and not a good will embodied in institutional forms. Speaking of the lessening influence of his early religious beliefs upon himself, Sumner said, "It was as if I had put my beliefs in a drawer, and when I opened it there was nothing there at all." [1] This reminds one forcibly of a similar confession by Darwin.

Certainly, the later Sumner was very unlike the youthful Sumner, and it is even more absurd in his case to cite his early utterances than it would be to cite passages from Comte's earlier work. Normal

---

[1] See *William Graham Sumner,* by Harris E. Starr, p. 543.

men change in the course of their intellectual and emotional life, and this was the case with William Graham Sumner.

Perhaps it is not unfair to cite Sumner's own words in support of the view that a man's social thinking is much determined by his social environment. "It is vain to imagine," Sumner says, "that a scientific man can divest himself of prejudice and put himself in an attitude of neutral independence toward the mores. He might as well try to get out of gravity or the pressure of the atmosphere."[2] If this statement were absolutely true, there could be no advance in social thinking until the conditions of life and civilization changed. Fortunately, we have seen that any such statement cannot be taken as absolute truth. Social thinking has developed, not so much upon the basis of the general conditions of civilization, as upon the basis of traditions in social thinking and the genius of exceptional minds. Perhaps again, however, it would not be unfair to say that Sumner's ardent advocacy of the philosophy of *laissez faire* was really an expression of the social complacency of the average educated New Englander of his time.

But, of course, Sumner got his main ideas from traditions in social thinking that had developed before his time. It is often denied that Herbert Spencer had much to do in the shaping of Sumner's thought, but there is much evidence that Sumner was immersed in the reading of Spencer from the time

---

[2] Sumner, *Folkways*, p. 98.

that he was a student at Oxford. It could not have been an accident that he was the first to use Spencer's *Study of Sociology* as a text. But he was an ardent admirer of Spencer, rather than a disciple. It must be conceded that he was too big a man to be merely a disciple of any previous thinker, yet it is hard to point out wherein the originality of his work consisted. His *laissez-faire* attitudes were almost exactly the same as Spencer's, except with relation to general public education and several governmental functions. However, he did not follow Spencer in the attempt to make a physical interpretation of human society. Sumner's interpretation was in terms of social conventions and social customs. Neither did he follow Spencer in the use of the organic analogy. In some ways, he was much closer to the social Darwinists, who wished to interpret society in terms of individual and group conflict. There can, at any rate, be no question as to the influence of Darwin's work upon Sumner's thinking. He accepted natural selection and the struggle for existence, even though he emphasized the power of convention and custom.

Probably Lippert's *Culture History of Mankind* gave Sumner many suggestions. At any rate, he came to perceive in the development of culture the supreme factor in social development. Gumplowicz's theory of group conflict also had much to do in the shaping of his thought. Thus Sumner's thinking, which in many respects seemed to many of his contemporaries so un-American, was, after all, rooted in the traditions of the social thought of his time.

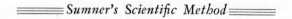

Sumner's Scientific Method

We are sometimes told that Sumner's method of thinking was somewhat vague and even mysterious. But he has left us clear statements as to what he considered to be a proper scientific method in sociology. He said that "the way to build a science of sociology is to build it in the same fundamental methods that have proved so powerful in the other sciences. I mean the more or less exact sciences."[3] It is clear, therefore, that his effort was to develop sociology as a purely natural science. His biographer tells us, "Sumner had no use for philosophy; he had studied it long and thoroughly in his youth, and had been throwing it overboard, as he said, ever since. It dealt with abstractions and phantasies, in his opinion, was altogether speculative and unverifiable, and never got anywhere."[4]

Sumner openly acknowledged that he got his method, the ethnographic or anthropologic method, from Herbert Spencer.[5] He insisted in his courses at Yale that the students use works in anthropology and ethnography as the foundation for the courses in the science of society. His *Folkways* has very few

---

[3] *American Journal of Sociology*, Vol. XII, p. 598 (March, 1907).
[4] Starr, *op. cit.*, p. 341.
[5] *Ibid.*, p. 395.

references except to anthropological and ethnographical literature. One exception must be made; Sumner made far more use of recent history than did Spencer. Much of his illustrative material in the *Folkways* is historical rather than ethnographic. He had, moreover, a keen appreciation of the principles of historical criticism.

But Sumner said publicly that he had no use for psychology in the giving of his courses in sociology. He even went so far as to say that he preferred that his students should know nothing of psychology. In the *Folkways,* he does not mention a single of his great contemporaries in scientific psychology, not even William James. However, he developed a very considerable psychology of his own. It was essentially a psychology of habit, and, in some respects, in the emphasis upon the unconscious and the automatic nature of processes of adjustment, it was a near approach to modern behaviorism. However, Sumner was careful to say that the mode of adaptation of human beings in society is mental, not physical. He seemed to consider that a physiological statement of the process of adjustment was altogether inadequate.

A striking peculiarity about Professor Sumner's work is that he apparently paid no attention to the work of his other colleagues in sociology, with the exception of the few whom we have already mentioned. The names of Comte, Ward, and Giddings do not appear in his bibliography or his index. In this matter of ignoring the work of his contemporaries, Sumner presents a striking parallel to Vilfredo

Pareto. This is true also in many other matters, such as the general attitude of both Sumner and Pareto toward present society, and their emphasis upon the study of the remote in time or space.

The most significant point about Sumner's method, however, is his wish to divorce sociology from all connection with social reform or reorganization. He wished to make sociology a pure science upon a purely naturalistic foundation, even though it could not be made as exact as some of the natural sciences. He was not so foolish as to think that scientific truth could be arrived at only by exact observation. His large use of the historical and the comparative method, as well as of deductions from the general theory of evolution by natural selection, shows this conclusively enough. However, like Spencer and Pareto, he depended upon a monumental accumulation of facts, making as little use of psychology as possible for their interpretation. On the whole, therefore, his method must be characterized as essentially the same as that of Herbert Spencer, without the use of any pet theory, such as evolution by the equilibration of energy, in order to sustain the facts that were selected. If Sumner had any such theory, it seems to have been simply the general Spencerian attitude that human society could be described, but not intelligently controlled, and that all attempts at control were bound to be either futile or detrimental. Thus Sumner's science of society was developed even more than Spencer's, free from any bias that might be entailed by the consideration of practical moral and social problems.

Sumner's Social Philosophy

Doctrine of social origins. Sumner tells us, at the very beginning of his *Folkways,* that all social origins are lost in mystery, and "it seems vain to hope that from any origin the veil of mystery will ever be raised."[6] Nevertheless, he speaks of men having been guided at the beginning by some instinctive tendencies and by natural needs. Moreover, he finds that there are four socializing or group-making forces: "These are hunger, sex-passion, vanity, and fear (of ghosts and spirits). Under each of these motives there are interests. Life consists in satisfying interests."[7] Hence, "Men begin with acts, not with thoughts." Ways of action were turned into customs and became mass phenomena. "Instincts were developed in connection with them. In this way folkways arise. The young learn them by tradition, imitation and authority. The folkways provide for all the needs of life then and there. They are uniform, universal in the group, imperative and invariable. . . . The folkways, therefore, are not creations of human purpose and wit; they are like products of natural forces which men unconsciously set in operation, or they are like the instinctive ways

---

[6] Sumner, *Folkways,* p. 7.
[7] *Ibid.,* p. 18.

of animals."[8]   From needs arise habits for the individual and customs for the group, "but these results are consequences which are never conscious and never foreseen or intended." Nevertheless, when reflected upon, these group habits become customs that are sacred. "When conviction as to the relation to welfare is added to the folkways, they are converted into *mores,* and by the virtue of the philosophical and ethical element added to them, they win utility and importance and become the source of the science and art of living."[9]

Sumner's description of the mores is worth quoting in full:

> We must conceive of the mores as a vast system of usages, covering the whole of life, and serving all its interests; also containing in themselves their own justification by tradition and use and wont, and approved by mystic sanctions until, by rational reflection, they develop their own philosophical and ethical generalizations, which are elevated into "principles" of truth and right. They coerce and restrict the newborn generation. They do not stimulate to thought, but the contrary. The thinking is already done and is embodied in the mores. They never contain any provision for their own amendment. They are not questions, but answers, to the problem of life. They present themselves as final and unchangeable, because they present answers which are offered as "the truth."

Again, he says, "The mores are the folkways, including the philosophical and ethical generaliza-

---

8 *Ibid.,* pp. 2 and 4.
9 *Ibid.,* p. 3.

tions as to societal welfare which are suggested by them, and inherent in them as they grow." [10] However, Sumner warns us against thinking that primitive men philosophized about their welfare. "They did not formulate any propositions about the causes, significance, or ultimate relations of things." [11] Nevertheless, they mythologized the mores. Apparently the mind of primitive man worked somewhat differently from the minds of present men. Finally, "In the early stages mores are elastic and plastic; later they become rigid and fixed. They seem to grow up, gain strength, become corrupt, decline, and die, as if they were organisms." The whole process, therefore, according to Sumner, is a natural and automatic one.

On the practical side, the process by which mores or customs are developed and established is "ritual." From this point of view, "The mores are social ritual, in which we all participate unconsciously." [12] There is, of course, a constant selection going on among the mores, especially in their early and plastic stage, but the selection is "mainly automatic and unplanful." Institutions and laws are produced out of the mores. As the mores, according to Sumner, include all primitive morals, primitive religion, and primitive law, they form the matrix out of which all culture has grown. But they are themselves the products of the unconscious needs,

10 *Ibid.*, p. 30.
11 *Ibid.*, p. 31.
12 *Ibid.*, p. 62.

interests, and habits of the mass of the people. Professor Keller has summed up Sumner's thought well when he says, "All of society's forms and institutions are found, when reduced to lowest terms, in custom. . . . The study of custom is, for the science of society, what the study of the cell is to biology. . . . The folkways and mores are institutions in their lowest terms." [13]

After all it appears that Sumner did have a very definite doctrine of social origins, and one which was not based upon mere observation.

Doctrine of social development. We have already seen that Sumner spoke of the mores as growing, declining, and dying like organisms. They present variability. And, like all organic growth, they are acted upon by natural selection. Most of the changes that are effected in the mores are, therefore, brought about by natural conditions, and unpremeditatedly. Many things in the natural environment and in the internal condition of the group can, therefore, affect the mores. But usually any attempt to change them through rational thought ends in failure. Cases when this has apparently been done are to be explained by the fact that conditions were ready for a change. "All these cases go to show that changes which run with the mores are easily brought about, but that changes which are opposed to the mores require long and patient effort, if they are possible at all." [14] Revolutions rarely effect any persistent change in the

---

[13] Sumner and Keller, *The Science of Society*, Vol. I, p. 31.
[14] *Folkways*, p. 94.

Henry Holt and Company

WILLIAM GRAHAM SUMNER

mores, but end in reaction when they introduce innovations to reconstruct the mores of the people. Even changes in religion in many cases do not result in changes in the mores. The mores may become corrupt, and it is possible to arrest such an aberration in its early stages. "It is, however, very difficult to do so, and it would be very difficult to find a case in which it has been done. Necessarily the effort to do it consists in a prophecy of consequences. Such prophecy does not appeal to anyone who does not himself foresee error and harm. Prophets have always fared ill, because their predictions were unwelcome and they were unpopular." [15] Every social group almost necessarily develops the conviction that its own customs are best. From this fact grows up a different set of attitudes toward those within one's own group and toward those outside. This has had the utmost effect upon social development. Out of this fact has grown the differences in sentiments in the in-group and toward the out-group, and Sumner strongly implies that these differences have had the utmost consequences in human history.

> The relation of comradeship and peace in the we-group and that of hostility and war towards others-groups are correlative to each other. The exigencies of war with outsiders are what make peace inside, lest internal discord should weaken the we-group for war. These exigencies also make government and law in the in-group, in order to prevent quarrels and enforce discipline. Thus war and peace have reacted on each other and de-

[15] *Ibid.*, p. 102.

veloped each other, one within the group, the other in the intergroup relation. The closer the neighbors, and the stronger they are, the intenser is the warfare, and then the intenser is the internal organization and discipline of each. Sentiments are produced to correspond. Loyalty to the group, sacrifice for it, hatred and contempt for outsiders, brotherhood within, warlikeness without,—all grow together, common products of the same situation. These relations and sentiments constitute a social philosophy. It is sanctified by connection with religion. Men of an others-group are outsiders with whose ancestors the ancestors of the we-group waged war. The ghosts of the latter will see with pleasure their descendants keep up the fight, and will help them. Virtue consists in killing, plundering, and enslaving outsiders.[16]

Unfortunately, Professor Sumner never adequately developed this idea, or applied it to the interpretation of human history as a whole.

Sumner's sociology is concerned mainly with a theory of social development or evolution. What we have just said lays merely the groundwork of his theory. Space forbids that we should attempt to give more than the salient points. In the main, his theory of social development is in materialistic terms: the relation of man to the earth; the uniformity of human nature; the belief in imaginary spiritual beings; and the ruling motives of human conduct— hunger, sex love, vanity, and fear. Sumner held that geographical conditions and the ratio of population to natural resources had much to do with the

---

16 *Ibid.*, pp. 12, 13.

development of human society. But what raised man above the brute was the accumulation of capital. By "capital" Sumner meant any product of labor that is used to assist production. This is the instrumentality by which, from the beginning, man has won and held every step in the development of civilization. It has created wealth; it has sustained labor; because it has given man leisure, it has made possible the development of science and art. It has not, however, freed man from the struggle for existence, because men by their very nature are driven into competition with one another for the possession of the means of subsistence. This competition is a natural law that results from the same forces in nature that we see at work in the world below man. It leads to co-operation, so that men may combine their forces against nature or against other human groups. Such co-operation is not based upon sympathy and mutual understanding, but is in its essence "antagonistic co-operation." In their efforts to control nature and their own life, men appeal to imaginary spirits with superhuman powers. Religious rites thus become a means of controlling failure, loss, and calamity. They also become the means of enforcing the folkways and the mores. Thus mystical and practical elements blend in creating ideas of social welfare. Finally, all of the four major motives of human nature already mentioned continually enter into and modify the process of social development. Thus, for example, not only may hunger and sex passion produce conflict and wars, but also vanity and religion. These sources of conflict among men, so far as we can see, will be perpetual. The enlargement of the peace group is not a promise that universal peace will ultimately prevail. It means only that larger units will enter into competition and possibly into war. At this point, Sumner's ideas are much like those of Gumplowicz.

Social development is centered in the satisfying of organic needs, especially hunger. Therefore, it is centered in economic processes, the production and distribution of material goods. Maintenance customs, or mores, change with changing conditions, and, through the accumulation of knowledge and technical inventions, their tendency is to change for the better. Social advance finds its basis in material civilization. On the other hand, the nonmaterial part of civilization for the most part simply shows fluctuations. "The useful arts," Sumner says, "do show an advance. The fine arts do not. They return to the starting point, or near it, again and again." [17] And Sumner adds that the general morals of societies have the same trend. They show ups and downs, fluctuations, but no certain advance.

Class distinctions are inevitable and "simply result from the different degrees of success with which men have availed themselves of the chances which were presented to them." There is, therefore, no natural equality in human society and no trend toward equality. The same might be said of liberty

---

[17] *Ibid.*, p. 604.

and fraternity. We have established democracy in our mores; but Sumner implies that most of its ideals are impossible of realization. "It is impossible to discuss or criticize it," he says. "It is glorified for popularity, and is a subject of dithyrambic rhetoric. No one treats it with complete candor and sincerity. No one dares to analyze it as he would aristocracy or autocracy. He would get no hearing, and would only incur abuse." [18]

In general, the process of social development is an automatic development of the mores that cannot be ascribed to intelligent purposes, and that cannot be made to conform to any intelligent plan of control. While some intelligent selection plays a part in the maintenance mores, yet, even here, the industrial system is mainly "automatic and instinctive in its operation." Forms of the family, of government, of religion, and of art are even more so. The general picture that Sumner would present of social development, to use his own words, is that "all the life of human beings, in all ages and stages of culture, is primarily controlled by a vast mass of folkways handed down from the earliest existence of the race, having the nature of the ways of other animals, only the topmost layers of which are subject to change and control, and have been somewhat modified by human philosophy, ethics, and religion, or by other acts of intelligent reflection."

Doctrine of social organization. In a general way,

---

[18] *Ibid.*, p. 77.

Sumner's doctrine of social organization has already been treated. Social organization is the result of the great forces of social development, the relation of man to natural resources, the uniformity of human nature, the fear of supernatural beings, and the effort to gratify the primary impulses of hunger, sex love, vanity, and fear.

Social institutions group themselves around these interests. The basis of an institution is always a concept, but institutions that are determined by concrete interests also have structure. The concepts and interests that underly institutions are born from the mores, and these are rooted in the general life conditions. There are, therefore, institutions for societal self-maintenance, institutions for societal self-preservation, institutions for self-gratification, and, finally, institutions for religion. All these institutions must rest upon the system of maintenance that largely coincides with the economic system.

As we have already seen, Sumner makes no use of the organic analogy. But he holds that there is a close interrelation and interaction between the different systems of mores and institutions. This he calls "the strain toward consistency" among the mores.[19] He is rather vague as to how far other institutions must adapt themselves to the institutions of maintenance; but he says that the different classes of mores and institutions must work together and must have a certain consistency with one another. Therefore, a certain economic system will tend to

---

19 *Ibid.*, pp. 5 and 6.

produce a certain type of family life, of government, and of religion. But Sumner implies that this strain toward consistency has rather wide limits. While the whole structure of society is roughly determined by its material basis in the maintenance mores, yet a certain latitude in the type of family life, of government, or of religion is possible. There is no rigid determinism, but there must be a consistency of other institutions with those that are concerned with maintenance, because "the first task of life is to live."

Thus it is evident that Sumner looks upon the organization of human society as largely a work of nature, or of unconscious forces. Attempts at the reorganization of society through intelligent planning, Sumner says, are, in most cases, bound to fail. In a very characteristic statement he says, "We can judge of the amount of serious attention which is due to plans for 'reorganizing society,' to get rid of alleged errors and inconveniences in it. We might as well plan to reorganize our globe by redistributing the elements in it." [20]

Doctrine of social progress. There can be no doubt that Sumner was very sincere in his belief that a system of *laissez faire,* or of natural liberty, would be the surest way to insure social progress. Approaching the whole problem from the standpoint of economics, rather than from the standpoint of a general theory of evolution, he came to believe that a system of natural liberty with its competition and

---

[20] *Ibid.,* p. 95.

selective influence upon individuals, classes, and in-stitutions was the best way to secure human develop-ment. It is wrong, therefore, to say that Sumner had no theory of social progress, or that he was not interested in progress. He did not believe that prog-ress could be brought about by governmental inter-ference or by collective planning. To be sure, he was somewhat sceptical of the possibility of progress in the general mores of society. We have already seen that he affirmed the reality of progress only in the maintenance mores. But his theory that there was a strain toward consistency in the mores led him to imply that if general social progress is in any degree possible, it is through the change in the use-ful arts and in the maintenance mores.

While Sumner's *laissez-faire* attitude rested upon a somewhat different basis than Spencer's, he reached practically the same conclusion. For he condemned not only all forms of socialism and trade-unionism, but also all social legislation, all attempts at govern-ment control over industrial conditions, even child-labor laws. Because he believed in natural liberty, he was opposed to all protective devices like the tariff, and was equally opposed to plutocracy, or combinations of capitalists, because, again, they in-terfered with natural liberty.

His main departure from Spencer in the matter of *laissez faire* was in regard to popular education, and this perhaps was not at bottom a radical departure, because he looked at the matter from the standpoint of individual liberty and competition. ''The one thing," he said, "which justifies popular education for all children, is the immense value of men of genius to society." But he was a strong believer also in the diffusion of knowledge, and, therefore, added, "If there is any salvation for the human race from woe and misery, it is in knowledge, and in training to use knowledge."

But Sumner considers that attempts to make the world over through religious systems and beliefs are absurd, because they do not go deep enough to affect vitally the great mass of mores. He illustrates this from the effects of Christian missions and other religious movements. He says that when the later Jewish prophets attempted to introduce a religion of righteousness, instead of a religion sanctifying existing customs, they also failed, and the implication seems to be that any such attempt at the building of an ideal or ethical society through religion is bound to fail. For, he says, "The religious system of the Jewish prophets never has become the actual popular religion of any people." [21]

Equally improbable is it that the world can be made over by scientifically ascertained facts and values. The mores, according to Sumner, are made by the masses, and the masses are little, if at all, influenced by scientific thought. The mores are automatic products of life's conditions. Therefore, "The mores made by any age for itself are good and right for that age." The mores make the standards of right for every people and every age. "The

[21] *Ibid.*, p. 558.

mores can make anything right."²² This famous
aphorism of Sumner is implied or repeated again
and again in the *Folkways*.   There is dispute among
his admirers as to just what he meant by it.   Probably he did not mean that the highest standard of
right was customary right, but evidently he did mean
that any higher standard of right could not be made
to prevail.   "Morals," he tells us, "are historical,
institutional and empirical."²³ He uses dozens of
illustrations to enforce his argument, one of which
is slavery.   Slavery was once universally considered
to be right; now it is universally condemned because
the mores have changed, and the mores changed because the conditions of life changed.   Again, when
Sumner says "Nothing but might ever made right,"
he undoubtedly refers to the power of society.   However, it is clear that he holds out no hope of the
establishment of standards of right through science,
and their diffusion through education.   This again
is one of those illusions of superficial students of
human social life who fail to see the facts.   All that
has just been said helps to interpret Sumner's book,
What Social Classes Owe to Each Other.   There he
marks out no program of education, legislation, or
sanitation to diffuse the goods of culture.   On the
contrary, he would rely entirely on natural competition between individuals and classes.   Free this natural process, he says, in effect, and things will take
care of themselves.   "Instead of endeavoring to re-

²² *Ibid.*, Chapter XV.
²³ *Ibid.*, p. 29.

distribute the acquisitions (wealth, culture, etc.) between the existing classes, our aim should be to *increase, multiply, and extend the chances.*" This is the only way we can further progress.[24]

Professor Keller seems to have accurately expressed Sumner's thought about social progress when he says, "The vast impersonal forces have always wrought out what is, in the end, expedient and rational."[25] Sumner himself expressed the same thought in his article on "The Absurd Effort to Make the World Over." It is worthy at least of partial quotation:

> If this poor old world is as bad as they say, one more reflection may check the zeal of the headlong reformer. It is at any rate a tough old world. It has taken its trend and curvature and all its twists and tangles from a long course of formation. All its wry and crooked gnarls and knobs are therefore stiff and stubborn. If we puny men by our arts can do anything at all to straighten them, it will only be by modifying the tendencies of some of the forces at work, so that, after a sufficient time, their action may be changed a little and slowly the lines of movement be modified. This effort, however, can at least be only slight, and it will take a long time. In the meantime spontaneous forces will be at work, compared with which our efforts are like those of a man trying to deflect a river, and these forces will have changed the whole problem before our interferences have time to make themselves felt.[26]

---

[24] *Op. cit.,* p. 167.

[25] See Keller, *Societal Evolution* (revised edition), p. 402.

[26] In *War and Other Essays,* pp. 208–210; quoted by Dr. Fay B. Karpf, in *American Social Psychology,* p. 244.

===== *Criticism* =====

Although Sumner developed a cultural interpretation of human society, he was too much under the
influence of the general trend of thought of the nineteenth century, and especially of Spencer, to see that
human society is essentially an artificial creation,
built up by the gradual learning of human groups
from experience. He failed to see that the mode of
transmission of the mores was essentially through
communication or tradition, much more than through
unconscious habituation. He failed to see, in other
words, that the customs and institutions of human
groups are always upheld by group traditions, that
the essence of these traditions is certain folk beliefs,
and they are inculcated in the young by communication and teaching. Sumner, in other words, tried to
assimilate the cultural processes of human society
to the blind forces of nature.

As his biographer says, "Sumner beheld societal
phenomena as an aspect of the earth's history." [27]
Consequently, he threw his whole faith upon automatic natural forces. In this respect, he was not far
from Spencer. He distrusted human intelligence, at
least when it manifested itself in a collective way.
The great culture-building factors in human society,
such as art, science, and religion, could hardly be
trusted. Sumner's trust was, if anywhere, not in

---

[27] Starr, *op. cit.*, p. 399.

the constructive intelligence of man, but in the natural competition of life, and in the slow modifying effect of natural forces in human society.

Admirers of Sumner have not hesitated to say that scientific sociology begins with his work. If "scientific" means "resting upon accurate observation," the claim can hardly be successfully defended, and it might be doubted at the beginning if mere observation of social facts could ever yield any large scientific generalizations concerning human society. Professor Giddings, after Sumner's death, went so far as to say, "We are beginning to recognize him as perhaps the most consistently sociological, if not the greatest of sociologists." [28] There can be no doubt about the value of Sumner's work, but Sumner himself would probably be the first to ridicule the idea that it was the beginning of scientific sociology. Sumner himself, on one occasion, went so far as to speak of his work as "a philosophy of society."

Sumner's sociology was the foil of Ward's, whose system we are about to consider. These two systems of sociological thought, both produced by the forces of the nineteenth-century American life, stand in sharp antithesis to one another. Both were rooted, however, in the English thought of the nineteenth century—Sumner's in Spencer's thought and in the system of natural liberty sketched by the early English economists; Ward's, also in Spencer's thought, but a typical American reaction to the Spencerian philosophy of *laissez faire.*

---

[28] Giddings, *Studies in the Theory of Human Society*, p. 293.

CHAPTER XXIX

Lester F. Ward and Planned Progress

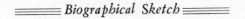

=== *Biographical Sketch* ===

WE NOW COME TO the man who is best entitled to be regarded as the chief founder of sociology in the United States, though none of his works were even published when Professor Sumner at Yale taught classes in sociology. The man is Lester Frank Ward. He was born on a farm near Joliet, Illinois, in 1841. His boyhood was spent in great poverty, with little or no opportunities for education, but he showed from his earliest youth an insatiable thirst for knowledge, and proceeded to educate himself perhaps in a way better than most educational institutions of his time could have educated him. He became interested very early in botany and zoology, interests that remained with him throughout his life. He began to prepare for college in a small institution in Pennsylvania in 1861–1862, but in 1862 he entered the Union Army and served as a soldier until he was wounded at the Battle of Chancellorsville. In 1865 he was appointed to the Treasury Department in the United States Civil Service. In 1867 he entered the night classes of Columbian University, which he himself was instrumental in founding, and graduated two years later with the A. B. degree. Later, at Columbian University, now George Washington University, he took a Master's degree and also degrees in law and medicine. He did not, however, attempt to practice these professions. In 1881 he was made a geologist on the United States Geological Survey, and soon achieved a great reputation in this field. In the meantime, he had acquired distinction for his botanical surveys, both of living and fossil plants. In 1883 he was appointed Chief Paleontological Botanist of the Geological Survey, a position which he retained as long as he was in government service. In the meantime, however, he had become interested in the social sciences, particularly in the work of Comte and Spencer. Almost from the first, he began to disagree with Spencer's practical conclusions, although accepting for the most part his mechanistic theory of evolution as a mechanical redistribution of matter and energy. Even as early as 1869, Ward tells us in his diary, he began the writing of his *Dynamic Sociology* to correct the erroneous conclusions of Herbert Spencer. Although Ward revolted at Spencer's conservatism and *laissez-faire* individualism, he was Spencerian in his early life in his philosophical point of view. Because he had the same general point of view as Spencer, he was perhaps of all men best fitted to reply to Spencer. It was the case of a Spencerian refuting Spencer. May we add that Ward was fully the equal of Herbert Spencer in intellectual power and penetration? Ward's *Dynamic Sociology,* on which he had been laboring since 1869, was published in two volumes in 1883, the year after Spencer's visit to the United States. As it was a refutation of Spencer by a Spencerian, it at once produced a sensation among Spencer's followers.

Ward now began to elaborate his sociological views. In 1893 he published an epoch-making work on *Psychic Factors of Civilization,* in which he laid the foundations for a psychological interpretation of human society. Inconsistently with his Spencerian philosophy, he attempted in this book to show that mind had been the foremost factor in the evolution not only of human society, but also that it was one of the foremost factors in organic evolution. In Ward's thinking, this work marks the turning point from a materialistic way of looking at life and mind to a spiritualistic monism. In many respects, it is the greatest of his works, and through it he must be regarded as a pioneer in social psychology. In 1898, Ward published a little book summarizing his sociological system, entitled *Outlines of Sociology.* This remains one of the most useful books for obtaining Ward's point of view in a short compass. Beginning with the first day of the twentieth century, he

LESTER F. WARD

tells us, he set to work to restate and revise his system of sociology. In 1904, he published the first part of his revision in a large volume entitled *Pure Sociology*. This was followed in 1906 with his *Aplied Sociology,* which, he declared, completed his system. During the same year, he was called to a chair in sociology in Brown University, largely because of the influence of Professor J. Q. Dealey. He taught at Brown until his death in 1913.

We may add that Professor Ward received many honors and recognitions during his lifetime. In 1903, he was made president of the International Institute of Sociology, then located in Paris. In 1906 he was made the first president of the American Sociological Society. We have already spoken of the recognition which he received in botany, zoology, paleontology, and geology. He was a most prolific writer, and during his lifetime wrote no less than six hundred articles and books.

It should also be added that Ward was of a deeply sympathetic and passionate nature. This he frequently admitted himself. His early experience with poverty made him especially sympathetic with the masses, whom he styled "the fourth estate." To emancipate the masses from ignorance and poverty became one of the great aims of his life. His deep sympathy, then, may explain in part his opposition to *laissez faire* and his devotion to democracy and to humanitarianism.

══ *Ward's Scientific Method* ══

Like Spencer, Ward remained in the realm of social philosophy, though he declared that sociology was both a science and a philosophy. In the early development of his system, he used philosophical terms and made his sociology a part of a universal system of philosophy. At first, Ward was a materialistic monist of a rather crude sort, but, before he reached the end of his sociological thinking and writing, he was emphasizing more than any other writer the part that intelligent, purposive activity plays in human society. He, of course, had much trouble reconciling purposeful activity in social progress with his belief in a general mechanistic determinism. It is not unfair to Ward to say that his philosophy, psychology, and sociology are a chaos of contradictions, if we take all of his writings as a unit. Ward was too big a man, perhaps, to permit contradictions to trouble him. His common sense always came to the rescue and made it impossible for him to overlook any real human values. Perhaps it was this realistic common-sense attitude that led him to emphasize the role of mind in organic and social evolution. However, he had his own way of explaining this seeming contradiction; for a central feature of Ward's philosophy was his doctrine of "creative synthesis." Through creative synthesis he found that the evolutionary process was constantly bring-

ing forth new factors that could not be foreseen in
the lower stages of development. Thus he held that
mechanism produces chemism, chemism produces life,
life produces mind, and mind produces society.
This we would now recognize as the doctrine of
"creative" or "emergent" evolution. However,
Ward would not admit that life and mind were not
derived from the forces active at lower levels of
development. He found some evidence of mind, he
acknowledged in later life, in every atom and mole-
cule. Therefore, in time, he became fond of speaking of a "world-soul" that represented creative striving in almost every direction. It is not surprising,
perhaps, that the later Ward used to tell his friends
that he was a "spiritualistic monist," because he
found an element of spirit or mind in every atom of
matter. Evolution, accordingly, becomes with Ward
not merely a redistribution of matter and motion, as
it was with Spencer, but the creation of new processes.

Ward's biology was also somewhat uncertain.
Although, in general, he accepted evolution by natural selection, as set forth by Darwin, he also held
to Lamarck's view of the inheritance of acquired
traits, even to the inheritance of intelligent adaptations. While accepting Spencer's mechanistic, hedonistic, and sensationalistic psychology, Ward also
insisted that purposive striving was at the very bottom of life processes, and particularly of human
behavior. He accepts, however, Spencer's general
view that in consciousness there are only two funda-

mental elements—feelings and the relations between feelings. From these he derives all other psychological traits. Feeling, Ward held, is at the bottom of purposive striving. It is to be explained as a protective device, brought forth by organic evolution to protect and guide delicate organisms. Thus Ward has, implicit in his philosophy, a hedonistic psychology as well as a hedonistic ethics.

Ward accepted Comte's hierarchy of the sciences and defended it against Spencer's criticism. He held, however, that Comte meant by this hierarchy not an absolute dependence of the higher and more complex sciences upon the lower and simpler sciences, but rather a filiation of the higher with the lower. The lower did not dominate the higher, but the higher had to take into account the bases laid by the lower sciences. Therefore, while physics and chemistry, geology and geography, were all useful to the sociologist, his chief help would come from biology and psychology. Ward insisted that sociology could not be constituted by the mere observation of social facts. It could be constituted only by the discovery of the laws and principles that would interpret these facts. These laws and principles could be discovered, according to Ward, only by the method of synthesis, by taking into account all that the lower sciences might bring to the aid of the sociologist. It was, however, knowledge of mind, and especially of the human mind and its workings, that would be of most use to the sociologist. These processes of the human mind, Ward contended, in the

form of human feelings, desires, purposes, and intelligence, are everywhere and always at work in
human relations. Human society can no more be
understood without attention to these psychic or
psychological factors than life can be understood
without attention to chemical factors. Therefore,
while Ward would not neglect human history or the
study of present human society, he would throw emphasis upon the evolutionary view, and particularly
upon the part that conscious factors play in social
evolution. He would emphasize, moreover, the comparative method of the study of many human societies in order to get a clearer view of the working of
all factors in social evolution, particularly the psychic
factors.

As Professor J. Q. Dealey has said, Ward, in his
Dynamic Sociology, was the first American social
thinker to turn away definitely from the biological
bias of Spencer and to suggest a psychological basis
for sociology. According to Ward, the feelings,
especially the simple, fundamental feelings connected
with hunger and sex, were primitive in the development of mind, and from them developed the mass of
emotions, interests, and desires that characterize
man. Feeling, therefore, he finds to be "the dynamic agent in both animals and men." It was
created as an inducement to functional activity, as
well as a protective device. When feeling is acted
on by memory, it becomes desire. The desires of
individuals are "the social forces." These are of
two sorts: the life-preserving forces, such as the de-

sires connected with food and sex; and the life-mitigating forces, such as aesthetic, moral, and intellectual desires. Desires are, so to speak, the steam in the boiler that makes the engine go. However, they would conflict and make a chaos of activity or function if nature had not evolved something to guide them. As a guide to the feelings and the desires, intellect or intelligence was evolved; first in its unconscious, intuitional form, and finally in the form of fully conscious reasoning and of insight into truth. While the intelligence or intellect is not a force in the true sense of the word, according to Ward, yet it does direct and control action, and so makes possible human achievement.

Primitively, all desires are blind. They impel to direct action toward the objects of desire. If obstacles intervene, they are simply arrested and never attain their objects. It is the function of the intellect to institute the transition to indirect methods. By slow evolution, the intellect perceives ways and means of attaining ends, and so shows ultimately the advantage of individual self-restraint and social co-operation. Hence intelligent purposes tend in the course of social evolution to take the place of blind desires. The pure processes of nature can never account for social phenomena. It is teleological forces that preside over, control, limit, and direct the affairs of men to progressive ends. The very idea of teleological force is an anthropomorphic conception. Man would never have attributed intelligent purposes or teleology to his gods, Ward says, if he had not experienced the working of intelligent forces in his own behavior. Intelligence simply guides desires in their course. Ultimately its office is to direct society into unobstructed channels, to enable the social forces to continue in free play and yet prevent them from being neutralized by collision with obstacles in their path. Interposed barriers are thus evaded by circuitous routes of approach, and so intelligence makes it possible to work out intelligent purposes and bring about essentially artificial progress in human society.

Because Ward emphasized that mind is the controlling factor in evolution, especially in social evolution, he has been called "the mind-intoxicated man," even as Spinoza was called "the God-intoxicated man." At any rate, Ward made the Spencerians sit up and take notice, because here was one, supposedly of their number, setting up the idea that mind, in the broad sense of psychic factors, had controlled human social evolution in the past and might, through the development of intelligence, bring about a planned, artificial progress in the future that would make past social evolution seem almost negligible. As Professor Small said in his *General Sociology* (p. 82):

> Ward's distinctive effort was to get for the psychic factors in social reactions due recognition and adequate formulation. . . . He first published when the influence of Herbert Spencer was probably at its height. In sociology that influence amounted to obscuration of the psychic element and exaggeration of the physical factors concerned

in shaping social combinations. . . . While the Spencerian influence was uppermost, the tendency was to regard social progress as a sort of mechanically determined redistribution of energy which thought could neither accelerate nor retard. Against this tendency Ward opened a crusade. He undertook to show that mind can control the conditions of human life to such an extent that it is possible to inaugurate a new and better era of progress.

But it is not the idea of automatic progress that Ward defended. On the contrary, if social progress takes place, it must be through intelligent effort, effort so highly intelligent that it may be said to be scientific. This is the social purpose implied in the development of science itself. In the preface to his *Dynamic Sociology,* Ward does not hesitate to say "The real object of science is to benefit man. A science which fails to do this, however agreeable its study, is lifeless. Sociology, which of all sciences should benefit man most, is in danger of falling into the class of polite amusements, or dead sciences." [1] And then with sublime self-confidence he adds: "It is the object of this work to point out a method by which the breath of life can be breathed into its nostrils."

While Ward would have been perhaps more successful in his attempt to humanize sociology if he had had a different philosophical point of view and a different psychology, yet, as we have already said,

---

[1] Ward, *Dynamic Sociology,* pp. vi, vii of Vol. I.

he can scarcely be charged with failing to recognize and to find a place in his methods of thinking for the higher social values. It is for this reason that Ward's approach to human social problems has proved an inspiration to all who, like himself, wish sociology to be a science to benefit man.

Ward's Social Philosophy

We have already seen that Ward would emphasize the study of social evolution in any scientific approach to human social problems. Like Comte, he considered that these problems were not understandable or solvable without an evolutionary approach. However, before we take up this evolutionary approach, we must first understand Ward's later conception of human society.

The nature of human society. It has been repeatedly said that there is nothing in Ward's later writings that we do not find in his *Dynamic Sociology.* Perhaps this is true by implication. But if we take into account explicit statements, then there is a great change indeed because, between the *Dynamic Sociology* and the *Pure Sociology,* there is the transition from a purely naturalistic view of human society to an almost completely cultural view. For in his *Pure Sociology* Ward tells us that the subject matter of sociology is human achievement; and achievement he identifies with invention, "the artificial modification of natural phenomena.'' ''No animal,'' Ward says, ''is capable of this.'' [2] Hence Ward would rule out of consideration in human sociology animal societies altogether. He denies that they are true societies, even though they are the result of blind adaptive processes. Man alone achieves, and it is by achievement or invention that he has built up civilization. Thus, in effect, Ward, in his *Pure Sociology,* holds that sociology is a science of civilization. This does not prevent the recognition of the fact that, in the past, social progress has been more or less accidental. From the sociological point of view, it has been accidental because it was not deliberately socially planned. It was the result, Ward holds, of ''individual telesis,'' or purposes, and not of ''collective telesis,'' or intelligent social purposes. It is necessary to emphasize this shift in Ward's thought. It has usually been neglected or overlooked by most of his interpreters. It perhaps adds to the inconsistencies in his social philosophy, but it should, by all means, be noted.

Doctrine of social origins. Even in the *Dynamic Sociology,* Ward refused to make any use of animal societies to explain the origin and nature of human institutions. Consequently, he was thrown back essentially upon Hobbes's theory of the origin of human society. Man, according to Ward, was not originally social by nature, and society did not exist at the beginning of human history. But it has arisen through the efforts of men to preserve themselves, to

---

[2] Ward, *Pure Sociology*, Chapter III, pp. 15, 16, 17.

protect themselves. In other words, it has arisen
through egoism and through natural selection.
Ward does not believe that man had any gregarious
instinct or tendency at the beginning. He formed
societies in consequence of perceiving the advantages
of association, and he tended to become social only
in consequence of the socializing processes set up
by society. Thus human history becomes essentially
a transition from unsocial man to social man; and we
may add that thus Ward perpetuates the mistakes in
social philosophy of the seventeenth and eighteenth
centuries.

In the evolution of the state, for example, Ward
finds that there are four stages.[3] The first was the
solitary, or *autarchic,* stage, in which men lived
relatively solitary, or as nearly so as was consistent
with the propagation of the species. The second,
or *anarchic,* stage was a stage of forced union,
in which early men lived in groups to defend
themselves. These groups became larger and
larger. The third stage, or *politarchic,* arose
when the rudimentary forms of law and government
were instituted. Thus tribes and nations had their
origin. The larger groups were formed by one group
conquering other groups. According to the *Dynamic
Sociology,* this is the stage in which we are now living. But ahead there is a fourth stage, the *pantar-
chic,* or cosmopolitan, which will result from the
further integration of conflicting groups or nations
and through the lessening of inter-group wars.

---

[3] Ward, *Dynamic Sociology,* Vol. I, pp. 464–467.

This stage will be an achievement of superior intelligence. Ward admitted that this final stage of political development was as yet only an ideal that would be realized through the triumph of humanitarian sentiments and practical interests that would sweep away the present barriers between nations, such as language, national pride, and difference of culture, and unite all nations in one vast political organization. It is fair to add that, in his *Pure Sociology,* Ward does not emphasize this theory, but he still holds that the social man is in a process of creation through the various socializing agencies of human society.

Doctrine of social development. As we have already seen, Ward holds that all distinctively human social development has come as the result of the power of man's mind to transform the material environment and, at the same time, human behavior. It is the gradual invention and achievement of man, handed down by what he calls "social heredity," that have resulted in the social development that has hitherto taken place.[4] He enumerates and discusses such forms of achievement as language, the invention of tools, utensils, weapons, literature, art, philosophy, and science. It is through all of these that human society has gradually developed to become what it is today. In his *Outlines of Sociology* he tells us:

> In so far as man has progressed at all, he has done so by gaining little by little the mastery in this struggle with the iron law of nature. In the

---

[4] Ward, *Pure Sociology,* p. 34; also Chapter XI.

physical world he has accomplished this through inventions, from which have resulted the arts. Every artificial form that serves a human purpose is a triumph of mind over the physical forces of nature. In the social world it is human institutions, religion, government, law, marriage, customs, that have been thought out and adopted to restrain the unbridled individualism that has always menaced society. And finally the ethical code and the moral law are simply the means employed by reason, intelligence and refined sensibility to suppress and crush out the animal nature of man.

In a famous passage, Ward seems to agree with the historical materialists in holding that the spiritual part of civilization needs no special cultivation. He argues that the spiritual part of civilization is conditioned upon material civilization. This much we can admit. But he goes on to argue further that the spiritual part of civilization "requires no special attention." [5] This position that Ward takes in his *Pure Sociology* is, however, entirely inconsistent with his emphasis upon the importance of science, knowledge, and socialized purposes in human social development. Both in his *Dynamic Sociology* and in his *Applied Sociology* he throws the whole emphasis upon mass education as the indispensable condition of social progress. This is surely inconsistent with any materialistic conception of history, or even with emphasis upon the primacy of material civilization.

Another doctrine of social development developed by Ward is the doctrine of the cross-fertilization of

[5] *Ibid.*, p. 18.

cultures or civilizations resulting in a new and higher civilization. This doctrine is really taken over from biology, and Ward fails to show for it an adequate psychological foundation. He says that cross-fertilization starts new processes of life, and that, in the case of civilizations, it makes the union of the best elements in both civilizations possible. Other interpretations of the development of civilization in human history are, however, possible. This particular doctrine results also from Ward's general doctrine of creative synthesis, and especially the doctrine of the union of opposites bringing about social evolution.

One of Ward's most fruitful perceptions in the matter of social evolution is that such evolution has been sympodial; that is, not like a tree, but like a vine.[6] This perception he got from his careful study of the geologic history of plant and animal fossils. He saw that the conception applied easily and directly to man's tool-making, and he gradually broadened it to include the development of social institutions and all social evolution. The perception has been accepted by practically all students of the evolution of culture.

Doctrine of social organization. Ward holds that "Synergy is the principle that explains all organization and creates all structures,"[7] both in the natural world and in human society. Synergy is the process that involves the union of opposing elements and

---

6 *Ibid.,* pp. 71–79.

7 *Ibid.,* pp. 171 f.

their combination and assimilation. Successively
higher and higher social structures are thus created
by a process of synthesis, and society evolves from
stage to stage. This is the same process of which
we have just spoken as the cross-fertilization of cultures. Ward also likened it to a process of equilibration. "Human institutions," he says, "are all
the means that have come into existence for the control and utilization of social energy." Thus have
resulted law, government, religion, morals, and all
other social institutions. In particular, existing
states and governments have thus come into existence through the fusion of unlike elements. In
this, Ward follows the theories of Gumplowicz and
Ratzenhofer.

Ward's theory of religion, as he came to develop
it finally, illustrates also his general theory of social
organization. Religion, law, morality, he tells us,
all develop out of "the group sentiment of safety."[8]
They are all devices to restrain the individual and to
hold him in his place with reference to institutions
and social organizations generally. In general,
Ward sees only the restraining or conservative side
of religion and morals in particular. In his *Dynamic Sociology*, he seems to regard them as having
no socially adaptive value, but of value only for the
gratification of individuals. Both religion and
morals, he holds, have a negative social utility rather
than a positive one. But in his later life, Ward

---

[8] *Ibid.*, p. 179.

holds altogether different views, especially regarding religion. He never sees religion as a progressive force or factor in human society; but he does appreciate its great value as a conservative force. In fact, he likens it to an instinct of race safety and says that its purpose is to prevent the elimination of the wayward in human society. Finally he speaks of it, in an article published in 1898, as "the force of social gravitation that holds the social world in its orbit." [9] This same conception, he acknowledges, might be extended both to morals and to law. It is worthy of remark, therefore, that, while the youthful Ward emphasized almost exclusively the problem of social progress, the mature Ward came to appreciate also the problem of social order and the means of preserving it.

Doctrine of social order. It is unnecessary to elaborate further Ward's conception of the part that religion and ethics might play in the establishment of an ideal social order. It will be sufficient for our purposes to elaborate the part that he conceived government might play. This Ward elaborated in the famous chapter on "Sociocracy," the final chapter of his book on *Psychic Factors of Civilization*. "Sociocracy" was a term that Ward borrowed from the writings of Auguste Comte, and he defined it as "the rule of society, by society, and for society." He conceived of it as a true democracy functioning intelligently for the welfare of all classes. It could

---

[9] "The Essential Nature of Religion," in *International Journal of Ethics,* Vol. VIII, pp. 169–92.

not come about, however, except through the development of the social sciences. Essentially, it could come only through the socialization of achievement and the diffusion of the results of achievement to all classes of the population. It was to be a government whose aim should be the social welfare of all classes. Ward recognized it as essentially a form of collectivism, and acknowledged that it could be established only through a just distribution of the products of all labor or effort. The history of the world, he said, shows that the masses of mankind have not participated fully in the results of achievement. Society as a whole now secures only so much of these results as cannot be prevented from filtering through the economic sieve, which is often very fine. Hence unsocialized individualism in the appropriation of the fruits of achievement has often resulted. Even those who have achieved most for human society, the inventors, the leaders, have often profited nothing by what they have achieved. The fruits of their labors have gone to a predatory few. This has resulted in underpaid labor, prolonged and groveling drudgery, wasted strength, misery, squalor, disease, and premature death. All of this might be prevented by a just distribution of the products of intelligent labor and effort.

Socialists have not been slow to claim that Ward's sociocracy is synonymous with socialism. But Ward, in his *Outlines of Sociology,* took pains to refute the idea that sociocracy was to be identified with the prevailing socialism. He contrasted sociocracy both with individualism and socialism. Individualism, he said, creates artificial inequality and confers benefits only on those whose superior cunning, intelligence, or accident of position, enables them to appropriate the benefits. Socialism creates, instead of artificial inequalities, artificial equality, and confers, according to Ward, the same benefits on all alike. Sociocracy, in distinction from both individualism and socialism, recognizes natural inequalities and aims to abolish artificial inequalities and to remove all artificial barriers between classes. It aims to confer benefits in strict proportion to merit, but insists that this can be done only if there is equality of opportunity to determine merit.

The truth seems to be that "sociocracy" is such a broad term that it could be used to designate many conceptions of a socialized government and of the diffusion of the results of achievement to all classes. Certainly, in Comte's use of the word, it had no connection with Marxian socialism. In fact, it was used by Comte before Marxian socialism was born. Undoubtedly, as Ward used the concept, it also had no connection with Marxian socialism, though no one can criticize socialists for appropriating the term. Sociocracy would certainly retain present forms of government in democratic states. As a government of society, by society, and for society, it would abstain from dictatorship and from any form of aristocratic or oligarchical rule.

Doctrine of social progress. Perhaps the most distinctive part of Ward's social philosophy, as we have already seen, is his doctrine of social progress. He does not deny that there has been social progress in the past. But he holds that it has been largely unconscious and accidental—not a planned, intelligent progress. One of the most distinctive things in Ward's social philosophy is his passionate affirmation of the possibility of intelligent social progress or improvement in the future. Society, he believes, can direct or at least greatly modify its own evolution for the benefit of man. This belief, he holds, comes from his demonstration of the superiority of the artificial over the natural in social evolution. Hence the immediate conclusion that nurture rather than nature is to be relied upon for social progress. Social improvement is possible through the socialization of achievement, through increasing social regulation, through social invention, and, finally, through collective intelligent purposes. But again it follows that such social improvement necessitates the elevation of the well-being of the masses, the universalizing of individual well-being. If we assume that men are substantially equal in native capacities, this method of improvement must operate through universal education. In his *Applied Sociology,* Ward examines the assumption that men are substantially equal in their native capacities. He finds that only about one tenth of one per cent are born geniuses, while defectives form about one half of one per cent. But Ward holds that the manifestation of genius depends upon social conditions. He thinks that, in at least half of the large residue that are now not designated as either geniuses or defectives, there is a great amount of special talent. The main problem before society, therefore, is to find this talent in the masses and to utilize it by fitting individuals for achievement and leadership. Society must first of all develop its human resources through the abolition of stunting poverty and other untoward social conditions and through the development of universal education.

The relation of universal education to planned social progress is simply this: Progress, according to Ward, means the increase of happiness in human society.[10] Human happiness is the ultimate end of effort, and progress is a direct means to happiness. Education is therefore the proximate means to progress, because education gives to the masses the knowledge that will result in progressive opinion, which will in turn result in progressive action, and so finally in social progress.

Unfortunately, Ward defines education as simply the diffusion of knowledge.[11] He holds that the diffusion of knowledge will be sufficient to result in dynamic or progressive opinion, and so sooner or later in dynamic or progressive action. This view, of course, goes back to Socrates's contention that knowledge would ultimately lead to virtue or to right social relations. Perhaps we can no longer hold to such an easy-going psychology. If Ward had only appreciated and studied carefully Aristotle's con-

---

[10] Ward, *Dynamic Sociology*, Vol. II, pp. 108–110.
[11] *Ibid.*, p. 568.

ception of education as involving not only the training of intelligence, but also habituation or training in
character, he would not have accepted such an inadequate view of the nature of that universal education
that he declared would be the means to progress. If,
however, we broaden Ward's conception of education, which in many ways was inconsistent with his
own conception of human nature, to include the education of the habits and emotions as well as the
education of the intellect, we may agree with Ward
that education is the indispensable and proximate
means of social progress; in fact, the only way of
elevating and universalizing the culture of the
masses. Certainly there is as yet no scientific reason for lack of faith in such an education as a means
of social progress, if not the only sure means.
Ward, at any rate, laid a foundation for a scientific
meliorism regarding social conditions, and, as Professor Hankins says, it is to his undying fame not
only to have elaborated the *rationale* of the scientific
view of the world, but to have preached so eloquently
in his social philosophy the doctrine of scientific
meliorism against the pessimism of *laissez-fairism.*[12]

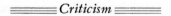

Criticism

Ward's sociology in his first book, *Dynamic Sociology,* was based upon a general cosmic philosophy.

---

[12] See *The History and Prospects of the Social Sciences,* edited by
H. E. Barnes, p. 307.

But the chapters on Cosmogeny, Biogeny, Psychogeny, Anthropogeny, and Sociogeny have scarcely any bearing upon Ward's ultimate social philosophy. It is true, also, that Ward tried to incorporate his system of sociology into an extreme naturalism, but hardly consistently, because Ward made mind and intelligent purposes central in human social evolution. His faith in the human mind, in human intelligence, in the possibility of planned progress and of intelligent control—in brief, in intelligent social purposes and values—stands in sharpest contrast to Sumner's faith in the slow working of natural forces. As we have already said, Sumner was the foil of Ward, and Ward the foil of Sumner. Each virtually ignored the work of the other. Even today, the social philosophy of each man stands in sharpest contrast to the other's. Not only do American sociologists find themselves divided by the issues that these two social philosophies present, but also virtually the whole American people. It may seem that Sumner's system of natural liberty is practically in eclipse, but if his general point of view, that social development is automatic and largely unconscious, prevails in the social sciences, then Sumner will in the long run triumph over Ward. Certainly his social philosophy was more consistent than Ward's.

The obvious weakness of Ward's social philosophy was its inconsistency. He did not have the insight to break with the extreme naturalistic point of view. His sociology proved inadequate for the higher cultural life of human society. He failed, for example, to appreciate even as much as Comte the role of religion and of an ethics of social order and progress in human society. He might have added very greatly to Comte's work at this point by showing how his sociology furnished a scientific basis for a social religion and a social ethics. But, to tell the truth, Ward appreciated these aspects of culture hardly more than did Sumner.

We must always remember that the most distinctive thing in Ward's social philosophy is his passionate affirmation of the possibility of intelligent social progress or improvement in the future. It is possible, of course, that Ward's attitude here was only one of wishful thinking. It will be very difficult, however, to find social facts to warrant such a conclusion. In spite of Ward's mistakes, we must consider him to have been the great fertilizing thinker produced by America in the nineteenth century. Even European writers, like Professor Leonard T. Hobhouse, acknowledge their indebtedness to him. Probably nothing would do so much to encourage the production of first-class works in social philosophy as the revival of his spirit.

Shortly after Ward's death in 1913, the author of this book said in the *American Journal of Sociology*: [13]

> The passing of Lester F. Ward removes from the scene of action the last of the great sociological giants of the Nineteenth Century. Professor

[13] Vol. XIX, July, 1913.

Ward will always rank with the other two great
founders of our science—Comte and Spencer. In
some ways his work for sociology was second only
to that of Auguste Comte. If there were errors in
both his premises and generalizations, as I believe
there were, this fact in no wise detracts from the
epoch-making character of his work, nor does it
give him any lesser place than we have indicated. . . .   The distinctive significance of Ward's
work was . . . to get for the psychic factor in
human society due recognition. . . .   Ward undertook to show that the psychic factor is the dominant one in human society, that it is the factor
which must receive chief attention from sociologists.

Professor Edward A. Ross, in the same issue of
the same journal, said, even more pointedly:

Few realize that Ward's daring arraignment of
the supposedly perfect methods of Nature and his
justification of the ways of mind in his *Psychic
Factors of Civilization,* published in 1893, furnish
the philosophy that lies at the base of the recent
great extension of functions by contemporary
governments.

Certainly, the judgment of the author of this book
has not changed since 1913, and it is doubtful if
Professor Ross' has.

CHAPTER XXX

Epilogue

WE HAVE COME a long way. We have seen the great currents of social thought that have accompanied, and, to some extent, shaped the development of western civilization for the last twenty-two hundred years. It is hardly necessary to say to any intelligent student of human society that practically all of these social doctrines are still living in our present civilization and contending for mastery. In a few countries, some very distinct social philosophy has come to dominate, such as Marxism in Russia, and Gobineauism in Germany. In most countries, however, these various social philosophies have become the tools of classes or parties. Sometimes the acceptance of a social philosophy seems grotesquely inconsistent with the professions and practices of an individual. For example, it is not unknown that ministers of religion accept a conflict or a purely naturalistic theory of human society. It is

553

surely time that the leaders, if not the masses, in western civilization should have some critical intelligence regarding these various philosophies of life. The conflicts of our world are not simply conflicts of practical interests. They also represent conflicts of ideas and ideals. If the present crisis of our civilization is leading again to a world conflict, that will be the result quite as much of the clash of philosophies as of practical interests.

We have also seen, to some extent, how these social doctrines took on the form that they did in the minds of individual thinkers. There is no evidence that any general law or principle has governed the development of social thought, except, indeed, the general principle of learning by trial and error. Most of the thinkers we have studied had little or no conception of the complex methods necessary for the understanding of human relations. Most of them made use simply of the method of fumbling and success, which is, we may say in justice, the method of undisciplined minds. Most of them sought for some single key to unlock the mystery of human relations and human development. Some, like Turgot, seemed to have had an almost miraculous insight; but many used the clews they discovered as weapons for some party. There is no Hegelian dialectic in the history of social thought, save only as ignorance had led from one extreme view to another. There has, however, been a steady process of learning by trial and error, fumbling and success. More and more, too, views have broadened, and the distinctive factors and traits that make human society have come into clearer view. More and more, also, there has been a movement away from arbitrary and fictitious thinking to matter-of-fact thinking based upon some understanding of scientific method.

As to the sociologists of the present, it is notorious that they are not agreed as to social philosophy or even as to concrete methods of studying social problems. Many repudiate the very idea that there is any connection between social philosophy and their work. In general, it must be said that they have not taken very seriously Comte's injunction that "A new science must be pursued historically, the only thing to be done being to study in chronological order the different works which have contributed to the progress of science."[1] They wish it, therefore, distinctly understood that present-day sociology is something very different from the social philosophy of the past.

In discussing standards of scholarship among sociologists at present, Professor P. A. Sorokin, of Harvard University, asks "whether at the present moment we have among the outstanding leaders of the social sciences men of as high a calibre as the leaders in this field during the nineteenth and early twentieth century."[2] His answer is an emphatic negative, and he points out that this is due in large

---

[1] See *The Positive Philosophy*, Martineau's translation, Introduction, Chapter I.

[2] See Professor Sorokin's article on "Improvement of Scholarship in the Social Sciences," in *Journal of Social Philosophy*, April, 1937, pp. 237–245.

part to the fact-finding character of present-day social science. He shows that in the history of science there is a kind of alternation between "synthesizing" periods and the "fact-finding" periods. Fact-finding study, he says, is unfavorable to broad generalization, to original synthesis, or to dazzling originality. In any such atmosphere, the self-respecting scholar tends to avoid a large synthesis and large vistas as he would the worst plague. "Pure thought is regarded suspiciously, while the tabulating machine, the coefficient of correlation, or a 'mental test' are believed to be patented ways to the kingdom of truth." Professor Sorokin also points out that, paradoxical as it may appear to be, it is true that the fact-finding periods are marked by far smaller findings of new relevant facts than are the synthetic periods. Thus he explains the lack of new syntheses in the sociological field at the very time when we need them most, and why present-day sociology is so often "thoughtless" sociology.

In spite of these severe strictures on present-day sociology, it must be said that Professor Sorokin himself illustrates in the most brilliant way the possibility of combining fact-finding with philosophical syntheses. Many other thinkers of the present, who are doing the same, might be mentioned. These bold social thinkers of the present are surely showing us the way out. The way is not new. It is the careful combination of fact-finding with generalization and interpretation. Many years ago, my teacher, Professor Albion W. Small, at the University of Chicago, used to say to his classes, "sociology, to deserve respect, must become not only a science, but an accredited section of general philosophy." This statement needs emphasis today, for the very aims of sociology are negatived unless it furnishes a foundation for a scientific social philosophy.[3] Most of the worthwhile problems in human social evolution cannot be solved by narrow scientific methods. For example, Ward's problem as to whether intelligent, planned social progress is possible is such a problem. Again, if progress of any sort is possible, the further question arises as to the direction it should take. Should our planned progress be toward a free democratic society? Or in the direction of Fascism, or of Soviet Communism? These questions, and questions like these, are the ones that the man on the street looks to the social sciences to solve. The social sciences cannot possibly avoid questions that concern human values, because social values are the very subject matter with which they deal.

Professor Sorokin demands for students of sociology, instead of so much training in "techniques" of

---

[3] In a recent book on *Human Affairs* my colleague, Professor William McDougall, in a chapter on "Philosophy and the Social Sciences," says, "It is right and well nigh inevitable that the social scientist shall be also a philosopher, or, at least, interested in social philosophy and its problems. And it is a mistaken policy to aim at raising up a tribe of pure social scientists who shall be blind and deaf to social philosophy; it is futile and worse than futile to carp at the social scientist who mingles philosophical considerations with his scientific observations and reasonings. Nevertheless, it is desirable that the social scientist shall understand what he is doing, shall recognize the distinction and the difference between the two kinds of enquiry, and shall understand the relations between them."

social investigation, more training in systematic thinking, logical principles, and philosophical methods. The time is surely ripe to take such a step if we are to escape from the paralysis that comes from devoting all of our energy to fact-finding. Modern philosophy is not antagonistic to co-operation with the social sciences. Philosophy no longer proceeds by reasoning from *a priori* principles. On the contrary, it reasons from the facts of experience. Much of the best philosophical method of the present time may be characterized as critical realism. A scientific critical realism should be of much aid to sociology.

But, of course, we should never forget another frequent remark of Professor Small, and that is that "students of sociology should always keep both feet on the ground." He did not mean by this that they should take into account only the facts and processes of present society, as the German school inclines to do. Neither did he mean by it that only those social facts should be taken into account that can be observed by sight. Rather, he meant that sociology should be based upon all of the facts of human experience, past and present, tangible and intangible, objective and subjective. Such facts as sentiments, beliefs, and traditions are not observable in the scientific sense of the word, but they are, nevertheless, real facts.

The true course of future progress for the science of sociology, as well as for social philosophy, is beginning to become discernible. The first fact that human sociology has to take into account is the difference between human society and the rest of nature.[4] We might as well have said the difference between human society and nature; because all of nature, as studied by the natural sciences, is ruled by blind, unconscious forces, but human society has been built up by the human mind and its intelligent purposes. That is, it has, so far as it differs from animal society. There is no mysticism in finding a sharp line of demarcation between the two. Animal societies are still ruled by the blind forces of nature. Let us take the usual example of two ant eggs of different sex and of the same species. From these two eggs, under proper conditions, every trait of ant society of that species will be reproduced. The same might still be said if, instead of taking two ant eggs, we took two baby gorillas of different sex. They too would reproduce, without any appreciable diminution, every trait of gorilla society, and that without the benefit of any traditions from previous gorilla societies.

There is, therefore, a great gulf between the natural condition of all animal groups and the relatively artificial condition of all human groups. Man has escaped from the leash of heredity, instinct, and natural selection, and it is sheer superstition to say

---

[4] A fuller statement of the point of view set forth in the remaining pages of this book will be found in an article on "Culture as an Elementary Factor in Human Social Life" in *Social Science*, Autumn No., 1935, pp. 313–318. This was a paper presented by the author to The International Congress of Sociology held at Brussels, Belgium, August, 1935.

otherwise, though some so-called scientific men seem very ambitious to uphold this superstition.

What has made the difference between man and the other animals? As far as we can answer in a single sentence, it is man's much greater learning capacity, and especially the capacity to learn from members of his own species. This has given him an indefinite capacity to acquire habits, to acquire sentiments, and to acquire beliefs and ideas. But all of these acquirements of man, except those of habit, depend upon language and other means of symbolical communication. In other words, man is an animal, not only built to live by learning, but built to live by learning from his fellow creatures. The whole development of human society, so far as it is *human,* has depended upon learning processes in individuals, and interlearning processes among individuals.[5] It has depended upon the learning of groups, as well as of individuals, and any such process of group learning is possible only to a very limited extent in the animals below man.

It is this process that has built up what we call "culture," or civilization, and that has given to human society its relatively artificial character. No animal group below man possesses culture, because none possesses the means of artificially storing up and communicating experience by means of symbols. All human groups, however, have culture, that is to say, language, traditions, customs, tools, institu-

[5] See Spiller, *The Origin and Nature of Man,* Chapters IV and V.

tions. Their culture, or what the group has learned, increasingly patterns and determines their social interactions and behavior. That is the whole difference between modern civilized man and primitive man. Through learning and interlearning, human groups have accumulated experience, knowledge, values by which they come to control their conduct. All human institutions, and nearly all interactions between civilized human beings, are learned adjustments, derived for the most part from the general culture of the group. This is the cultural view of human society that is revolutionizing the social sciences.

This is not saying that physical conditions and biological traits should not be taken fully into account in human sociology. Even though man is transforming his environment, both objective and subjective, both physical and social, as Ward proclaimed, no one has yet proposed to start orange culture in Greenland. Physical conditions and biological traits form the background, or, if you wish, the basis, of human culture. They are, however, more and more modified as culture advances. Moreover, the study of the limits that these natural conditions impose is always a legitimate part of the human social sciences. If some of the philosophers of the nineteenth century who tried to assimilate human society to nature, had said that they were studying merely the framework or limits within which human social development took place, there could be little objection to their thinking. However, it seems to the author that the sociologist is more interested in the development of group culture in its myriad forms than he is in the framework or limits that nature imposes.

Again, this does not mean that human instinctive tendencies or organic urges should not be taken fully into account. Man shares most of these with the brutes. Hunger and sex, as well as land and natural resources, are real conditions modifying human association. But again, no one has proposed that these should be ignored. Like the conditions of physical nature, they afford certain limits, or a framework within which processes of human association go on. But again, it seems to the author that the sociologist is more interested in the cultural modifications brought about in man's natural tendencies and animal impulses than he is in the limits that these organic conditions impose. If it is a mistake to ignore these conditions, it is an even greater mistake to ignore the possibility of their cultural modification.

Now, if we reach the conclusion that social forms and institutions are products of culture and have been made by man, we must also reach the conclusion that they can be unmade by man. If human customs and institutions are learned adjustments, they can be unlearned. This is not saying that every new adjustment that may be tried will work equally well. The steam engine is a tool made by man, but if it is to work well, the conditions afforded by nature and human nature must be taken fully into account. So it is with human institutions. Probably, under given conditions, certain forms, or possibly a single form, will work better than others. Hence the need of studying both the facts of human nature and of human society. But they should be studies with reference to possibilities as well as with reference to past and present experience. The very fact that civilized human behavior represents a learned adjustment throws a considerable burden of proof upon those who claim that customs and institutions cannot be changed. Those who claim, for example, that war and military systems cannot be abandoned by civilized nations through the change of their culture and social traditions have the burden of showing that there are forces in nature and in human nature independent of all culture and learned social adjustment that cannot be controlled, and that inevitably produce wars. The presumption would seem to be that relatively durable peace might be produced by a change in our social traditions and better control over natural conditions.

From the standpoint of social philosophy, this cultural approach to human social problems does not mean that all the social philosophies of the past were vain and just so many errors. On the contrary, there has been a steady approach to this cultural, psychological view. Even Sumner was not so far from wrong. His error consisted in throwing the emphasis upon the relatively unconscious and automatic nature of changes in custom. If he had thrown his emphasis upon social tradition, and pointed out that all social traditions are taught, his conclusion might have been very different. For tradition is psychological, and the only way that we know of conveying a tradition is by a process of teaching and learning. If this process can be controlled, then the growth and development of the social tradition of every group can be controlled. Ward was, therefore, nearer right when he emphasized that human social development was a matter of achievement, and that achievement could be raised to the level of intelligent purpose, and even to that of a collective program of social progress. Perhaps Sumner was coldly and dispassionately intelligent in his study of human society; but Ward saw the possibilities involved in the process of human social development, and in thus laying the foundations for a scientific, an educational, and a political meliorism, he gave us a sounder, more enduring social philosophy.

APPENDIX

Suggestions for Further Reading

(These suggestions are meant to guide readers of this book to certain works, especially to the original sources, which are relevant to the interpretation presented in the chapters. They form an outline of readings suitable to accompany the text.)

General Bibliography

Barnes, H. E., and Becker, Howard, *Social Thought from Lore to Science,* two vols., 1938.   An encyclopedic work covering the social philosophy of all peoples, especially European and American.

Bogardus, E. S., *A History of Social Thought,* Second Edition, 1928.

Cook, Thomas I., *History of Political Philosophy,* 1937.

House, F. N., *The Development of Sociology,* 1936.

Lichtenberger, J. P., *Development of Social Theory,* 1923.

Small, A. W., *The Origins of Sociology,* 1924.

The following books are valuable for certain phases of social philosophy:

Bristol, L. M., *Social Adaptation,* 1915.

Bury, J. B., *The Idea of Progress,* 1921.

Flint, Robert, *History of the Philosophy of History,* 1894.

The histories of political science and of economics frequently contain valuable material for the study of the development of social philosophy. This is especially true of the histories mentioned below:

Dunning, W. A., *A History of Political Theories,* three vols., 1908–1920.

Engelmann, G., *Political Philosophy from Plato to Jeremy Bentham,* with Introductions by O. Jaszi, 1927.

Contemporary social philosophy has been adequately dealt with by Sorokin, P. A., *Contemporary Sociological Theories,* 1928.

The reader will find valuable sketches of the life and work of the social thinkers included in this book in *The Encyclopedia of the Social Sciences,* twelve vols., 1930–1935.

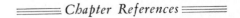

Chapter References

CHAPTER I

Compare Chapters II, III, IV of Bogardus, *A History of Social Thought,* with the text.

Chapter II

Read Books IV and V of Jowett's translation of Plato's *Republic*; also Book III of Plato's *Laws*.

Chapter III

Read Books I, II, VII, VIII of Jowett's translation or Welldon's translation of *The Politics of Aristotle*.

Chapter IV

Read from Lucretius' poem, *De Rerum Natura*, the section on Primitive Man, Book V, beginning Verse 800.

Chapter V

Read Part XIII, Chapters I–VI of Augustine's *City of God*.

Chapter VI

Read Machiavelli, *The Prince*, Chapters XV, XVI, XVII, XVIII, XIX; also Book II of More's *Utopia*.

Chapter VII

Read Chapters XII, XIV, XV, XVI, XVII, XVIII in Hobbes' *Leviathan*.

Chapter VIII

Read Chapters I, II, III, IV of Locke's *Second Treatise of Government*.

Chapter IX

Read Chapters XIII and XV of H. P. Adams, *The Life and Writings of Giambattista Vico*.

Chapter X

Read Books I–XVII, inclusive, of Montesquieu's *Spirit of the Laws.*

Chapter XI

Read Turgot's entire Second Discourse, "On the Progress of the Human Mind," translated by McQuilkin De Grange. (The Sociological Press, Hanover, N. H., 1929.)

Chapter XII

Read pp. 281, 282 of Durant, *The Story of Philosophy.*

Chapter XIII

Read entire *A Discourse on the Origin of Inequality* and Book I of *The Social Contract,* by J. J. Rousseau. (In Everyman's Library.)

If possible, the lectures on Voltaire (VI) and on Rousseau (VII) in Hearnshaw, *The Social and Political Ideas of Some Great Thinkers of the Age of Reason,* should also be read.

Chapter XIV

Read Condorcet's *Outlines of an Historical Picture of the Progress of the Human Mind* (English translation); or, better yet, Schapiro's *Condorcet and the Rise of Liberalism.*

Chapter XVI

Read Chapter VIII of Book I of Smith's *Wealth of Nations.*

Chapter XVII

Read pp. 1–82 of Hegel's *Philosophy of History,* Sibree's translation.

Chapter XVIII

Read Nietzsche's *Will to Power.*

Chapter XX

Read Chapter II of Buckle's *History of England.*

Chapter XXI

Read *The Communist Manifesto*; also, the author's preface of Marx's *Critique of Political Economy*; also, Chapter XXXII of *Capital.*

Chapter XXIII

Read Chapters I and II of Harriet Martineau's translation of *Comte's Positive Philosophy*; also Chapters I–VI of Book VI of the same book; also, Chapters I and II of Vol. I of Comte's *System of Positive Philosophy* and Chapter I of Vol. III.

Chapter XXIV

Read Tarde's *Social Laws,* entire book.

Chapter XXV

Read Spencer's *Principles of Sociology,* Vol. I, Parts I and II.

Chapter XXVIII

Read Sumner's *Folkways,* Chapters I and II.

Chapter XXIX

Read Ward's *Dynamic Sociology,* pp. 1–81 of Vol. I and pp. 100–110 and 540–636 in Vol. II; read also Chapter XV of *Psychic Factors of Civilization.*

Index

A

Absolutism, 80, 83, 94, 107, 124, 125, 212, 287–289
Adaptation, social, 338, 420, 424, 445, 448, 475, 507
Agriculture, 31, 47, 208, 221, 253, 316, 317, 496
Alexander the Great, 36, 38, 39
Altruistic impulses, 256, 266, 301, 390, 394
American Indians, 4, 264
Analogy, as a scientific method, 248, 456, 466, 471, 474, 478
Anarchism, philosophical, 109, 133, 212, 215, 299, 457
Ancestor worship, 5, 451
Animal societies, 44, 243, 373, 448, 538, 560
Animism, 381, 384
Anthropology, 231, 241, 263, 373, 422, 446, 506
Aquinas, Thomas, 79, 81–84, 110, 287
Aristocracy, 20, 28, 33, 35, 50, 51, 104, 111, 125, 144, 155, 299–301
Aristotle, 33, 36–60, 62, 64, 67, 81, 82, 99, 100, 103, 298, 367, 548

Athens, 9, 10, 11, 12, 14, 19, 40, 41, 50, 64
Augustine, Saint, 35, 72–79, 83, 333, 414
Authority, 60, 78, 83, 140, 147, 221, 278, 287

B

Bacon, Francis, 58, 60, 114, 115, 117
Bagehot, Walter, 418
Baldwin, J. M., 419
Barnes, H. E., 549
Behaviorism, 178, 371, 507
Bible, the, 74, 78, 82, 109, 414
Bodin, John, 94, 98–106, 141, 142, 193, 220, 266, 312
Bogardus, E. S., 3
Bolshevists, 34, 339
Bristol, L. M., 431, 481
Buckle, Henry Thomas, 256, 313–323
Bury, J. B., 54, 63, 78, 107, 277, 351

C

Calvin, John, 79, 108, 110–113
Campanella, Thomas, 114